THE Essential
SAN JUAN
ISLANDS
GUIDE

D1372175

THE *Essential* SAN JUAN ISLANDS GUIDE

4th Edition

MARGE & TED MUELLER

Neither the authors nor the publisher of this book received money, goods, or services as compensation for the inclusion or description of any facility in this book. The authors are entirely responsible for research in this book. We have done our best to fully gather information on each business. If there are factual errors, we regret it and apologize. *Any errors are the responsibility of the authors, not of the businesses represented.*

Our goal in this book is to be as complete as possible. If we have overlooked any businesses, we regret it. If you will let us know, we will do our best to include that business in our next reprint or edition, if it is appropriate to the content of the book. Please contact us via the internet at *margeted@comcast.net*, or by U.S. mail at Marge and Ted Mueller, 1440 NW Richmond Beach Road, Suite 202, Shoreline, WA 98177.

—Marge & Ted Mueller

Published by
JASI
P.O. Box 313
Medina, Washington 98039
(425) 454-3490

First Edition 1994. Second Edition 1996. Third Edition 2000. Fourth Edition 2007.

Printed in the United States of America

Cover, book design, and layout by Marge Mueller, Gray Mouse Graphics
All photos by the authors except as noted
Cover photo: *Fisherman Bay, Lopez Island*
Frontispiece: *A Washington State Ferry in the San Juan Islands. Photo by Bob and Ira Spring.*

Mueller, Marge
The Essential San Juan Islands Guide / Marge & Ted Mueller: 4th ed.

ISBN: 9781881409342
Library of Congress Control Number: 2003209244
International Standard Serial Number: 1546-3990

CONTENTS

◆

◆

LIST OF MAPS

SIDEBARS

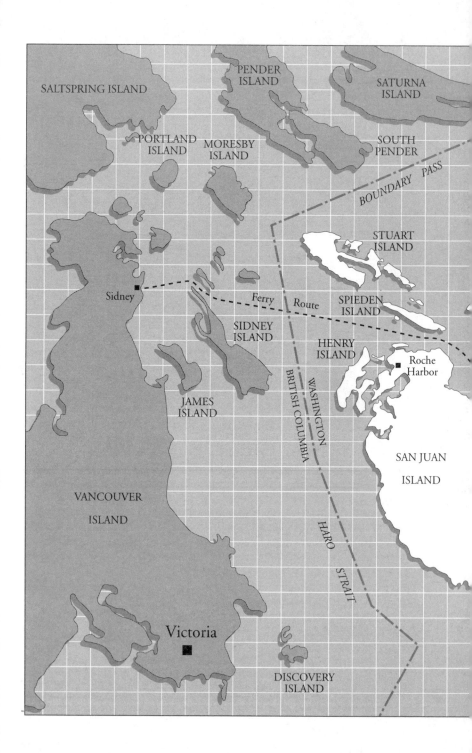

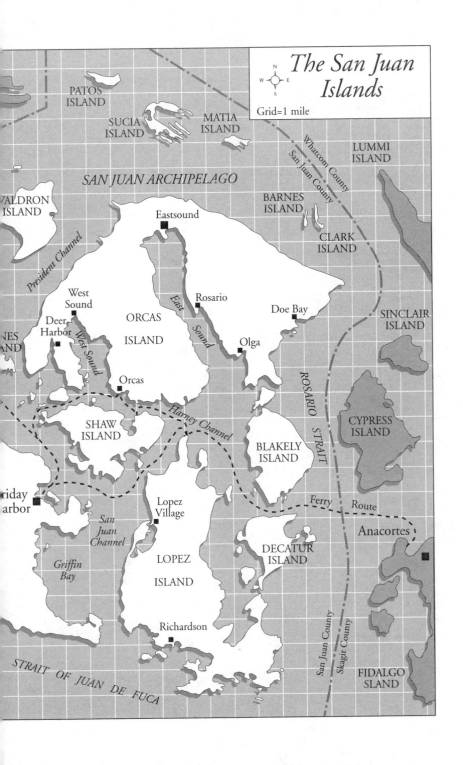

The San Juan Islands

Grid=1 mile

PATOS ISLAND

SUCIA ISLAND

MATIA ISLAND

LUMMI ISLAND

Whatcom County
San Juan County

SAN JUAN ARCHIPELAGO

BARNES ISLAND

ALDRON ISLAND

CLARK ISLAND

President Channel

Eastsound

SINCLAIR ISLAND

West Sound

Rosario

Doe Bay

Deer Harbor

East Sound

ORCAS ISLAND

NES ND

Olga

West Sound

Orcas

ROSARIO STRAIT

CYPRESS ISLAND

SHAW ISLAND

Harney Channel

BLAKELY ISLAND

riday arbor

Lopez Village

Ferry   Route

Anacortes

San Juan Channel

DECATUR ISLAND

Griffin Bay

LOPEZ ISLAND

Richardson

STRAIT OF JUAN DE FUCA

San Juan County
Skagit County

FIDALGO SLAND

CONTENTS BY CATEGORY

A family explores tidepools at Obstruction Pass on Orcas Island.

Bakeries, Delis & Take-Out (Continued)

Bed & Breakfast Inns

Bicycle & Moped Rental

Boats—Tours, Cruises, Charters & Rentals

Books, Videos & Music—New & Used

LODGING AT A GLANCE

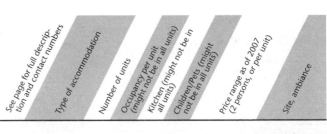

LOPEZ ISLAND	See page for full description and contact numbers	Type of accommodation	Number of units	Occupancy per unit (might not be in all units)	Kitchen (might not be in all units)	Children/Pets (might not be in all units)	Price range as of 2007 (2 persons, or per unit)	Site ambiance
Aleck Bay Inn	80–81	B&B	4	1–2		C	$98–$198	Water view, beach
Amy's House at Hunter Bay	81–82	Home	1	1–7	K	C	$450, $1200 wk	Water, views
The Bay House and Garden Cottages	82	Home, cottages	3	1–7	K	C	$150-$200	Marine views
Blue Fjord Cabins	82	Cabins	2	1–4	K	C/P	$125, $795 wk	Forest, water
The Cabin on Lopez	83	Home	1	1–5	K	C	$125	Forest
Channel View Farm	83	Home	1	1–4	K	C	$135	Farm and garden
Cozy Cabin on Lopez Island	83–84	Cabin	1	1–2	K		$85	Woods, privacy
Edenwild Inn ♿	84	B&B	8	1–3		C	$165–185	Village
Flat Point Beach Cabin	84–85	Cabin	1	1–4	K	C	$150, $875 wk	Beach
The Inn at Swifts Bay	85–86	B&B	5	1–2			$110–$210	Forest
Islands Marine Center	86	Apartments	3	1–3	K	C	$95–$130	Village
A Little Red House	86	Home	1	1–4	K	C	$135, $825 wk	Yard, view
Lopez Farm Cottages	87	Cottages	4	1–3	K	C	$160–$180	Country
Lopez Islander Bay Resort	88	Rooms/suites	30	1–4	K	C	$98–335	Village, beach

- *Pricing policies vary.* In general, prices given on this table are summer rates, per day, double occupancy. However, cottages and vacation homes usually rent for the entire unit, so basic occupancy might be for four or more on those units. Weekly rates are noted. If weekly rates are not shown, sometimes they can be negotiated.

- Prices are as of spring, 2007, and are subject to change. Lower rates are usually offered off-season.

- A tax of 9.7 percent is additional. For a general discussion of lodging, see Lodging Details, page 35–36.

- Prices listed are the range between the lowest-priced unit and the highest-priced unit. For some lodgings the weekly or monthly rates are also indicated.

- Some units might accommodate additional persons with a roll away, futon, or fold-out sofa. Where space allows, an added fee, ranging from $15 to $30, is usually charged for additional persons.

- Where pets are permitted, an added fee might be charged for them. If pets are allowed, it usually is only in select lodgings, so allergy-prone persons are assured of pet-free accommodations.

- Disabled accessible lodging is noted with a ♿ symbol after the name; however, not all units might have disabled access, or in some cases units might not be fully ADA compliant. Inquire for full information.

LODGING AT A GLANCE

	See page for full description and contact numbers	Type of accommodation	Number of units	Occupancy per unit (might not be in all units)	Kitchen (might not be in all units)	Children/Pets (might not be in all units)	Price range as of 2007 (2 persons, or per unit)	Site, ambiance
Lopez Island Getaway	88–89	Home	1	1-4	K	C	$350, $950 wk	Marine views
Lopez Lodge	89	Rooms	3	1-4	K	C	$60–125	Village
Lopez Retreat	89	Home	1	1-4	K	C	$200, $1200 wk	Bay view
MacKaye Harbor Inn	90	B&B	5	1-2		C	$139-195	Country, beach
Meadow Wood Cottage	90	Cottage	1	1-4	K	C	$145, $945 wk	Forest
Peninsula Home	90–91	Home	1	1-8	K	C	$2500 wk	Waterfront
Ravens Rook Guest Cabin	91	Cabin	1	1-5	K	C	$ 130, $875 wk	Quiet woods
Rustic Elegance	91–92	Home	1	1-8	K	C	$165	Forest
Sunset View House	92	Home	1	1-9	K	C	$205–$245	Meadows, sunset views
Three Seasons on Lopez	92–93	Home	1	1-4	K	C	$275, $675 wk	In Village
Village Guest Home	93	Home	1	1-4	K	C	$90, $525 wk	Village, beach

ORCAS ISLAND

Abigail's Beach Home	121	Home	1	1-12	K	C	$200–700	Beach, wetland
Abode	121–122	Apartment	1	1-2	K		$88	Garden, walk to Eastsound
All Dream Cottages	122	Cottages	4	1-4	K	C	Contact owner	Pasture, waterfront
The Anchorage Inn	122	B&B	3	1-2	K		$199	Forest, water view
Bartwood Lodge	123	Rooms, suites	16	1-4		C	$149–179	Waterfront
Bayside Cottages	123–124	Cottages, suites	10	1-9	K	C	$175–$380, $1100–$1800 wk	Waterfront
Bayview Cottage	124	Cottage	1	1-6	K	C	$130–$800	Bay views
Beach Haven Resort	124–125	Resort	16	1–10	K	C	$115–$285	Waterfront
Beach House on Orcas	125	Suites	2	1-2			$169–$269	Waterfront, views
Blackberry Beach Cabins	125–126	Cabins	2	1-4	K	C/P	$80–150	Waterfront
Blacktail Ridge	126	Home	1	1-4	K	C	$250, $1500 wk	Forest and views
Blue Heron B&B	126–127	B&B	3	1-3		C/P	$95–$145	Water View
Blue Wisteria	127	Home	1	1-6	K	C	$275	Secluded acreage
Boardwalk on the Water	127	Cottages	4	1-4	K	C	$170–290	Village, water view
Brackenfern Lodge	128	Rooms	6	1-2	K		$350–$450 mo	Near Eastsound
Buck Bay Farm B&B	128–129	B&B	5	1-4		C	$109-199	Country, farm
Buckhorn Farm Bungalow	129	Cabin	1	1-4	K	C	$135	Country, farm
Cabins-on-the-Point	129–130	Cabins, home	5	1-6	K	C	$175–295	Waterfront, view

19

LODGING
AT A
GLANCE

	See page for full description and contact numbers	Type of accommodation	Number of units	Occupancy per unit (might not be in all units)	Kitchen (might not be in all units)	Children/Pets (might not be in all units)	Price range as of 2007 (2 persons, or per unit)	Site, ambiance
Casa Crayola	130	Cottage	1	1-2	K		$135	Village
Cascade Harbor Inn	130–131	Inn	45	1-4		C	$129–399	Forest, water view
Deer Harbor Inn	131	Rooms, home cottages	13	1-6	K	P	$139–325	Country, water views
Doe Bay Resort & Retreat Center	132	Cabins, house, hostel	49	1-24	K	C	$20–$180	Waterfront, forest
Double Mountain B&B	133	B&B	3	1-4		C	$95–160	Forest, view
Eastsound Landmark Inn	133–134	Inn	15	1-6	K	C	$161–189	Village, water view
Eastsound Suites	134	Suites	2	1-6	K	C	$295–395	Village
Evergreen at Rosario	134–135	Home	1	1-6	K	C	$250, $1500 wk	Bay view
Foxglove Cottage	135	Cottage	1	1-4	K	C	$200	Village, waterfront
Frog & Sparrow (to say nothing of Columbine)	135–136	Cottages	3	1-3	K	C	Contact owner	Beach
The Garden House	136	Suite	1	1-4	K	C/P	$150	Country
Glenwood Inn	136–137	Cabins	5	1-8	K	C	$850–$950 wk	Waterfront, farm
The Gnome House	137	Cabin	1	1-6	K	C/P	$185, $1100 wk	Forest, romantic
Heartwood House	137–138	Home	1	1-10	K	C/P	$2500 wk	Water view
The Homestead	138	Home	2	1-6	K	C	$350	Country, beach
Huckleberry House	138–139	Home	1	1-4	K	C	$160, $975 wk	Near village
The Inn at Ship Bay ♿	139	Inn	10	1-3		C	$195–295	Waterfront
The Inn on Orcas Island	139–140	B&B, cottages	8	1-4	K	C	$185–285	Water view
Kangaroo House B&B	140	B&B	5	1-4		C	$125–180	Country
Kingfish Inn B&B	141	B&B	4	1-4		C	$150–160	Village
Laughing Moon Farm	141	Cabins	3	1-8	K	C	$195, 1400 wk	Farm, wooded
Lieber Haven Marina Resort	142	Rooms, cabins	12	1-4	K	C	$125–165 (4 persons)	Waterfront
Madrona Hill B&B	142–143	B&B, cottage	5	1-3	K	C	$99–250	Wooded
Madrona House	143–144	Home, Cottage	2	1-6	K	C	$486 ($2700)	Waterfront
Maggie's Manor	144	Home	1	1-10	K	C/P	$375 ($2250)	Forest, views
Massacre Bay B&B & Cottage	144–145	B&B, Cottage	4	1-4	K	C	$105–$145, $695 wk	Beach access, water views
Meadowlark Guesthouse	145	Home	1	1-4	K	C/P	$135	Country, water view
North Beach Inn ♿	146	Cottages	13	1-7	K	C/P	$135–$240, $820–1525 wk	Waterfront

LODGING AT A GLANCE

	See page for full description and contact numbers	Type of accommodation	Number of units	Occupancy per unit (might not be in all units)	Kitchen (might not be in all units)	Children/Pets (might not be in all units)	Price range as of 2007 (2 persons, or per unit)	Site, ambiance
North Shore Cottages	146–147	Cottages	4	1–4	K	C/P	$255–$355	Waterfront, romantic
The Old Trout Inn	147	B&B, cottage	4	1-2	K		$110–$195, $860, $1200 wk	Country, pond
Once in a Blue Moon Farm	147–148	Homes, suites	6	1-5	K	C/P	$150–$800, dep. on size of group	Farm
Orcas Cottages	149	Cottages	2	1-6	K	C	$150–$200 $800–$1400 wk	Rural, views
Orcas Hotel	149	Inn	12	1–3		C	$89–$208	Village, waterfront
Orcas Island Vacation Home	150	Home	1	1-5	K	C	$985	Water views
The Orcas Tree House	150	Home	1	1-6	K	C	$210, $1260 wk	Woods, views
Otters Pond B&B	150–151	B&B	5	1-2		C	$150–$225	Forest, pond
Outlook Inn on Orcas Island	151–152	Inn	40	1–4		C	$84–$289	Village, water view
Palmer's Chart House	152	B&B	2	1-2		C	$80	Water View
Pebble Cove Farm	152–153	B&B	2	1-4		C	$150–$225	Beachfront
The Place at Cayou Cove	153	Cottages	4	1-4	K	C/P	$295–$425	Waterfront
Rosario Resort & Spa ♿	153–154	Resort	116	1–4	K	C/P	$219–$750	Waterfront, views
Rose Arbor Cottage	154–155	Cottage	1	1-5	K	C	$165, $960 wk	Near airfield
Sandcastle Guesthouse	155	Cottage	1	1-4	K	C	$140	Waterfront, wetland
Sand Dollar Inn B&B	155–156	B&B	3	1-2			$135	Country, water view
Seacliff Cotttage	156	Home	1	1-6	K	C	$310, $1890 wk	Water view
Smuggler's Villa Resort	156–157	Resort	20	1-6	K	C	$259–$325 $1599–2099 wk	Waterfront
Spring Bay Inn	157	B&B	5	1-2		C	$220–$260	Waterfront, forest
Swannies ♿	157–158	Suite	1	1-2	K	C	$90	Near village
Turtleback Farm Inn	158	B&B	11	1–3		C	$100–$245	Country
Walking Horse Country Farm	159	Home	1	1-4	K	C	$150	Country, farm
West Beach Resort	159–160	Resort	19	1-6	K	C/P	$149 ($1595)	Waterfront

SAN JUAN ISLAND

An Island Place to Stay	206	Homes	2	1-10	K	C/P	$155–300	Country
Argyle House B&B ♿	206–207	B&B, cottage	6	1-6	K	C	$135–$245	Town, quiet
Beaverton Valley Farmhouse B&B	207–208	B&B, cabin	5	1–4	K	C/P	$100–$170	Country

LODGING AT A GLANCE

	See page for full description and contact numbers	Type of accommodation	Number of units	Occupancy per unit (might not be in all units)	Kitchen (might not be in all units)	Children/Pets (might not be in all units)	Price range as of 2007 (2 persons, or per unit)	Site, ambiance
Best Western Friday Harbor Suites	208	Inn	57	1-4	K	C	$148–189	Town
Bison Island Bed and Bronze	208	Cottage	1	1-4	K	C	$175, $850 wk	Golf course and lake
Blair House B&B	209	B&B	3	1-4		C/P	$115–$195	Town
Courtyard Suites	209	Suites	2	1-6	K	C/P	$200–$225	Town
Discovery Inn	210	Inn	28	1-4	K	C	$119–$154	Town
The Dragonfly	211	B&B	4	1-2			$195–$230	Country, Japanese décor
Elements San Juan Island Hotel and Spa ♿	211–212	Inn, guesthouse	73	1-4	K	C/P	$189–$369	Town
Friday Harbor House ♿	212	Inn	23	1-2		C	$215–$360	Town, water view
Friday Harbor Lights	212–213	Suites	3	1-8	K	C	$185–$425	Town, waterfront
Friday's Historical Inn	213	Inn, guesthouse	18	1-2	K	C	$99–$345	Town
Halverson Home B&B	214	B&B, apartment	4	1-4	K	C	$145–$205	Pastoral
Harrison House Suites	214–215	Suites, cottage	5	1–10	K	C/P	$175–$375	Town
Haven on the Bay	215	Home	1	1-7	K	C/P	$195 $1295–2044 wk	Country, waterfront
Highland Inn	215–216	B&B	2	1–2			$275	Country, water view
Hillside House B&B	216	B&B	6	1–3		C	$125–$275	Town
Horseshu Hacienda ♿	217	Home	1	1-6	K	C/P	$275, $1400 wk 6 persons	Farm
Inn To The Woods B&B	217–218	B&B	4	1-2		C	$130–$230	Forest
Jensen Bay B&B	218	B&B	1	1–4	K	C	$195	Country
Juniper Lane Guest House	218–219	House, cabin, hostel	6	1-7	K	C	$30 1 person, $85–175 2-persons	Country
Kirk House	219	B&B	4	1-2		C	$180–$205	Town
Lakedale Resort	220–221	Lodge, cabins, home	17	1–8	K	C/P	$239–$329 2 persons, $489 4 persons	Forest, lakes
Lonesome Cove Resort	221	Resort	6	1–6	K	C	$125–$180	Waterfront

LODGING AT A GLANCE

	See page for full description and contact numbers	Type of accommodation	Number of units	Occupancy per unit (might not be in all units)	Kitchen (might not be in all units)	Children/Pets (might not be in all units)	Price range as of 2007 (2 persons, or per unit)	Site, ambiance
Longhouse B&B	221–222	B&B, cabin	3	1–4	K	C	$115–$130	Waterfront, artifacts
Mar Vista Resort	222–223	Cabins	8	1–4	K	C	$120–$195	Country, beach
Nichols Street Suites	223	Suites	2	1–6	K	C	$165–$185	Town
Oak Ridge Ventures	223–224	Home	1	1–8	K	C	$1975 wk	Country
Olympic Lights B&B	224	B&B	4	1–2			$140–$150	Country, view
The Orca Inn	224–225	Motel	75	1–2		C	$59–$104	Town
Pear Point Inn	225	B&B	2	1–4		C	$150–195	Country, bay view
Roche Harbor Resort ♿	225–227	Resort, rooms, suites, cottages	70	1–6	K	C	$99–$539	Waterfront
Sandpiper Condominiums	228	Condos	6	1–4	K	C/P	$85, $625 wk	Town
San Juan Suites	228	Suites	5	1–4	K	C	$139–$299	Town
San Juan Waterhouse	228–229	Home	1	1–6	K	C	$2750	Waterfront
Snug Harbor Marina Resort	229–230	Cottages, studios	10	1–4	K	C/P	$169–$229	Waterfront
States Inn & Ranch	230–231	B&B, suite, cottage	10	1–6	K	C	$99–$249	Country, farm
Tower House B&B	231	B&B	2	1–2			$160–$175	Country, romantic
Trumpeter Inn B&B	231–232	B&B	6	1–2		C	$155–$195	Country
Tucker House B&B	232	B&B, suites, cottages	10	1–6	K	C/P	$170–$250	Town
Two Private Vacation Homes	233	Homes	2	1–8	K	C/P	$1290/ $1660	Country, one with water view
Wayfarer's Rest	233	Hostel,	5	1–10	K	C/P	$30–$80	Town
Wharfside B&B: Aboard the *Slow Season*	234	B&B	2	1–2		C/P	$179–$289	60-foot sailboat
Wildwood Manor B&B	234–235	B&B	4	1–2		C	$195–$250	Forest
Yacht Haven Vacation Rental	235	Home	1	1–4	K	C	$350, $2100 wk	Waterfront

PREFACE

◆

IN THE MORE THAN 30 YEARS that we have been frequenting the San Juan Islands, and the 15 years since we wrote the first edition of this book, the area has seen some changes: growth, modernization, and an economic shift to tourism. Far more companies offer wildlife cruises, kayak tours, scuba diving, and other island-centric adventures. The tourist "shoulder" season has been extending beyond the prime season of June through September, with some visitors opting to arrive earlier or later to take advantage of the lack of crowds, better lodging rates, and spring or fall weather. However, in many ways the San Juans remain much the same—pristine forests and beaches still abound, there still is not a single stoplight and no four-lane highways, and during the tourist off-season dogs still doze in the sidewalks of Friday Harbor's main drag, Spring Street.

Where visitors *will* find an enormous change, however, is in the access to San Juan tourist information. Nearly every business has an internet web site where facilities and rates can be found, and each of the three major island has a Chamber of Commerce web site with general information and links to various businesses. Lodging web sites offer virtual tours that enable you to peek into their guest rooms from your computer. Email contacts and reservations are just a mouse click away. Maps often posted on web sites tell you how to get there.

With all that information at hand, do you need this guidebook? You certainly do. We have tried to make this book an adjunct to your internet search. It is organized to give you a quick overall look at everything that is available, even those businesses not listed on the internet. It will save you a lot of web surfing, will lessen the possibility of your missing just the spot you are looking for, and will give you an unbiased view of the facilities. In addition, it gives you information on the logistics of visiting the San Juans that you won't find on any web site, as well as insights we have gleaned from our intimate knowledge of the area. The numerous maps in this book help you orient yourself and locate sites in the islands.

Email addresses and web links listed here all worked for us at one time, but we don't guarantee they will when you try them. If you are unable to make quick contact, try searching for the business by name. A warning on web sites: They sometimes can be out of date. Facilities and rates might have changed, and hot-linked sites might have disappeared. Sometimes businesses create new web sites or close down, but their old web sites are still around. We had an unpleasant experience while staying at a San Juan hotel. The bill was larger than we expected, and when we mentioned a discount offered on the web site, the hotel manager cavalierly dismissed it by saying, "Oh, that's an old web site. Those discounts aren't correct." (And not even an apology.) We will not stay there again.

Be sure to confirm all information researched from the internet or other sources

Foot passengers disembark from the ferry at San Juan Island.

before going to the islands. The data in this book was gathered in 2006 and early 2007, so even with it as a reference you should directly contact businesses you are interested in for the most current data when planning your trip.

HOW TO USE THIS BOOK
◆

Our goal in writing this book, which provides information on San Juan facilities, is to help visitors plan their visit to the islands and more fully enjoy their stay once they arrive. We have not attempted to give a "rating" to any business listed. We recognize that different people are looking for different things in lodgings, restaurants, charters, tours, or even shopping. Therefore, we try primarily to give a complete, accurate picture so readers can best choose what suits their needs.

In addition to providing a wealth of internet information, this book gives you the tourist facts necessary to make use of any of the services the islands provide. It contains detailed information on resorts, motels, hotels, inns, and bed and breakfast inns; lists of boat tours and charter services; transportation options; keen places to shop; and restaurant descriptions. Along with these you'll find mention of the various festivals, fairs, and other events that occur in the islands year-round. Public and private campgrounds and parks are included here, as well as youth camps.

In this book, we have tried to include establishments that would be of interest to visitors. Most businesses are grouped by island and general categories of information, although there are some descriptions of off-island listings.

Any business community has a range of turnovers. Sadly, this is especially true of the San Juans, which is dependent on the seasonal vagaries of the tourist industry. Because of this, although we have made every effort to include current information, some of the businesses researched might not be operating by the time this book reaches bookstores, and new ones might have sprung up. Accommodations tend to be relatively stable, and long-established restaurants that have solved the problem of quiet-season survival should still be there.

———————————————————◆———————————————————

In 1979 we wrote a book called *The San Juan Islands, Afoot and Afloat*. It became—and remains—a bestseller, presently in its fourth edition and retitled *Afoot and Afloat: The San Juan Islands*. That book covers all the public parks, public nooks and crannies, and recreational possibilities in the San Juans. It is our hope that this book, a companion volume to that one, will help you plan your trip to the region and add to your enjoyment of these endlessly enchanting islands.

—Marge and Ted Mueller

INTRODUCTION

---◆---

THE STATE OF WASHINGTON CURVES INWARD at its far northwest corner, thrust back nearly 100 miles by a watery arm of the Pacific Ocean. Within this coastal embrace lie the San Juan Islands—a cluster of several hundred rocks, reefs, and by-gosh good-size islands that are year-round home for around ten thousand people. To this remote destination flock several hundred thousand visitors each year.

What draws these people, and why do many return year after year, like pilgrims to their personal Mecca? Recreation certainly is one answer. Nearly every type of boating flourishes here—sailing, cruising, kayaking, canoeing—as well as other water-related adventures such as fishing, clam digging, crabbing, scuba diving, and beachcombing. Camping, picnicking, hiking, bicycling, horse riding, sightseeing, birdwatching, wildlife viewing . . . the recreation list goes on and on.

The unparalleled beauty of rocky shores, forest-draped hills, pastoral valleys, soothing mists, and rose-tinged sunsets brings those who seek nourishment for their souls. Tranquility draws others to shore-side resorts, where the soft lap of waves and cries of sea birds replace jarring telephone rings and computer beeps. The pace is clearly slowed, even in the islands' few small villages, where at the height of the tourist season a dog can snooze undisturbed on a sunny sidewalk, and the major excitement is the coming and going of the ferry.

In the preface we described changes to the San Juans that we have witnessed over some 40 years. Another change in the San Juans that visitors might note is the growing awareness—and concern—among residents for the need to preserve this fragile area. With the pressure of population growth and increased tourism, along with the global problems of pollution and climate change, residents have become willing to tax themselves, and remove land from their tax base as well, to protect their environment. The San Juan Preservation Trust, the San Juan Land Bank, the Friends of San Juan, Wolf Hollow Wildlife Rehabilitation Center, and the Whale Museum, as well as several other environmentally concerned programs and organizations have been established. Recently, more than 1500 acres of land that encompass Turtleback Mountain on Orcas Island were purchased by the citizens through the Land Bank and Preservation Trust, saving it from real estate development. The push to preserve the islands continues.

Step Up & Take a Bow, San Juan Islands

Island. Fantasy Island, Treasure Island, Gilligan's Island. Just the word "island" conjures up visions of romantic getaways, vacation retreats, or childhood escapes. The San Juans are just such a mystical destination—remote, unknown,

Spencer Spit State Park is one of the popular destinations on Lopez Island.

mysterious. There's no denying they'd be far less alluring if there were bridges and a freeway leading into their heart.

As far as basic statistics go, the San Juan archipelago covers an area some 25 by 30 miles. Of its several hundred islands, islets, rocks, and reefs (some of which disappear at high tide), fewer than two-hundred are officially named, and of these, only a handful have the size and potable water necessary to make them habitable.

Through the island group thread the Washington State ferries, nosing into landings at the four major islands: Lopez, Shaw, Orcas, and San Juan. San Juan and Orcas Islands are just a bit under 60 square miles of land each, Lopez is about half that size, and Shaw is a scant 7¾ square miles. Roads run the length of the ferry-served islands and circle their edges, but you'll find no four-lane highways here, and not a single traffic light. Villages on San Juan, Orcas, and Lopez have restaurants, lodging, and shops. Your car will get you around any of these places, but a bicycle or moped will serve just as well, if you're of the athletic bent.

The San Juans were once heavily agricultural, providing grain and fruit to Washington markets. However, when the Grand Coulee Dam was built in the 1950s, irrigation of huge areas of arid land in the eastern part of the state made it impossible for this tiny corner to compete. Today, most locally grown produce is sold right here on the islands, and tourism has replaced farming as the economic mainstay.

A good reason for the islands' popularity is their balmy weather. The massive bulk of Vancouver Island and the Olympic Mountains to the west cause many storms and cold weather fronts to be shunted north or south. The sun shines an average of nearly 250 days a year, and the average annual rainfall is only 29 inches; Friday Harbor residents can be slathering on sunscreen when Seattleites are popping up umbrellas. Temperatures range in the 70s during the day in summer, rarely rising to the 80s. Summer evenings might occasionally call for a light sweater. Spring arrives early, and fall lingers late; these "shoulder" months might well be the best times of all to visit the islands, as the heavy crush of tourists is gone. Residents are even more friendly and relaxed during the quiet season, and ferries are uncrowded.

Year-round residents are ordinary folk—farmers, shopkeepers, fishermen, doctors, and lawyers. There are a lot of resident retirees who see the casual pace and mild climate as the ideal antidote to years in the rat race. You'll also find a good many artists, craftspersons, writers, and musicians who nurture their creative muse in the tranquil islands. San Juan Islanders often consider themselves a breed apart, and a world apart, from mainlanders. Signs on shop doors might say, "Closed for today, gone to America." Posted business hours might list times, with an addendum of, "Or whenever I'm there." You'll find these islanders uncommonly friendly, although their patience might be tested by the summer onslaught of tourists and the occasional demanding boor.

Wild Things

The variety of wildlife is a remarkable feature of the San Juan Islands. There's an ample number of creatures to excite the most ardent binocular-wielding nature lover. Often you'll see seals and sea lions on reefs and rocky shores, and otters in quiet coves. Deer frequently appear at dusk in orchards, meadows, and parks, and if you don't take care of your campsite groceries, you are almost assured of being visited by raccoons.

WHALES. You'll see the likeness of orca whales (called killer whales by some) on T-shirts, coffee mugs, mailboxes, and postcards everywhere—you'll think they are the local logo. If you're lucky, you'll even see live ones! Three resident orca family groups, known as "pods," totaling about 80 individuals, have been identified in Puget Sound waters. These three pods are most frequently seen in the San Juans, making the area a destination for wildlife watchers. The Whale Hotline, operated by the Whale Museum in Friday Harbor, tracks the pods for research purposes. Tour boat operators utilize this information to give their clients a reasonable chance of seeing these magnificent mammals. Dolphins, minke whales, and gray whales, which make seasonal trips through these waters, also might be sighted.

BIRDWATCHING. The islands are a Mecca for bird lovers. Some 300 different species of birds have been identified in the San Juans. Because the archipelago lies on the Pacific Flyway, hundreds of thousands of migratory birds pass through here annually, and some species use the offshore islands as breeding and nesting sites. To protect these sea birds, 84 of the rocks, reefs, and islands have been designated as the San Juan Islands National Wildlife Refuge. Glaucous-winged gulls, cormorants, pigeon guillemots, and rhinoceros auklets are among the predominant species.

Land-based birds include spectacular bald eagles. Some 50 pairs are year-round residents, nesting in tall tree snags throughout the islands. They represent about one-third of the total number of breeding pairs in the entire country, outside of Alaska. Golden eagles and osprey are also seen, and some nest here as well. Other birds of prey include hawks, harriers, owls, and even vultures.

Beaches, marshes, thickets, and meadows host even more birds, ranging from great blue herons to wrens and wild turkeys. Wild turkeys? Yes. They were introduced in the San Juans many years ago, and have thrived—visitors are sometimes startled to spot them foraging along the roadside.

Numerous tour boats take visitors to spots where orca whales might be seen.

MARINE LIFE. Sea life is so abundant and so unique that all of the shores and the entire seabed of the San Juan archipelago, along with nearby Cypress Island, have been designated as a marine biological sanctuary. The University of Washington's laboratories at Friday Harbor are dedicated to studying this habitat. Be aware that the taking or killing of any marine life, except for food use, is strictly prohibited. If you fish or gather shellfish or seaweed for food, you are required to have a valid Washington State License, and you must observe all state regulations.

Scuba divers and beachcombers congregate here to view rocky undersea walls and tide pools plastered with rainbow-hued anemones, sea stars, and all manner of curious creatures. Old pilings boast collections of barnacles and tube worms that extend delicate tentacles to capture free-floating plankton. Clams, abalone, mussels, shrimp, sea urchins, and (the gourmet's favorite) Dungeness crab attract foragers who come with buckets, shovels, and trap-like "pots" seeking food for the dinner table.

Eager anglers drop lines from boats at reefs, shoals, and current-swept points for salmon and bottomfish that feed on the rich habitat. Commercial fishing, primarily for salmon, was once an economic mainstay of the San Juans. However, because of depleted runs (largely due to overfishing, loss of spawning areas, and pollution), the industry is now much reduced. Sport fishing, fortunately, remains some of the best to be found in the state, and for some visitors it is the prime reason for coming here. A number of fishing charters operate out of San Juan harbors or nearby mainland ones.

Because of the confined nature of the islands and the fragile habitat, use of personal watercraft (jet skis) has been legally banned in all waters of San Juan County. Violators face a stiff fine.

YOU'LL WANT
TO KNOW...

◆

THE VERY REMOTENESS OF THE ISLANDS, THEIR MYSTERY, poses a number of logistical problems. Unless you are willing to place your fate (and your hard-earned two-week vacation) in the hands of the gods, you still get caught up in the mundane: Where do I stay? Where do I eat? What's there to do? And even the most practical question of all: How do I get there?

Because of the islands' isolation, reaching them takes a little planning. Most visitors opt for the Washington State ferry. Others pilot their own boats or charter them off-island. Some people drop in via airplane, enjoying the scenic view en route. Several airlines have regularly scheduled runs with small planes, and charters are also available. Transportation options are covered in other chapters of this book.

About Your Trip

Even a book as comprehensive as this cannot fully prepare tourists for their first visit to the San Juans. Perhaps the hardest thing to grasp is "island time." Visitors arrive with a full itinerary, planning to see everything and do everything in a two-day weekend, only to find themselves sitting in ferry lines while all their expectations go out the window. "Island Time" recognizes that no matter how much you rush around, the ferry schedule controls everything. Tight itineraries have no meaning when you might not make it onto the next ferry—or even the one after that.

Because of the time spent on transportation, a minimum of three days is needed, especially in summer, to give you a nice, relaxed experience and enable you to do even a portion of the things there are to do. A full week is even better—you'll leave satisfied that you've had time to soak up island magic and enjoy many activities.

It is possible to visit more than one island on each visit, but there are those ferry lines again! If you are staying on one of the islands, it is possible to walk aboard the ferry (no lines there) or bring a bicycle, and leave the ferry on a different island, spend several hours, then return to your home base via another ferry. On San Juan Island there are lots of things to see within walking distance of the ferry terminal. At the other islands, you will need a bicycle or some other transportation. (See On-Island Transportation, pages 104–106, 185–191, and 272–274.) Another nice way to see the islands is to spend two or three days on one of the islands, then move to a different one for a few more days.

By taking the international ferry, which makes one round-trip through here daily in the summer, it also is possible to combine a trip to the San Juan Islands with a jaunt to Victoria, British Columbia. That beautiful city, which touts itself as "a little bit of Britain," offers a wealth of restaurants, sights, and activities. A visit there really is like a tour abroad.

Going Through U.S. Customs

For Canadian neighbors or other visitors from foreign ports, San Juan Island has a Customs office. Check-in points for boaters are at Friday Harbor and Roche Harbor. Airport check-in is at the Friday Harbor Airport. For information, call:

United States Customs
> Anacortes: (360) 293-2331
> Friday Harbor and Roche Harbor: (360) 378-2080

The U.S. has specific restrictions on importing certain food and agricultural products, and on the amounts of alcoholic beverages and tobacco products that may be imported. Check with the Customs service for current regulations. Pets must have current certificates of rabies vaccination.

Persons arriving in the San Juan Islands from Canada via the Washington State ferry must clear U.S. Customs before disembarking at Friday Harbor. Those continuing east to Anacortes without leaving the vessel in Friday Harbor, or those boarding the international ferry at Friday Harbor must clear Customs at Anacortes.

BOAT ARRIVALS. Privately owned or chartered foreign boats, or U.S. boats returning from a visit to Canada, must clear U.S. Customs prior to docking, anchoring, or touching another boat within U.S. waters. The boat's skipper must report to Customs at a port of entry immediately upon arrival. No one else may leave the boat, and no baggage may be removed, until clearance is granted. The U.S. Customs offices at Roche Harbor and Friday Harbor operate during normal business hours.

If checking in by telephone, you must provide the following information:

- Vessel identification number. This is the user-fee number on the decal issued by the home port province, or the documentation number for documented vessels.
- Vessel name and length.
- Names, addresses, photo ID, and birth or naturalization certificates for all passengers. Tentatively, as of 2009 passports or visas will be required.
- If you're returning to the U.S. from a visit to Canada, you must also have available the clearance number issued to you when you entered Canada.
- An estimated date of departure, if returning to Canada.

Once you've completed an arrival report and clearance is granted, you must record the clearance number in the ship's log and retain it there for a minimum of one year. Pleasure boats over 30 feet in length entering the U.S. must pay an annual processing fee of $25 on or before the first entry into the U.S. each year. A non-transferable decal is issued to the boat upon payment of the fee.

To streamline border crossing, under the I-68 program (in Canada, the NEXUS program), boaters with small pleasure craft can pre-register and receive a single permit for the entire boating season. Registrants returning to the U.S. need only report by telephone, during business hours, to (800) 562-5943. All passengers on board must also have I-68 permits. To enroll in I-68, you must be interviewed in person at a Customs Border Protection office, undergo law enforcement checks, and provide proof of citizenship. A fee of $16 is charged for a 12-month permit.

Hours & Seasons

For most of the businesses included here we have not listed specific hours or seasons that they are open because they often change radically from season to season, and can even vary due to the weather or personal needs of the owner. In most cases, stores are open daily from 10 A.M. to 5 or 6 P.M. from July through September. For restaurants, we have indicated which meals are served, although this, too, can change by season. Before planning to dine at a restaurant, or heading for a particular shop, it is wise to call to check their current hours of operation.

In April, May, and June, businesses are just beginning to gear up for the tourist season. In October they gear down, with some open only on weekends, or their hours shortened. From Thanksgiving through the end of February, a lot of restaurants and stores shut their doors completely. However, if you are visiting during that time you won't have any difficulty finding lodging, and there are always enough businesses and restaurants open providing service to the year-round residents that you'll be able to meet your basic needs.

If you're looking for a real away-from-it-all vacation, the quiet season is the time to go. You'll be able to write the Great American Novel or relax to near-oblivion as the islands settle into a cocoonlike state, waiting for spring and their beautiful "butterfly" stage.

Wireless and TV Reception

Cell phone reception is fairly good on Lopez and San Juan Islands. However, due to Orcas Island's mountainous nature, reception there tends to be iffy in spots. A number of lodgings include land-line phones with their accommodations so you can stay connected with the outside world, if you want. Some lodgings boast that they have no telephone and no TV, so you can truly get away from it all. Most have a phone available at a central location in case of emergency.

If you rely on your laptop, many lodgings also have computer wi-fi connections, and a number of cafés and coffee shops also offer this service.

General TV reception in the islands tends to be crummy. Unless a lodging has cable or a satellite dish, you'll have trouble keeping up with your favorite programs or watching ball games. Some places that list TV availability have only CD or VCR movies for you to watch. TVs are often in a common area, not in your room. If it is important to you, inquire.

Rates & Prices (& Taxes)

Any time of year, but especially in summer, you will find that prices for many goods and services range a bit higher in the San Juans than on the mainland. Because little is produced locally, virtually everything on the islands, from toilet paper to tractors, must be brought in by boat or small plane, adding to their cost.

CHARTERS, TRANSPORTATION. In this book we have included general price ranges for individual businesses such as boat charters, air services, and transportation. However, these are only estimates, since these change from season to season and year to year. Additionally, most businesses have a range of fees depending on the client's needs. For current rates, and any added information you might want, contact them directly or check their web site. Rates listed are for adult fares; children usually are less and discounts are sometimes given for seniors. If rates are not listed in this book, we were unable to obtain that information in time for this printing.

RESTAURANTS. A general range of prices is indicated for restaurants:

$ Inexpensive   Most dinner entrées under $12
$$ Moderate   Most dinner entrées $12 to $25
$$$ Expensive   Most dinner entrées $25 and up

Please be aware that by state law, smoking is prohibited in all indoor public places in Washington, including restaurants and bars. Outside, smoking is prohibited any place that is less than 25 feet from building entrances and exits, ventilation intakes, or openable windows.

LODGING. Island places of lodging usually have a range of accommodations and facilities, and a variety of prices. In this book we have indicated the low to high range of facilities. Prices quoted for summer accommodations are, in general, summer rates, double occupancy. However, cottages and vacation homes usually rent for the entire unit. Prices are as of early 2007, and are subject to change. Lower rates are usually offered off-season. Tax is not included.

When a location offers many different kinds of lodging and the facilities are complex, we have used bulleted lists to help you sort them out.

Lodging accommodations are quite variable and therefore are difficult to quantify. Is a stunning view worth more than fancy décor and a jetted bathtub? Is forested privacy more valuable than walking distance to restaurants? Would you rather sit on a beautiful antique couch or stretch out on a modern sofa from Ikea? Because of this, we haven't attempted to give readers a value rating. We hope that by reading the descriptions you can select the lodging that best fits your needs as well as your budget.

TAXES. The combined state and county sales tax in San Juan County is 7.7 percent. Sales tax is not levied on food purchased in grocery stores, nor on prescription drugs. An additional 2 percent use tax is levied on lodging.

Taxes are levied on the following:
     Beer, wine, soft drinks sold in grocery stores and restaurants
     Non-food grocery items such as soap, cosmetics, and toilet tissue
     Goods such as clothing, non-prescription drugs, sundries, newspapers
     Food and beverages served in restaurants
     Lodging

Any applicable taxes are already included in the price of:
     Packaged hard liquor purchased in state-owned liquor stores
     Entertainment (boat tours, theater tickets)
     Fuel (including marine fuel)
     Ferry fares
     Boat charters
     Airplane fares or charters
     Boat moorage

Lodging Details

The range of prices quoted for lodging are summer rates, double occupancy; however, cottages and vacation homes usually rent for the entire unit. Prices are subject to change. Quiet-season rates, except for holidays, generally are lower by 10 or 20 percent, or the second or third day will be offered at a significant reduction.

Reservations are required. In summer, most accommodations are booked well in advance. A deposit, usually by credit card, is normally required at the time you make your reservation in the event of a cancellation or no-show. If a site does not take credit cards, they will usually hold your reservation for a short period of time until your check arrives. Many of the rental homes also require a security deposit. We have indicated which accommodations accept credit cards, although some might not take every major credit card.

All accommodations are open year-round, unless otherwise noted. However, innkeepers take a break, too, and some might be closed for short periods during the quiet season.

As with accommodations everywhere, some lodgings have restrictions on pets and children. Even if a facility is listed as accepting pets, when you make your reservation be sure to confirm that it is OK to bring your animal. If you are allergic to animals, even though an establishment does not accept pets, the innkeepers might have pets of their own, so be sure to check if there are animals on the premise.

By state law, public lodgings, such as motels and hotels, must have at least 75 percent of their facilities nonsmoking. Some are completely nonsmoking. If this is a concern for you, either pro or con, be sure to inquire.

Tower House, on San Juan Island, is one of many fine B&Bs in the islands.

Finding the Ideal Lodging

Because there is such a range of types of accommodations, in this book they have been categorized to help you find what best suits your needs

BED & BREAKFAST INNS ⊨▬◀ These are two or more rooms in a large home, usually in a beautiful setting. Bathrooms, in nearly all cases, are private. In a few cases a "dedicated" bath might be indicated, which means it is not immediately adjoining your room—you have to step into a hall to reach it, but it is for your use alone during your stay. If rooms share a bath, that is noted. Although guests have plenty of privacy, some facilities are shared, such as B&B sitting rooms, decks, and hot tubs.

Bed and breakfast inns provide the ultimate in pampering, with multi-course breakfasts and maid service for your room. You can chat with your host or other guests, or find a quiet niche to yourself, if you prefer. Some facilities deliver breakfast to your room where you can eat it on your private deck, or in your nightie and robe without rushing your day.

Complimentary wine and snacks might be offered. There might be a guest refrigerator where you can get ice and keep mixes to prepare drinks (you provide the liquor). If you have special dietary needs, your hosts will make every effort to accommodate you, but be sure to let them know when you make your reservations.

COTTAGES, VACATION HOMES, GUEST SUITES, CONDOMINIUMS & HOSTELS ⌂ Most often favored by families, these are separate units with private entrances and private baths. All linens are provided, but not daily maid service. Usually they include kitchenettes, with refrigerator, microwave, coffeemaker, and sink, or full kitchens. Basic cooking utensils and dishes are provided. Food staples are not included unless noted (some provide breakfast makings such as coffee, cereal, milk, and yogurt). In addition to the stated sleeping accommodations, often they can accommodate additional persons on a hide-a-bed or futon. Some have additional roll-aways or cribs.

All units have heat of some sort to soften any evening chill, but some cottages might have only wood stoves (wood provided). These stoves are not the rustic kind one associates with a fishing cabin, but are clean, modern versions (essentially enclosed fireplaces or wood-burning heaters) that offer a cozy glow. If heat is by wood stoves, so far as we know, it is noted here. Gas or electric fireplaces might also provide heat and cheer.

RESORTS, HOTELS, MOTELS & INNS 🏨 These usually include a large building, or several large buildings, with many private rooms, each with private baths. Suites have a separate sitting area. Often they have private view decks, fireplaces, wet bars, and hot tubs. Unless otherwise noted, hotels and motels always have maid service, with towels and linens changed daily. Resorts frequently have their own spacious beach and such things as tennis courts, children's play area, pool, and restaurant. A complimentary continental breakfast is usually provided.

VACATION HOME RENTAL FIRMS. These businesses maintain extensive listings, but available lodgings vary from year to year. Most lodgings have a one-week minimum rental clause, although some might be available for shorter times.

Joyous Events: Weddings, Vow Renewals & Commitment Ceremonies

What spot could be more romantic for a special joyous event than the gorgeous San Juans? Your guests will especially enjoy the location, as they can combine your festivities with a personal weekend getaway. Book well in advance and inform your guests, so those planning to stay over can get lodging reservations.

Marriage licenses obtained anywhere in the state of Washington are valid in the San Juans. Locally, licenses can be obtained from the San Juan County Auditor's office in Friday Harbor; phone (360) 378-2161. There is a three-day waiting period.

Numerous restaurants have banquet rooms, special facilities, and catering

The Episcopal Church in Orcas Island's Eastsound is one of the San Juans' many beautiful houses of worship.

available for celebration parties. In addition, there are catering companies that specialize in such group gatherings. If you have a spirit of adventure, consider an unconventional spot for your ceremony—the top of Mount Constitution, English Camp, Lime Kiln State Park (maybe whales will cavort offshore), or a charter boat. Before planning a group ceremony in any public spot, check with the proper authorities regarding any restrictions.

A number of San Juan lodgings do weddings and other ceremonies, although you will need to plan well in advance, as they tend to be heavily booked with regular customers during the summer. Some have catering facilities on hand; others can suggest local sources. The skilled staffs at both Rosario Resort and Roche Harbor Resort will assist you in planning a memorable event at their facilities. Lodgings that are especially popular are Kangaroo House on Orcas Island and Trumpeter Inn on San Juan Island. The 64-foot charter boat, *Odyssey*, operated by San Juan Excursions, and the 56-foot *Orcas Express* operated by Orcas Island Eclipse Charters both do weddings at sea. Outlook Inn, Victorian Valley, The Hotel de Haro at Roche Harbor, Lakedale Resort, and San Juan Vineyards all have wedding chapels. Spring Bay Inn does weddings in kayaks. One of the innkeepers, Sandy Playa, can perform the ceremony.

Some Northwest couples have their ceremony on the mainland and then escape to one of the islands' exquisite bed and breakfast inns or resorts for romantic seclusion. Several lodgings have honeymoon suites and offer special packages. Inquire when you check for reservations.

A web site, *thesanjuans.com*, lists accommodations and wedding related services such as florists, caterers, officiants, musicians, and photographers. The chambers of commerce or information bureaus on the major islands should also be able to provide information.

Event Planners

Lopez Island Celebrations
P.O. Box 565; Lopez Island, WA 98261
(360) 468-3140

San Juan Wedding and Event Planning
Becki Day, P.O. Box 3335; Friday Harbor, WA 98250. Phone: (360) 378-9519; fax: (360) 378-3648; email: *beckiday@rockisland.com*; web site: *sanjuanislandweddings.info/services*

Officiants

Local judges can preside over weddings. The following persons also will officiate.

Ament, Rita
Phone: (360) 378-9628

Rev. Archie Brooks
P.O. Box 3135, Friday Harbor, WA, 98250.
Phone: (360) 378-2789; email:
   weddingarch@hotmail.com

Rev. Jean Hendrickson
Phone: (360) 378-7712

Carla Higginson
175 2nd Street North, Friday Harbor, WA
98250. Phone: (360) 378-2185

Playa, Sandy
(360) 376-5531; web site: *weddingsonorcas.com*

Rev. Dorothy Stone
P.O. Box 1034; Friday Harbor, WA 98250;
Phone: (360) 378-6663; email:
choose love@rockisland.com

Churches & Houses of Faith

For a church ceremony, contact one of the island churches of your faith, or a non-denominational church, and inquire about their services.

Lopez Island

Grace Episcopal Church
Phone: (360) 468-3477

Lopez Island Community Church
Phone: (360) 468-3877

Orcas Island

Eagles Rock Church
Phone: (360) 376-6332

Emmanuel Episcopal Parish
Phone: (360) 376-2352

Orcas Island Community Church
Phone: (360) 376-6422

Orcas Island Seventh-Day
Phone: (360) 376-6683

St. Francis Catholic Church
Phone: (360) 376-6301

Seventh Day Adventist
Phone: (360) 376-6683

Victorian Valley Chapel
P.O. Box 261; Orcas, WA 98280. Phone: (866) 424-2735; email: sara@chapelvalleycorp.com; web site: victorianvalleychapel.com

Another option for your ceremony is this intimate little site in Victorian Valley on Orcas Island. The quaint country chapel has arched, stained glass windows and antique pews that seat 75 guests.

San Juan Island

Assembly of God of San Juans
Phone: (360) 378-2789

Calvary Chapel San Juan
Phone: (360) 378-7267 or (360) 378-7268

Christian Science
Phone: (360) 378-4773

Church of Jesus Christ of Latter Day Saints
Phone: (360) 378-4162

Faith and Hope Fellowship
Phone: (360) 378-2789

Family Life Foursquare
Phone: (360) 378-3072

Friday Harbor Presbyterian Church
Phone: (360) 378-4544

Friday Harbor Seventh Day Adventist Church
Phone: (360) 378-4164; web site: rockisland.com/~fhsda/

Islands Community Evangelical Church
Phone: (360) 378-4154

Jehovah's Witness
Phone: (360) 378-2861

Lutheran Church in the San Juans
Phone: (360) 378-4855; web site: lutheransonline.com/

St. David's Episcopal Church
Phone: (360) 378-5360; web site: saintdavidsepiscopal.org

St. Francis Catholic Church
Phone: (360) 378-2910

Sakya Kachod Choling Tibetan Buddhist
Phone: (360) 378-6938

San Juan Unitarian Universalist Fellowship
Phone: (360) 378-5473

Seventh Day Adventist
Phone: (360) 378-4164

Word with Power Christian Center
Phone: (360) 378-2122

Additional Lodging Information

Both Orcas Island and San Juan Island have associations that maintain a lodging hotline in the summer. If you are unable to find lodging, or arrive and find the space you've reserved is not suitable for your needs, they will try to find a spot for you. They are dedicated to helping innkeepers deliver the best possible service in the highest quality inns. Be aware there are times when absolutely everything is filled.

Lopez Island does not maintain a hotline. However, general lodging information can be obtained from the Chamber of Commerce. The following web sites provide links to some of the accommodations.

Bed & Breakfast Association of San Juan Island

P.O. Box 3016; Friday Harbor, WA 98250. Phone: (866) 645-3030 or (360) 378-3030; web site: *san-juan-island.net*

Lopez Island Chamber of Commerce

Lopez Village, Old Post Road; Lopez Island, WA 98261. Phone: (877) 433-2789 or (360) 468-4664; email: *lopezchamber@lopezisland.com*; web site: *lopezisland.com*

Orcas Island Chamber of Commerce

P.O. Box 252; Eastsound, WA 98245. Phone: (360) 376-2273; web site: *orcasislandchamber.com*

Orcas Island Lodging Association

Phone: (360) 376-2175; email: *info@orcas-lodging.com*; web site: *orcas-lodging.com*

San Juan Chamber of Commerce

135 Spring Street; Friday Harbor, WA 98250. Phone: (360) 378-5240; email: *chamberinfo@sanjuanisland.org*; web site: *sanjuanisland.org*

ABOUT PETS

For some people, dogs are an integral part of their family, and their pets accompany them on car or boat trips. If you bring Bowser to the San Juans, be forewarned that by county ordinance, dogs must be confined or kept on a leash in rural areas. The meeting of city dogs with country cows or sheep has at times had very tragic results—generally for the livestock. By law, any unlicensed dog roaming free in rural areas may be shot.

Also, some accommodations do not allow pets. If you wish to stay the weekend in a lovely bed and breakfast inn, or go on one of the wildlife cruises, several boarding kennels offer animal care. Consider one of the following rather than miss a wonderful opportunity. The place where you make lodging reservations might also recommend a kennel. No pet boarding is available on Lopez Island.

PET BOARDING
◆

Animal Inn (San Juan Island)

497 Boyce Road; Friday Harbor, WA 98250. Phone: (360) 378-4735

Eastsound Kennels (Orcas Island)
186 Dolphin Bay Road, Route 1, Box 78H; Eastsound, WA 98245. Phone: (360) 376-2410

Sunnyhill Kennels and Cattery (Mainland)
8033 Summit Park Road; Anacortes, WA 98221. Phone: (360) 293-3434

ON-ISLAND TRANSPORTATION

Lopez, Orcas, and San Juan Islands have taxi services, although they are much more casual than similar services you might be accustomed to on the mainland. You might find a taxi or two waiting at the ferry terminal when the ferry arrives, but if you need one, usually you will have to phone ahead of time of your arrival or upon your arrival. Even then, service can be sporadic.

Some island businesses have rental cars or bicycles available for your use. A few lodgings are within walking distance of the ferry. Those that are farther away might pick you up at the ferry, the airport, or even your marina, or suggest suitable transportation. Inquire when you make your lodging reservation. In the chapter on each island, see On-Island Transportation, pages 104–106, 185–191, and 272–274.

Bicycles are another option for touring the islands. Rental shops are near the ferry landing in Anacortes, at Orcas Landing, and Friday Harbor. Friday Harbor and Orcas Island also have moped and scoot cart rentals. Scoot carts are small two-passenger, three-wheeled vehicles, much like a golf cart. They are permitted on San Juan roads. You must have a valid driver's license to operate either a moped or a scoot cart. State law requires that bicycle riders wear a helmet on public roads. If you do not have one, rental of a bicycle usually includes a helmet.

SHOPPING

This book focuses on stores that will be of the most interest to visitors. We have tried to note when businesses are open only at limited times, although for any store on the islands hours might vary from summer to winter. Shops are listed alphabetically, by island. For ease in locating a particular shopping category, consult the listing in the front of the book for facilities by type.

When a shopping location is some distance from the main center of business, we have provided driving directions.

As any shop-oholic knows, the joy of browsing through stores is in finding that unique "something" that you might not find elsewhere, happening on an especially good buy, or celebrating your visit with a remembrance that embodies the particular character of the spot. Beyond the usual souvenir T-shirts, postcards, and salt and pepper shakers, there are specialty items that draw shoppers to the islands.

FINE ART & CRAFTS. Many artists make their homes in the islands. Look for top-notch paintings, limited-edition art prints, fine art photographs, stained glass, pottery, porcelain, sculpture, woodcrafts, metalwork, furniture, handmade musical instruments, and jewelry ranging from inexpensive to quite luxurious. Some items can be custom made to your taste and needs.

You might discover unusual items such as baskets woven from dried kelp and chairs fashioned from driftwood. Many artists rely on local shops to sell their goods, although some artist's studios are open for retail business year-round, or at least during summer months. San Juan Island has an artist's studio open house the first weekend in June every year, where you can tour the studios and purchase work directly from the artists.

A recent term on the art scene, giclee (zhee-klay), is popping up regularly. A giclee (sometimes spelled glicee) is a type of inkjet print that is, essentially, a computer printout—although a very high quality one. An original painting or drawing is photographed digitally or scanned. In some cases it might be created on a computer, or the scanned art is digitally enhanced. The art is carefully color matched and printed out with archival inks on quality, acid-free paper or canvas, usually in a smaller size than the original. The specialized printers used can accommodate large dimension materials, and typically have eight or 12 inkjets to ensure perfect color, as opposed to your color inkjet printer at home that has four. Sometimes the printout is individually artistically enhanced. The artist hand signs and dates each print. These prints are less expensive than the original, but nonetheless are of excellent quality and are very much worth owning.

FIBER ARTS. Sheep, llamas, and alpacas are raised on the San Juans, and yarn spun from their wool finds its way into local studios and shops. However, because the islands' source is not adequate or varied enough to support the prolific work of local fiber artists, raw materials are also imported. You'll find tapestries, rugs, soft sculpture, and unique "wearable art." If you're a knitter or weaver, you'll revel in stores that are filled with feather-soft skeins of yarn.

NORTHWEST NATIVE ART. Early Northwest Native culture in the region that today is Washington and British Columbia, developed an exceptionally powerful art style, utilizing natural and symbolic forms blended in a complex imagery. Totem poles are the most commonly recognized representatives of this art. Small versions of totems can be found for sale. However, you'll also discover wonderful carved boxes, masks, sculptures, paintings, and prints utilizing Northwest Native art forms. Some of the art found in shops is done by tribal members, while other pieces are by non-natives with a good knowledge of the art form. Some modern artists incorporate these motifs in contemporary paintings or sculptures. There are also "knock-offs," although even an inexpensive, foreign-made totem pole makes an interesting souvenir. If you're looking for a collector's item, we recommend you have a knowledge of the art, shop in a store that specializes in it and can advise you on your purchase. An excellent one is Arctic Raven Gallery in Friday Harbor.

FOOD & DRINK. Numerous "cottage industry" food producers thrive on the islands. Look in gift shops and grocery stores for local brands of island- produced jellies, honey, and preserves. There's a local brand of coffee (not grown here, of course, but locally roasted). An excellent microbrewery and two local wineries have their devotees. Several sauces, salsas, and other condiments are locally made with loving care. Fresh and dried herbs and herb-flavored vinegars come from local farms.

Pelindaba, which has a store in Friday Harbor and a farm on San Juan Island, is a spot you won't want to miss. Their inventive use of lavender and other herbs in everything from décor to food to cosmetics is inspiring. Any of these items make an excellent souvenir to take back home—and an excellent reason to return.

Lopez Village, Eastsound, and Friday Harbor all have farmers' markets in the summer on Saturday, and sometimes on other days. There you can buy fresh-baked goods, and locally-grown produce, garden plants, and cut flowers, as well as the work of local craftspeople. You never know exactly what you'll find, because the selection varies. It's a terrific way to sample the bounty of the islands, as well as to chat with the people who produce it. The location of the markets might change from year to year, but you'll usually find them near the center of town, and signs usually tell of their location.

SEAFOOD. Salmon, Dungeness crab, clams, mussels, oysters, shrimp, abalone—there's no denying these are locally "grown." In Friday Harbor you can usually buy fresh salmon right at the docks, and crab, clams, and shrimp are often available as well. If you're not from the Northwest and have never had local Dungeness crab, don't miss it. It's the best crab in the world. Even Julia Child sang its praises.

You'll find fresh seafood in the grocery stores, too. Local people know top-quality seafood, and no merchant would consider offering anything but the best. Some stores will pack it in ice or dry ice and ship it to friends or to your home for you, guaranteeing that it will arrive fresh. You'll also find locally smoked or canned seafood—another excellent gift.

BOOKS. Statistics say that Northwesterners read more books per capita than people from any other place in the U.S. (it must be those gray winter days). They

Northwest Flavor—Shopping for Memories

If you're from Connecticut or Chattanooga, what do you shop for that embodies the San Juan Islands and the Pacific Northwest? Wind kites (flag-like wind socks adapted from Japanese fish kites), usually fashioned from brightly colored nylon, are very popular. You'll find them representing nearly everything from ladybugs and pansies to dragons or rainbows. Boaters love to tie them on their rigging to trail colorfully in the wind. They also look great on a patio or in a child's room.

Seagulls, seashells, starfish, and other nautical gewgaws are in abundance. They may not hold much fascination if you already live in a seacoast city, but if you're from the Midwest, they'll certainly be a nice remembrance of your trip.

Anything adorned with an orca whale is popular. It can't be just any whale, it's got to be one of those majestic black and white mammals. With the advent of the "Free Willy" movies (which, by the way, were filmed here in the San Juans and nearby British Columbia), there's more orca motif paraphernalia than ever before, especially for kids. San Juan Islanders like to call these whales their own, even though they roam throughout most of the Northern Hemisphere.

You'll find salmon-decor items everywhere, and in everything from pillows to potholders to women's purses and men's ties. The perfect item for the fish lover! And finally, anything with a ferryboat motif attracts buyers. Christmas tree ornaments, posters, potholders, and children's toy ferries are a few of the renditions for sale in shops throughout the islands.

also write a lot of them. Island bookstores carry an extensive selection of those of local interest and by local authors. You'll find gorgeous volumes of photography picturing local scenery as a souvenir of your trip.

San Juan Special Events

Numerous special events and public celebrations take place on the islands throughout the year. Many center around a particular San Juan recreation—there are fishing derbies as well as bicycling, running, and sailing races, July sees a summer arts fair and lavender festival. The three large islands have 4th of July parades, and San Juan Island has a county fair. You might want to pick a particular event to include in your vacation. For many years the San Juan Island Jazz Festival was a popular feature. However, it drew such large crowds at a time when the island was already overwhelmed with tourists that it became impossible to manage, and it had be discontinued. Several smaller festivals of different natures now take its place.

Descriptions of many of the events are listed with the information on a particular island under Events & Attractions, pages 103, 183, and 266. The various Chamber of Commerce web sites can also let you know what's going on.

Yacht Clubs & Annual Boating Events

It's no secret that the San Juans are a boater's paradise. The three major islands have yacht clubs, and in addition there's the Friday Harbor Sailing Club and the Sailing Foundation. These organizations sponsor parades, races, regattas, and other rivalry and revelry throughout the year. Some races are white-knuckle serious, while others are just for fun. Members of other yacht clubs may join in many of the events. They are a perfect way to get to know other boaters and enjoy the terrific boating in the islands.

For non-boaters, the races and parades are grand spectator events. Two of the major events are:

Opening Day of Boating Season

WHEN: The first Saturday of May.

Oil the teak and shine the brightwork! The yacht clubs of Orcas, Lopez, and San Juan Islands kick off the boating season with local yacht parades. Boats are decorated for display and competition. Sailboat races and all-around parties are part of the festivities. You can register and compete for one of the prizes, or just get in line and join the fun.

The Lopez Island parade takes place in Fisherman Bay, the Orcas Island one in West Sound is by the yacht club dock, and the San Juan Island parade is right in Friday Harbor.

Shaw Island Classic Sailboat Race

WHERE: The race begins and finishes at the Port of Friday Harbor docks.
WHEN: The second weekend in August.

The Shaw Island Classic is one of the "for fun" races. Slack and flaky winds at times result in few of the boats being able to finish the race in the prescribed time. The objective is to navigate the 16-or-so nautical miles around Shaw Island by whatever route the skipper chooses, depending on an assessment of tidal currents, winds, and the fickle finger of fate. Whether they finish or not, most skippers and crews take it in a lighthearted spirit, and all participants join in a dinner sponsored by the San Juan Island Yacht Club to cap off the race and to award trophies. The event usually attracts more than a hundred entrants from all over the Northwest. It's a wonderful race to participate in as well as to watch. A portion of the course is along the ferry route, so the ferries can provide good vantage points.

TENNIS & GOLF

If you want to make tennis part of your vacation, lodgings that have courts for the use of their guests are listed in the index. All three of the large islands have tennis courts at the high schools. These courts might be busy when school is in session, but often are available at other times.

- Lopez Island has newly refurbished tennis courts at the high school in the middle of the island, at Center Road and School Road.
- On Orcas Island, tournament-quality tennis courts are at Buck Park, on the north side of the Orcas Island High School. To reach Buck Park, drive north out of Eastsound on either Lover's Lane or North Beach Road and turn east on Mount Baker Road. You'll find the tennis courts in about a mile, on the south side of the road. A path for jogging and bicycling runs along the side of the road.
- On San Juan Island, the excellent courts at Friday Harbor High School are at 45 Blair Avenue.
- San Juan Golf and Country Club, at 806 Golf Course Road on San Juan Island, has tennis courts available to the public, for a fee and by reservation.

GOLF COURSES

Lopez Island Golf Club

Airport Road; Lopez Island, WA 98261. Phone: (360) 468-2679; web site: *lopezislandgolfclub.com*

🚗 Drive south from Lopez Landing, and in 2 miles turn west on Fisherman Bay Road. Continue to Lopez Village and follow the road as it curves south around Fisherman Bay. At 7¼ miles from the ferry landing, head west on Airport Road. The entrance road is in another ½ mile. If you reach the airport, you've gone too far.

This 9-hole, par 33 golf course sits on the southwest side of Lopez Island, near the airport. The 40-acre public facility enjoys a pastoral setting. Hawks nest nearby, and deer sometimes roam the fairways.

Because the course is lightly played, you don't need reservations. Only the tee boxes and greens are irrigated, and by late summer the fairways can become very dry. The clubhouse, which is open from March to October, has golfing supplies as well as rental clubs and pullcarts. Quiet-season green fees are paid on an honor system.

Orcas Island Golf Course

2171 Orcas Road, Route 1, Box 85; Eastsound, WA 98245. Phone: (360) 376-4400; email: *golf@orcasgolf.com*; web site: *orcasgolf.com*

🚗 From the ferry landing, head north on Orcas Road. The course lies on the west side of the road, 6 miles from the landing.

Orcas Island's 9-hole, par 36 course gets very busy in the summer, so make reservations in advance. During the quiet season there rarely is a problem getting playing time. Several holes cross a hilltop and some ponds to make the course interesting, as well as a real physical test. An alternate 9 holes makes an enjoyable 18-hole challenge.

The clubhouse has a pro shop, lounge, and scenery-encompassing patio. You can rent clubs and either power or pull golf carts.

San Juan Golf and Country Club

806 Golf Course Road; Friday Harbor, WA 98250. Phone: (360) 378-2254; fax: (360) 378-3107; email: *sjgolf@rockisland.com*; web site: *sanjuangolf.com*

🚗 From Spring Street in Friday Harbor, turn south on Argyle. Follow this road as it turns west and then T's into Cattle Point Road. Follow Cattle Point Road south, and in 2 miles, as it bends west, Golf Course Road heads straight south to the clubhouse.

Great golfing and a superb marine view, too! This 9-hole, par 35 course is the best, most popular course in the San Juans. Its 6508 yards make it the longest 9-hole venue in Washington. The particularly delightful course boasts well-kept greens, beautiful flowers, and an overlook of Griffin Bay. Reservations are suggested for weekends during the summer.

The pro shop stocks a complete range of golfers' needs, including rentals. Tennis courts are also available to the public. The bar and restaurant are open from May through September, and feature soups, salads, and sandwiches. A celebrity tournament is held here every year in early June. See Events & Attractions in the chapter on San Juan Island, page 266.

SAN JUAN CAMPS & OUTDOOR EXPERIENCES

The San Juan Islands are a destination for vacationing families and adults. It figures that they have wonderful summer camps, too. All the islands' youth camps offer an exciting gamut of outdoor fun ranging from swimming, hiking, rock climbing, and horseback riding to photography and theater arts. Kids will discover they can have a blast without the benefit of electronic gadgets. Older youths have opportunities for out-of-camp trips to remote islands. One camp offers a mountain climb to the top of Mount Baker. Many kids return year after year, working up in the programs, and some eventually become counselors.

All youth camps offer the basic staples of camping and camaraderie, and are well supervised by counselors, instructors, and other staff. Private camps are more expensive than the YMCA camp, but in general they provide more personal instruction, and smaller staff-to-camper ratio. Transportation from nearby cities is generally available; specific information is available from the respective camps, which are described in the chapters on specific islands.

CAMPS & ADVENTURES
Camp Nor'wester

Summer: P.O. Box 4395; Roche Harbor, WA 98250. Winter: P.O. Box 668; Lopez Island, WA 98261. Phone: (360) 468-2225; fax: (360) 468-2472; email: *camp@norwester.com*; web site: *norwester.org*

AGES: Boys and girls ages 9 to 16.

FACILITIES: Lodging in 16-person units (including tents or teepees) with counselor and assistant, restrooms and showers, main lodge, dining hall, saltwater swimming pool, barn, stables with 28 horses, riding ring, rifle and archery ranges, craft center, adobe oven, health center, trading post, playfields, trails, rock-climbing areas, dock, beach, 35-foot Indian-style canoe.

ACTIVITIES: Camping, swimming, nature study, sailing, rowing, canoeing, soccer, baseball, basketball, volleyball, music, drama, crafts, photography, baking, bicycling, archery, riflery, hiking, rock climbing, mountain climbing, ropes and challenge course, out-of-camp trips, and more.

FEES: 2-week session (ages 9-10) $1750; 4-week session (ages 11-16) $3350; Additional deposit at camp store for laundry and sundries.

For more than 50 years Camp Nor'wester held forth on a beautiful peninsula on the tip of Lopez Island. Unfortunately, the property was sold, and anguished youngsters and their parents were faced with the loss of their beloved camp. However, Camp Nor'wester was able to locate an ideal new site on Johns Island, south of Stuart Island.

Once youngsters enter Camp Nor'wester, the everyday world vanishes, and only the realm of outdoor adventure remains. The camp's distinctive Northwest bent reflects the culture of Native Americans who lived here long before the San Juans became a summer playground for youngsters. The camp's 35-foot canoe is carved in the authentic Haida manner.

Extended trips, available to older campers, include bicycle treks to Canada's Gulf Islands, alpine hiking in Mount Baker–Snoqualmie National Forest, and a real mountain climb to the glaciated summit of Mount Baker. The season is divided into two-week and four-week sessions, beginning mid-June and ending mid-August. Campers may sign up for one session or two.

Canoe Island French Camp

P.O. Box 170; Orcas, WA 98280-0370. Phone: Canoe Island: (360) 468-2329; fax: (360) 468-302; email: *info@canoeisland.org*; web site: *canoeisland.org*.

AGES: Boys and girls ages 9 to 15.

FACILITIES: Lodging in 3–4-person teepees with counselor, restrooms, and heated swimming pool, dining room, library, health center, social room, photography darkroom, craft room, program building with stage, tennis court, archery range, volleyball court, dock, beach, canoes, kayaks, sailboat.

ACTIVITIES: French-based singing, dancing and cultural activities, camping, crafts (including pottery and photography), sailing, canoeing, kayaking, swimming, archery, fencing, drama, music, tennis, volleyball, campfires, nature study, out-of-camp trips.

FEES: 2-week session $1885; 3-week session $2585; weekend family camp $215 per person; discounts for early payment of tuition, sibling, and multiple sessions.

Has there ever before been such a great way for a kid to learn a language? French Camp is located on Canoe Island, its own private 50-acre island immediately south of Shaw Island. For more than 30 years this camp has used the French language and culture as a unique springboard for summer activities.

Each two-week session has special activities relating to a session theme. La Révolution Française campers explore the founding of the French Republic, storm the Bastille and search the island for Marie Antoinette. Les Voyageurs campers explore neighboring islands by canoe, bike, or sailboat, practice Voyageur and Indian living skills and participate in a Native potlatch. Les Chevaliers campers follow clues around the island to find the holy grail, use a trebuchet to bombard a fortress, and engage in kayak jousting. Le Tour du Monde campers try African and Vietnamese cuisine, play Caribbean and Cajun music, and participate in a world's fair of culture, food, music, and sports.

Four Winds * Westward Ho

286 Four Winds Lane; Deer Harbor, WA 98243. Phone: (360) 376-2277; email: *abby@ fourwindscamp.org*; web site: *fourwindscamp.org*

AGE: Boys and girls ages 7 to 16; counselor training program ages 16 to 18.

FACILITIES: Lodging in 4- to 6-person cabins or wall-tents with counselor, restrooms and showers, dining lodge, stables with 26 horses, crafts cabins, dance court, dock and boathouse, amphitheater, infirmary, archery range, tennis courts, basketball court, badminton court, sports field, beach.

ACTIVITIES: Rowing, sailing, canoeing, bicycling, hiking, fishing, tide-pool exploration, horse riding (English and Western, trail riding, cart driving), tennis, archery, soccer, lacrosse, volleyball, basketball, crafts (woodcarving, weaving, photography, painting, more), drama, music, folk dancing, campfires, out-of-camp trips.

FEES: 1 week Junior Session $875; 4 week sessions for older campers $3800; financial aid grants are available.

Four Winds Camp was founded for girls in 1927, and its boys' counterpart, Westward Ho, opened three years later. Today they are joined as a single, large, co-ed camp on the west shore of Orcas Island's West Sound. The camp's several dozen rustic buildings are casually scattered around 150 wooded acres that encircle Four Winds Bay.

Mid-June to late August camp sessions are divided by age group. A low-key, one-week session offers beginning campers, ages seven to nine, a chance to live together and gain outdoor knowledge. Close staff supervision ensures these youngsters a positive camp experience. For more seasoned campers, four-week sessions for ages eight to sixteen provide greater freedom and individual growth. A counselor training program is offered for sixteen- to eighteen-year-old experienced campers.

Gnats Nature Hikes

P.O. Box 272; Deer Harbor, WA, 98243. Phone: (360) 376-6629. Web site: *orcasislandhikes.com*

SUMMER RATES: Half day $30 per person, boat trip for half-day outer island marine park hike $65 per person, custom hikes available.

This business is the only one of its kind in the San Juans—and what a great idea! Natalie Herner offers customized guided nature hikes in Orcas Island's Moran State Park for intermediate-level hikers, and shares her knowledge of the island's natural history. Boat trips for hikes to outer island marine parks are also offered. Hikes are available daily year-round. Snacks are provided. Backpacks and water bottles are available.

YMCA Camp Orkila

P.O. Box 1149; Eastsound, WA 98245. Offices: 909 Fourth Avenue; Seattle, WA 98104. Phone: Eastsound: (360) 376-2678; Seattle: (206) 382-5009, (206) 382-5001; fax: Eastsound: (360) 376-2267; Seattle: (206) 382-4920; email: *colemanorkilainfo@cs.seattleymca.org*; web site: *seattleymca.org*.

AGE: Boys and girls grades 1-12; families.

FACILITIES: Lodging in rustic open-air cabins with counselor, restrooms, dining hall, heated outdoor swimming pool, playing fields, archery range, rifle and BB range, nature trails, beach, basketball court, baseball and softball diamonds, volleyball court, indoor climbing wall, high and low ropes course, BMX track, horses, riding arena, corrals, forest riding trails, dock with floats, rowboats, kayaks, canoes, sailboats, craft center, chapel, small animal farm, food and vegetable gardens, marine life tanks, riding arena and trails, 45-foot cruiser, Marine Salmon Center, remote camps at Satellite Island and Twin Lakes.

ACTIVITIES: Swimming, fishing, nature study, crafts, music, drama, hiking, rock climbing, camping, bicycling, horse riding and care, farming, gardening, sailing, kayaking, canoeing, river rafting, skateboard camp, marine biology, basketball, volleyball, soccer, campfires, horse pack trips, out-of-camp trips.

FEES: Sessions vary from 10 to 22 days; fees range from $635 to $1950; financial aid is available.

Several generations of Northwest campers fondly recall their sun-drenched summers at Camp Orkila. The YMCA camp, based on Orcas Island's northwest shore, has been holding forth since 1906. Youngsters acquire new skills and develop positive values—and all the time they think they are just having fun!

Sessions ranging from seven to twenty-two days for youngsters from sixth through twelfth grades offer a broad range of experiences. Programs include such varied offerings as Seekers, Explorers, and Trekkers (the traditional camping program); Pioneer Camp (farming, gardening, and animal care), Horsemasters (equine care and riding techniques); Adventure Trips (wilderness skills for teens); and Bikers, Kayakers, Mariners, and Rock Climbers. Special sessions are offered for children with diabetes.

GETTING THERE
FERRYBOATS, PLANES, BUSES & BICYCLES

THEY COME HAULING KAYAKS, canoes, trailers, bicycles, mopeds, suitcases, backpacks, camping gear, and kids: The vacationing throngs descend on the San Juans every year. The Washington State ferry system records more than 1.5 million riders to the islands yearly. Of that, the majority are visitors, bent on enjoying this vacationland for a day, or a week, or even the summer. Washington State's ferry system is the largest and finest of its kind in the nation. For many, especially those who are not already familiar with it, the ferry ride is nearly as great an adventure as the ultimate destination. It is, indeed, one of the best (and definitely cheapest) ways to tour the islands. In addition to the state ferries, a few private ferries provide regular service to the islands, taking passengers from and to destinations not served by the state ferry system.

FERRY SERVICE

Washington state ferries traveling to the San Juans originate in the city of Anacortes (on the mainland, 86 miles north of Seattle), and travel to the four largest islands: Lopez, Shaw, Orcas, and San Juan. Anacortes is reached by driving I-5 north from Seattle or south from Vancouver, B.C. Just north of Mount Vernon, take Exit 230/Highway 20 West and head west to Anacortes. The ferry terminal is on the far west side of town, 4 miles from the city center. Watch for signs that direct you there.

A number of different ferryboats operate on the San Juan runs, and their sizes vary. Most are three-deck ships ranging between 250 and 400 feet in length and holding from 75 to 160 vehicles. The largest accommodates several thousand passengers.

DISABLED ACCESS. Facilities for physically disabled passengers are available on most ferries that make San Juan runs, with the exception of the inter-island ferry. A small elevator operates between the car deck and observation levels.

If you are physically disabled, or are traveling with a disabled person, and want to be able to leave your car to go to the observation deck, inform the attendant when you purchase your ticket. The crew will attempt to see that your vehicle is parked near the elevator, and that there is room to unload a wheelchair. If traveling without a car, wheelchairs can easily negotiate the overhead passenger ramp that links the terminal and boat at Anacortes. You will need to take the elevator down to the car deck to leave the boat at any of the island landings.

Comfortable inside seating and large windows, as well as outside viewing areas, offer visitors grand views of island scenery.

Reading the Ferry Schedule

Three types of ferry runs operate to, and within, the islands: a regular domestic run, an international run, and an inter-island run. Schedules change slightly every three months, and from year to year. During times of very heavy traffic, extra sailings might be added that will not appear on the schedule. Sailing times generally are closely met, except for unforeseen circumstances such as fog or other weather problems, or the very rare equipment failure.

Regular domestic runs originate in Anacortes and travel to Lopez, Shaw, Orcas, and San Juan Islands. These ferries leave Anacortes approximately 16 times a day in summer, 12 times in winter. The trip to Lopez Island takes about 45 minutes, and Friday Harbor is reached in approximately 1 hour and 15 minutes. However, not all ferries go to every island, so check carefully that the one you are planning to be on will take you to your desired destination.

International runs also originate in Anacortes, but end in Sidney, B.C., near Victoria, on Vancouver Island. This ship runs once a day in summer, and does not operated from January through the end of March. The one-way trip lasts 3 hours. Car space can be reserved on this ferry in summer for those traveling to Sidney; therefore, summer can be the most difficult run in which to get vehicle space to the islands on this particular run. If you board an eastbound ferry at Friday Harbor that originated in Sidney, you will be subject to Customs inspection when you disembark at Anacortes. This is necessary because this ship and some of its passengers cross the Canadian border, even though you did not leave the U.S. yourself. See Going Through U.S. Customs on page 32.

Inter-island runs travel between the four ferry-served islands, but are never scheduled to go to a mainland destination. The ships on the inter-island runs are smaller than those on other runs and hold fewer cars and passengers. The inter-island route between Orcas Island and Friday Harbor is the most splendid of all the runs, although it is not usually taken by the regular ferry runs from Anacortes. It is here, in tight little Wasp Passage, that the ferry threads its way through "the rock pile" of smaller islands. Some of these islets are privately owned and have quaint cabins or elegant homes, while some are marine state parks. As the westbound ferry hangs a left to the south, Yellow Island, one of the preserves held by The Nature Conservancy, is in view off the starboard (right) rail.

Fares

As of summer 2007, round-trip ferry fares for a vehicle under 20 feet plus the driver were:

Lopez Island
$23.95 to $26.55 ($32.35 to $35.90 peak season)
Shaw and Orcas Islands
$28.65 to $31.85 ($38.70 to $43.00 peak season)
San Juan Island (Friday Harbor)
$34.05 to $37.85 ($46.05 to $51.10 peak season)
Intersland
$15.85

Passengers, whether walk-on or in a car, pay $9.85 to $13.15 to all destinations; children under 11 and senior citizens pay half fare; children under five are free. There is an added charge for trailers and overlong RVs; the fee varies according to length. Motorcycles are charged about half the auto rate. There is a charge of $2.05 to $4.10 for bicycles walked on; however, there is no tariff for boats or bicycles that are mounted on vehicles, provided the overall height is less than 7½ feet. There might be slight increases to all fares annually.

Because it is assumed nearly everyone will be making a round-trip, with the exception of those going to Vancouver Island, in British Columbia, all tolls are round-trip, and are collected only on westbound runs. If you stop at one island and then later continue west, you'll pay a small additional toll.

For schedules, fares, or other information, contact the Washington State Department of Transportation.

Washington State Ferries

2901 Third Avenue, Suite 500; Seattle, WA 98121-3014
Administrative offices: (206) 515-3400
24-hour schedule information: (888) 808-7977, (800) 843-3779 (automated)
Seattle: (206) 464-6400
TT/TDD relay services for the hearing impaired: (800) 833-6385; Seattle: (206) 587-5500
Web site: *wsdot.wa.gov/ferries*
Web camera view of Anacortes. Orcas, and Friday Harbor terminal lots: *wsdot.wa.gov/ferries/cameras*

Getting On Board

If you walk on board, you will not need to worry about long ferry waits. Although there is no regular bus service on any of the islands, several hotels are within walking distance of the Friday Harbor ferry landing, and one at the Orcas ferry landing. A few other hotels and resorts will pick you up at the ferry terminal. In summer, there is scheduled bus service on Orcas Island, and on San Juan Island between Friday Harbor and Roche Harbor. Other transportation options are described later in this chapter.

If you take your vehicle to the islands, you will be told to park in a lane at the ferry landing according to your destination because the ferries make stops at several islands. This strategy facilitates unloading at each island. It is important that you follow the parking directions of the ferry crew. When leaving an island, signs in the parking area tell you which lane to park in, according to your destination. *Heed them!*

In the height of summer, catching a ferry can be stressful due to the heavy volume of ferry traffic. Plan ahead, go prepared, and you'll enjoy the trip much more. In summer, if you're driving your car, expect there will be a wait in the ferry line whether you are going to the islands or leaving them, so arrive at least an hour early. On sunny weekends in July and August you might wait . . . and wait . . . and wait—it might be several hours. Bring something to read, games for the kids, a pillow for a nap, or lunch. Once properly parked, you will not have to move your car until the ship is ready to load, so you can leave it to browse nearby shops or grab a quick snack at a café. If a ferry employee is around, you would be wise to check how long the wait will be before you go very far. If you order food at a nearby restaurant, tell your server what ferry you will be catching, and they will try to expedite your order. Above all, stay near enough to watch for approaching ferries and to hear loudspeaker announcements. You should be in your car at least 30 minutes before scheduled departure time. If you are not there when boarding time arrives, traffic will be detoured around your vehicle, you will incur the silent (or not-so-silent) scorn of fellow passengers, and you will be fined and your car towed.

You Made It!

Once on board, you may leave the car deck to go to the observation levels (we recommend you take your camera along). Seats inside and on outside decks provide perfect views of the ever-changing scene as the ship slides past picturesque islands. Early morning and late afternoon provide drifting mists and dramatic lighting. You might spot bald eagles perched in tall tree snags on nearby islands. You could even

Safety on the Washington State Ferries

- Smoking anywhere on the ferries is strictly prohibited, even in your car, because of the potential hazard. Extinguish all smoking materials before boarding or loading your vehicle.
- Cans of gasoline are not permitted on the ferry. Propane tanks on campers must be shut off and sealed with a red tag procured from the tollbooth before boarding.
- Animals must be confined to cars or kept on a leash on the car deck. In the terminal waiting area and on the passenger decks, animals must be confined to cages, with the exception of service animals.
- To avoid interfering with on-board communications systems, do not use your cellular phone during loading.
- Trained security dogs, along with their handlers, might patrol the loading areas. In normal situations this will not slow any ferry operations.

Ferry decks provide fresh-air views of scenery, and possibly wildlife.

sight whales—if the captain knows they are in the vicinity he will usually slow the ship. Sandwiches, beverages, and other snacks are available from a small restaurant on the upper level, and from vending machines. A loudspeaker will announce when it is time to return to the car deck.

When driving vehicles off the ferry, follow the crew's directions. At any of the intermediate stops (Lopez, Shaw, and Orcas) it might be necessary to back vehicles off or on. At Orcas Landing and Shaw, this procedure is relatively easy. However, at Lopez, a steep uphill incline can make it complicated for those trying to back up with trailers.

Finally, unless you really will need your vehicle for transportation on the islands, consider leaving it at Anacortes. Vehicles can be left at large parking lots adjoining the ferry terminal, although there is a charge for parking there.

PRIVATE PASSENGER FERRY SERVICE
◆

Island Transport Ferry Service, Inc.

Skyline Marina, 1909 Skyline Way; Anacortes, WA 98221. Phone: (360) 293-6060; cell: (360) 941-6060; fax: (360) 293-8674; email: *info@island-transporter.com*; web site: *island-transporter.com*

Island Transport Ferry Service offers a high-speed "Taxicat" passenger and cargo service that links Skyline Marina in Anacortes to the San Juans. The company's six-passenger catamaran will deliver you and up to 100,000 pounds of cargo to any of the San Juan Islands, either to a dock or directly onto an island beach.

Pacific Sea Taxi

Bellweather Hotel; 1 Bellweather Way; Bellingham, WA 98225. Phone: (360) 393-7123; email: *sean@pstaxi.com*; web site: *pstaxi.com*

SUMMER RATES: From $20 to $110 per person, depending on group size and destination.

The 30-foot *Triton* can deliver up to six passengers to any of the San Juan islands on a demand scheduling basis. You name the island and the departure time, and you and your group can be delivered to your destination.

Victoria–San Juan Cruises

Bellingham Cruise Terminal; 355 Harris Avenue, Suite 104; Bellingham, WA 98225. Phone: (800) 443-4552 or (360) 738-8099; email: *tours@whales.com*; web site: *whales.com*

SUMMER RATES: One way Bellingham to Friday Harbor: Adult $39, child 6-12 $19.50. Round trip: Adult $49, child 6-12 $24.50. Whale watch tour: Adult $49, child 6-12 $29, under 6 free.

Victoria–San Juan Cruises is the parent company of a varied group of tour operations that provide shuttles to the San Juan Islands and Victoria, as well as tours of Bellingham Bay. The *San Juan Island Commuter* provides daily ferry service to Orcas Island and Friday Harbor. The 50-foot boat departs from Bellingham daily at 9:30 A.M. makes a stop at Orcas, then continues on to Friday Harbor, arriving at 11: 45 A.M.

It then offers an optional three-hour whale watch tour before departing Friday Harbor at 4:30 P.M. After a stop on Orcas it arrives back at Bellingham at 7 P.M. Snack bar service is available; some cruises offer lunch buffets. Bicyclists, kayakers, and hikers can be dropped off or picked up by another of the company's vessels at Eliza, Sinclair, Blakely, or Lopez Islands in summer.

OTHER TRANSPORTATION: PLANES, BUSES, BICYCLES & MOPEDS

Visitors can charter or rent planes for touring the islands, or catch a scheduled flight from nearby cities. Many flights are very reasonably priced, and, considering the convenience and time saved, they are not significantly more expensive than driving from Seattle or similar points and then taking the ferry. Even chartering is usually very reasonable when the cost is divided among several people, and in addition you have the advantage of traveling on your own schedule.

San Juan, Orcas, and Lopez Islands all have small airports; you can usually arrange transportation from the airport to your island destination. Wheeled aircraft can land at the public airstrips on the major islands; seaplanes provide versatility for reaching remote spots.

Several companies provide regularly scheduled flights to the San Juan Islands. They also offer charters, sightseeing, and cargo flights. Virtually any company in the Pacific Northwest that charters planes will fly you to the San Juans or take you on sightseeing flights. Some are listed below. You'll find many more listed in phone books or online yellow pages of cities such as Seattle, Tacoma, Bellingham, Oak Harbor, Port Townsend, and Olympia, as well as in Victoria and Vancouver, British Columbia. In the summer, book your flight well in advance to ensure room.

SCHEDULED AIRLINES
◆

Kenmore Air

6321 NE 175th, P.O. Box 82064; Kenmore, WA 98028. Phone: (866) 435-9524, (866) 359-
2842; fax: (425) 485-4774; web site: *kenmoreair.com*
Lake Union Terminal: 950 Westlake Avenue North; Seattle, WA 98109
Kenmore Air Harbor Terminal: 6321 NE 175th Street; Kenmore, WA 9028
Boeing Field Terminal: 7277 Perimeter Road S; Seattle, WA 98108
Eastsound Airport: 147 Shoen Lane; Eastsound, WA 98245
Friday Harbor Airport: 800 Franklin Drive; Friday Harbor, WA 98250.

RATES: Seattle to San Juans $196 to $221 round trip, depending on season and day of week.

Kenmore Air schedules four daily seaplane flights from Lake Union, in downtown
Seattle, and six daily wheeled-plane flights from Boeing Field to several destinations
on Lopez, Orcas and San Juan Island, and limited schedules to Deer Harbor and
Decatur Island. Schedules vary seasonally. The airline will make other stops for two
or more persons, and charter service is available. Overnight lodging packages with
various San Juan hotels are offered.

San Juan Airlines

4000 Airport Road, #A; Anacortes, WA 98221. Phone: (800) 874-4434; email: asi@rockisland.com;
web site: *sanjuanairlines.com*

RATES: Scheduled flights $44 to $59 one-way, depending on destination. Charter rates begin at
$80 per person.

San Juan Airlines offers five daily flights each from Anacortes and Bellingham to
the San Juans, with stops in Friday Harbor, Eastsound, Lopez, and Roche Harbor.
Flights are also available to Boeing Field and Renton Airport and various other
destinations.

AIR CHARTERS & SCENIC FLIGHTS
◆

Aeronautical Services, Inc.

112 Airport Circle Drive; Friday Harbor, WA 98250. Phone: (800) 345-9867 or (360) 378-
2640. *Eastsound phone:* (360) 376-5730. *Lopez Island phone:* (360) 468-2486; email: *asi@
rockisland.com*; web site: *rockisland.com/~asi*

SUMMER RATES: Fares depend on destination and number of passengers.

This company provides charter and daily air freight services between Mount Vernon,
Seattle, Eastsound, Friday Harbor, Lopez, and Canadian locations. Charter flights
accommodate up to nine passengers. Sightseeing flights are also available.

Island Air

72 Airport Circle Drive; Friday Harbor, WA 98250. Phone: (888) 378-2376 or (360) 378-2376; fax:
(360) 378-3199; email: *reservations@sanjuan-islandair.com*; web site: *sanjuan-islandair.com*

SUMMER RATES: Depending on the number of people on a flight and the destination, fares range from $90 (to Anacortes) to $579 (to Portland). Charter rates for three-passenger plane are $150 per hour, five-passenger plane $250 per hour.

Island Air offers scenic flights in the San Juan Islands as well as charter flights anywhere within the U.S. and Canada. The service has four aircraft: two single-engine planes carry three passengers each, one larger single-engine craft carries five passengers, and a twin-engine carries four passengers.

Northwest Seaplanes

860 West Perimeter Road, Renton, WA 98057. Phone: (800) 690-0086, or (425) 277-1590; fax: (425) 277-8831; email: *info@nwseaplanes.com*; web site: *nwseaplanes.com*

SUMMER RATES: $550 per hour for 6-passenger planes.

Northwest Seaplanes, based at Renton airport, just a few minutes from SeaTac International Airport, offers charters and scenic flights to the San Juan Islands and B.C. Northwest Seaplanes is also an owner of San Juan Airlines, which offers scheduled flights between Anacortes and Bellingham and the San Juans. Ground transportation from Renton to Seattle destinations is also available, for an additional charge.

Northwest Sky Ferry

4167 Mitchell Way, Bellingham, WA 98226. Phone: 360-676-9999; email: *info@ northwestskyferry.com*; web site: *northwestskyferry.com*

SUMMER RATES: $39 per person for a scenic ride; other rates depend on length of flight and number of passengers.

Shared-seat discounts on flights between the San Juan Islands and Bellingham, as well as charters and scenic flights throughout the Northwest and Canada are provided by Northwest Sky Ferry. The company flies Cessnas.

Regal Air

10217 31st Avenue, Hanger C51, Paine Field; Everett, WA 98204. Phone: (800) 337-0345. *Everett phone:* (425) 743-9123. *Seattle phone:* (425) 353-9123; fax (425) 347-4507; email: *fly@regalair.com*; web site: *regalair.com*

SUMMER RATES: From $190 round-trip to the San Juans (in same day).

Regal Air offers charter flights to airstrips in the San Juans, as well as scenic and photographic flights.

Rose Air

Hillsboro/Portland Airport. Phone: (503) 675-7673; cell: (503) 860-6389; email: *roseair@ comcast.net*; web site: *roseair.com*

SUMMER RATES: $200 per hour. Hillsboro/Portland airport to the San Juans is a 1½ hour flight.

Jane Roosevelt provides charter flights in a Cessna TR 182 from Hillsboro/Portland airport to the San Juan Islands and other northwest destinations. She also has a package rental of a vacation house, the Rose Arbor Cottage in Eastsound. For details see Orcas Lodging, page 58–59.

Sound Flight

300 Airport Way, P.O. Box 812; Renton, WA 98057. Phone: (800) 921-3474 or (425) 254-8063; fax: (425) 254-8065; email: *info@soundflight.net*; web site: *soundflight.net*

SUMMER RATES: Depend on number of passengers and destination.

Seaplane charter flights from Renton, on the south end of Lake Washington, will take you to any island in the San Juans as well as various points in British Columbia, Washington, Oregon, and Idaho. There is one scheduled round-trip flight each day Thursday through Sunday. Cessna 206's can carry up to four passengers; the larger Beavers accommodate six persons. A wheeled Cessna 182 can carry up to three passengers to those islands that have landing strips.

Bus Services
◆

Scheduled bus service is the answer for visitors who are looking for connecting transportation between major airports and the ferry. Some travel companies also offer bus tours of the islands. For information, contact your travel company.

Airporter Shuttle/Bellair Charters

1416 Whitehorn Street; Ferndale, WA 98248. Phone: (866) 235-5247 or (360) 380-8800; fax: (360) 380-1538; email: *shuttle@airporter.com*; web site: *airporter.com*

SUMMER RATES: One way Seattle to Anacortes: Adult $33, senior/military $31, youth $20. Round trip fares are available.

The Airporter Shuttle has several route connections along the I-5 corridor, including one direct connection between SeaTac and the Anacortes ferry terminal, with intermediate stops at Skyline Marina, Anacortes Shell Station, Farmhouse Inn, and Mount Vernon. There are 12 runs daily, but because of the early and late ferry schedules, only ten northbound and nine southbound runs connect to the ferry terminal daily.

Island Airporter

139 Tarte Road; Friday Harbor, WA 98250. Phone: (360) 378-7438; web site: *islandairporter.com*

SUMMER RATES: $39.95 to $54.95.

Monday through Saturday the Island Airporter provides non-stop transportation between Roche Harbor and Friday Harbor and SeaTac Airport and return. The coach departs Roche Harbor at 5 A.M., and Friday Harbor at 5:45 A.M. to arrive at SeaTac at 9:30 A.M. On the return leg the coach leaves SeaTac at noon, and arrives at Friday Harbor at 3:15 P.M. and Roche Harbor at 4 P.M. Check with the company to confirm current schedules.

Off-Island Bicycles
◆

Several companies that rent both bicycles and mopeds on the islands are listed under On-Island Transportation in the chapters on specific islands.

Skagit Cycle Center

1620 Commercial; Anacortes, WA 98221; (360) 588-8776; email: *info@skagitcyclecenter.com*; web site: *skagitcyclecenter.com*

SUMMER RATES: Roughly $30 a day per bike, $18 a day for trailers. Group discounts can be negotiated.

This full-service bike shop in Anacortes rents quality bicycles for all your family for your San Juan trip. For super fun, try a tandem bike. Small folks or gear can be hauled in one of their bike trailers. Bring your own helmets and shoes, although a few used helmets are available for rental. Reservations are required, of course, so call or email ahead.

A unique service of the store is bike assembly: Ship your bicycle to the store from home, and one of their experienced staff will assemble it and have it ready when you arrive. At the end of your vacation, drop it off at the shop and they will disassemble it and ship it back home for you. The store carries a full line of parts and gear, including helmets and clothing, and also does repairs.

Two-Wheel Courtesy & Safety

Bicycles and mopeds are wonderful (and very popular) ways to see the islands. However, because the roads are often narrow and winding, persons who choose either of these modes of transportation should make sure they do not endanger themselves, impede the pleasure of other visitors, or rankle the residents. Ferries unload bicycles, mopeds, and motorcycles first. Hot on their heels follow the four-wheeled vehicles, so take care and stay to the right. At both Lopez and Orcas, there is a long uphill pull from the ferry landing, and laboring cyclists can cause traffic to back up. When cycling in the San Juan Islands, please observe the following rules of safety and courtesy:

- Ride in small groups of three or four, and space groups widely apart.
- Stay well to the right side of the road and ride single-file to allow motor vehicles an opportunity to pass.
- Make stops on the straightaway, rather than on a bend in the road or the crest of a hill, where it is difficult for motorists to see you. On Orcas Island bicycle pulloffs are located near the top of steep hills.
- When stopping to rest, move completely off the road.
- Do not trespass. Use the public restrooms in the villages, and camp only in designated sites.
- Do not litter.

Boating
Tours, Cruises, Charters & Marinas

◆

ALTHOUGH THE MAJORITY OF VISITORS TO THE SAN JUANS arrive by ferry, Northwest boaters know well the accessibility of the islands from any of the mainland ports. The trip doesn't require a yacht—even small boats and kayaks with experienced paddlers can make the trek from Anacortes or Victoria in good weather.

The table below shows the distance by water to Friday Harbor from nearby ports and landmarks in Washington and British Columbia. If you are coming into the U.S. from a foreign port, or planning to leave the U.S. and then return, read the information regarding going through U.S. Customs on page 32.

DISTANCES TO FRIDAY HARBOR BY WATER (IN NAUTICAL MILES)			
Anacortes, WA	18	Port Angeles, WA	37
Bellingham, WA	28	Port Ludlow, WA	44
Blaine, WA	37	Port Townsend, WA	30
Bremerton, WA	76	Seattle, WA	67
Cape Flattery, WA	87	Tacoma, WA	86
Eagle Harbor, WA	67	Vancouver, B.C.	62
Everett, WA	62	Victoria, B.C.	30
Olympia, WA	112		

Several marinas on the islands provide moorage, fuel, and services for boaters. Numerous public boat launches are nearby on the mainland. There are launch ramps on San Juan, Orcas, and Lopez Islands, although trailered boats are best put in on the mainland rather than ferried to the islands for launching. Good anchorages are abundant, especially at the marine state parks.

If you are planning to fish, crab, or gather shellfish, you are required to have a valid Washington State License. In addition, you must have catch record cards for salmon, halibut, sturgeon, steelhead, and Dungeness crab. Anglers, scuba divers, beach users, and boaters must observe all state regulations on the taking of any food animal. Many sporting goods stores sell licenses. A pamphlet listing regulations is available at sporting goods stores, or rules are posted online at *wdfw.wa.gov/fishcorn. htm*, and can be downloaded. If you are chartering, the company you charter from can inform you what you will need and where it can be purchased. The taking of shellfish and seaweed is also regulated, and a license, to be worn on the outside of

Boating in the San Juan Islands can take you to sublime spots such as Echo Bay at Sucia Island Marine State Park. Mount Baker is in the distance.

clothing when harvesting, must be purchased. A catch record card must be filled out for Dungeness crab. If fishing in one of the island lakes, freshwater licenses are required, except for those lakes on private land.

As of 1995, the operation of jet skis (personal watercraft) is banned in San Juan County. This action was taken because of concern over noise and hazards to boaters and marine life. If you had planned to use such craft in the islands, you cannot.

BOAT TOURS, CRUISES, CHARTERS & RENTALS

Tours, cruises, charters, and rentals are ways to enjoy the islands by boat if you don't own a vessel. Negotiating around the interior of a boat can involve a bit of physical activity. Some boats can accommodate disabled persons or persons who have some physical limitations. If you have any concerns, discuss them with the company at the time you rent or charter a boat.

If you plan to go on one of the boats:

- Take along an extra sweater or jacket and head covering. Boating often is cool, and you probably will welcome an extra layer of clothing.
- It is unlikely you will get seasick, but if you are prone to motion illness, or if the day is a bit windy, which might cause some roughness, take some motion sickness medication. A pharmacist can advise which is best for you. Ideally, it should be taken an hour before your trip.
- Use sunscreen and wear sunglasses. Even if the day is overcast, reflection off the water can cause a burn.
- Brisk sea air can make you hungry. Most boats offer food and beverages, or at least snacks are available.
- Be sure to take your camera and binoculars, if you have them. You should use a fast film, such as 400 ASA, to minimize the motion of the boat and the movement of wildlife you see. If your camera is digital and has adjustable settings, you should use a reasonably fast shutter speed, along with the appropriate ISO for the available light.

TOURS AND CRUISES. Tours and cruises are, in general, the same thing, although a tour usually has a guided narration explaining such things as the wildlife or natural history of the area. A cruise might just be a nice ride without a narration. Skippered tours and cruises that leave at scheduled times and follow a specific itinerary or a defined goal—fishing, diving, or whale and wildlife watching—are all popular in the San Juans. Boat size varies from small vessels that accommodate a few people to large yachts complete with dining room and bar that entertain more than a hundred.

Of course, none of the fishing or wildlife cruises can guarantee that you'll catch salmon or see whales, but the folks that run these boats are well versed in the islands and will offer you a better chance than you might have on your own. They will, as well, provide you with in-depth knowledge of the area itself. In summer, when whales frequent the region, cruises usually have around a 90-percent success rate, although any cruise that tours the beautiful islands, whales or no whales, is most certainly a treat.

Numerous tours to and through the islands originate in nearby cities. Those that are specifically focused on the San Juans are listed in this book; others can be located by checking with local travel agents. There is considerable overlap between businesses that list themselves as tours or cruises, and those that describe themselves as charters. If you're looking for a skippered boat trip around the islands, check out all descriptions.

BOAT RENTALS AND CHARTERS. All the nearby major cities, as well as several San Juan harbors, have businesses that offer boat charters and rentals. With any type of rental or charter, be sure to inquire as to exactly the type of boat, its size, its power, how enclosed it is, sleeping accommodations, and what is included in the way of both marine and personal supplies. *Rentals* are generally small boats for day use, and range from kayaks and rowboats up to small outboards for fishing or island exploring. *Charters* are larger boats that are contracted for a weekend or up to several weeks. They can be sailboats, cruising houseboats, or powerboats ranging up to posh yachts. These are classified as either *bareboat* or *skippered*.

On a *bareboat charter*, you are the skipper; you plan your itinerary and are fully responsible for the safety and well-being of yourself, your crew, and the boat. By law, chartered boats must be fully equipped with all U.S. Coast Guard-required safety devices such as fire extinguishers, life jackets (personal flotation devices, or PFD's), and other flotation devices, such as cushions and life rings. They usually have fuel, a radio, charts, and cooking utensils—everything necessary for a comfortable voyage. You provide your own food, bedding, and fishing gear, although these might be available through the company for an additional charge. Typically, rowing dinghies are provided, and outboard motors can be rented at an additional charge.

If this is your first time chartering with a company, you will normally be given a short "checkout" cruise to assure the company of your boat-handling abilities and to familiarize you with your craft. If you have questions or want suggestions about cruising in the islands, be sure to ask. Then you're on your own.

On a *skippered charter*, you are essentially a guest. Unless your own group is large, there might be other guests along. The boat owner is in charge of the boat, although some skippers will be happy to let you crew, or even take a turn at the

The Morning Star, *a Chesapeake "Bugeye" 56-foot ketch, seen here headed for the Rosario Resort Marina, can be chartered for skippered sails.*

helm. Meals and bedding are provided. Although the captain might have particular destinations in mind, the itinerary is usually flexible. If fishing is your goal, or if you're not an experienced boater, a skippered charter is a good way to go because the boat owner knows all the best spots and will make sure you enjoy your cruise. Some charters specialize in other recreation where the skipper has particular experience or knowledge, such as scuba diving. *Learn-to-sail skippered charters* include lessons, giving you the skills to captain your own ship next time.

RATES. Fees for boat rentals, charters, or tours range from around $25 for an afternoon to $18,000+ for a week! If you want to play like the Great Gatsby, rates for a skippered, crewed sailing yacht go into the stratosphere. However, there are many quite reasonable boats available, so somewhere in that range there must be a boat to match your needs and budget. Quiet-season rates might be lower on rentals, charters, and tours.

Skippered tours and charters begin at about $45 for a half day and range up to $70 to $150 for a full day. The price depends on the services offered and the size, type, and comfort of the boat. Group rates are available on large boats. Vessels range from a 16-foot outboard for two, up to 100-foot yachts that can accommodate up to 50 guests for the day or 17 overnight guests. Some charters provide drinks and light meals for half-day or sunset cruises, or full meals on all-day or overnight trips.

Bareboat charters run between $700 weekly for a basic, comfortably equipped boat, into the $10,000 range for a large, posh yacht. Rates for companies listed below are prime season rates, and lower rates are generally available at other times. All require a security deposit and insurance.

OFF-ISLAND BOAT & KAYAK TOURS, CRUISES & CHARTERS

ABC Yacht Charters
3001 R Avenue, Suite #106, P.O. Box 129; Anacortes, WA 98221. Phone: (800) 426-2313 or (360) 293-9533; fax: (360) 293-0313; email: *info@abcyachtcharters.com*; web site: *abcyachtcharters.com*

ABC has both power cruisers and sailing yachts, from 30 to 72 feet, available for bareboat charter from Skyline Marina in Anacortes. Larger custom yachts, ranging from 50 to 120 feet, are chartered only with skipper and crew. Many items of equipment beyond USCG requirements are included with all boats. The company has staples and provisioning packages available on request, and will rent items such as bedding, barbecues, outboards, and fishing gear. One of their boats is specially equipped with wheelchair ramps and lifts to accommodate boaters with physical limitations.

Advance Entertainment and Affordable Dream Sailing
P.O. Box 581; Ferndale, WA 98248-0581. Phone: (800) 354-8608 or (360) 739-1814; email: *captsails@aol.com*; web site: *hometown.aol.com/captsails/myhomepagenwcharterprices*

A variety of this company's skippered cruises originate from the Bellingham/Anacortes area. Power yachts range from 32 feet to 61 feet ($5400 to $18,000 per week).

Sailing yachts range from 32 feet to 57 feet ($5100 to $8900 per week). Food provisions not included in this price.

Anacortes Yacht Charters

Anacortes Marina, Suite 2, P.O. Box 69; Anacortes, WA 98221. Phone: (800) 233-3004, (360) 293-4555; email: *info@ayc.com*; web site: *ayc.com*

SUMMER RATES: Bareboat power $280 to $525 per day; bareboat sail $120 to $285 per day. A few vessels are available for day rental year-round, ranging from $225 to $450 per day. 7-day minimum during prime season, 4-day minimum off-season. For crewed yachts, call for rates.

This firm offers more than 80 powerboats and sailboats. Bareboat power boats range from 28 feet to 66 feet; bareboat sailboats are from 24 to 51 feet. Day rentals are sized from a 15-foot Boston Whaler to a 26-foot Sea Ray power boat. Crewed power yachts range from 80 feet to 125 feet. Most are less than five years old. Clients can purchase supplies, groceries, and liquor within walking distance of the moorage, or on request the company will arrange for meals, staples, and bedding to be on board.

Bellhaven Charters

714 Coho Way; Bellingham, WA 98225. Phone: (800) 542-8812 or (360) 733-6636; fax: (360) 647-9664; email: *bellhaven@bellhaven.net*; web site: *bellhaven.net*

SUMMER BAREBOAT RATES: Sail $1600 to $2650 per week; power $1850 to $9000 per week.

Bellhaven Charters offers both power boats and sailboats. Bareboat sail charters are from 32 to 42 feet, and power charters range from 27 feet to 60 feet. Provisions for your trip are readily available from nearby Bellingham supermarkets. The company also offers sailing courses certified by the American Sailing Association.

Bellingham Yachts

Squalicum Harbor Center; 1801 Roeder Avenue, Suite 174; Bellingham, WA 98225. Phone: (800) 671-4244 or (360) 671-0990; fax: (360) 671-0992; web site: *bellinghamyachts.com*

SUMMER RATES: $2650 to $9500 per week.

This company charters a complete line of powerboats between 36 and 53 feet. They will provide training in boat handling for bareboat charters, or year-round can provide a skipper and crew for trips to the San Juans, Gulf Islands, or farther north in Canadian waters. Quiet-season discounts are available.

Clipper Navigation, Inc.

Pier 69, 2701 Alaskan Way; Seattle WA 98121; *Seattle phone*: (800) (888) 2535, (206) 448-5000, *Victoria phone*: (250) 382-8100; email: *reservations@victoriaclipper.com*; web site: *victoriaclipper.com*

Clipper Navigation operates daily round-trip service between Seattle and Victoria, with intermediate stops in the San Juan Islands. The passenger vessels *Victoria Clipper* and *Victoria Clipper IV*, both high-speed catamarans, operate year-round. Between April and September, two other passenger vessels, *Victoria Clipper II* and

Victoria Clipper III, provide additional trips to Victoria, Rosario Resort, and Friday Harbor. There are one or two sailings daily during the quiet season, and up to six round-trip sailings daily in summer. Travel time each way is two to three hours on the catamarans, slightly longer on the other vessels.

Between April and September, the *San Juan Explorer* offers a three-hour whale and wildlife tour out of Friday Harbor, departing at 11 A.M. daily. A naturalist provides interpretation, and a hydrophone permits passengers to listen to whales communicate among themselves. The company also offers tour packages that include hotel rooms, multiday tours in the San Juans, guided kayaking trips, and side trips to other destinations. Tours can interconnect with B.C. ferries, floatplane flights, bus lines, and Amtrak. They have car rentals as well—a full transportation package.

Discovery Charters
P.O. Box 636; Anacortes, WA 98221. Phone: (360) 293-4248

Sail from Cap Sante Marina in Anacortes aboard the *Discovery* for live-aboard two- to seven-day scuba diving tours in the San Juan and Gulf Islands. Anchor in quiet harbors each night. Air fills to 3000 PSI, low side exits, and an easy-boarding ladder add to the comfort and safety of dives. Three "home-cooked" meals a day, plus snacks, take care of creature comforts. Each dive explores different sites. The vessel accommodates up to 12 divers on trips of more than three days. Shorter whale watch and marine birdwatching charters are also available.

Island Adventures, Inc.
1801 Commercial Avenue; Anacortes, WA 98221. Phone: (800) 465-4604 or (360) 293-2428; fax: (360) 299-8708; email: *whales@islandadventurecruises.com*; web site: *island-adventures.com*

SUMMER RATES: Adults start at $64, children $49.

You have your choice of two different types of vessel. The 65-foot *Island Explorer II* offers a heated cabin with inside booth-type seating, a snack bar, and a full walk-around second deck with outside covered seating. An underwater hydrophone listens for the calls of the whales. The *Island Whaler,* one of the fastest in the whale-watch fleet, is an ultra-fast catamaran that cruises at 35 knots. Seating is outside on glass-shielded open deck seating.

In summer, the two vessels make five departures daily from docks on Commercial Street in Anacortes. Sunset cruises are a special treat. Trips might include exploring Deception Pass in addition to whale watching and nature tours. The company claims better than 90 percent success at sighting whales on their trips.

Island Mariner Cruises
5 Harbor Loop, Squalicum Harbor; Bellingham, WA 98225. Phone: (877) 734-8866, or (360) 734-8866; fax: (360) 734-8867; email: *mariner@orcawatch.com*; web site: orcawatch.com

SUMMER RATES: $75. Inquire about charters, group rates, and discounts for seniors and children.

From mid-May through mid-September, come aboard the 110-foot *Island Caper* for a 90-mile, seven-hour whale search and nature watch cruise through the San Juan

Islands. "Captain Trivia," who has been the company's on-board naturalist/story-teller since 1985, provides an entertaining, informative narration. The vessel, one of the finest tour boats on Puget Sound, can carry up to 149 passengers (a minimum group of 20 is required), and is wheelchair accessible. Group charters for weddings, receptions, company picnics, and similar gatherings are also available. On board are a hot tub, a complete galley, a portable bar you can stock, a sound system, a TV, and a VCR. Extended custom cruises can be accommodated using the seven two-person bunkrooms below deck.

Mosquito Fleet

1724 W Marine Drive; Everett, WA 98201. Phone: (800) (888) 2535, (425) 252-6800; email: *reservations@victoriaclipper.com*; web site: *whalewatching.com*

SUMMER RATES: One way: Adults $77, children $38.75. Round trip: Adults $110, children $55.

The jet catamaran *Orca Song* can take up to 149 people for an eight-hour adventure-filled day. The vessel leaves the Everett Marina, north of Seattle, for a cruise through cliff-rimmed Deception Pass, and on to the San Juans. A naturalist on board makes your trip more interesting, and the vessel participates in a whale-spotting service, which increases your chances of being in the right spot at the right time.

Weekend tours are offered during May, and sailings are daily from the end of May through the end of October. Sandwiches, soft drinks, beer, wine, and snacks can be purchased aboard.

Mystic Sea Charters

Cap Sante Marina, Dock A; 710 Seafarers Way; Anacortes, WA 98221. Phone: (800) 308-9387 or (360) 466-3042; email: *mystic@ncia.com*; web site: *mysticseacharters.com*

The MV *Mystic Sea* is a 100-foot vessel operating out of either Anacortes or Coupe-ville. During the orca whale season (May through October), the vessel sails from Anacortes, but during the gray whale season (March through May) it sails out of Coupeville on Whidbey Island. Charter it for a host of activities such as large group meetings and parties, long-distance sightseeing trips, wildlife tours, scuba diving expeditions, fishing trips, or inter-island transportation.

The vessel sleeps up to 14 persons for overnight trips and accommodates up to 42 guests for shorter cruises. A TV/VCR, a stereo system, a wet bar, an espresso bar, and fully catered meals are among its creature comforts.

NW Explorations

2623 South Harbor Loop; Bellingham, WA 98225. Phone: (800) 826-1430 or (360) 676-1248; fax: (360) 676-9059; email: *charter@nwexplorations.com*; web site: *nwexplorations.com*

SUMMER RATES: $3400 to $10,815 per week.

Thirteen prestigious Grand Banks power yachts, ranging from 36 to 52 feet are available for either bareboat or skippered charter. Towels, linens, sleeping bags, and fishing gear may be rented from the company.

Par Yacht Charters

2620 North Harbor Loop Drive, Harbor Mall Suite 1; Bellingham, WA 98225. Phone: (360) 752-5754; fax: (360) 752-0454; email: *info@paryachtcharters.com*; web site: *paryachtcharters.com*

SUMMER RATES: Bareboat power charters to $4750 per week, bareboat sail $1500 to $3250 per week.

This company's fleet consists primarily of the very popular Bayliners. The vessels range from 32 to 47 feet for power craft and 32 to 50 feet for sailboats.

Paraclete Charter Service

Berth TB, Skyline Marina; Anacortes, WA 98221. Phone: (800) 808-2999 or (360) 293-5290; email: *skip@paracletecharters.com*; web site: *paracletecharters.com*

Paraclete Charter Service offers 24-hour transportation throughout the San Juans on three boats, the 34-passenger *Paraclete*, which has deck space for carry-on cargo such as bicycles, the 48-passenger *Kiononia*, or the 64-passenger *Sylvan Spirit*. Groups can arrange for catered meals or lunches to be served in the limited galleys of either of the larger boats.

Penmar Marine Company

2011 Skyline Way; Anacortes, WA. Phone: (800) 828-7337 or (360) 293-4839; fax: (360) 293-2427; email: *penmar2@fidalgo.net*

Penmar, based at Skyline Marina in Anacortes, offers year-round skippered or bare-boat charters for one- or two-week trips to the San Juans or into Canadian waters. Powerboats run in the range of from 15 to 44 feet, and sailboats between 26 and 52 feet. Either type boat will provide never-to-be-forgotten vacation trips to the San Juans, Gulf Islands, or Desolation Sound. Extensive yacht accommodations, over and above USCG requirements, are provided with each boat. On bareboat charters, linens, galley basics, provisions, fishing gear, and outboard motors can be supplied at extra cost.

Puget Sound Express

Point Hudson Marina; 227 Jackson Street; Port Townsend, WA 98368. Phone: (360) 385-5288; fax: (360) 732-0448; email: *info@pugetsoundexpress.com*; web site: *pugetsoundexpress.com*

SUMMER RATES: Port Townsend to Friday Harbor one way: Adult $49.50, child $39.50. Round trip: Adult $67, child $49. Bicycles and kayaks: $12.50. Wildlife tour: Adult $65, child $49.

The 64-foot *Glacier Spirit* departs daily from Port Townsend, crosses the Strait of Juan de Fuca, and passes close by the south side of Lopez Island. You are treated to a description of the region's natural history as you view marine mammals and birds. After a cruise up San Juan Channel, the boat docks at Friday Harbor. You can go ashore or remain on board for a two-hour whale watch excursion. The boat returns to Port Townsend via the west side of San Juan Island. Up to 72 passengers can enjoy large viewing windows, snacks, and beverages throughout the trip. Overnight packages with San Juan Island bed and breakfast inns can be arranged.

Cruisers such as this 24-foot Nordic Tug, which sleeps four, are offered for bareboat chartering by numerous companies.

R & R Charters

Skyline Marina; Anacortes, WA 98221. Phone: (360) 293-2992; cell: (360) 708-7423; email: *rnj17@comcast.net*; web site: *rrcharters.com*

SUMMER RATES: Shared charter: $140 per person, minimum of 2, maximum of 4. Exclusive use of boat with captain: 1 to 2 persons $400, 3 to 4 persons $560.

This charter is strictly about fishing, not sightseeing, although you might see orcas and other marine life on the trip. The *No Regrets*, a cuddy cabin, 24-foot Bayliner Trophy, can take two to four persons out of Skyline Marine for a six- to eight-hour fishing trip for salmon, halibut, or lingcod, depending on the season and what is running. All fishing gear, bait, and tackle are provided.

Sailnorthwest Charters, LLC

P.O. Box 5084; Bellingham, WA 98227. Phone: (360) 840-1698 or in western Washington (360) 305-6169 or (707) 245-7490; email: *info@sailnw.com*; web site: *sailnw.com*

SUMMER RATES: Bareboat: *Hopscotch* $3350, *Spotlight Gal* $1500. Skippered: $225 additional per day. Additional charge for linens and provisioning.

This company has two sloops available for charter, either bareboat, or crewed. The 50-foot Beneteau Oceanis, *Hopscotch*, can accommodate up to eight guests; the 32-foot Islander, *Spotlight Gal*, sleeps five. For a modest fee they will even provision the galley with foods of your choice, so all you need do is check in and step on board.

They also offer sailing lessons, including a weeklong Cruise 'N Learn Class for a maximum of three people, ensuring you'll get plenty of time at the helm. Their instructors are certified by the American Sailing Association.

San Juan Sailing

2615 South Harbor Loop, Suite 1; Bellingham, WA 98225. Phone: (800) 677-7245 or (360) 671-4300; fax: (360) 671-4301; email: *charter@sanjuansailing.com; web site: sanjuansailing.com*

SUMMER RATES: Bareboat: $1075 to $3950. Skippered: $4475. Additional charges for dinghy outboard, saltwater fishing gear, and meal provisioning, if desired.

Sailing out of Bellingham, you're only two hours away from the San Juans, where you can sharpen your sailing skills in its broad channels and relax at anchor in one of its marine state parks. Thirty-five sailing yachts, from 28 to 49 feet, are available for bareboat charter, and a 42-foot sailing catamaran is for skippered charter. All are equipped for safety and living comfort and include sheets, blankets, towels, and crab rings. See their sister company, San Juan Yachting, for power boat charters.

San Juan Yachting

2615 South Harbor Loop, Suite 1; Bellingham, WA 98225. Phone: (800) 670-8089 or (360) 671-4300; fax: (360) 671-4301; email: *charter@sanjuanyachting.com*; web site: *sanjuanyachting.com*

SUMMER RATES: $2750 to $10,570. Additional charges for dinghy outboard, saltwater fishing gear, and meal provisioning, if desired.

This companion company to San Juan Sailing charters 12 power boats ranging from 34 to 64 feet. All sail out of Bellingham, a short hop to the San Juans. Charter fees include sheets, blankets, towels, and crab rings.

Ship Harbor Yacht Charters

2201 Skyline Way; Anacortes, WA 98221. Phone: (877) 772-6582 or (360) 299-9193; fax: (360) 588-8833; email: *info@shipharboryachts.com*; web site: *shipharboryachts.com*

SUMMER RATES: Bareboat sail $2698 to $4590; bareboat power $1586 to $8990; crewed power $4112 to $8990.

This charter company has an extensive fleet of luxury yachts available for charter out of Skyline Marina. For bareboating, Beneteau and Jeanneau sailing yachts range from 40 to 52 feet. Power boats range from 26 feet to 54 feet. Also available are crewed charters on yachts ranging from 50 to 54 feet. The firm's web site provides a virtual tour of each vessel.

Viking Cruises

109 North First Street, P.O. Box 327; LaConner, WA 98257. Phone: (888) 207-2333 or (360) 466-2639; email: *cruise@vikingcruises.com*; web site: *vikingcruises.com*

SUMMER RATES: One-day cruises: $12.50 to $55 per person, depending on duration; lunches can be ordered. 3-day, 2-night San Juan cruise: $614, double occupancy $220, single supplement.

You'll skip the ferry lines by boarding the modern, 58-foot cruiser *Viking Star* in LaConner, 60 miles north of Seattle, and taking off for scenic adventures. The beautifully appointed vessel, which holds up to 49 passengers, has an enclosed, heated cabin with large viewing windows, and spacious outside decks. Up to a dozen people can join the captain in the upper deck wheelhouse. A variety of tour options are available, ranging from one- to five-hour cruises in the Swinomish Channel, Padilla Bay, Skagit Bay, Deception Pass, and the eastern Strait of Juan de Fuca.

A three-day tour of the San Juans includes overnight stays at Rosario Resort on Orcas Island and Elements San Juan Island Hotel and Spa on San Juan Island. You can add a crab-fest lunch during a cruise through Deception Pass.

Also available are private charters where catering services can serve sit-down meals for up to 36 persons.

SCUBA DIVING SUPPLIES
◆

You'll find scuba air refills at a few spots in the San Juans; however, equipment and repairs can be hard to come by. Stop at either of these two mainland shops to be sure you're fully outfitted before heading for those prime dive spots.

Anacortes Diving and Supply, Inc.

2502 Commercial Avenue; Anacortes, WA 98221. Phone: (360) 293-2070; fax: (360) 293-8822; email: *andive@fidalgo.net*; web site: *anacortesdiving.com*

This comprehensive diving supply offers extensive dive training from snorkeling through advanced open water, master diver, and Nitrox diving. The shop offers rentals of tanks, wetsuits, dry suits, regulators, weight belts, fins, underwater photo dive cases, and more. Tank refills are available.

Washington Divers, Inc.

903 North State Street; Bellingham, WA 98225. Phone: (360) 676-8029; cell: (360) 920-0269; fax: (360) 647-5028; email: *info@wadivers.com*; web site: *washingtondivers.com/*

Operating since 1973, this is one of the oldest dive stores in the country. It offers classes ranging from introductory courses to open water certification, specialty courses, and dive leadership. A comprehensive supply of quality diving equipment is sold. They offer scheduled weekend shore dives and boat dives.

OFF-ISLAND MARINAS
◆

Anacortes Marina

2415 T Avenue, P.O. Box 846; Anacortes, WA 98221. Phone: (360) 293-4543; fax: (360) 293-7013; web site: *anacortesmarina.com*

FACILITIES: Fuel dock (gas, diesel, propane), pumpout station.

This privately owned, breakwater-protected marina on Fidalgo Bay handles haulouts to 60 tons and offers marine services, repairs, and supplies. Yacht charter and yacht sale companies are based at the marina. No guest moorage is available.

Blaine Harbor

235 Marine Drive; Blaine, WA 98230. Phone: (360) 647-6176; email: *blaineharbor@portofbellingham.com*; web site: *portofbellingham/blaine_harbor*

FACILITIES: 1000-foot guest float, restrooms, showers, wireless broadband, fuel dock (gas and diesel), pumpout station, launch ramp.

The city of Blaine sits on the U.S.–Canada border, 15 nautical miles from the San Juans. The marina, operated by the Port of Blaine, can launch or haul out boats up to 150 tons, and there is adjacent dry storage. Land facilities include a marine chandlery. Fishing charters also operate out of the port facilities. From the harbor, the San Juan Islands are a leisurely day-cruise away.

Cap Sante Boat Haven

1st and Commercial Avenue, P.O. Box 297; Anacortes, WA 98221. Phone: (360) 293-0694; fax: (360) 299-0998; VHF channel 66; email: *marina@portofanacortes.com*; web site: *portofanacortes.com*

FACILITIES: 150-200 guest slips with power and water, wireless broadband, restrooms, showers, coin-operated laundry, fuel (gas, diesel, premix, kerosene, propane), pumpout station.

The Port of Anacortes operates Cap Sante Boat Haven, on Fidalgo Bay. Haulouts to 30 tons can be handled, and a full range of boat maintenance and repair services are available. The basin hoist launch takes boats up to 26 feet; dry storage is ashore. Groceries, ice, bait, hardware, and electronic gear are sold at the marina store. Downtown Anacortes, just a few blocks away, has restaurants and shops. Companies at the marina offer boat rentals and charters.

Point Roberts Marina Resort

713 Simundson Drive; Point Roberts, WA 98281. Phone: (360) 945-2255; fax: (360) 945-0927; email: *prmarina@pointrobertsmarina.com*; web site: *pointrobertsmarina.com*

FACILITIES: Guest moorage with power and water, restrooms, showers, coin-operated laundry, wireless broadband, fuel (gas, diesel, propane), U.S. Customs.

A rock breakwater on the south side of Point Roberts shelters the entrance to a cozy, but fully outfitted marina. Along the entry channel are guest moorages, with permanent moorages and a hoist boat launch farther into the yacht basin. Ashore, the marina offers a complete range of marine repairs, a chandlery, grocery, pub, and restaurant.

Semiahmoo Marina

9540 Semiahmoo Parkway; Blaine, WA 98230. Phone: (360) 371-0440, VHF channel 68; fax: (360) 371-0200; email: *semimarina@bbxmail.net*; web site: *semiahmoomarina.com*

FACILITIES: Guest slips with power and water, wireless broadband, fuel dock (gas, diesel, propane), pumpout station, restrooms, showers, coin-operated laundry.

Semiahmoo Marina, part of the extensive Semiahmoo Resort, lies on Drayton Harbor, near Blaine. Although it is primarily a permanent moorage marina, guest slips are available by reservation. The facility has security gates. The marina offers haulouts to 35 tons, dry storage, and a full range of marine maintenance, repair, and service. Shore-side shops carry groceries, gifts, bait and tackle, and marine hardware and supplies.

Skyline Marina

Flounder Bay; 2011 Skyline Way; Anacortes, WA 98221. Phone: (360) 293-4839; fax: (360) 293-9458; email: *betty@skylinemarinecenter.com*; web site: *skylinemarinecenter.com*

FACILITIES: Guest moorages with power and water, wireless broadband, restrooms, showers, coin-operated laundry, fuel (gas, diesel, CNG, propane), pumpout station.

For many boaters, Skyline Marina is the jumping-off point for their trip to the San Juans. The full-service marina is conveniently located on Fidalgo Island, at the north end of Burrows Bay. The marina can do haulouts to 35 tons and has dry storage and a complete range of marine repair and maintenance services.

Nearly everything a boater needs is right at hand. Shops in the marina complex sell marine hardware, groceries, ice, fishing tackle, bait, and licenses. A restaurant, yacht brokers, yacht charters, boat rentals, and fishing charters are within the marina complex, and a supermarket and liquor store are within walking distance.

Squalicum Harbor

722 Coho Way, P.O. Box 1737; Bellingham, WA 98225-1737. Phone: (360) 676-2542; email: *squalicum@portofbellingham.com*; web site: *portofbellingham.com/squalicum_harbor_home_page*

FACILITIES: Guest moorage with power and water, wireless broadband, restrooms, showers, coin-operated laundry, fuel (gas, diesel), pumpout stations, boat launch ramp.

The third largest marina complex in Washington is on the north end of Bellingham Bay. Only the Port of Everett Marina and Seattle's Shilshole Marina are larger. Two adjacent moorage basins have more than 1700 feet of guest moorage. The older of the two basins, on the west, fronts on Squalicum Mall and Harbor Mall; both have a number of marine-oriented businesses offering parts and supplies, bait and tackle, haulouts, boat maintenance and repair, hoist launching, yacht sales, and charters. Two fuel docks and two pumpout stations complete the facilities.

The main moorage dock leads ashore to Harbor Center, a covered esplanade with more marine-oriented shops, including boutiques, tackle and bait shops, a small grocery, a marine chandlery, restaurants, and yacht sales and charters. On one corner of the basin is a four-lane boat launch ramp.

OFF-ISLAND LAUNCH RAMPS & PUT-INS

All the launch ramps described below are within 18 miles of the San Juans, making them ideal put-ins for day trips. They are listed from north to south.

Lighthouse Marine County Park Boat Launch

This Whatcom County park is on the southwest tip of Point Roberts. To reach it, take Tyee Road south from the U.S.–Canada border to Marina Drive, turn west and follow Marina Drive, then Edwards Drive, to the park. The ramp has two lanes and an adjacent boarding float. The ramp is 12 nautical miles north of Patos Island.

Port of Bellingham, Blaine Marina Boat Launch

A two-lane concrete ramp, with a loading float between lanes, drops to the jetty-protected basin on the east side of the Blaine Marina. From the north side of the town of Blaine, turn west from Peace Portal Drive onto Marine Drive. Follow it to the first intersection, then turn south on Milhollin Drive, which ends at the launch ramp parking area. From here, Patos Island is 16 nautical miles to the south.

Port of Bellingham, Squalicum Harbor Boat Launch

A four-lane concrete launch ramp with two boarding floats is immediately east of the Harbor Center buildings at Squalicum Harbor. From downtown Bellingham, head northwest on Holly Street to C Street. Turn left on C, and in one block, right on Roeder. Follow Roeder to the first entrance to Squalicum Harbor. There is ample parking above the ramp and to the south, beyond the Coast Guard station. The ramp is 13 nautical miles from the west tip of Orcas Island.

Larrabee State Park, Wildcat Cove Boat Launch

Larrabee State Park has a single-lane launch ramp on its north shore. To reach it, from the south side of Bellingham, follow signs to Highway 11 and Chuckanut Drive. Turn west on Cove Road ¾ mile north of Larrabee State Park; at a T-intersection, the road south leads to the steep launch ramp on Wildcat Cove, a tiny inlet on Samish Bay. The west tip of Orcas Island is 11 nautical miles away.

Bay View Boat Launch

Because the portion of Padilla Bay by the small community of Bay View becomes a mudflat at minus tides, this ramp is usable only at high tide and by shallow-draft boats. To reach the ramp, take the Bay View–Edison Road north from Highway 20 to Bay View. A single-lane concrete ramp is just north of the intersection with Wilson Road. The ramp is 15 nautical miles from the entrance to Thatcher Pass.

Swinomish Channel Boat Launch

An excellent two-lane concrete ramp with a boarding float is located on the east side of the Swinomish Channel, beneath the Swinomish Channel Bridge. Head west on Highway 20, and just before it starts over the Swinomish Channel bridge, turn right onto a road paralleling the north side of the highway. From here, Thatcher Pass in the San Juans is just 14 nautical miles away.

Washington Park Boat Launch

This popular ramp at Sunset Bay in Washington Park is only 6 nautical miles from Thatcher Pass. At Anacortes, follow Highway 20 west toward the ferry terminal. Where the road heads downhill to the terminal, continue west on Sunset Avenue to Washington Park. The launch ramp is on the north shore, just inside the park.

Pioneer City Park Boat Launch

This ramp drops into the east side of the Swinomish Channel at LaConner. At the south side of LaConner, turn south on Second, then west on Sherman, to reach the concrete launch ramp. There is ample parking above the ramp. It is 17½ nautical miles to Thatcher Pass, via the Swinomish Channel.

Deception Pass State Park, Bowman Bay Boat Launch

Deception Pass State Park has two launch areas, one on the west side of the pass, and one on the east. To find the launch area on the west side, take Highway 20 south toward Deception Pass State Park. At the south end of Pass Lake, turn west on Rosario Road, to the park's Bowman Bay area. A large parking lot and a single-lane concrete launch ramp are near the center of the bay. The ramp is 8 nautical miles from Lopez Pass.

Deception Pass State Park, Cornet Bay Boat Launch

The eastern Deception Pass launch site is in the Cornet Bay marina area. At the main entrance to the park, turn west from Highway 20 onto Cornet Bay Road and follow it to the park. Just inside the park boundary are four ramps with two boarding floats. The launch area is 9 nautical miles from Lopez Pass.

LOPEZ ISLAND
THE FRIENDLY ISLE

◆

SKIP LOPEZ ISLAND IF YOU'RE LOOKING FOR A SWINGING SCENE; but, if you want to laze away to a near-jellyfish state, you'll adore this place. Lopez, the first landing to be reached from Anacortes by the Washington State ferry, is less tourist-oriented than either Orcas or San Juan Islands. First-time visitors will find that facilities at the ferry landing at Upright Head are surprisingly sparse. The small ferry office with outside waiting area and small inside space might be staffed only when a boat is due. A phone booth offers solace to stranded travelers.

Green forest flanks Ferry Road as it stretches south from the landing. Is there anything beyond? It depends on what you're looking for. This is the most slow-paced, most pastoral, and friendliest island of all. It boasts some outstanding lodging and restaurants, a few interesting shops, and, of course, the exquisite scenery that pervades the entire archipelago. Bicyclists revel in the light traffic and gently rolling roads (don't be deterred by that short uphill grind from the ferry landing). Kayakers flock to the rugged, cove-riddled shores on the island's south flank.

Midway down the west shore of the island, one small hamlet, known as Lopez or Lopez Village, offers some limited services. Fisherman Bay, a well-protected anchorage, holds two excellent marinas that meet most boating needs. Overnight lodgings

Quiet village roads and scenic country lanes provide terrific bicycle tours on Lopez Island.

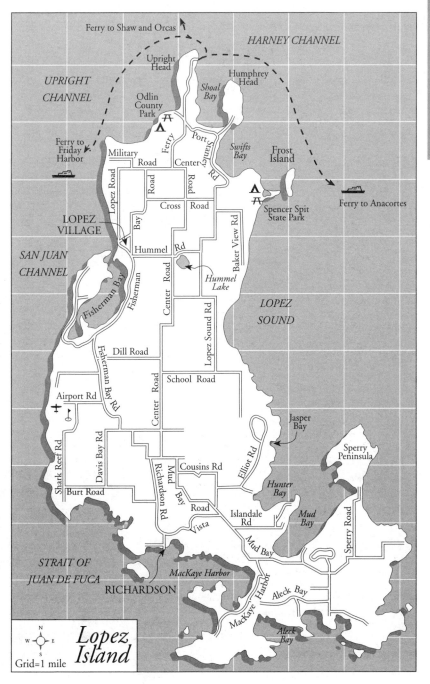

Ferry to Shaw and Orcas

HARNEY CHANNEL

Upright
Head

Humphrey
Head

UPRIGHT
CHANNEL

Shoal
Bay

Odlin
County
Park

Port Stanley Rd

Swifts
Bay

Frost
Island

Ferry to
Friday
Harbor

Military
Road

Center

Ferry

Road

Ferry to Anacortes

LOPEZ
VILLAGE

Bay

Cross   Road

Spencer Spit
State Park

SAN JUAN
CHANNEL

Hummel   Rd

Baker View Rd

Fisherman

Fisherman Bay

Center Road

Hummel
Lake

LOPEZ
SOUND

Dill Road

Lopez Sound Rd

Fisherman Bay Rd

Airport Rd

Davis Bay Rd

Center Road

School   Road

Jasper
Bay

Sperry
Peninsula

Shark Reef Rd

Burt Road

Cousins Rd

Elliot Rd

Hunter
Bay

Mud Bay Rd

Richardson Rd

Road

Islandale
Rd

Mud
Bay

Sperry Road

Vista

Mud Bay

STRAIT OF
JUAN DE FUCA

MacKaye Harbor

RICHARDSON

MacKaye Harbor

Aleck Bay

Aleck
Bay

N
W   E
S
Grid=1 mile

Lopez
Island

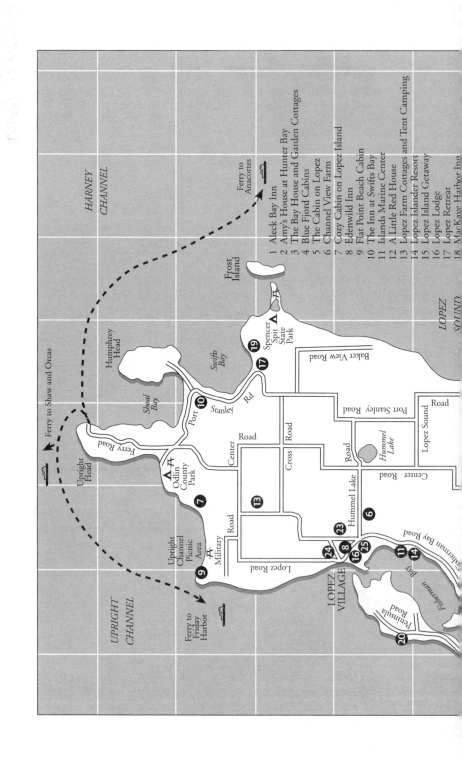

1 Aleck Bay Inn
2 Amy's House at Hunter Bay
3 The Bay House and Garden Cottages
4 Blue Fjord Cabins
5 The Cabin on Lopez
6 Channel View Farm
7 Cozy Cabin on Lopez Island
8 Edenwild Inn
9 Flat Point Beach Cabin
10 The Inn at Swifts Bay
11 Islands Marine Center
12 A Little Red House
13 Lopez Farm Cottages and Tent Camping
14 Lopez Islander Resort
15 Lopez Island Getaway
16 Lopez Lodge
17 Lopez Retreat
18 MacKaye Harbor Inn

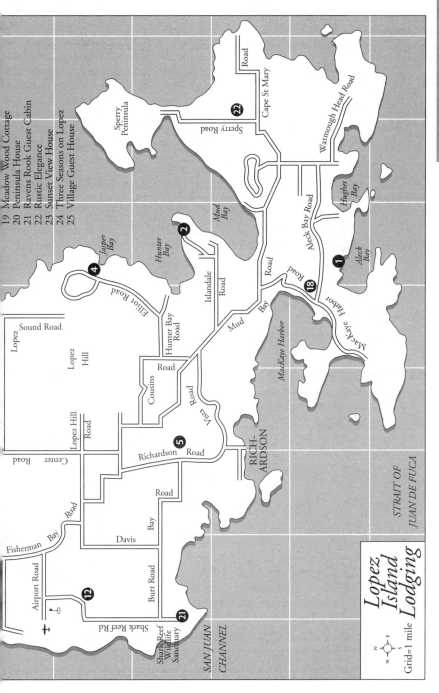

19 Meadow Wood Cottage
20 Peninsula House
21 Ravens Rook Guest Cabin
22 Rustic Elegance
23 Sunset View House
24 Three Seasons on Lopez
25 Village Guest House

Lopez
Island
Lodging

Grid = 1 mile

are scattered throughout the island, while two parks beckon campers.

The handful of Lopez Island shops are largely concentrated in Lopez Village. Here you'll find Old Town (a few buildings on a spur road that dead ends at the water), Lopez Plaza (a long, low building on the southwest side of Lopez Road that holds a few shops), and a cluster of businesses and stores gathered on the northeast side of Lopez Road. A few additional businesses are scattered south, along Fisherman Bay Road.

And that's about all. For many visitors, it's quite enough.

LODGING

Prices quoted for accommodations are summer rates, per day, double occupancy. However, cottages and vacation homes usually rent for the entire unit. Prices are as of 2007, and are subject to change. Lower rates are usually offered off-season. A tax of 9.7 percent is additional. For a general discussion of lodgings, see Lodging Details, pages 35–36.

     = Bed and breakfast inns

     = Cottages, vacation homes, guest suites, condominiums, and hostels

     = Resorts, hotels, motels, and inns

     = Camping (see full descriptions under Parks & Campgrounds)

     = Children OK, however there might be some restrictions

     = Pets OK, however there might be some restrictions

Aleck Bay Inn

45 Finch Lane; Route 1, Box 1920; Lopez Island, WA 98261. Phone: (360) 468-3535; fax: (360) 468-3533; email: *abi@centurytel.net*; web site: *interisland.net/abi*

ACCOMMODATIONS: B&B inn with 4 rooms, all with queen-size beds, private baths and Jacuzzis, fireplaces, some with TV and VCR.

RESTRICTIONS: Children by arrangement, no pets, no smoking.

EXTRAS: Full breakfast, afternoon tea, sun deck, hot tub, beach, table tennis, billiards, games, croquet, badminton, volleyball, music, TV in sitting room, meeting room, bicycle and kayak rentals, facilities for small groups and weddings.

SUMMER RATES: $98 to $198; 2-night minimum June to September. Major credit cards accepted.

From the ferry landing, follow Ferry Road south for 2 miles to a T-intersection and turn left (east) on Center Road, which shortly turns south. In another 5½ miles, at a T-intersection, turn left (east) on Mud Bay Road. Follow Mud Bay Road southeast for 3 miles to MacKaye Harbor Road. Turn right (south) on MacKaye Harbor Road and in 1 mile turn left (east) on Aleck Bay Road. In ¼ mile, at a sign for the inn, turn right on Wren Road. At a junction in a short distance, continue straight ahead on Finch Road to the inn. By boat, the inn lies on Aleck Bay on the south end of Lopez Island. Good anchorages are available offshore, and dinghies can be landed on the beach.

Aleck Bay Inn provides gracious accommodations for your vacation, weekend getaway, wedding, or honeymoon. The facilities are ideally suited for a small group gathering—the spacious, sunny game room also serves as a meeting room. Guests who want more than reading on the sun deck or beachcombing will enjoy kayaking, bicycling, or games. Evenings might bring music fests around the piano. Snacks are always available; on request, dinner can be served.

The inn has easy access to the beach. Exquisite Aleck Bay has good anchorages for boaters who want to come ashore for a weekend stay, or who use the inn as a base for island excursions.

Amy's House at Hunter Bay

24 Crab Island Road; Lopez Island, WA 98261-8060. Phone: (253) 735-1390, (253) 307-7742, or (253) 874-3246 (ask for Amy); email: *amydmv@yahoo.com*; web site: *amys@emeraldweb.biz*

ACCOMMODATIONS: Rental home with 2 queen-size beds, 2 twin beds, full-size futon in a sleeping loft. 2 bathrooms, one with shower and jetted tub, one with shower, fully equipped kitchen.
EXTRAS: TV/VCR/DVD, stereo, deck, large deck, fenced yard.
SUMMER RATES: Weekend $450; week $1200.
Immediately adjacent to the county dock on the south end of Lopez Island.

Up to seven visitors can enjoy this modern guesthouse on the southeast side of Lopez Island. It features a prime location with northerly views of Lopez Sound, the ferry lanes, and Mount Baker. It offers easy beach access to a protected cove, along

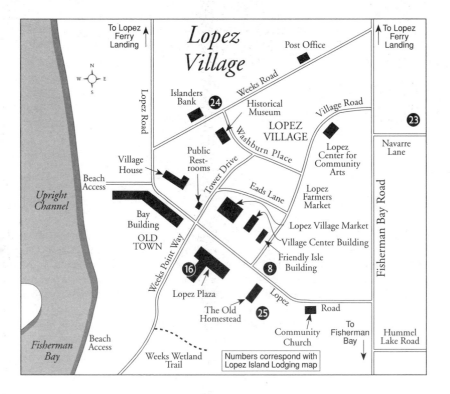

with ample opportunities for seal and otter watching. You can arrive by car, or tie your boat short-term to the dock, or anchor just offshore in the spacious bay.

Large windows take in the view, and the modern kitchen is fully equipped for whipping up meals. Enjoy watching boats and birds while your soul is restored.

The Bay House and Garden Cottages 🏠 👪

P.O. Box 602; Lopez, WA 98261. Phone: (360) 468-4889; email: *cc@interisland.net*; web site: *interisland.net/cc*

ACCOMMODATIONS: Rental home and 2 cottages.
- *Bay House:* 2 bedrooms, hide-a-bed, kitchen, bath, hide-a-bed, kitchen, bath. hide-a-bed, kitchen, bath.
- *2 cottages:* Queen-size beds, kitchens, bath.

EXTRAS: *Bay House:* Fireplace, stereo, CD collection, TV/VCR, deck with umbrella table. *Cottages:* Wood stoves.

SUMMER RATES: *Bay House:* $200 per night, double occupancy $15 per extra person. *Cottages:* $150 per night, double occupancy.

🚗 Guests will be given driving directions.

Golden knotty pine paneling accented by crisp, airy curtains greets visitors at the guesthouse and cottages of these accommodations. Wood stoves warm chilly evenings; the one in the guesthouse is on a fieldstone hearth. Sitting on the south end of Fisherman Bay, Lopez Village is just a pleasant walk away.

The landscaped yard that brims with seasonal flowers includes a goldfish pond and fountain, and has plenty of space for sunbathing. The water view sweeps west and north across Fisherman Bay, with glimpses of the Strait of Juan de Fuca.

Blue Fjord Cabins 🏠 👪 🐎

862 Elliott Road; Lopez Island, WA 98261. Phone: (888) 633-0401 or (360) 468-2749; email: *bluefjordcabins@yahoo.com*; web site: *interisland.net/bluefjord*

ACCOMMODATIONS: 2 cabins, each with queen-size bed, bath, kitchenette.
RESTRICTIONS: Children OK, depending on age; additional charge for pets, non-smokers preferred.
EXTRAS: TV, shoreline deck and beach gazebo, beach, trails.
SUMMER RATES: $125, 3-night minimum July through September and holidays, 2-night minimum at other times. Stay for a week, and your seventh night is free. No credit cards.

🚗 Confirmed reservations will be sent a map.

These Nordic chalet-style cabins are in a woodland setting that fronts on a remote cove on the east shore of Lopez Island. The units are well separated, and each enjoys forest views and seclusion. The cabins comfortably accommodate one or two persons. The beautiful, modern lodgings feature log walls with open-beam ceilings, skylights, carpeting, kitchens, and decks. Comfortable brass beds have featherbeds, and down duvets. The kitchens come fully equipped—just bring your own groceries.

A short nature trail leads to Jasper Bay, a sheltered cove that holds a romantic waterside viewing deck with a gazebo, ideal for a private picnic.

The Cabin on Lopez 🏠 👪

1005 Richardson Road; Lopez Island, WA 98261. Phone: (360) 468-2088; email: *stonem@ rockisland.com*; web site: *rockisland.com/~stonem*

ACCOMMODATIONS: Cabin with 2 queen-size beds, 1 daybed, full bath, kitchen, spacious deck.
RESTRICTIONS: No pets, no smoking.
EXTRAS: TV/VCR, barbeque.
SUMMER RATES: $125 per night, $795 per week double occupancy, 3-night minimum.
🚗 Guests will be given driving directions.

Cedar shake siding, natural cedar interior, and lots of windows that open to forest and water views make this cabin right at home in its setting on the southwest side of Lopez Island. Stretch out on the deck to sunbathe in the day or to listen to woodland sounds at night. Views extend out to Victoria, B.C. on distant Vancouver Island.

Channel View Farm 🏠 👪

444 Hummel Lake Road, P.O. Box 800; Lopez Island, WA 98261; (866) 489-4414 or (360) 468-4415; email: *stay@channelviewfarm.com*; web site: *channelviewfarm.com*

ACCOMMODATIONS: Rental home with queen-size bed, bath, sleeping loft with twin beds, kitchen.
EXTRAS: Satellite TV/DVD, barbeque, patio, pond.
RESTRICTIONS: No pets, no children under 12, no smoking.
SUMMER RATES: $135 per night, 2-night minimum.
🚗 From the ferry landing, follow Ferry Road south for 2 miles and turn right onto Military Road. In ½ mile, at an intersection, head south on Fisherman Bay Road, and in 1¾ miles turn left on Hummel Lake Road. In ¾ mile look for the farmhouse on the right.

The view to the channel is a bit distant, but the farm and garden ambience, along with its relaxation, is right outside your door. The airy, modern cottage will sleep four; a ladder leads to a sleeping loft. Walk to Lopez Village for shopping or a meal. Bring your bicycles or rent some in Lopez Village to tour the level country roads.

Cozy Cabin on Lopez Island 🏠

244 Shady Lane; Lopez Island, WA 98261. Phone: (360) 468-3347; cell: (360) 298-0209; fax: (775) 269-0869; email: *wogcw@rockisland.com*; web site: *cozycabinonlopezisland.com*

ACCOMMODATIONS: Cabin with queen-size bed, ¾ bath, kitchenette.
EXTRAS: Deck, complimentary bicycles available.
RESTRICTIONS: No smoking, no pets.
SUMMER RATES: $85 double occupancy, 2-night minimum.
🚗 From the ferry, follow Ferry Road south for 2 miles to a T-intersection. Turn right (west) on Military Road, and follow it for ¾ miles as it turns north. At the next corner turn east on Coho Lane, and then north on Shady Lane (the third driveway). At a fork head northwest; the cabin is on the right after a wooden gate. Check in at the owner's residence, downhill.

You'd never guess its origins in the 1920s from the look of this beautifully restored cabin with new pine interior and comfortable accommodations. The woodsy setting is perfect for a romantic getaway. A sliding double door near your bed opens onto the deck, letting in the sounds and scents of the forest as you drift off to sleep. Lopez Village is just five minutes away by car, or ten minutes using the bicycles the owners have available for use.

Edenwild Inn ⊨ ♛ ♿

Lopez Village; 132 Lopez Road, P.O. Box 271; Lopez Island, WA 98261. Phone: (800) 606-0622 or (360) 468-3238; fax: (360) 468-4080; email: *edenwild@rockisland.com*; web site: *edenwildinn.com*

ACCOMMODATIONS: B&B inn with 8 suites, king- and queen-size beds, all with private baths, some rooms with fireplace, all with either water or garden views, some with disabled access.

RESTRICTIONS: No children under 12, no pets, no smoking.

EXTRAS: Sumptuous continental breakfast, afternoon tea, honeymoon suite, bicycles, wireless internet access. Kayak and boat rentals nearby.

SUMMER RATES: $165 to $185. Visa and MasterCard accepted.

🚗 Located in the heart of Lopez Village, south of Lopez Plaza.

Although fashioned after a Victorian-era country inn, Edenwild Inn is recently built, providing charm along with modern conveniences. Soft flower tones of violet, rose, and blue sweep down the walls and over the elegantly furnished rooms. The comfortable living room boasts a huge fireplace. Bright flowers and a pretty arbor leading to the front door add to the charm. The veranda and patio offer ring-side seats for viewing sunsets over Fisherman Bay. Enchanting is the only word for it.

Edenwild Inn, in Lopez Village, is one of the island's excellent B&Bs.

With prior arrangements, the inn can pick you up at the ferry, Lopez airport, or from a boat or seaplane in Fisherman Bay. The Lopez Village location is handy for shopping and dining, or as a base for island exploration. Bicycles are available for guest use, while kayak guided trips are right across the street.

Flat Point Beach Cabin 🏠 ♔

Lopez Island, WA 98261; (360) 468-3105; email: *jlmal@rockisland.com*; web site: *rockisland.com/~jlmal/lopez_island_beach_rental*

ACCOMMODATIONS: Cabin with 2 bedrooms, one with queen-size bed, one with bunk beds, bath with shower, kitchen.

RESTRICTIONS: No smoking, no pets.

EXTRAS: Deck, phone, TV/DVD, CD, stereo, barbeque, clam shovel. Mooring buoy available with advance notice.

SUMMER RATES: $150 per night, $875 per week, 4 people maximum.

🚗 ⛵ Guests will be given driving or boating directions.

Even though this modern cabin is really nice and well appointed, you won't want to spend much time indoors. Flat Point is one of the premier sites on Lopez Island, with views to the north, south, and west, and one of the best beaches on the island. The wetland behind the cabin is home to otters, heron, waterfowl, and songbirds. At low tide the beach can be walked south to Lopez Village or east and north to Odlin County Park.

Hand-carried boats are easily launched from the beach, or you can tie your boat up to the owner's mooring buoy, with advanced permission, and take your dinghy ashore.

The Inn at Swifts Bay 🛏

856 Port Stanley Road; Lopez Island, WA 98261. Phone: (800) 903-9536 or (360) 468-3636; fax: (360) 468-3636; email: *inn@swiftsbay.com*; web site: *swiftsbay.com*

ACCOMMODATIONS: B&B inn with 5 rooms and suites, each with queen-size bed, 3 with private bath and fireplace, 2 share a hall bath.

RESTRICTIONS: No children, no pets, no smoking.

EXTRAS: Full breakfast; exercise room with sauna; hot tub, robes and slippers; 2 common areas with fireplaces, VCR, music and movie videotapes; walk to private beach.

SUMMER RATES: $110 to $210. Major credit cards accepted.

🚗 From the ferry landing, follow Ferry Road south for 2 miles to a T-intersection and turn left (east) on Port Stanley Road. In about ¾ mile, as the road bends south, the mailbox and the sign for the driveway to the inn is on the right.

World-class pampering marks this top-rated bed and breakfast inn on quiet Lopez Island. The Tudor-style brick home, embraced by three acres of lush forest and rhododendrons, exudes Northwest hospitality and grace. The inn sits on a hillside, across the road from Swifts Bay; a short walk provides beach access.

Each of the splendid rooms has an individual character; one opens onto a patio, an attic room has an antique sleigh bed and skylights for star viewing. Reserve the outdoor hot tub for private soaking—robes and slippers are available. Evening brings romantic hand-holding on the quiet patio, or casual gatherings around the fireplace in one of the two common rooms. Enjoy a sherry along with a chat with other guests and your hosts. The gourmet breakfasts match the sublime accommodations.

Islands Marine Center 🏠 ♀♂

2793 Fisherman Bay Road, P.O. Box 88; Lopez Island, WA 98261. Phone: (360) 468-3377; fax: (360) 468-2283; email: *imc@rockisland.com*; web site: *islandsmarinecenter.com*

ACCOMMODATIONS: Building with 3 units, 2 with queen-size bed, and single bed, 1 unit that can only be rented with another (no separate entrance); all with private bath, kitchens, fireplace, view deck.

RESTRICTIONS: Children OK, no pets, no smoking.

EXTRAS: TV, Dish network, barbeque pit, picnic tables. Bicycle and kayak rentals next door. Moorage and boat launch available.

SUMMER RATES: 1 bedroom $95, second connecting bedroom $35; 2-night minimum on 3-day weekends. Major credit cards accepted.

🚗 Located on Fisherman Bay Road, immediately south of Lopez Village, on the second floor of the Islands Marine Center.

These spacious, modern apartments are centrally located to all the marine activity on Fisherman Bay, making them an ideal base for visitors who want to take advantage of the San Juan's superb boating or fishing.

One suite that sleeps up to six has a hide-a-bed, trundle, and separate bedroom with a queen-size bed. Another unit that has no separate entrance can be rented as an additional bedroom for guests in either of the two main suites. Each room looks west over Fisherman Bay, offering prime views of the islands' spectacular sunsets.

A Little Red House 🏠 ♀♂

177 Starkman Lane; Lopez Island, WA 98261. Phone: (360) 468-2903; email: *starkman@ rockisland.com*; web site: *lopezvacationrental.com*

ACCOMMODATIONS: Rental home with 2 bedrooms with queen-size beds, 1 double sofa bed, 1 full bath, kitchen.

RESTRICTIONS: No pets, no smoking.

EXTRAS: Satellite TV/VCR, washer, dryer, barbeque, picnic area, porch swings. Close to golf course and Shark Reef Wildlife Sanctuary.

SUMMER RATES: $135 per night, $825 per week.

🚗 From the ferry landing, follow Ferry Road south for 2 miles to a T-intersection and turn right (west) onto Military Road. In ½ mile, at the intersection of Military Road and Fisherman Bay Road, head south on Fisherman Bay Road. In 4½ miles turn right (west) on Airport Road (signed to the golf course and airstrip). In ½ mile turn left (south) on Shark Reef Road, and in another ¼ mile follow the road southwest. At the next corner, where Shark Reef Road turns west, go south on Starkman Lane to the house.

Here's a charming house, with a second story over the main house, and a nice large yard where you can turn the kids loose. The modern kitchen is fully furnished, including a microwave and dishwasher. The washer and dryer are great for grubby clothes after a busy day of exploring. In the evening, relax on the porch swings.

Lopez Farm Cottages and Tent Camping 🏠 ⋀ 🏕

555 Fisherman Bay Road, P.O. Box 610; Lopez Island, WA 98261. Phone: (360) 468-3666; (800) 440-3556; fax: (360) 468-3966; email: *johnwarsen@centurytel.net*; web site: *lopezfarmcottages.com*

ACCOMMODATIONS: 4 cottages (1-bedroom) , 1 with king-size bed, the others with queen-size beds, futons available for a child, private bath, kitchenettes .

RESTRICTIONS: 1 child OK, no pets, no smoking.

EXTRAS: Continental breakfast, hot tub (one shared, one private and secluded), farm atmosphere, barbeques. 13 wooded tent sites. Winery nearby.

SUMMER RATES: $160 to $180. Futon available for $25 per night. Tent sites $36 to $65, double occupancy. Visa and MasterCard accepted.

🚗 From the ferry landing, follow Ferry Road south for 2 miles to a T-intersection and turn right (west) onto Military Road. In ½ mile, at the intersection of Military Road and Fisherman Bay Road, head south on Fisherman Bay Road. The driveway leading to the inn is on the left in ¼ mile, across from Lopez Island Vineyards.

This historic family farm provides just what you're looking for in a getaway. Sheep graze in the pastures, and you're almost sure to see deer foraging in the farm's 100-year-old orchard. The modern, newly built guest cottages, nestled in an old cedar

The charming cabins at Lopez Farm Cottages are one of the many kinds of lodgings available in the San Juan Islands.

grove near the back of the 40-acre farm, are designed to fit right in with the rural ambiance, with country casual furnishings, charming front porches and back decks, and lots of privacy. The generous Continental breakfast of muffins, jam, fruit, and other country goodies are on hand right in your cottage. There's no need to even get out of your PJs to chow down.

Immediately across the road is Lopez Island Vineyards, where you can visit the tasting room, and then pick up a bottle of their award-wining wine to sip on the porch of your cottage as evening settles over the farm. Bliss!

A fine campground, some distance from the cottages, offers tent sites for tourists seeking slightly more rugged accommodations. Three more campsites are snuggled in the woods beyond the cottages. See Parks & Campgrounds, pages 107–108.

Lopez Islander Bay Resort 🏠 ⋀ ⚥

2864 Fisherman Bay Road, P.O. Box 459; Lopez Island, WA 98261. Phone: (800) 736-3434 or (360) 468-2233; fax: (360) 468-3382; email: *desk@lopezislander.com*; web site: *lopezislander.com*. Marina: (360) 468-3383, monitors VHF channel 78

ACCOMMODATIONS: Resort.
- 28 rooms with king- or queen-size beds.
- 2 suites with 3-bedrooms, some with kitchenettes.
- Economy rooms with shower only in bathroom.

RESTRICTIONS: Children OK, no pets, no smoking.

EXTRAS: TV in all rooms, many rooms with kitchenettes , wet bars, and microwaves. All rooms have water views. Heated swimming pool, Jacuzzi, coin-operated laundry, restaurant (lunch, and dinner), meeting and banquet facilities, beach, bicycle and kayak rentals. Marina, charters (fishing, diving, or wildlife viewing). RV park and camping.

SUMMER RATES: $98 to $125, suites $210 to $335. Major credit cards accepted.

🚗⛴⫪ The resort is immediately south of Lopez Village on Fisherman Bay Road. By boat it lies just inside the entrance to Fisherman Bay. The marina has a small seaplane float.

The Lopez Islander offers a full range of facilities, making it ideal for boaters' rendezvous and company retreats. Rooms are in long, 1- or 2-story buildings across the road from the marina and restaurant..

Lopez Village is just a stroll away, and various rental or chartering opportunities are right at hand. Boaters will welcome a chance to steady their sea legs in one of the comfortably furnished units, and soak in the resort hot tub. See also Restaurants & Cafés, page 96, Marinas, Launch Ramps & Put-Ins, page 106, and Camping, pages 107–108.

Lopez Island Getaway 🏠 ⚥

Lopez Island, WA 98261. Phone (425) 788-4338; email: *reservations@lopezgetaway.com*; web site: *lopezgetaway.com*

ACCOMMODATIONS: Rental home with 2 queen-size beds, 2 single beds in a loft, 2 baths, kitchen.

EXTRAS: Espresso machine, TV/VCR, CD, washer, dryer, wood stove, deck, barbeque.

SUMMER RATES: Weekly $950, weekend $350.

🚗 Guests will be given driving directions.

A weekend, week, or longer spent in this peaceful home on Lopez Island is sure to sooth nerves frayed by civilization's demands. The modern, architect-designed three-story house is situated so its cathedral windows take advantage of views out to Lopez Sound. Whether you want to whip up a gourmet meal, or just make popcorn, all the kitchen gear you need is there.

Lopez Lodge 🏠 ⚥

Lopez Village, P.O. Box 117; Lopez Island, WA 98261. Phone: (360) 468-2816; email: *needle@ rockisland.com*; web site: *lopezlodge.com*

ACCOMMODATIONS: Building with 3 rooms (1 or 2 queen-size beds), private or shared baths; all have kitchenettes.
RESTRICTIONS: Children OK, no pets, no smoking.
EXTRAS: All have TV, microwave, small refrigerator. Bicycle, kayak, and boat rentals nearby.
SUMMER RATES: $60 to $125. Major credit cards accepted.
🚗 In Lopez Village, next to Lopez Plaza.

These second-floor rooms above a small shopping plaza in Lopez Village are just the ticket for people looking for comfortable, reasonably priced accommodations. Furnishings are utilitarian, but all rooms are spacious and clean, and have water views of the end of Fisherman Bay. The largest unit has two beds, kitchenette, a small living area, and private bath. The two smaller units (one with one bed, one with two) share a bath (shower only). Coffeemakers are provided in each unit.

Lopez Retreat 🏠 ⚥

1795 Port Stanley Road; Lopez Island, WA 98261. Phone: (360) 410-9149; email: *katie@ lopezretreat.com*; web site: *lopezretreat.com*

ACCOMMODATIONS: Rental home with 2 bedrooms with queen-size and double beds, 2 baths, 4 person occupancy, kitchen.
RESTRICTIONS: No smoking, no pets.
EXTRAS: Deck, barbeque, satellite TV/DVD, stereo, washer, dryer, public beach access, mooring buoy.
SUMMER RATES: $1200 per week, daily (on special request) $200 per night, 3-night minimum.
🚗 ⚓ From the ferry landing, follow Ferry Road south for 1¾ miles to a T-intersection and turn left (east) on Port Stanley Road. Follow it for 1 more mile to the house at 1795.

This modern, two-bedroom home on the northeast end of Lopez Island overlooks Swifts Bay. A large deck and cathedral ceilings emphasize the gracious home's spaciousness. It comes fully equipped with everything you will need for your visit. There's access to the pebbled beach, and a mooring buoy offshore is available for tying up your vessel, if you arrive by boat.

MacKaye Harbor Inn ⊫ 🏌

949 MacKaye Harbor Road; Lopez Island, WA 98261. Phone: (360) 468-2253; fax: (360) 468-2393; email: *mackaye@rockisland.com*; web site: *mackayeharborinn.com*

ACCOMMODATIONS: B&B inn with 2 suites and 3 rooms (2 rooms with private baths, 3 rooms share 2½ baths).

RESTRICTIONS: Children over 8 OK, no pets, no smoking.

EXTRAS: Full breakfast, afternoon tea, guest refrigerator, barbecue, complimentary bicycles, kayak rentals (for guests only), kayak instruction and tours, binoculars, garden.

SUMMER RATES: $139 to $195. Major credit cards accepted.

🚗 From the ferry landing, follow Ferry Road south for 2 miles to a T-intersection and turn left (east) on Center Road, which shortly turns south. In another 5½ miles, at a T-intersection, turn left (east) on Mud Bay Road. Follow Mud Bay Road southeast for 3 miles to MacKaye Harbor Road.Turn right (south) on MacKaye Harbor Road. The water is reached in less than 1 more mile. The inn is on the left, at the end of the beach.

The lovely Victorian farmhouse facing on MacKaye Harbor is one of the best-known and most highly praised of Lopez lodgings—and deservedly so. Morning salt breezes drifting through lace curtains; languid, sunny afternoons; evenings by the fireplace with a good novel—what could be nicer? Although a country road separates the inn from the bay, the shore is part of the property. As a guest, you can stroll on the driftwood-strewn beach. For exercise, kayaks and bicycles are available for a turn around the island, either by water or land.

Because of its popularity, the inn is heavily booked in summer. But don't forget that the quiet season is a terrific time to visit the San Juan Islands, too.

Meadow Wood Cottage 🏠 🏌

252 Coyote Lane; Lopez Island, WA 98261. Email: *joann@rockisland.com*; web sites: *rockisland.com/~joann*

ACCOMMODATIONS: Cottage with 2 bedrooms, 2 baths, kitchen.

RESTRICTIONS: No smoking, no pets.

EXTRAS: TV/VCR/DVD, wood stove, barbeque, deck, beach access.

SUMMER RATES: Daily $145 per person for 2 persons; weekly $135 per day for 2 persons, extra guests $15 a day per person. 4-day minimum in summer, 3-day minimum in winter.

🚗 North of Spencer Spit State Park, above Swifts Bay. Guests will be given driving directions.

Enjoy five acres of meadow and forest all to yourself (except for the neighboring wildlife) while staying in this cheerful, modern cottage on the north end of Lopez Island. Stroll down to the beach at Swifts Bay, or take an easy walk to Spencer Spit State Park. Lopez Village is just 3½ miles away.

Large windows that stretch to the top of the cathedral ceiling let in San Juan sunshine. Enjoy cocktails and meals on the deck, or by the cozy wood stove.

Peninsula House 🏠 🏌

887 Peninsula Road, P.O. Box 6; Lopez Island, WA 98261; email: *jml@rockisland.com*; web site: *peninsula-house.com*

ACCOMMODATIONS: Rental home with 4 bedrooms, including master suite with king-size bed and Jacuzzi, 3 baths, kitchen.

EXTRAS: 3 view decks, washer, dryer, barbeque, hot tub private beach, satellite TV/DVD/VCR, CD, mooring buoy, bicycles.

SUMMER RATES: $2500 per week, 3-night minimum.

🚐 From Lopez Village, drive south on Fisherman Bay Road for 2 miles, and then turn right (west) on Bayshore Road. Follow Bayshore around Fisherman Bay for 1¼ miles and take the first left turn after crossing the spit, which is Peninsula Road. Follow this road to its end at 887.

This very special waterfront estate is beautifully suited for small weddings and family reunions. It looks out to boating traffic in San Juan Channel, and is not far from the driftwood-piled beach of Otis Perkins Park.

The master suite fills the entire top floor, and includes a custom-built king-size bed, Jacuzzi spa, and its own private deck. What could be more luxurious? The kitchen, fully equipped for family feeds, includes a dishwasher. Original works of art throughout complement the modern décor.

Ravens Rook Guest Cabin 🏠 👫

58 Wild Rose Lane; Lopez Island, WA 98261; email: *ravensrook@rockisland.com*; web site: *rockisland.com/~ravensrook*

ACCOMMODATIONS: Rental home with 2 queen-size beds, sleeping loft, extra sleeping mat, bath with shower, kitchen.

RESTRICTIONS: Children OK, no toddlers, no pets, no smoking.

EXTRAS: Oil heat, wood stove, stereo, CD, small pond, deck, bicycles, walking distance to Shark Reef Wildlife Sanctuary.

SUMMER RATES: $100 per night in June, $130 per night, July and August. 2-night minimum. $875 per week July and August. 4-person maximum.

🚐 Guests will be given driving directions.

If you ever dreamed of a rustic cabin in the woods, this is the one for you. It's an affordable getaway in the cozy comfort of quiet woods—and really nice. The post-and-beam cabin is light and airy, with large windows looking out to the forest, and skylights looking out to the sky and stars.

The sleeping loft, which holds two queen-size beds, is reached by a ladder. A sleeping mat is provided for an additional child, or take the mat out to the deck to snooze in the fresh air.

Rustic Elegance 🏠 👫

90 Sperry Road; Lopez, WA 98261. Phone: (360) 435-8065; email: *info@lopezrusticelegance. com*; web site: *lopezrusticelegance.com*

ACCOMMODATIONS: Rental home that sleeps 6 to 8, full bath with double-size shower and antique claw-foot tub, 1½ baths, kitchen.

RESTRICTIONS: No smoking, no pets.

EXTRAS: Wet bar, TV/VCR, satellite dish, stereo, deck, 6-person hot tub, outdoor firepit, outdoor hammocks, badminton net. Walking distance to public beach.

SUMMER RATES: Up to 4 adults $165 per night, additional adults $15 per night, 2-night minimum.

🚐 From the ferry landing, follow Ferry Road south for 2 miles to a T-intersection and turn left (east) on Center Road, which shortly turns south. In another 5½ miles, at a T-intersection, turn left (east) on Mud Bay Road. In 5 miles this turns into Sperry Road. The house is on the right side of Sperry Road.

This three-story-tall, shake-sided home sports a wide deck encircling the second story. The home, sitting in open forest on the southeast end of Lopez Island, holds all the ingredients for a really great stay: hot tub, outdoor firepit with benches, wet bar, and forest ambience.

Sunset View House 🏠 🕴

43 Navarre Lane; Lopez Island, WA 98621; email: *stay@sunsetviewhouse.com*; web site: *sunsetviewhouse.com*

ACCOMMODATIONS: Rental home with 3 bedrooms with queen-size beds, loft sitting area with futon, 2 full baths, kitchen.
RESTRICTIONS: No smoking, no pets.
EXTRAS: TV/VCR/DVD, deck. Short walk to Lopez Village.
SUMMER RATES: Sunday through Thursday $205, Friday and Saturday $245, 1 to 4 persons; $15 per night for each additional person, 9 persons maximum; $25 cleaning fee and $100 security deposit per reservation. 6 percent discount for full week.

🚐 From the ferry landing, follow Ferry Road south for 2 miles to a T-intersection and turn right (west) onto Military Road. In ½ mile, at the intersection of Military Road and Fisherman Bay Road, head south on Fisherman Bay Road. Follow Fisherman Bay Road for 2 miles, passing Village Road on the right, and in a short distance turn left (east) on Navarre Road. Turn onto the first unmarked dirt road to the left and follow it to the house.

A big family or group of up to eight people will delight in this fine home. Aptly named, the house sits on a slight hill, surrounded by four acres of meadows and woods, and looks out to stunning sunset views over Fisherman Bay. You might well see bald eagles; deer are your neighbors. The spacious home is 2100 square feet, not including the large deck. Lots of room for fun!

Three Seasons on Lopez 🏠 🕴

95 Weeks Road; Lopez Island, WA 98261. Phone: (206) 214-8551; email: *contact@threeseasonsonlopez.com*; web site: *threeseasonsonlopez.com*

ACCOMMODATIONS: Rental home with 1 bedroom, 1 bath, kitchen.
RESTRICTIONS: No smoking, no pets.
EXTRAS: Small deck, TV/VCR, stereo, gas stove, soaking tub, washer, dryer, barbeque. Within walking distance of shops and restaurants in Lopez Village.
SUMMER RATES: $675 per week, $275 per weekend, 1-week minimum stay.

🚐 From the ferry landing, follow Ferry Road south for 2 miles to a T-intersection and turn right (west) onto Military Road. In ½ mile, at the intersection of Military Road and Fisherman Bay Road, head south on Fisherman Bay Road, and follow it for 3¾ miles to Weeks Road. Turn right onto Weeks Road. The house is in 2 blocks, on the right, at 95 Weeks Road.

Sited right in the heart of Lopez Village, this fine, contemporary home boasts vaulted ceilings, tall windows, and hardwood floors. The home's deck overlooks a landscaped, flower-edged yard. Walk to shops, restaurants, and beaches, and pick up some steaks at the market for grilling on the barbeque. Or, grab binoculars and head down to Weeks Wetland Trail for birdwatching and looking for marshland critters.

Village Guest House 🏠 👫

Route 1, Box 2358; Lopez Island, WA 98261. Phone: (360) 468-2191

ACCOMMODATIONS: Rental home with 2 bedrooms, 1 bath, kitchenette.
RESTRICTIONS: Children OK, no pets, no smoking.
EXTRAS: Deck, barbecue, TV/VCR, beachfront. Walk to Lopez Village. Bicycle, kayak, and boat rentals nearby.
SUMMER RATES: $90 to $525 weekly (includes tax). 1-week minimum in summer. No credit cards.
🚗 Located on the water, two houses north of Old Town.

Your family can have a grand vacation in this nice cottage at the mouth of Fisherman Bay. Steps lead down the moderate bank to the beach. The shops and restaurants of Lopez Village, and kayak and bicycle rentals are right down the road.

The cottage sleeps four comfortably and has a spacious living room. Grill your burgers on the outside barbecue and relax in lawn chairs as you enjoy the sea breeze and spectacular sunsets. Boats negotiating the narrow channel into Fisherman Bay seem just an arm's length away from your front yard.

VACATION HOME RENTAL FIRMS
◆

Realtors on Lopez and the other islands have listings of various residences you can rent for a week or longer. There you can enjoy all the comforts of home, and can fantasize about being one of those very fortunate San Juan Islands property owners—and then go home at the end of your vacation and not have to worry about such mundane things as upkeep and property taxes. Or, maybe you'll decide this is the life for you, and you'll go real estate shopping. If so, check their web site.

Windermere Vacation Rentals

Friendly Isle Building #A, P.O. Box 27; Lopez Island, WA 98261. Phone: (360) 468-3344, (360) 468-3177; fax: (360) 468-3632; email: *gortons@rockisland.com;* web site: *windermerevacationrentals.com*

RESTAURANTS, CAFÉS & TAKE-OUT
◆

$	Inexpensive	Most dinner entrées under $12
$$	Moderate	Most dinner entrées $12 to $25
$$$	Expensive	Most dinner entrées $25 and up

🍾 = Beer and wine 🍸 = Full bar

What could be nicer than a sunny deck and fine food at the Bay Café in Lopez Village?

The Bay Café $$$ 🍷

9 Old Post Road, Lopez Village; Lopez Island, WA 98261. Phone: (360) 468-3700; email: *thebaycafe@aol.com*; web site: *bay-cafe.com*

HOURS: Dinner. Reservations recommended. Major credit cards accepted.

The setting is typical San Juan: a cheery room amply decorated with fresh flowers and an eclectic assortment of memorabilia. Windows spreading along one side of the room overlook the entrance to Fisherman Bay, and an outside deck adds summer seating.

And the food is straight from heaven! The cafe's wide range of innovative dishes draw on a variety of cuisines. The menu might include Dungeness crabcakes warmed with herbed tomato vinaigrette, a filet of aged beef tenderloin with wine demi-glace, a seafood curry, or ocean-caught prawns. The dessert menu is equally dazzling.

Bucky's Lopez Island Grill $ 🍷

Lopez Plaza; Lopez Island, WA 98261. Phone: (360) 468-2595

HOURS: Breakfast, lunch, and dinner.

Sit inside this cozy café, or grab one of the tables on the open deck overlooking Fisherman Bay. Stop by for lunch to find out what a Black and Blue Chickenburger is, or to check out their claim that they make the best fish and chips in the San Juans. Dinner choices include ribs, fresh seafood, chicken, steak, burgers, and another chance to feast on fish and chips. Bucky's is the only place on Lopez you're sure to find open early for breakfast. All items are available for take-out.

Café La Boehme $

Lopez Plaza; Lopez Island, WA 98261. Phone: (360) 468-2257

The espresso craze is as strong on Lopez Island as it is in the rest of Western Washington. At Café La Boehme you can complement your latte or mocha with tasty fresh-baked goods. Settle down at one of the tables on the outside covered deck and soak up your morning caffeine and calories.

Chuck's Wagon—Espresso to Go $

Sunset Builders Supply parking lot, intersection of Center and Schoolhouse Roads; Lopez Island, WA 98261. Phone: (360) 468-2193

After you have tried out the high school tennis courts, or bicycled along Center Road, stop here for an iced espresso and hot dog. You might not always find them open.

The Galley Restaurant and Lounge $ ⊻

3365 Fisherman Bay Road; Lopez Island, WA 98261. Phone: (360) 468-2713; lounge: (360) 468-2874; email: *galley@rockisland.com*; web site: *rockisland.com/~galley*

HOURS: Breakfast, lunch, and dinner. Major credit cards accepted.

Here's where many local people hang out—what better recommendation can there be? Visiting boaters can tie up to the restaurant's dock on Fisherman Bay (moorage is free for patrons), saunter across the road, and chow down on a steak, burger, chicken, shrimp, or Mexican fare. Down a cool one in the lounge and shoot pool or play the pinball machine.

Isabel's Espresso $

Village House, 308 Lopez Road; Lopez Island, WA 98261. Phone: (360) 468-4114; email: *Isabel@rockisland.com*

HOURS: Daily from 7:30 A.M. to 5 P.M.

If you can't begin your day without a hot double tall skinny latte with Amaretto flavoring, whipped cream, and a dusting of cinnamon, you'll be able to get it here at Isabel's. There are also bagels, cookies, other nibblies, and a selection of teas. This small spot, with only six tables, is ideal for good conversation mixed with great coffee.

Lopez Island Creamery Café $

3185 Fisherman Bay Road; Lopez Island, WA 98261. Phone: (360) 468-2051; web site: *lopezislandcreamery.com*

HOURS: Lunch in summer, pizza in evenings. Monday through Saturday 11:30 A.M. to 8 P.M.; Sunday 1 P.M. to 6 P.M.; closed Wednesday. Weekends only off-season.

Gourmet hand-made ice cream in 28 different flavors, made right on the premises! What more need we say? Ice cream is the mainstay, but in summer, lunch and dinner offerings are burgers: beef, veggie, and (where else but in the San Juans?) wild salmon. Pizza's on the menu, too.

The café is a bit south of Lopez Village on Fisherman Bay Road. A few tables are inside, and picnic tables are on the patio.

Lopez Island Soda Shop (Lopez Island Pharmacy) $

Lopez Village; 157 Village Road; Lopez Island, WA 98261. Phone: (360) 468-4511; email: *sodafountain@lopezislandpharmacy.com*; web site: *lopezislandpharmacy.com*

HOURS: Breakfast and lunch daily except Sunday; fountain treats all day. Major credit cards accepted.

You might not drive up in your pink Chevy BelAir, but you'll still enjoy the nostalgia trip as well as the good food. The 1950s-style soda fountain has been a long-time standby at the Lopez Island Pharmacy—so much so that when they moved to new digs some time ago, they packed up the fountain and its 15 stools and moved them, too. Lunch fare includes sandwiches and burgers to go with your soda, float, malt, or banana split. Enjoy coffee and a pastry for breakfast. See also Shopping, Galleries & Artists, page 101.

Lopez Islander Bay Resort $$ Y

Fisherman Bay Road, P.O. Box 197; Lopez Island, WA 98261. Phone: (360) 468-2234 (restaurant), (360) 468-2333 (resort), (360) 468-3383 (marina); web site: *lopezislander.com*

HOURS: Lunch and dinner. Lounge, catering facilities. Major credit cards accepted.

The sweeping marine view from the spacious dining room and open patio is decidedly San Juan, and so is its menu, with its emphasis on fresh Northwest cuisine. An iced drink and hot appetizer start your meal. Then, on to the main menu, which ranges from sandwiches to salmon, with a nice assortment of chicken and beef dishes in between. Try seafood pasta (local seafood, of course), prime rib, scallops, or shrimp. A children's menu is available.

This restaurant is part of the Lopez Islander Bay Resort complex, which has lodging and moorage facilities. See also Lodging, page 88, Marinas, Launch Ramps & Put-Ins, page 106, and Parks & Campgrounds, pages 107–108.

Love Dog Café $$ 🍷

Lopez Village; 1 Village Center; Lopez Island, WA 98261. Phone: (360) 468-2150; email: *lovedogcafe@rockisland.com*; web site: *lopezisland.com/members/lovedog*

HOURS: Breakfast, lunch, and dinner. Open daily 8 A.M. to 8 P.M.; closed Wednesday. Major credit cards accepted.

A large, eclectic menu features tasty, well presented dishes. It includes the usual fare of soups, salads, burgers and sandwiches, steaks, and ribs. There are also more exotic dishes such as shrimp benedict, eggplant parmesan and portobello quiche. A deli case features wines, imported beers, and dessert offerings such as a rich mousse and bread pudding with raisins and whiskey.

Seating is in the spacious main room or outside on a long deck overlooking the village and Fisherman Bay.

Vortex Café and Juice Bar $

The Old Homestead, 135A Lopez Road, Lopez Village; Lopez Island, WA 98261. Phone: (360) 468-4740

HOURS: Open Monday through Saturday 10 A.M. to 6 P.M.

The small café is found in the Old Homestead, a gray clapboard house across from Edenwild Inn. It's a great place to stop for healthy, organic vegetable drinks, cookies, vegetable wraps, burritos, soups, salads, and teas. A few tables are tucked inside and a few more are on a covered outside deck.

GROCERIES, BAKERIES, DELIS & LIQUOR
✦

Blossom Natural Foods

The Old Homestead; 135B Lopez Road, Lopez Village; Lopez Island, WA 98261. Phone: (360) 468-2204; email: *blossomlopez@rockisland.com*

Before heading out for your day of bicycling, hiking, or paddling around Lopez Island, you'll want to stop at this shop in a gray house across from Edenwild Inn to stock up on energy food. The shop carries a great range of natural and organic foods such as dried fruits, nuts, bulk cheese, protein bars, and other nutritious snacks. Pick up some organic beer or wine, fair-trade coffee and tea, local seafood, or organically grown meat.

Holly B's Bakery

Lopez Plaza; Lopez Island, WA, 98261. Phone: (360) 468-2133; web site: *hollybsbakery.com*

Holly Bower has been purveying scrumptious fresh-baked goodies to tourists and islanders for more than 15 years. Pick up some of her legendary cinnamon rolls or chocolate chip cookies to spirit back to your boat for breakfast, or enjoy them with coffee from a nearby espresso shop. Closed in winter, alas.

Islandale/Southender

3024 Mud Bay Road, Route 1, Box 1650; Lopez Island, WA 98261. Phone: (360) 468-2315; web site: *lopezisland.com/islandale*

Open Monday through Saturday 7 A.M. to 2:30 A.M.

This small gas station and general store serves people on the south end of the island, providing groceries, videos, and a small assortment of basic needs, including ice. It's just the place to stop for picnic makings and cold beer after the bicycle trek downisland. A small deli offers sandwiches and burgers.

Lopez Village Market

Lopez Village; 214 Lopez Road; Lopez Island, WA 98261. Phone: (360) 468-2266; fax: (360) 468-2445; email: *lvmarket@rockisland.com*

HOURS: 8 A.M. to 8 P.M. ATM. Major credit cards accepted.

This is the largest, most complete grocery on Lopez Island. You'll find all you need here to restock your boat galley or go with dinner back in your weekend cottage. They have ice and an excellent collection of beers and wines. The store also carries a selection of basic drug, toiletry, hardware, and kitchen items; you should be able to find here whatever it was you forgot to bring from home. Outside are gasoline, diesel, propane, and firewood.

Vita's Wildly Delicious

Lopez Village; 77 Village Road; Lopez Island, WA 98261. Phone: (360) 468-4268; email: *vitas@ rockisland.com*

This upscale deli offers tasty dishes such as macaroni and cheese with Villard cheese, chicken satay, feta timbale, bacon-wrapped pork medallions with apricot glaze, and mouthwatering cakes and cookies. Eat at a small inside counter, a picnic table out front, or combine your selection with a bottle of one of their excellent vintages and slip off for a private picnic.

Washington State Liquor Store

Lopez Village; 3 D Washburn Place; Lopez Island, WA 98261. Phone: (360) 468-2407

HOURS: Tuesday through Saturday 10 A.M. to 6 P.M.

The Lopez Island liquor store is located in the new section of Lopez Village on Washburn Place, immediately across the street from the historical museum.

SHOPPING, GALLERIES & ARTISTS

Archipelago

Lopez Plaza; Lopez Island, WA 98261. Phone: (360) 468-3222

This interesting little shop offers women's casual wear along with some dressier clothing. You won't be able to resist the soft fabrics, knitwear, and purses. You'll also find a nice selection of imported jewelry and an occasional hat.

Bay Electronics and Toys

Lopez Village; 9 Old Post Road, Suite 9; Lopez Island, WA 98261. Phone: (360) 468-3541; fax: (360) 468-3581; web site: *fishbayelectronics.com*

The gearhead in your crowd will want to stop here for quality electronics, including batteries, cables, iPod accessories, and home theater and security packages. There are educational and fun electronic toys to keep the kids entertained, and everyone can enjoy DVD rentals.

Chimera Gallery (A Lopez Artists Cooperative)

Lopez Plaza; Lopez Island, WA 98261. Phone: (360) 468-3265; email: *gmgildea@rockisland.com*; web site: *chimeragallery.com*

More than 20 local artists and craftspeople display their work at this long-time gallery. It is one of our favorite places to stop. You'll see a wide range of artworks of uniformly high quality, including blown glass, pottery, wood, paintings, block prints, metal sculpture, jewelry, masks, handmade clothing, photo prints, and more. The constantly changing offerings include items you are unlikely to find elsewhere. You might see glass by Lark Dalton and Corrie Haight or amazing woodworks by Bruce Parker.

Colin Goode Gallery and Studio

Lopez Village; 95 Village Road; Lopez Island, WA 98261. Phone: (360) 468-4715; email: *goodegallery@hotmail.com*

Not all artists can do justice to Northwest scenery, but Colin Goode does so beautifully. His art is available as original oils, or as high quality prints of his paintings. His gallery at the edge of Lopez Village features a few other local artists. He also offers painting classes in the rear of the gallery.

Congregation Studio

Lopez Village; 25 Eads Lane; Lopez Island, WA 98261. Phone: (360) 468-3173

Linda Koenig makes wonderful mosaics from shells, mirrors surrounded by buttons, shells, other beach findings, and driftwood.

Copper Creations

Lopez Village; 25 Eads Lane; Lopez Island, WA 98261. Phone: (360) 468-4803; email: *copper@ rockisland.com*

Fiber artist Sue Noble spins her own yarns from rayon, linen, silk, and cotton fibers, then weaves one-of-a-kind designs. Her amazingly soft scarves and tableware boast lovely textures and color combinations.

Dancing Trees Framing and Gallery

Lopez Village; 25 Eads Lane; Lopez Island, WA 98261. Phone: (360) 468-3967

Karen Hartman's studio occupies one of the shops in an historic building in Lopez Village. The interesting building, formerly Benson Hall, was moved to its present site from Eastsound on Orcas Island. Hartman can create the perfect framing for that work you purchased from a local artist.

Earthwise Clothing and Body Care

The Old Homestead, Lopez Village; 135 Lopez Road; Lopez Island, WA 98261. Phone: (360) 468-3199; email: *blossom@rockisland.com*

Earthwise is one of a small cluster of shops in The Old Homestead that are oriented to natural products. The shop carries gauzy women's clothing, hats, candles, and organic body lotions.

Gallery 10, Colleen James Fine Art

Lopez Village; 265 Lopez Road; Bay Building, Suite B & C; Lopez Island, WA 98261. Phone: (360) 468-4910, fax: (360) 468-4767; email: *gallery10@rockisland.com*

Owner Colleen James presents fine art by local artists for yourself or your home. Offerings include fanciful clothing, romantic dresses, hand-knit sweaters, unique lamps, wall decorations, and much more. You're certain to find a particular piece of art, clothing, or furnishings to match your personal flair.

The Village Center Building, which houses Village Apparel and Islehaven Books and Borzoi, sports colorful flags.

Islehaven Books and Borzoi

Village Center Building; 210 Lopez Road; Lopez Island, WA 98261. Phone: (360) 468-2132; email: *islehaven@rockisland.com*

For your reading needs, Islehaven is the spot. Kids can read or play a quiet game in a corner while parents browse. The store's excellent selection includes hardbound books and paperbacks. You'll also find a good selection of children's books and regional guides as well as cards, prints, posters, cassette tapes, CDs, and maps.

Keep it Clean Laundry

864 Fisherman Bay Road; Lopez Island, WA 98261. Phone: (360) 468-3466

After a couple of days of bicycling Lopez and tent camping, this self-service laundry one mile north of Lopez Village might prove appealing for sudsing your duds.

Lopez Island Farmers Market

In Lopez Village at the intersection of Eads Lane and Village Road

HOURS: Saturday 10 A.M. to 2 P.M. and Wednesday 3 P.M. to 6 P.M., May through Labor Day.

There's nothing like a farmer's market to get the flavor (literally) of an area. From food to flowers, jellies to jewelry, this one has loads of irresistible goods displayed in picturesque kiosks. Select fresh produce for your boat's galley or vacation cottage, or find a treasure to remind you of your visit. Many Lopez Island artists offer their work at the market, rather than maintain studio hours. It is a great place to see how amazingly talented many of the resident artists are.

Lopez Island Pharmacy

Lopez Village; 157 Village Road; Lopez Island, WA 98261. Phone: (888) 325-3269, (360) 468-2616, (360) 468-4511 (soda fountain); fax: (360) 468-3825; email: *rhp@ lopezislandpharmacy.com*; web site: *lopezislandpharmacy.com*

Lopez Pharmacy is well-known for its 1950s-style soda fountain. The store stocks the standard drugs and sundries as well as a line of gift items, including some very nice things by local craftspeople. The fountain offers sandwiches and sodas. See also Restaurants & Cafés, page 96.

Lopez Island Vineyards

724 Fisherman Bay Road, Route 2, Box 3096; Lopez Island, WA 98261. Phone: (360) 468-3644; email: *winery@lopezislandvineyards.com*; web site: *lopezislandvineyards.com*

HOURS: Wednesday, Friday, and Saturday, from Memorial Day through Labor Day, noon to 5 P.M. Off-season (Labor Day to Christmas, and mid-March to Memorial Day) open Friday and Saturday only, or by appointment. Closed Christmas to mid-March.

In early days, the San Juan Islands were widely known for the orchards that flourished here. Lopez Island Vineyards, a small family-run vineyard, continues this heritage by producing premium wine from grapes grown on their own estate on Lopez Island, and in eastern Washington. You can stop by to pick up a bottle or two, or you can dally in the wine-tasting room and tour the vineyards.

Lopez Island Vineyards offers a sunny spot to sample a glass of vino.

Martin and Malay Studios

341 Shoal Bay Lane; Lopez Island, WA 98261. Phone: (360) 468-2159; email: *m2arts@ centurytel.net*

Drop by on a summer Saturday, or call for an appointment at other times to see the work of Christa Malay. You can select from pastels, watercolors, oil paintings, limited edition etchings, serigraphs, and giclees. The studio is on the north end of the island off Port Stanley Road.

Rita Elliott Studio

Lopez Village; 25 Eads Lane; Lopez Island, WA 98261. Phone: (360) 468-2911

Artist Rita Elliott creates original jewelry, primarily in silver and gold. The studio is open by appointment, or during the Labor Day artist's open house.

Sticks and Stems Floral and Gift Shop

189 Hummel Lake Road, P.O. Box 694; Lopez Island, WA 98261. Phone: (360) 468-4377; fax: (360) 468-4378; email: *mambaso@rockisland.com*; web site: *lopezisland.com/member/stick*

When you are touring Lopez Island, you'll probably stumble on this pretty garden shop on Hummel Lake Road. Be sure to stop. In addition to garden supplies, they carry a nice selection of home decorating items such as garlands, wreaths, dried and silk flowers, ceramic pots, baskets, glass and metalwork items, birdhouses, soap, and candles.

Village Apparel

Village Center Building; Lopez Island, WA 98261. Phone: (360) 468-2022

Spiff up your vacation wardrobe at this women's clothing shop, or find a personal gift for a friend back home. There is a little something for every member of the family. Maybe a colorful top, a scarf, or some bright jewelry is just the finishing touch you're looking for. Their selection of children's clothing is especially nice.

Wren Studios, Inc.

Lopez Village; 352 Lopez Road; Lopez Island, WA 98261. Phone: (360) 468-3368; email: *art@ leonardwren.com*; web site: *leonardwren.com*

Leonard Wren's oil paintings reflect scenes from the San Juans as well as sun-dappled cottages, vineyards, and villages of France and Italy. His studio, right on Lopez Road as you enter Lopez Village from the north, exhibits his original oils and giclees. He also offers workshops demonstrating his artistic techniques. If you don't stop at his studio, you should check out his web site. It's beautiful and unique.

EVENTS & ATTRACTIONS

5K/10K Fun Run/Walk on Lopez Hill

Email: *dianaz@lopeztrails.org*; web site: *lopeztrails.org*

This event, sponsored by the Lopez Trails Cooperative, began in 2007, but is expected to occur annually. It is held in early April, when spring weather guarantees at least passable weather. It is non-competitive—the goal is good health and a good time. Proceeds benefit the Friends of Lopez Hill, who are dedicated to seeing the hill's 400 acres preserved as open, public space.

Fourth of July Parade

If you're jaded by mega-events such as the Rose Bowl Parade or Macy's Thanksgiving Parade, stop by the San Juans to discover what a hometown Fourth of July parade is really meant to be. The whole island turns out to either participate or watch, as the marchers join ranks and wend along the two-mile parade route. Fireworks! Flags! Clowns! Hometown bands! Kids in costumes! Funny old cars! Hot dog carts! Ice cream vendors! Where else could you have so much fun? Or eat so much?

Lopez Island Historical Museum

Lopez Village; 28 Washburn Place, P.O. Box 163; Lopez Island, WA 98261. Phone: (360) 468-2049; email: *lopezmuseum@rockisland.com*; web site: *rockisland.com/~lopezmuseum*

HOURS: Noon to 4 P.M. Friday through Sunday, May, June, and September; open Wednesday through Sunday, July and August. A $2 donation is requested.

For insights into early island life stop at the historical museum in Lopez Village. Old farm machinery, boating and fishing paraphernalia, household goods and gadgets, photographs, and several ship models are beautifully displayed to portray long-ago residents and their daily activities. The large mail-sorting desk from the original Port Stanley post office is especially interesting.

Outside, you'll find a couple of picnic tables, and on the lawn is a Puget Sound gillnetter, hay baler, leaning wheel grader, and Native American racing dugout.

Tour de Lopez
P.O. Box 102, Lopez Island, WA 98261: web site: *lopezisland.com/tour*

On an island that is said to offer the best bicycling in the San Juans, it's to be expected they'll have an annual tour. In 2006 more than 650 participants registered for the fun, non-competitive event, which is held the last Saturday in April. The short tour encompasses about 10 miles, the long tour runs the length of the island and back, a distance of some 26 miles. Sponsors are the Chamber of Commerce and local merchants.

The number of participants is limited, so preregister by going online for a form, or writing them requesting one.

ON-ISLAND TRANSPORTATION
◆

Lopez Bicycle Works
2847 Fisherman Bay Road; Lopez Island, WA 98261. Phone: (360) 468-2847; web site: *lopezbikeworks.com*

Lopez Island has been referred to as the "Aspen of bicycling," and this shop provides for cyclists' every need. For those who want to sample the sport, there are more than 100 bicycles for rent. A fully equipped repair shop can assist you with problems. The shop sells custom-built bikes and they carry a full line of bicycle products and accessories. You'll find the shop just south of Lopez Village, on Fisherman Bay Road, across the street from the Lopez Islander Marina.

BOAT & KAYAK TOURS, CRUISES & CHARTERS
◆

Cascadia Kayak Tours
Water Tower at The Old Homestead; 135 Lopez Road; Lopez Island, WA 98261. Phone: (360) 468-3008, cell: (360) 298-2075; web site: *cascadiakayaktours.com*

SUMMER RATES: Sunset $35 per person, ½ day $65 per person, 2-day $250 per person, 3-day $375 per person, custom $125 per person per day.

This family-owned business offers half-day, full-day, sunset (breathtaking!), 2-day, and 3-day trips, as well as longer trips customized to your particular interest. Explore wave-worn caves and cliff sides; observe sea birds, seals, and whales with a naturalist guide. Routes cover from five to nine miles a day. All skill levels are welcome. Multi-day trips reach small islands for camping under the stars; kayak and camping gear is provided, as are gourmet meals.

Harmony Charters

973 Shark Reef Road, Box 2314; Lopez Island, WA 98261. Phone: (360) 468-3310; email: *countess@interisland.net*; web site: *interisland.net/countess*

SUMMER RATES: $325 per person, per day.

Join the captain and crew aboard the 63-foot motor yacht *Countess* for a tour of your choice. Pick a secluded anchorage to try your hand at crabbing, clamming, or fishing. Guest amenities include one stateroom with a queen-size bed, and two staterooms each with a double berths and single bunk. All have private bathrooms. Gourmet meals are designed to your tastes. Added attractions include a ski boat.

Kismet Sailing Charters

P.O. Box 100; Lopez Island, WA 98261. Phone: (360) 468-2435; email: *sailkismet@rockisland. com*; web site: *rockisland.com/~sailkismet*

SUMMER RATES: $195 per person, per day.

Take a three-day sail aboard the 36-foot ketch *Kismet*. The yacht accommodates four to six guests for cruises in the San Juans or Gulf Islands. The spacious lounge has a wrap-around couch and a piano. All meals are included.

Lopez Kayak Adventures

P.O. Box 36; Lopez Island, WA 98621. Phone: (360) 468-5020; web site: *lopezkayakadventures.com*

SUMMER RATES: Southender $75 per person, Sunsetter $35 per person. Call for private lesson prices.

Two different guided paddle adventures can be had with these folks. The Southender challenges tidal currents to view wildlife, culture, and natural history. The Sunsetter paddles Fisherman Bay to watch glorious sunsets. Private lessons turn a novice into a paddler in three 3-hour sessions.

Lopez Island Sea Kayaks

2847 Fisherman Bay Road; Lopez Island, WA 98261. Phone: (360) 468-2847; email: *info@ lopezkayaks.com*; web site: *lopezkayaks.com*

SUMMER RATES: Rentals: $15 to $35 per hour, depending on kayak type; half-day $30 to $70; full day $40 to $90; multidays half-price for all days past the first. Guided trips: South End $75 per person, Sunsetter $35 per person.

The south end of Lopez Island, is one of the most breathtaking areas in the San Juans to explore by kayak. Lopez Island Sea Kayaks, located at Lopez Bicycle Works on Fisherman Bay Road, rents boats for individual use for a short spin around local waters, or longer, multi-day trips. Single and double sea kayaks are available; all come equipped with dry bags, hatch tarps, and safety equipment. For $10 additional they will deliver your kayak to wherever you are staying on the island. In addition to rentals, the company offers guided half-day and sunset tours.

The firm are also a retail paddleshop, offering new and used kayaks for sale, as well as paddling apparel and accessories, maps, books, and gifts.

MARINAS, LAUNCH RAMPS & PUT-INS
◆

Islands Marine Center

2793 Fisherman Bay Road, P.O. Box 88; Lopez Island, WA 98261. Phone: (360) 468-3377 or
(360) 468-2279; fax: (360) 468-2283, VHF channels 16 and 69; email: *imc@rockisland.com*;
web site: *islandsmarinecenter.com*

FACILITIES: 50 guest slips with power and water, restrooms, showers, coin-operated laundry,
launch ramp, pumpout station.

This full-service marina on Fisherman Bay, on the west side of Lopez Island, has
both moorage and repair and maintenance. Haulouts to 15 tons and dry storage
are available. The marine center sells and services small boats and outboard motors,
carries marine hardware and supplies, bait and tackle, and ice. On request, courtesy
van service is provided to Lopez Village, the airport, the golf course, and the ferry
landing. See also Lodging, page 86.

Lopez Islander Bay Resort

2864 Fisherman Bay Road, P.O. Box 459; Lopez Island, WA 98261. Phone: (800) 736-3434 or
(360) 468-2233, (360) 468-3383 (marina), (360) 468-2234 (restaurant); VHF channel 78;
email: *desk@lopezislander.com*; web site: *lopezislander.com*

FACILITIES: 50 guest slips with water, power, and high-speed wireless internet service, fuel dock
(gas), restrooms, showers, coin-operated laundry.

The marina at Lopez Islander Bay Resort is part of a resort complex on Fisherman
Bay, on the west side of Lopez Island. The recently rebuilt moorage is excellent. The
resort's restaurant and lounge sit above the moorage. Overnight accommodations
are available at the resort; moorage guests may use the heated swimming pool and
hot tub. Groceries and bicycle rentals are nearby in Lopez Village. The office of the
Islands Marine Center, which carries marine supplies, is just across the road. See also
Lodging, page 88, Restaurants & Cafés, page 96, and Camping, pages 107–108.

Odlin County Park Boat Launch

Route 2, Box 3216; Lopez Island, WA 98261. Phone: (360) 468-2496

This single-lane launch ramp faces on Upright Channel, on the northwest side of
Lopez. To reach it from the ferry landing, follow Ferry Road south to the intersection
with Port Stanley Road. Turn west and follow the road downhill to Odlin County
Park. The ramp is on the north side of the park, just as the road meets the water.
Boat trailer parking is in a lot near the park entrance.

Hunter Bay Boat Launch

The Hunter Bay launch ramp is adjacent to a county dock on the southeast side of
the island. To find it, take Center Road south down the middle of Lopez Island to
Mud Bay Road. Head east on this road, and in 2 miles turn east on Islandale Road.
Follow this downhill to its end at the dock and the single-lane launch ramp. Parking in the vicinity is limited.

MacKaye Harbor Boat Launch

Kayakers especially like this launch ramp, as it allows them access to several bays and islands on the south end of Lopez. Reach the ramp by following Ferry Road south and then turning left on Center Road, which becomes Mud Bay Road. Follow this road east to Islandale, then turn south on MacKaye Harbor Road. After a few hundred feet, head west on Norman Road (gravel), which leads to a single-lane concrete launch ramp with a boarding float on the northeast side of MacKaye Harbor. Parking is just uphill in a gravel lot.

PARKS & CAMPGROUNDS

Lopez Farm Cottages and Tent Camping ⋔

555 Fisherman Bay Road, P.O. Box 610; Lopez Island, WA 98261. Phone: (800) 440-3556
    or (360) 468-3666; fax: (360) 468-3966; email: *johnwarsen@centurytel.net*; web site:
    lopezfarmcottages.com

FACILITIES: 13 wooded campsites, each with level space, hammock, 2 chairs, table. Shared camp
    buildings with barbecues, picnic tables, restrooms, showers, complimentary coffee and tea,
    telephone, badminton net.
RESTRICTIONS: No children under 14, no pets.
SUMMER RATES: $33 to $65 per site, double occupancy. Open from April 15 to September 30.
    Visa and MasterCard accepted.
🚐 From the ferry landing, follow Fisherman Bay Road south. The driveway leading to the camp-
    ground is on the left, across from the winery, in 2½ miles.

Campers couldn't ask for nicer places than these secluded, wooded campsites. They are just the spot to settle in after a day of touring the island. The well-planned facility includes private baths and showers. The parking area is far enough away so your evening won't be disturbed by cars and headlights, and wheelbarrows are provided for you to ferry your gear to your site. Cooking is at barbecues by the shared camp buildings; you can eat there and enjoy the camaraderie of fellow campers, or take your meal back to your campsite for evening solitude.

Each site offers its own charms. The most private are the three beyond the cottages, and one in the main tenting area that looks out to a pasture where sheep graze. See also Lodging, pages 87–88.

Lopez Islander Bay Resort ⋔

2864 Fisherman Bay Road, P.O. Box 459; Lopez Island, WA 98261. Phone: (800) 736-3434
    or (360) 468-2233; fax: (360) 468-3382; email: *desk@lopezislander.com*; web site:
    lopezislander.com. Marina: (360) 468-3383, monitors VHF channel 78

FACILITIES: Standard campsites on lawn with picnic table and firepit. RV sites with water and
    electricity hookups. Seasonally heated swimming pool, Jacuzzi, showers, restroom.
SUMMER RATES: RVs $35 per night, 3-person occupancy, 1 vehicle per site. Extra person over age
    3 or extra vehicle $5 per day. Campsites $25 per night. Pets $5 by prior arrangement.
🚐 On the east side of Fisherman Bay, immediately south of Lopez Village.

In addition to its lodging, restaurant, and marina, Lopez Islander Bay Resort has a small campground in the forest, across the road from the marina. Tent sites, which are scattered about a grassy lawn, include picnic tables and firepits. Some have adjacent parking, but a few require a short walk from your vehicle. RV sites have water and electric service. Guests have the use of the swimming pool and Jacuzzi, as well as the hot showers that go with them. See also Lodging, page 88, Restaurants & Cafés, page 96, and Marinas, Launch Ramps & Put-Ins, page 106.

Odlin County Park ⛺ ♿

148 Odlin Park Road, Route 2, Box 3216; Lopez Island, WA 98261. Phone: (360) 468-2496 (park office), (360) 468-1842 (reservations only), (360) 378-8420 (information); email: *parks@co.san-juan.wa.us*; website: *co.san-juan.wa.us*

FACILITIES: 24 vehicle campsites, 6 hiker/biker campsites (2 are Cascadia Marine Trail campsites), picnic shelters, picnic tables, fireplaces, disabled accessible vault toilets, boat launch ramp, dock, 4 mooring buoys, sports field, children's play equipment, hiking trails.

SUMMER RATES: Per night for up to 4 persons: Vehicle sites $15; hiker/biker sites $10; additional adults $3 each, additional children $2 each. Maximum of 8 persons per site; one additional vehicle per site $5. Reservations available.

🚗 ⛴ The park is 1¼ miles from the ferry landing. To find it, turn west off Ferry Road onto Odlin Park Road (well signed) and follow it 300 yards downhill. By boat, the park is on the far northwest end of Lopez Island, immediately south of Upright Head.

This pretty little county park holds 30 campsites on an 80-acre wooded site. The protected, sandy beach offers excellent wading and swimming. A baseball diamond, oodles of picnic tables, picnic shelters, and fireplaces attract daytime users, too. A boat launch ramp and dock sit at the north edge of the property. DNR property, adjacent to the south, has some nice forest trails.

Spencer Spit State Park ⛺

521A Bakerview Road, Lopez Island, WA 98261. Phone: (360) 468-2251, reservations: (800) 452-5687; web site: *parks.wa.gov*

FACILITIES: 30 standard campsites, 7 hiker/biker campsites, 3 Cascadia Marine Trail campsites, picnic shelters, picnic tables, fireplaces, restrooms and pit toilets, trailer dump, 16 mooring buoys, hiking trails. Camping open March to November. Reservations available.

🚗 ⛴ From the ferry landing, drive 1¼ miles south and turn east on Port Stanley Road, which curves south. At 3¾ miles, head west on Baker View Road and follow it to the park. Total distance is 5 miles.

The fascinating sandy spit that wraps around a saltwater lagoon is the premier attraction of this fine park on Lopez Island's northeast side. You'll find campsites on the hill above the beach, and picnic tables along the shore. For boaters, there are numerous mooring buoys for tying up, and when those are filled there's ample room for anchoring.

SIMPLY SHAW

ALTHOUGH THE FERRIES TOUCH DOWN AT SHAW, the island doesn't offer much for tourists. Residents stoutly resist any commercialization of their corner of the archipelago. However, it's an interesting spot, and if you have time, you'll probably enjoy a brief turn around its roads before going on to the larger islands.

For many years the island was renowned because nuns, members of the Franciscan Order, operated the ferry terminal and Shaw's sole commercial enterprise, the marina and store at the ferry landing. However, with advancing age, the three nuns operating the enterprise decided to sell it. The marina and store are now run by a family; they also hold the contract for operating the ferry landing.

Most Shaw Island roads are inland, rarely offering scenic glimpses of the water. You'll discover an interesting museum and an historic schoolhouse at a crossroads near the middle of the island. There are no commercial lodgings on Shaw; the only overnight "facility" for visitors is a small campground facing on Upright Channel. Canoe Island, off the southeast shore of Shaw Island, is the site of a youth camp.

The island's web site is *shawislanders.org*.

SHOPPING & FOOD

Shaw General Store

37 Blind Bay Road; Shaw Island, WA 98286. Phone: (360) 468-2288

HOURS: Monday through Saturday 9:30 A.M. to 5 P.M.

The many hats worn by this combination ferry terminal/general store/gas station/marina/post office contribute to its rustic country store atmosphere. You'll find aisles and walls lined with tourist trinkets along with living necessities ranging from garden tools to pantyhose. Snacks and sandwich fixings are available.

ATTRACTIONS

Little Red Schoolhouse

At the intersection of Blind Bay Road and Hoffman Cove Road

Your great-grandparents might have learned their three R's in a one-room schoolhouse similar to the one that sits mid-island. This Shaw Island building, which is on

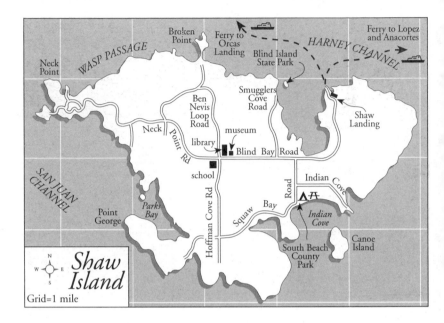

the National Register of Historic Places, is a still-operating example of these classic schools. A modern wing has been added.

Across the road's intersection is the island library. A tiny log cabin that adjoins it houses historical displays of earlier island times.

MARINAS & LAUNCH RAMPS

Shaw General Store

37 Blind Bay Road; Shaw Island, WA 98286. Phone: (360) 468-2288

This little marina on Harney Channel, adjacent to the Shaw Island ferry landing, offers a limited number of guest moorage slips by advance arrangement. You can tie up briefly to shop for groceries, hardware, bait, and tackle at the small store at the head of the dock. Fuel is not available. Store hours are Monday through Saturday 9:30 A.M. to 5 P.M.

South Beach County Park Boat Launch

The only public launch ramp on Shaw Island is at South Beach County Park. To reach it from the ferry landing, continue on Blind Bay Road to its intersection with Squaw Bay Road. Turn onto the latter and follow it south to Indian Cove Road. Here turn west, and shortly reach the county park and a single-lane launch ramp into Indian Cove. Because of the long shallow beach, the ramp is only usable at high tides.

An historic log cabin on the grounds of the Shaw Island public library holds displays of early times.

PARKS & CAMPGROUNDS

South Beach County Park

San Juan County Parks and Recreation; Friday Harbor, WA 98250. Phone: reservations: (360) 378-1842; information: (360) 378-8420; email: *parks@co.san-juan.wa.us*; web site: *co.san-juan.wa.us/parks/shaw.html*

FACILITIES: 11 campsites, 2 Cascadia Marine Trail campsites, group camp, water, pit toilets, picnic shelter, fireplaces, picnic tables, boat launch ramp.

SUMMER RATES: Up to 4 persons and one vehicle per site $13; each additional adult $3, each additional child $2, to a maximum of 8 persons per site. Maximum of 2 additional vehicles per site at $5 each. Reservations accepted.

Head south from the ferry landing on Blind Bay Road, and in 1¼ miles, turn left onto Squaw Bay Road. In ¼ mile, a side road to the left, which is usually signed, leads to the park.

This small park, tucked in a remote corner of Shaw, is often bypassed in favor of larger, better-known campgrounds. As a result, you might find space here when other areas are filled. Even if you don't plan to camp, it's a great place to stop; the beach is one of the best in the San Juans, and in summer the shallow water often warms enough for wading or swimming.

Boats with minimum draft can easily be beached on the shore, but the bay is so shallow that those that draw more water must anchor well out and dinghy ashore.

ORCAS ISLAND
TOURIST NIRVANA

◆

IF ASKED TO CHOOSE THE BEST of the San Juan Islands, many visitors would undoubtedly say it is Orcas. While that assessment could be argued long and passionately, there is no question about Orcas' many offerings to tourists: superlative scenery, terrific recreation, and a diversity of accommodations, restaurants, and shopping.

The island's three small "centers of commerce" are at Orcas Landing, Eastsound, and Deer Harbor. A few restaurants and other businesses are scattered about at other spots on the island, mostly at the intersections of main roads. The several shops and eateries at the village of Orcas attract departing tourists who (wisely) arrive early, in anticipation of the ferry. Overnight accommodations are also nearby. Deer Harbor, on the west side of the island, has a few facilities for people who stop at the marina found there. Olga, east of Moran State Park, has a small grocery that is open in summer and a public dock with a float for boaters. Nearby, in a large building that formerly housed a strawberry processing plant, an excellent café and an art gallery featuring the work of island artists are popular destinations, both for tourists and residents. Farther east, beyond Olga, the eclectic Doe Bay has a offerings ranging from a campground, yurts, and hostel lodgings to family-sized cabins, along with clothing optional group hot tubs and a sauna.

The largest village—and major business center—is Eastsound, at the head of the long, fjordlike waterway named East Sound. The extreme head of the waterway, which ends in Fishing Bay and Ship Bay, is quite shallow. However, boaters wanting to stop at Eastsound can anchor in Fishing Bay and take a dinghy to the public dock on the west side of Madrona Point. From there it's just a nice leg-stretch (about two blocks) to the shops, groceries, and restaurants of Eastsound.

A good deal of the eastern lobe of the island is devoted to Moran State Park, a 4600-acre mountainous treasure that provides recreation and scenic splendor to residents and visitors alike.

Orcas Island roads have more twists and turns and ups and downs than those on the other islands. That's part of its charm. Around any bend might lie a jewel of a bay, or at the top of a rise a breathtaking marine vista might appear. The perversity of the roads is not enough to deter bicyclists, who flock here by the thousands—some even make it to the 2407-foot-high top of Mount Constitution.

The island's somewhat unusual "saddlebag" shape makes getting around a bit complicated. The landmass is divided nearly in two by East Sound, and, to a lesser

The hamlet of Eastsound Village sits at the head of East Sound.   113

extent, is sliced again by West Sound and Deer Harbor. All roads must loop around these waterways; few roads go true east–west or north–south, thus getting from the far east side of Orcas to its far west side requires a somewhat circuitous route. The main road, Orcas Road (also known as the Horseshoe Highway), runs north from Orcas around East Sound to the village of Eastsound. In Eastsound it is labeled Main Street, then it continues east as Crescent Beach Drive. Shortly, at a T-intersection, it bends south as Olga Road, which continues through Moran State Park to end at the small community of Olga. Deer Harbor Road curves around the end of West Sound, heading for Deer Harbor, and Crow Valley Road provides an alternative north–south route on the west side of the island.

Getting Away, Pioneer Style

For at least several centuries Orcas has been a tourist destination. Although the long-ago Native Americans who originally summered here were, undoubtedly, most interested in tucking the local flora and fauna into their winter larders, they certainly must have appreciated the island's uncommon beauty.

In the late 1800s, the island became a getaway for mainland vacationers who came here to relax next to tents and campfires on the beach or in the cedar-scented forest, or to stay in one of the inns that had sprung up on the shores. Some of those inns still welcome visitors today.

The Orcas Hotel, at the Orcas ferry landing, has been hosting visitors since 1904

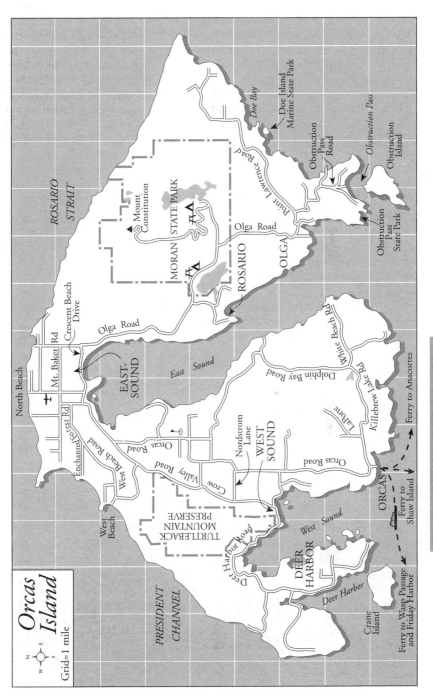

ORCAS ISLAND
Maps

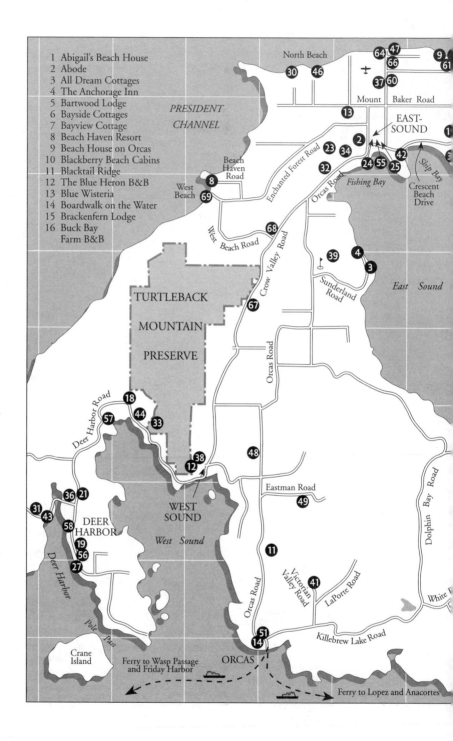

1 Abigail's Beach House
2 Abode
3 All Dream Cottages
4 The Anchorage Inn
5 Bartwood Lodge
6 Bayside Cottages
7 Bayview Cottage
8 Beach Haven Resort
9 Beach House on Orcas
10 Blackberry Beach Cabins
11 Blacktail Ridge
12 The Blue Heron B&B
13 Blue Wisteria
14 Boardwalk on the Water
15 Brackenfern Lodge
16 Buck Bay
   Farm B&B

PRESIDENT
CHANNEL

North Beach

Mount   Baker Road

EAST-
SOUND

Beach
Haven
Road

West
Beach

Crescent
Beach
Drive

Fishing Bay

Ship Bay

East   Sound

TURTLEBACK

MOUNTAIN

PRESERVE

Enchanted Forest Road

Orcas Road

West Beach Road

Crow Valley Road

Sunderland
Road

Orcas Road

Deer Harbor Road

WEST
SOUND

Eastman Road

DEER
HARBOR

West Sound

Dolphin Bay Road

Orcas Road

Victorian
Valley Road

LaPorte Road

White

Deer Harbor

Pole Pass

Crane
Island

Ferry to Wasp Passage
and Friday Harbor

ORCAS

Killebrew Lake Road

Ferry to Lopez and Anacortes

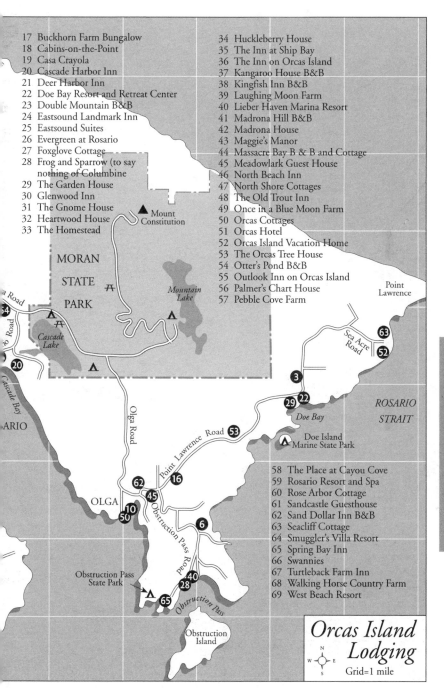

17 Buckhorn Farm Bungalow
18 Cabins-on-the-Point
19 Casa Crayola
20 Cascade Harbor Inn
21 Deer Harbor Inn
22 Doe Bay Resort and Retreat Center
23 Double Mountain B&B
24 Eastsound Landmark Inn
25 Eastsound Suites
26 Evergreen at Rosario
27 Foxglove Cottage
28 Frog and Sparrow (to say nothing of Columbine
29 The Garden House
30 Glenwood Inn
31 The Gnome House
32 Heartwood House
33 The Homestead

34 Huckleberry House
35 The Inn at Ship Bay
36 The Inn on Orcas Island
37 Kangaroo House B&B
38 Kingfish Inn B&B
39 Laughing Moon Farm
40 Lieber Haven Marina Resort
41 Madrona Hill B&B
42 Madrona House
43 Maggie's Manor
44 Massacre Bay B & B and Cottage
45 Meadowlark Guest House
46 North Beach Inn
47 North Shore Cottages
48 The Old Trout Inn
49 Once in a Blue Moon Farm
50 Orcas Cottages
51 Orcas Hotel
52 Orcas Island Vacation Home
53 The Orcas Tree House
54 Otter's Pond B&B
55 Outlook Inn on Orcas Island
56 Palmer's Chart House
57 Pebble Cove Farm

58 The Place at Cayou Cove
59 Rosario Resort and Spa
60 Rose Arbor Cottage
61 Sandcastle Guesthouse
62 Sand Dollar Inn B&B
63 Seacliff Cottage
64 Smuggler's Villa Resort
65 Spring Bay Inn
66 Swannies
67 Turtleback Farm Inn
68 Walking Horse Country Farm
69 West Beach Resort

Mount Constitution

MORAN STATE PARK

Mountain Lake

Cascade Lake

Point Lawrence

Sea Acre Road

ROSARIO STRAIT

Doe Bay

Doe Island Marine State Park

Olga Road

Point Lawrence Road

OLGA

Obstruction Pass Road

Obstruction Pass State Park

Obstruction Pass

Obstruction Island

ORCAS ISLAND Maps

Orcas Island Lodging

N W E S

Grid=1 mile

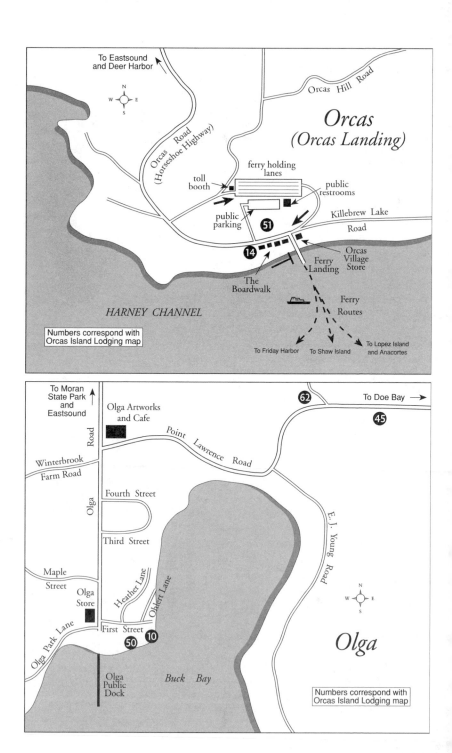

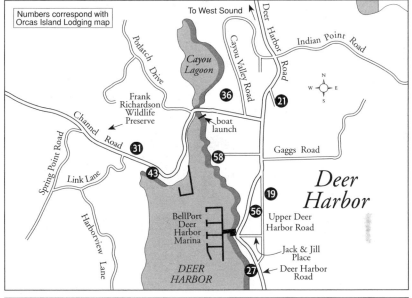

Numbers correspond with Orcas Island Lodging map

To West Sound

Cayou Lagoon

Potlatch Drive

Cayou Valley Road

Deer Harbor Road

Indian Point Road

36

21

Frank Richardson Wildlife Preserve

Channel Road

31

boat launch

58

Gaggs Road

43

Spring Point Road

Link Lane

19

56

Deer Harbor

Harborview Lane

BellPort Deer Harbor Marina

Upper Deer Harbor Road

Jack & Jill Place

DEER HARBOR

27

Deer Harbor Road

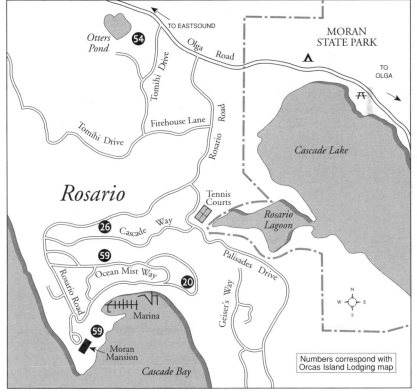

TO EASTSOUND

MORAN STATE PARK

Otters Pond

54

Olga Road

Tomihi Drive

TO OLGA

Firehouse Lane

Rosario Road

Tomihi Drive

Cascade Lake

Rosario

Tennis Courts

Rosario Lagoon

26

Cascade Way

59

Palisades Drive

Ocean Mist Way

20

Rosario Road

Geiser's Way

Marina

59

Moran Mansion

Cascade Bay

Numbers correspond with Orcas Island Lodging map

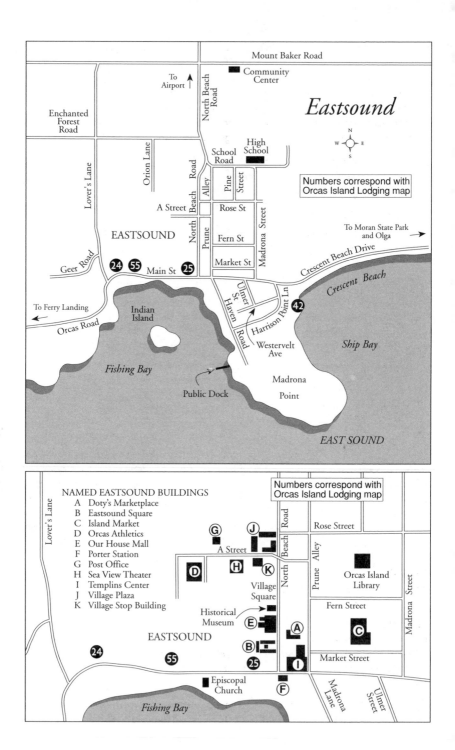

Eastsound

Mount Baker Road

Community Center

To Airport

North Beach Road

Enchanted Forest Road

Orion Lane

School Road

High School

North Beach Road

Pine Street

Alley

EASTSOUND

Lover's Lane

A Street

Rose St

Prune

Fern St

Madrona Street

Geer Road

24 **55** Main St **25**

Market St

To Moran State Park and Olga →

Crescent Beach Drive

Crescent Beach

To Ferry Landing ←

Orcas Road

Indian Island

Ulmer St

Haven

Harrison Point Ln

42

Ship Bay

Westervelt Ave

Fishing Bay

Public Dock

Madrona Point

EAST SOUND

Numbers correspond with Orcas Island Lodging map

NAMED EASTSOUND BUILDINGS

A Doty's Marketplace
B Eastsound Square
C Island Market
D Orcas Athletics
E Our House Mall
F Porter Station
G Post Office
H Sea View Theater
I Templins Center
J Village Plaza
K Village Stop Building

Numbers correspond with Orcas Island Lodging map

Lover's Lane

G **J**

A Street

D **H** **K**

North Beach Road

Prune Alley

Rose Street

Orcas Island Library

Madrona Street

Village Square

Fern Street

Historical Museum **E**

C

A

EASTSOUND

B

24 **55** **25**

I

Market Street

Episcopal Church

F

Madrona Lane

Ulmer Street

Fishing Bay

LODGING

Prices quoted for accommodations are summer rates, per day, double occupancy. However, cottages and vacation homes usually rent for the entire unit. Prices are as of 2007, and are subject to change. Lower rates are usually offered off-season. A tax of 9.7 percent is additional. For a general discussion of lodgings, see Lodging Details, pages 35 to 36.

▬	= Bed and breakfast inns
🏠	= Cottages, vacation homes, guest suites, condominiums, and hostels
🏨	= Resorts, hotels, motels, and inns
⛺	= Camping (see full descriptions under Parks & Campgrounds)
👫	= Children OK, however there might be some restrictions
🐕	= Pets OK, however there might be some restrictions

Abigail's Beach House 🏠 👫

412 Eastman Road; Eastsound, WA 98245. Phone: (360) 376-7035; fax: (360) 376-6500; email: *farmgirl@onceinabluemoonfarm.com*; web site: *onceinabluemoonbay.com/*

ACCOMMODATIONS: House with 5 bedrooms with 1 king-size and 5 queen-size beds, 3 double beds, 1 single bed, 3½ baths, kitchen.
RESTRICTIONS: No smoking.
EXTRAS: Tea balcony, satellite TV/DVD, phones, outdoor beach deck with furniture and grill, laundry. Walk to Eastsound.
SUMMER RATES: $200 to $700 per night, depending on number of guests.
🚗 On the north side of Orcas Island. Guests will be given driving directions.

Up to 12 people can enjoy this waterfront home surrounded by gardens. The décor has Victorian touches with flowered chintz, patterned wallpaper, and antiques, but the house itself is modern, including the gourmet kitchen. A boardwalk that crosses a bird sanctuary and wetlands leads to an expansive, private, black-pebbled beach. Views north to Sucia, Matia, and Patos Islands, and the night lights of the ski areas above Vancouver B.C. can be seen from almost every room in the home. However, you won't want to miss going out to the beach to feel ocean air in your face.

Abode 🏠

257 Geer Lane, P.O. Box 1342; Eastsound, WA 98245. Phone: (360) 376-6247; web site: *sanjuanweb.com/abode*

ACCOMMODATIONS: Apartment with queen-size bed, private bath, kitchenette.
RESTRICTIONS: No smoking.
EXTRAS: Flower and vegetable gardens, walking distance to Eastsound.
SUMMER RATES: $88 per night. Weekly and off-season rates available.
🚗 Guests will be given driving directions.

This bright, comfortable, new apartment in a wooded setting overlooking Eastsound will make a perfect base for your Orcas Island explorations. After your day's adventures relax by strolling down paths that wind through a garden of native and exotic flowers, and then curl up with a book to enjoy the solitude of your retreat.

All Dream Cottages 🏠 ☆☆

P.O. Box 85; Eastsound, WA 98245. Phone: (360) 376-2500; fax: (360) 376-3211; email: *alldreamorcas@hotmail.com*; web site: *alldreamcottages.com*

ACCOMMODATIONS: 4 cottages with queen or double beds, bath, kitchen or kitchenette, decks.
RESTRICTIONS: No smoking.
SUMMER RATES: Contact owner for rates and complete details.
🚗 Guests will be given driving directions.

Cottages at different locations on Orcas Island offer a range of lodging experiences.
- *Day Dream:* A cozy 2-bedroom cottage surrounded by 7 acres of pasture and wooded meadow. It has a roomy deck with a porch swing and mountain view.
- *Isle Dream:* Cottage with a deck with a water and sunrise view. A unique, huge skylight over the 2-person shower lets you suds under the stars.
- *Sea Dream:* 1-bedroom cottage with elegant country furnishings and sunset views. It is sited on a medium-bank lot with easy water access.
- *Tree House Suite:* Cottage designed just for two, sits on high-bank waterfront with beach access. The bed is raised so you can enjoy the views while snuggling under the comforter.

The Anchorage Inn ⊨

249 Bronson Way; Eastsound, WA 98245. Phone: (360) 376-8282; email: *sandrab@rockisland. com*; web site: *anchorageonorcas.com*

ACCOMMODATIONS: B&B inn with 3 suites (queen-size beds); each with private bath, kitchenette.
RESTRICTIONS: No children, no pets, no smoking.
EXTRAS: Microwave, coffeemaker, refrigerator, wireless internet, shared hot tub and barbecue, CD player, private beach. No TV.
SUMMER RATES: $199 per night, 2-night minimum in high season. MasterCard, Visa, Discover accepted.
🚗 From the ferry landing follow Orcas Road toward the town of Eastsound and in seven miles turn right on Sunderland Road (Crow Valley Pottery on the left and Orcas Golf Course on the right). The road goes through the golf course. In about 1 mile, at the end of Sunderland Road, Bronson Way heads left. Follow Bronson Way to its end at Anchorage Inn.

These beautiful, spacious accommodations on a wooded, sixteen-acre site would be ideal for three couples. Or, rent just one of the three suites and be assured of plenty of privacy from the other guests. Each of the three suites has a private stairway and deck, along with its own kitchenette stocked with juices, cereal, yogurt, coffee, and other breakfast makings.

You can spend the afternoon sunning on the inn's own beach, barbecue steaks or salmon from the local grocery, then settle into the two-person hot tub and watch the moon rise over East Sound. The inn is managed by Dick and Sandra Bronson, who did such a great job at the Old Trout Inn bed and breakfast. Their innkeeping expertise shines through with the special touches in these outstanding lodgings.

Bartwood Lodge 🏠 👫

178 Fossil Bay Drive; Eastsound, WA 98245. Phone: (888) 817-2242 or (360) 376-2242; email: *info@bartwoodlodge.com*; web site: *bartwoodlodge.com*

ACCOMMODATIONS: Motel with 16 rooms and suites with king-size, queen-size, and double beds, private bath; some rooms with water view, some with private patio; some suites with fireplace, one suite has kitchen and fireplace.

RESTRICTIONS: Children OK, no smoking.

EXTRAS: TV, championship tennis court, beach, boat dock, launch ramp, mooring buoys. Fishing charters available.

SUMMER RATES: $149 to $179. Major credit cards accepted.

🚗⛵ From Eastsound, drive north on North Beach Road to Bartel Road and head east for ½ mile. By boat, the lodge is on the north side of the island, west of Point Thompson.

Arrive either by car or boat at this small resort on Orcas Island's north shore. Comfortable, modern rooms and suites await you in a three-story building facing directly on the water. Patio Rooms, away from the water side of the lodge, have private patios where you can watch the evening stars. Waterfront Rooms and Fireplace Rooms all enjoy views north to Sucia and Matia Islands, Canada's Gulf Islands, and the peaks of Canada's Coast Range.

The rocky beach of the resort offers interesting tide pool exploration. Whales frequent these outer San Juan waters. Charter a boat to take advantage of some of the best fishing in the islands just offshore, or to take a trip to Sucia Island State Park.

Bayside Cottages 🏠 👫

65 Willis Lane; Olga, WA 98279. Phone: (360) 376-4330; fax: (360) 376-6516; email: *bayside@ orcas1.com*; web site: *orcas1.com*

ACCOMMODATIONS: 8 cottages and 2 suites. All units have electric heat as well as wood or gas stoves, full kitchens.

- *Beach House:* Waterfront with view of Mount Baker. Master bedroom with king-size bed, second bedroom with 2 twin beds, and glassed-in sunroom with double-bed futon. Accommodates 7.
- *Plum Tree Cottage:* Water view. 3 bedrooms, three baths; 2 king-size beds, 1 queen-size bed, single sofa bed. Accommodates 7 to 8.
- *Two Peapod Cottages:* Waterfront. One cottage with 2 bedrooms with queen-size beds; smaller cottage with 1 bedroom with queen-sized bed. Both have an additional daybed. Together they accommodate 9.
- *Bayside Cottage:* Waterfront. 1 bedroom with queen-size bed; a queen-size sofa bed and single daybed in living area. Accommodates 4 to 5.
- *Lummi and Cypress Cottages:* Water view. Queen-size beds. Each accommodate 2.
- *Wisteria Cottage:* Orchard view. 1 bedroom with queen-size bed, 1 bedroom with twin beds. Accommodates 5.
- *The Barn Loft:* Garden view. Suite with 1 bedroom with queen-size bed; queen-size sofa bed in living room. Accommodates 4.
- *The Mount Baker Suite:* The best mountain and water view. Attached to the main residence.

Private entrance and deck. 1 king-size bed in the bedroom, 1 queen-size hide-a-bed in the living area, and a double bed alcove. Accommodates 5.

RESTRICTIONS: Children OK, no pets, no smoking.

EXTRAS: Satellite TV/VCR, CD, all have easy beach access, private setting.

SUMMER RATES: $175 to $380 per night, $1100 to $1800 week, 4 persons. Third night free during the quiet season, except during holidays. Visa and MasterCard accepted.

🚗 From the ferry landing, drive to Eastsound Village and continue east then south through Moran State Park toward Olga. At the Olga Café, turn left on Point Lawrence Road, pass Buck Bay, and at a Y intersection go right on Obstruction Pass Road. After the power substation, go past three wide curves in the road until you see a road sign for Willis Lane. Turn left, then left again at the first driveway on the left, which takes you to the main house and office.

Water, views, privacy, and lovely accommodations—what could be nicer? Eight separate private cottages and two suites offer a range of choices, each beautifully decorated and boasting kitchens and maximum privacy. One of these accommodations on 12 waterfront acres might be just right for you.

Bayview Cottage 🏠 🕴

Eastsound, WA 98245. Phone: (360) 376-3870; email: *jaw@interisland.net*; web site: *orcasnet. com/bayview*

ACCOMMODATIONS: Cottage with loft bedroom (queen-size bed), kitchen, wood stove. Sofa bed in living area sleeps two.

RESTRICTIONS: No smoking, no pets.

EXTRAS: Deck, water view, walking distance to Eastsound.

SUMMER RATES: $130 per night, $800 per week, 2-person occupancy, 2-night minimum.

🚗 Guests will be given driving directions.

This cozy cottage offers terrific accommodations for two or four. An unusual feature is a loft equipped with a queen-size bed. Large windows opening onto the deck, and an unusual diamond-shaped window in the loft, take advantage of the views of East Sound and eagles soaring above the treetops. Stroll to the village of Eastsound for shopping or dining out.

Beach Haven Resort 🏠 🕴 ♿

684 Beach Haven Road; Eastsound, WA 98245. Phone: (360) 376-2288; fax: (360) 376-6183; email: *relax@beach-haven.com*; web site: *beach-haven.com*

ACCOMMODATIONS: Resort with 16 units. All have private bath, kitchen or kitchenette, wood stove.
- *Log cabins:* 1, 2, or 3 bedrooms, some with open loft, sleep 2 to 8.
- *Stargazers Cottage:* Secluded, with private Jacuzzi, skylights, beach cabana, sleeps 2.
- *Balcony View Apartments:* 2 modern apartments on 2nd floor, each sleep 2.
- *Beachfront Lodge Apartment:* Sleeps 6. Disabled accessible.
- *Beachcomber Home:* 4 bedrooms, sleeps 10. Disabled accessible.

RESTRICTIONS: Children welcome, no pets, nonsmoking rooms only; smoking OK outside.

EXTRAS: Beach, playground, rowboat and canoe rentals, free mooring buoys, romantic atmosphere, adult section. No TV.

SUMMER AND YEAR-ROUND WEEKEND RATES: Cabins $135 to $285, cottage $140, apartments $115 to $175. 1-week minimum mid-June through August reserved for repeat guests. No new guests accepted from mid-June through late August. Major credit cards accepted.

🚗 (Mileages given are total distance from ferry landing.) From the Orcas ferry landing, drive north on Orcas Road. In 2½ miles, turn left (west) on Deer Harbor Road. At 3¼ miles, at a T-intersection where there is a café, go right (north) on Crow Valley Road. After 6¾ miles, turn left at a stop sign by a hardware store onto West Beach Road. In 8 miles, at a T-intersection, turn right, and at 8¼ miles, turn left onto Beach Haven Road, which ends at the resort. Total distance from the ferry is 8½ miles.

Thirteen well-maintained log cabins, a Beachcomber cedar home, two modern apartments, and a romantic cabin are all just steps from a long, sloping pebble beach on Orcas Island's west shore. The cabins are completely furnished and have electric heat; wood-burning stoves (wood supplied) add a cheery note to chill evenings.

Here's the ideal site for either a secluded retreat or a family vacation. Cabins are well separated, with a family section and an adults-only section. Four one-bedroom cabins in the adult section offer privacy. Behind the family section lies a large playground, where children run, play, and easily become pals. The two-story fort set, Burma bridge, swings, slides, table tennis area, and horseshoe pits keep them busy all vacation long.

Beach House on Orcas 🏠

64 Fox Cove Court; Eastsound, WA 98245. Phone: (360) 376-4679; email: *paula@beachhouseon orcas.com*; web site: *beachhouseonorcas.com*

ACCOMMODATIONS: 2 waterfront view units in home; each with queen-size bed, private bath, private entrance.
RESTRICTIONS: No smoking, no pets.
EXTRAS: Living room or studio, fireplace, microwave, coffee pot, refrigerator, satellite TV/VCR/DVD, waterfront barbeque. Beach access, tennis court and dock available. Walk to Eastsound.
SUMMER RATES: $169 to $269. MasterCard and Visa accepted.
🚗 Guests will be given driving directions.

These accommodations on the north shore of Orcas Island overlook their namesake islands, as well as Mount Baker, the Gulf Islands, and British Columbia's Coast Range. The broad private beach outside your windows hosts seals and otters. Watch, and you'll spot eagles soaring by. Kayaks can be put in from the beach.

The roomy Matia Suite has a bedroom separate from the living room. The cozy Sucia View Studio has a private entrance and a yard on the waterfront.

Blackberry Beach Cabins 🏠

P.O. Box 102; Olga, WA 98279. Phone: (360) 376-2845; email: *caroljo@blackberry beach.com*; web site: *blackberrybeach.com*

ACCOMMODATIONS: 2 separate cottages with queen-size beds, kitchens, private baths.
RESTRICTIONS: Children and pets by permission, no smoking.
EXTRAS: Beach, one cabin with outdoor hot tub. Massage available.
SUMMER RATES: Waterfront Cabin $130 to $150, Garden Cabin $80 to $100. Pets $10 per night per pet. No credit cards.

🚗 Drive east through Eastsound Village and south on Olga Road through Moran State Park. At the Olga Café and Artworks intersection, continue straight ahead to the community of Olga. Take the last road on the left, just past the post office. Blackberry Beach is the second house on the right. Park on the road and walk through the breezeway on the right side of the owner's home to reach the cabins, which are on the beach, east of the public dock.

A waterfront cabin must be nearly everyone's idea of a perfect summer getaway. Either of these cozy, clean cottages would be perfect for a couple or single person to find peace and quiet away from the daily rat race. Waterfront Cabin has a kitchen, spectacular view, and a two-person hot tub. The more modest Garden Cabin has a kitchen/living room combination. You won't want to do all your cooking here, as the outstanding Olga Café is just a short stroll up the road.

Kayaks can be launched at the nearby public dock, and the trails, lakes, and views of Moran State Park are only a few minutes' drive or bicycle ride away.

Blacktail Ridge 🏠 ✜♀

Salem, OR 97308. Phone: (503) 871-2011; email: *info@orcasislandhome.com*; web site: *orcasislandhome.com*

ACCOMMODATIONS: Rental home with 2 bedrooms with queen-size beds, study with queen-size bed, 2 full baths, kitchen.
RESTRICTIONS: No smoking, no pets.
EXTRAS: Indoor Jacuzzi, fireplace, wood stove, barbeque, bicycles, pond.
SUMMER RATES: $250 per night $1500 per week.

🚗 From the ferry landing, take Orcas Highway for 1½ miles and turn right onto Victorian Valley Drive. Take the first driveway on the right (Blacktail Run), and continue left to the top of the hill.

Orcas Island's hills and ridges offer the most spectacular views in the San Juans. This newly-constructed home, sited on a 17-acre property, features large windows, decks, and a slate patio that look out to stunning views—forested islands, distant ferries, sailboats, and sunsets. The spacious home sleeps six and boasts high ceilings, luxurious furnishings, and a complete kitchen with a Dacor range and work island. You might even see a deer at your doorstep.

The Blue Heron Bed & Breakfast 🛏 ✜♀🐎

982 Deer Harbor Road; Eastsound, WA 98245. Phone: (360) 376-4198 (May to September), (760)212-8556 (October to April); email: *info@orcasblueheron.com*; web site: *orcasblueheron.com*

ACCOMMODATIONS: B&B inn with 3 rooms, 1 with queen-size bed and daybed, 1 with queen-size bed, 1 with double bed, all with private baths.
RESTRICTIONS: No smoking, pets welcome.
EXTRAS: Wireless internet access, coffee and tea available all day, fenced yard for dog, porch swing. Walking distance to restaurant, marina, and public dock.
SUMMER RATES: $95 to $145 per night, pets $10 per day. Visa, MasterCard, and Discover accepted.

🚗✜ From the ferry drive 2½ miles north on Orcas Road, and then turn west on Deer Harbor Road. The house is on the right side of the road in a little more than 1 mile.

This historic 1910 home has water views over West Sound Bay. You are sure to notice it if you drive by—it is painted the lovely blue gray of a great blue heron, and has crisp white trim. Accommodations are three cozy second-floor rooms, Pelican, Egret, and Walrus, each with a private bath. Pelican and Egret have offset sitting areas where you can enjoy a sunny cup of breakfast coffee, or an evening aperitif.

This is one of the few B&B's that permit pets, and it has a fenced yard for dogs to romp in. They offer transportation to and from the ferry, and their Romantic Package includes transportation on a charter plane from Anacortes or Bellingham.

Blue Wisteria 🏠 👫

1725 Mount Baker Road; Eastsound, WA 98245. Phone: (360) 376-4073; fax: (360) 375-7191; email: *stay@bluewisteria.com*, web site: *bluewisteria.com*

ACCOMMODATIONS: Rental home with 3 bedrooms, king-, queen-size, and bunk beds, 2 full baths, kitchen.
RESTRICTIONS: No smoking, no pets.
EXTRAS: Satellite TV/VCR, stereo, washer, dryer, wood stove, central solarium with hot tub, tennis court.
SUMMER RATES: $275.
🚗 Drive north on Orcas Road to Lovers Lane, turn right on Mount Baker Road to the property at 1725.

There's plenty of room for the entire family in this three-bedroom vacation home sited on five wooded acres on the northwest side of Orcas Island. Whip up meals for the gang in the spacious, fully equipped kitchen. Two living rooms means there's one for the kids, one for the grown-ups. The two-story solarium features a cedar hot tub—just the thing after a brisk bicycle tour of the island.

Boardwalk on the Water 🏠 👫

8292 Orcas Road, P.O. Box 73; Orcas, WA 98280. Phone: (877) 376-2971 or (360) 376-2971; email: *mamie@orcasislandboardwalk.com*; web site: *orcasislandboardwalk.com*

ACCOMMODATIONS: 4 separate cottages, 2 with one bedroom. All have queen-size beds, baths with shower. 2 with kitchen, 2 with microwave and refrigerator, 1 with washer, dryer.
RESTRICTIONS: Children OK, no pets.
EXTRAS: Decks, air conditioning, satellite TV, honor bar, wireless internet hot spot. Catering and host service bar available.
SUMMER RATES: $169.95 to $289.95, additional $45 to $75 per person for 1-night stays; discount for multinight stays. Major credit cards accepted. $15 fee for launching your own kayak.
🚗 On the bank, a block to the west above the ferry landing.

What could be more convenient? Walk off the ferry and then walk right into your reserved lodging. Four pretty vacation cottages, The Rose, Odella's, Mamie's Place, and Grandma's Little House are clustered just above the ferry landing. You'll be right in the heart of Orcas Landing's fun activity, yet snug in your own cottage.

ORCAS SLAND
Lodging

Brackenfern Lodge 🏠 ♥♥🐄

32 Brackenfern Lane; Eastsound, WA 98245. Phone: (360) 376-4090; email: *dpage@rockisland. com*; web site: *brackenfernlodge.com/*

ACCOMMODATIONS: Shared house with 6 unfurnished rooms, 3 shared bathrooms, shared kitchen.

RESTRICTIONS: No smoking, pets by arrangement.

EXTRAS: Shared living rooms, coin-operated laundry, spacious grounds, wi-fi hotspot, cable outlets for TV with HBO in each room, all utilities except phone, DSL wired in every room. Walking distance to Eastsound.

SUMMER RATES: $350 to $450 per month.

🚗 Take Crescent Beach Drive east from Eastsound to the intersection with Olga Road and Terrill Beach Road. Turn north on Terrill Beach Road; Brackenfern Lane is the first road on the left in less than ¼ mile.

This lodging is a bit unusual among vacation rentals, but it might be just what you are looking for. Brackenfern Lodge, a two-story house, offers six very reasonably priced rooms for rent. Although the common areas are fully furnished, the rooms themselves are not. You provide your own bed, sleeping pad, futon, or whatever, and your own linens. Each room is separately keyed, so you are assured of security. Rental is monthly or long term. The rooms are intended for single persons, but an addition person might be considered, and visitors are permitted, under particular conditions. TV hookups are provided—you provide the TV.

Buck Bay Farm Bed & Breakfast 🛏 ♥♥♿

716 Point Lawrence Road; Olga, WA 98279. Phone: (888) 422-2825 or (360) 376-2908; email: *angie@buckbayfarm.com*; web site: *buckbayfarm.com*

ACCOMMODATIONS: B&B inn. Rooms on the lower level are disabled accessible.
• 2-bedroom suite with queen-size beds, 1 in-suite bath.
• 4 bedrooms with queen-size beds, private baths.

RESTRICTIONS: Children OK, no pets, no smoking.

EXTRAS: Full breakfast, sunroom, hot tub, satellite TV/DVD, VHS, CD in each room, firepit, barbecue for guest use, wireless internet, guest laptop available, unlimited long distance telephone, horseshoes, badminton, bocce, and croquet, bottomless cookie jar. Near Moran State Park.

SUMMER RATES: $109 to $199. Major credit cards accepted.

🚗 Follow Crescent Beach Drive east from Eastsound, then continue south on Olga Road through Moran State Park. At the Olga junction, head west on Point Lawrence Road. The inn is on the right, ¾ mile from the junction. Total distance from Eastsound is 7 miles.

This airy, elegant inn boasts wide decks overlooking meadows, and an orchard where guests can bask in the summer sun or marvel at the evening starlight. Common areas include a sunroom and a sitting room, so there's plenty of room to socialize with other guests or to find your own private niche for reading or zoning out.

Natural wood ceilings provide a fresh counterpoint to walls of deep rose, burgundy, and white. Alder and Rose Rooms are exceptionally spacious; each has a sitting area and a daybed that can accommodate an extra guest. The Berry Suite, consisting of the Blueberry and Raspberry Rooms share a bath. Maple and Willow Rooms each have a private bath and queen-size bed.

The home-style breakfast might feature a quiche or pancakes, French toast, and eggs to order, along with fresh fruit, sausage, hash browns, hot muffins, and jam.

Buckhorn Farm Bungalow 🏠 👫

17 Jensen Road; Eastsound, WA 98245. Phone: (360) 376-2298; email: *rental@buckhornfarm. com*; web site: *buckhornfarm.com*

ACCOMMODATIONS: Rental cottage with queen-size bed, queen-size futon couch in living room, kitchen, wood stove.

RESTRICTIONS: Children OK, no pets, no smoking.

EXTRAS: Barbecue, satellite TV/VCR, stereo, CD player. Close to beach, walk or bicycle to Eastsound Village.

SUMMER RATES: $135 per night, 2-night minimum; single nights are accepted at a slightly higher rate. Visa or MasterCard accepted.

🚗 From the ferry, follow Orcas Road to Eastsound Village. Take the Crescent Beach Drive east from town to a T-intersection and turn left onto Terrill Beach Road. In 1¼ mile, turn right on Buckhorn Road to arrive at the bungalow in another ¼ mile.

This charming, 1940's cottage, beautifully updated, will take you back to the time when the San Juan Islands were Washington's "Orchard Capital." Fruit trees, berries, and a garden grace the farm, and deer saunter through the grounds.

After a day of exploring nearby Moran State Park, you'll love relaxing in the cozy cottage, grilling a salmon on the barbecue, and watching evening settle over the island. How long has it been since you've heard crickets? The owner's home is a short distance away, on the farm, assuring you plenty of solitude.

Cabins-on-the-Point 🏠 👫

2101 Deer Harbor Road; Eastsound, WA 98245. Phone: (360) 376-4114; web site: *cabinsonthepoint.com*

ACCOMMODATIONS: 3 cabins and 2 rental homes.
* *On West Sound:* 3 cabins (Heather, Primrose, and Willow) on 3 acres of a waterfront estate on West Sound. 1 with 2 bedrooms; all have queen-size beds, private baths, kitchens. Heather and Primrose share a 2-person hot tub.
* *Highlands House:* Near Rosario. 2 bedrooms with queen-size beds, 2 baths, fireplace, kitchen, barbeque, TV/VCR, CD, hot tub. Walk to Moran State Park or Rosario.
* *Sunset House:* East Sound waterfront, queen-size beds, fireplace, TV/VCR, kitchen, barbeque, deck.

RESTRICTIONS: Children OK, no pets, no smoking.

EXTRAS: All cabins have TV/VCR, CD, wood fireplaces, private beach. Grounds are available for weddings. Dock moorage by arrangement.

SUMMER RATES: $175 to 295 per night, 3-night minimum.

🚗⚓ Guests will be given driving or boating directions.

Cabins that carry the names of Heather, Willow, and Primrose can't help but be beautiful, and these certainly live up to their names. Any of these romantic Cape

ORCAS ISLAND
Lodging

Cod–style cottages facing on West Sound would make a wonderful honeymoon nest or weekend retreat. There's no end of ways to relax: a soak in the hot tub, a snooze in the hammock, a fire on the beach, a picnic on the flower-edged lawn. Weddings are a specialty!

Heather and Primrose have queen-size beds tucked into bay windows, so you can drift off to sleep while watching the stars. Willow has two comfortable bedrooms.

Highlands House and Sunset House are located elsewhere on Orcas Island, but have a common management and the same attention to your vacation needs.

Casa Crayola 🏠

79 Upper Deer Harbor Road; Deer Harbor, WA 98243. Phone: (360) 376-5540; email: *casacrayola@rockisland.com*; web site: *casacrayola.com*

ACCOMMODATIONS: Studio apartment with queen-size bed, bath, kitchenette.
RESTRICTIONS: No smoking.
EXTRAS: Private patio, skylight. Walk to commercial facilities in Deer Harbor.
SUMMER RATES: $135 per night, 2-night minimum.

🚗 Follow Deer Harbor Road northwest from West Sound for 4 miles; at the entrance to Deer Harbor take Upper Deer Harbor Road, on the left. Casa Crayola is on the uphill side of the road in a few hundred yards.

This is truly a special place. A bright yellow wrought iron gate opens to a patio fronting a small cottage brightly painted in blue, purple, orange, gold, and aqua. This is aptly named Casa Crayola—it can't help but cheer your spirits. Flowers nod over the edge of the flagstone patio, a skylight over the bed brings in moonlight. Through the trees are water views of Deer Harbor.

Cascade Harbor Inn 🏠 ⚥♿

1800 Rosario Road; Eastsound, WA 98245. Phone: (800) 201-2120 or (360) 376-6350; fax: (360) 376-6354; email: *cascade@rockisland.com*; web site: *cascadeharborinn.com*

ACCOMMODATIONS: Inn with 45 units that can be combined into 5 different 1-, 2-, and 3-room arrangements, most with queen-size beds, some with double Murphy bed, some with kitchen, some with fireplace, all with private bath. Suites and rooms can be joined together to accommodate families or groups. Disabled accessible (bathrooms not ADA).
RESTRICTIONS: Children OK, no pets.
EXTRAS: All units have private view balconies. Walking distance to Rosario Resort and marina; trail leads to Moran State Park. Conference room for up to 20 people available.
SUMMER RATES: $129 to $399 per night, 2-night minimum. MasterCard, Visa, Discover cards accepted.

🚗 From Eastsound, continue east for 4 miles and go right (south) on Rosario Road. Follow it downhill for 1¼ miles to Rosario Resort and turn left at the bottom of the hill, continue along, parallel to the water. At a Y in the road, stay right. The office is in the Port Building.

Relax on your private balcony as you watch eagles wheeling above the treetops, or curl up by the fireplace with a book and a bowl of popcorn. These well-appointed, modern waterfront units overlooking Cascade Harbor will beautifully fill your needs for an overnight, weekend, or extended stay. Boaters coming into the Rosario marina can easily walk up to the inn for a luxurious stay away from cramped berths. Various combinations of adjoining rooms allow for creating larger suites for families or groups.

You can whip up a meal in your kitchen or stroll down to Rosario Resort, just below, to dine in their restaurant. (The other facilities of the resort are available for a fee.) More restaurants, as well as shopping, are in Eastsound. Moran State Park, with its hiking, swimming, biking, fishing, sightseeing, birdwatching, and wealth of other recreation, is just up the road.

Deer Harbor Inn 🏠 🏚 🐎

P.O. Box 142; Deer Harbor, WA 98243. Phone: (877) 377-4110 or (360) 376-4110; fax: (360) 376-2237; email: *stay@deerharborinn.com*; web site: *DeerHarborInn.com*

ACCOMMODATIONS: Inn with lodge, cottages, and rental home.
- Lodge Rooms: 8 rooms in a 2-story log lodge, private baths, refrigerators, shared sitting rooms.
- *Cottages:* 4 guest cottages (1- and 2-bedroom) with king-size beds, queen-size couches, private baths, refrigerator.
- *House:* 3 bedrooms, Jacuzzi, pool table.

RESTRICTIONS: No children, no smoking, pets OK in some cottages.

EXTRAS: Continental breakfast, some with gas or electric fireplaces, guest cottages have decks and private hot tubs, TV/VCR. Lodge rooms have common areas with TV/VCR, computer with internet access. Hot tub in a nearby gazebo, spa in a nearby cottage. Water view. Deer Harbor Inn serves dinner.

SUMMER RATES: $139 to $325 per night, 2-night minimum in cottages. Major credit cards accepted.

🚗 ⛴ From the Orcas ferry landing, head north on Orcas Road, and in 2½ miles turn west on Deer Harbor Road. Follow this road as it curves around West Sound. The entrance to the inn is on the left in 4 miles, about ¼ mile before reaching Deer Harbor. Guest who arrive by boat can moor at the BellPort Deer Harbor Marina and walk the short distance to the inn.

When tourists arrived at Deer Harbor Lodge in your grandfather's or great-grandfather's day, they stayed at the gracious lodge on the hillside above the harbor. Today, only the restaurant portion of the old inn still serves the public. A handsome two-story log lodge, log cabins, and a vacation home, all near the inn, now offer overnight rest to tourists. Fresh white muslin, puffy comforters, and rugged natural wood provide elegance with a country flair in all the accommodations. The lodge, constructed of huge peeled logs, has high ceilings and spacious rooms. Both of its floors share common sitting rooms and wide decks that look out to Deer Harbor and the surrounding forested mountains. On the grounds, the Ataraxia Spa cottage has self-serve hydro massage. A massage therapist can be scheduled.

Breakfast awaits in your room in a charming picnic basket, and juice chills in your small refrigerator, so you can enjoy your coffee and goodies in your PJs. For dinner, stroll through the old orchard to the inn to enjoy one of their outstanding meals. See also Restaurants & Cafes, page 162.

Doe Bay Resort and Retreat Center 🏠 🏨 ⋂ ☗☗☗

107 Doe Bay Road, P.O. Box 437; Olga, WA 98279. Phone: (360) 376-2291; fax: (360) 376-5809; email: *office@doebay.com*; web site: *doebay.com*

ACCOMMODATIONS: Resort with a wide range of accommodations, including camping. Guest kitchen with stove, refrigerator, and cookware, restroom. Linens provided except as noted.

- 10 cabins (1- to 3-bedrooms), queen-size, double, single, and futon beds, baths, kitchens.
- 7 cabins (1-room) with double beds, full bath, 4 with kitchen, 3 with microwave and mini refrigerator.
- 1 cabin (1-bedroom), double bed, futon, half-bath.
- 7 cabins (1-room) with double bed, wood stove, no running water, 4 with double futon.
- Hostel with 8 single beds and 2 rooms with double beds.
- Retreat House (2-bedroom) with 2 bedrooms can sleep 24. Queen-size or double beds, and futon and 8 hostel-style double beds upstairs, 1½ baths, kitchen.
- 8 yurts with double beds, no running water or electricity. Bedding provided in summer
- 14 tent and 5 RV campsites.

RESTRICTIONS: Children OK, pets on leash OK, no smoking.

EXTRAS: Hot tubs and sauna (clothing optional), massage available, convenience store, Doe Bay Art Café (breakfast, lunch, and dinner; vegetarian and seafood specialties), volleyball courts, 2 beaches, picnicking, trails, scuba diving, guided kayak trips, no TV.

SUMMER RATES: Major credit cards accepted.

- Cabins $80 to $180 per night.
- Rooms and hostel $20 to $50 per night.
- Retreat House $450 per night, based on 10 occupants.
- Yurts $70 per night.
- Campsites $30 per night $5 surcharge on Friday and Saturday in summer.

🚗 From Eastsound, drive east, following Crescent Beach Drive and then Olga Road and Point Lawrence Road for 18 miles to Doe Bay.

Doe Bay offers alternative accommodations for those seeking inexpensive lodgings and informal surroundings. This does not mean the setting is any less enticing—in fact, it is one of the most splendid, with cabins clustered in a wooded setting on the rim of a small, rocky cove. Some units have water views; all are permeated by the bracing scent of cedar, fir, and salt air. Although a few of the cabins have better appointments, accommodations tend toward the rustic and Spartan. The diversity of lodgings, ranging from dormitory-style single beds in the Retreat House to 3-bedroom cabins with kitchen and bath, assure you'll probably find something suitable for your needs. And Doe Bay is great for a gang, as some units sleep up to ten people. If you don't choose one of the units with a kitchen, you can eat at the café or cook your meals in the community guest kitchen.

There is a great sense of camaraderie—shared interests make for quick friendships. Due to its livelier atmosphere and lower cost, the resort attracts a younger crowd than more up-scale resorts elsewhere in the islands. Tubs and sauna are clothing optional. Non-guests may use the hot tubs for a fee. Seats and picnic benches above the beach invite a private afternoon with a favorite book or a snack with a gull or two.

Double Mountain Bed & Breakfast ⊨ ♀♀

P.O. Box 614; Eastsound, WA 98245. Phone: (360) 376-4570; email: *double@orcasonline.com*; web site: *doublemountainbandb.com*

ACCOMMODATIONS: B&B inn with 2 bedrooms and 1 suite.
- 1 bedroom with king-size bed and private bath, deck.
- 1 bedroom with king-size bed and bath in adjacent hall.
- 2-room suite with private bath, kitchen, deck, sleeps 4.

RESTRICTIONS: Children 8 years and older OK, no pets, no smoking.
EXTRAS: Full breakfast, views, birdwatching. Massage available by appointment. Golfing and Orcas Island Airport nearby.
SUMMER RATES: $95 to $160 per night. Major credit cards accepted.

🚗 From the ferry landing, follow Orcas Road for 7½ miles; 1 mile before reaching Eastsound, you'll see Double Hill Road, a road that angles up the hillside. Follow the road uphill for ¾ mile to the inn, on the right. Drivers unaccustomed to Orcas Island backroads might at first be intimidated by the steep drive up the gravel road. However, it's only a short distance, and the fine inn awaits. If you notice some large spaceship-type sculptures hanging in the trees to the left along Orcas Road, you have gone too far, and will soon be in Eastsound.

Double Mountain Inn has a breathtaking, 180-degree panoramic view that stretches from Canadian mountains down the length of East Sound to islands beyond. Across the valley, the tree-clad slopes of Buck Mountain and Mount Constitution rise. At night, lights of remote homes twinkle on Buck Mountain, and Eastsound Village glows below. Airplanes at the small airport look like children's toys.

This modern private home, situated on the side of Double Mountain, offers excellent accommodations in one of two spacious bedrooms on the main floor or a lower-level suite. Windows and a deck stretching along one side of the house take full advantage of the view. You'll feel at home instantly in the country modern furnishings. For breakfast, innkeeper Gail Koher might whip up some of her special "Dutch babies," with powdered sugar and homemade jam, as she did for us.

Eastsound Landmark Inn 🏠 ♀♀

67 Main Street; Eastsound, WA 98245. Phone: (800) 622-4758 or (360) 376-2423; fax: (360) 376-3769; email: *manager@landmarkinn.net*; web site: *landmarkinn.net*

ACCOMMODATIONS: Inn with 15 condo-style suites with 2 or 3 bedrooms, queen-size bed and hide-a-bed, private bath, kitchen, fireplace. 2 units have limited handicap access (not ADA).
RESTRICTIONS: Children OK, no pets, no smoking.
EXTRAS: All units have private decks, most have water views, all have cable TV/DVD/VCR, cribs available, bicycle storage, beach access. Wireless internet access.
SUMMER RATES: $161 to $189 per night; discount for full week. Prefer 2-night minimum. Major credit cards accepted.

🚗 From the Orcas ferry landing, follow Orcas Road north to Eastsound. The inn is on the left as you enter town.

This three-story complex offers large, fully equipped condominium units within easy walking distance of the restaurants and shopping of Eastsound. The largest unit, which has three bedrooms and 1¾ baths, sleeps eight vacationers. Bicycle storage is available for those who choose this mode of touring the islands. Immediately across the road from the inn is a small park with a beach and waterfront trail. Most units have water views, the balance look out to forest-embraced hills or the rooftops of charming Eastsound Village. Ground-level units will appeal to those who have difficulty negotiating stairs.

Eastsound Suites 🏠 ♯♀

269 Main Street; Eastsound, WA 98245. Phone: (360) 376-2887, (360) 622-6003; email: *info@ eastsoundsuites.com*; web site: *eastsoundsuites.com*

ACCOMMODATIONS: Condominium with 2 suites, each with king-size bed and queen-size sleeper sofa, bath with steam shower and jetted tub, kitchen. Additional bedroom with queen-size bed and ¾ bath can be opened to either of the suites. No daily housekeeping; for extended stays fresh linens delivered upon request.
RESTRICTIONS: No smoking, no pets.
EXTRAS: Sundeck, fireplace, radiant floor heat, washer, dryer, cable TV/DVD/VCR, stereo, CD, complimentary coffee, tea, and fresh fruit.
SUMMER RATES: 1 bedroom $295 per night, 2 bedroom $395 per night, 2-night minimum. 10 percent discount on stays of 5 or more nights. Visa and MasterCard accepted.
🚗 On Eastsound's Main Street, near the intersection of North Beach Road.

Right in the heart of Eastsound, these two modern condominium-style suites offer easy access to shopping and restaurants in the village. The spacious luxury suites are on the second floor of a recently constructed building, above small commercial businesses. The sundecks offer prime southerly views of Fishing Bay and fjordlike East Sound.

When you aren't out exploring the island, each suite has a large selection of books, magazines, movies, CD's and board games. Since the owners do not live in the building, you will have to make your own beds, but that's a minor inconvenience for these fabulous surroundings.

Evergreen at Rosario 🏠 ♯♀🐾

1229 Rosario Road; Eastsound, WA 98245. Phone: (360) 298-0047; fax: (650) 376-3477; email: *stay@evergreenatrosario.com*; web site: *evergreenatrosario.com*

ACCOMMODATIONS: Rental home with 2 bedrooms. 1 bedroom with queen-size bed, full-size futon sofa in living room; bedroom on upper level has a king-size bed that can be separated into 2 twin beds; 2 full baths, kitchen.
RESTRICTIONS: No smoking, pets only by previous arrangement, 6 guest maximum.
EXTRAS: Loft den, satellite TV/DVD/VCR, stereo, wrap-around deck with hot tub, barbeque. Complimentary guest passes to Rosario Resort pools, exercise facilities, and tennis courts.
SUMMER RATES: $250 per day, $1500 per week, 2-night minimum.
🚗 ⚠ From the ferry landing follow Orcas Road through Eastsound to Crescent Beach Drive and then Olga Road. Follow Olga Road to the Rosario Resort sign, turn right, and then stay on Rosario Road. Continue 2 miles to 1229. You can also arrive by boat or float plane to the docks at Rosario Resort. It's a short walk uphill, or arrange for a rental car or taxi.

You'll wish this cedar A-frame house set among towering trees were your permanent home. It is just above Rosario Resort, and overlooks the waters of Cascade Bay. Soaring ceilings and an open floor plan give an ethereal sense of freedom. Furnishings are modern, with big cushy chairs that invite curling up to read or take an afternoon snooze. There's ample room for every family member to find a getaway nook.

Although the home is not part of Rosario, rental includes paid access to most resort amenities, including both the indoor and outdoor pool. And, of course, the resort's restaurants are just a stroll away.

Foxglove Cottage 🏠 👪

P.O. Box 1390, Eastsound, WA 98245. Phone: (360) 376-6690; email: *mparnell@rockisland.com*; web site: *orcasisland.com/foxglove*

ACCOMMODATIONS: 2-bedroom cottage with queen-size bed, daybed with trundle, hide-a-bed in living room, kitchen, fireplace.
RESTRICTIONS: Children OK, no pets, no smoking.
EXTRAS: Deck overlooking the harbor, TV/VCR, path to beach.
SUMMER RATES: $200 per night, 4-night minimum May to September.
🚗 The cottage is immediately south of BellPort Deer Harbor Marina, on the west side of the road.

"Cute" is the best word to describe this pretty little cottage edged by a white picket fence. Its convenient location, right on the Deer Harbor waterfront, makes it handy to harbor activities and restaurants. Several businesses offer a variety of boats to charter or rent out of Deer Harbor, or you can put in your kayak at the marina launch ramp, for a fee.

The cottage provides a full, modern kitchen, fireplace, and a bedroom with queen-size bed. The daybed in another, smaller bedroom, and hide-a-bed in the living room, are ideal for children, making the accommodations great for a family. The deck is just the spot to enjoy your burgers while watching harbor activity. Or, stroll down the short path to the sandy beach.

Frog and Sparrow (to say nothing of Columbine) Vacation Homes at Obstruction Pass 🏠 👪

Obstruction Pass Road; Olga, WA 98279. Phone: (360) 376-4671; email: *jbates@interisland.net*; web site: *frogandsparrow.com*

ACCOMMODATIONS: 2 small rental homes and a 1-room cabin. Houses have kitchens, cabin has light cooking facilities; all with double bed, bath, and wood stove.
RESTRICTIONS: Children possible, no pets, no smoking.
EXTRAS: Beach, water views, woods nearby. Boat moorage and kayak rental within walking distance at Lieber Haven Marina.
SUMMER RATES: Call for current rates, no minimum stay, no credit cards.
🚗 Guests will be given driving directions.

The whimsical names give you a hint about these accommodations situated on Obstruction Pass, one of the most scenic corners of Orcas Island. Each of the little houses, with eclectic furnishings, has something unique. Sparrow, on a wooded hill with a lawn and small organic garden, has a sleeping loft for an extra person or two. Sheds and two decks (one large and curving), were built of split cedar and driftwood. Take a sleeping bag to the sleep shed, and awaken to the sounds of the water.

Frog, which sits right on the beach, is a shingled cottage dating from the 1940s. Directly behind Frog is Columbine, a one-room rustic cabin with a bath and a cedar and driftwood deck. The deck, fence, and cedar-slab counters were all built by local artists.

All three cottages have double beds, made up with flannel sheets and lots of pillows. Flowers are provided by the owner, and fresh organic vegetables can be gathered from the garden

The Garden House 🏠 ♀♀🐄

3222 Point Lawrence Road; Olga, WA 98279. Phone: (360) 376-4549; web site: *doebay. net/garden.html*

ACCOMMODATIONS: Home with 1 suite with queen-size bed, hide-a-bed, kitchen/sitting room, wood stove and electric heat. Crib and futon available.

RESTRICTIONS: Children OK, pets by advanced arrangement, no smoking.

EXTRAS: Hot tub, barbecue, CD player, access to private beach, 10 minutes from Moran State Park.

SUMMER RATES: $150 per night, 2-night minimum.

🚗 Guests will be given driving directions

You and your family will feel right at home in these fine guest quarters on wooded waterfront property at the east end of Orcas Island. It's not furnished as fancy as high-end, expensive bed and breakfast inns, but it's meticulously clean, well cared for, and is the perfect place to really kick back and relax. The suite is the top floor of a wood-framed home; dormers let in lots of light, and cathedral ceilings make it spacious and airy. The beach is a four-minute walk away, along a wooded trail. The suite sleeps four, or possibly a family of five. Guests are invited to cut flowers from the garden for a bouquet, or pick fruit or berries from the garden for their meals—proof your host wants you to feel right at home.

Glenwood Inn 🏠 ♀♀

546 Glenwood Inn Road, P.O. Box 110; Eastsound, WA 98245. Phone: (360) 376-2671

ACCOMMODATIONS: 5 waterfront cabins (largest sleeps 8), each with private bath, kitchenette, fireplace.

RESTRICTIONS: Children OK, no pets, no smoking.

EXTRAS: Beach, forest, llamas. No TV.

SUMMER RATES: $850 to $950 per week. Open end of May to October; 2-day minimum stay spring and fall, 1-week minimum in summer. No credit cards.

🚗 From Eastsound, drive north on either Lovers Lane or North Beach Road and turn west on Mount Baker Road. Follow this road and head north (right) on Glenwood Inn Road, which is the last road before YMCA Camp Orkila.

What greater testimonial is there for a resort than to have guests return year after year? That's the case for this quiet spot on a 75-acre forested enclave on Orcas Island's north shore. The five cabins, located above the beach and on a slight bluff, all boast water views. The largest A-frame unit, which sleeps eight, has a loft and both queen-size and single beds. Llamas kept on the property add a bucolic note.

The resort's ½-mile-long sandy beach faces north to Sucia Island and Canada's Gulf Islands. Walk the beach west to reach Point Doughty, a long rocky spit that attracts scuba divers. Eagles, which nest nearby, often are seen soaring overhead or perched in tall snags.

The Gnome House 🏠 ♛👫🐂

P.O. Box 148; Deer Harbor, WA 98243. Phone: (360) 376-4223 or (360) 376-2480; email: *connor@centurytel.net*; web site: *orcasrec.com/gnome*

ACCOMMODATIONS: Rental cabin with queen-size sleigh bed, queen-size alcove sleeping space, foldout double bed, private bath with sunken tub, kitchen, wood stove.
RESTRICTIONS: Children OK, pets by arrangement, no smoking.
EXTRAS: Private outside hot tub, view, garden, patio, barbecue, outdoor bar.
SUMMER RATES: $185 per night, 2-night minimum; $1100 per week. Major credit cards accepted.
🚗 From the ferry landing follow Orcas Road for about 2½ miles to Deer Harbor Road and turn left. Follow this road through West Sound toward Deer Harbor. Pass Deer Harbor Inn (on your left), and at the bottom of the hill turn right onto Channel Road and drive over a small wooden bridge. The Gnome House drive (signed "Connor") is in ½ mile at 704 Channel Road.

Straight out of a fairytale, a stay at the Gnome House is sure to be an experience you remember all your life. The cottage is a hand-crafted marvel, with massive timbers, cedar arches, stonework, and such fanciful touches as a spiral staircase with carved squirrel and acorn newel posts and a sunken tub with a peek-a-boo view of the garden. It accommodates up to four adults and two children. A sleigh bed is tucked into a loft, another is a Scandinavian alcove bed, complete with murals.

The cabin's surroundings are nearly as fanciful as its interior. It is sited on a 110-acre, bird-filled, nature preserve above Deer Harbor. Gardens surround the cottage, and a barbecue, picnic table, lawn furniture, and romantic outside hot tub help you fully enjoy this gorgeous natural environment. The same people who offer Maggie's Manor rent Gnome House. They know how to provide guests with truly memorable accommodations.

Heartwood House 🏠 ♛👫🐂

P.O. Box 1480; Eastsound, WA 98245. Phone: (360) 317-8220; email: *gretchen@ heartwoodconcepts.com*; web site: *heartwoodhouse.com*

ACCOMMODATIONS: Rental home with 2 bedrooms and studio/den. Queen-size beds, full futon, 2 twin beds, trundle bed, portable crib, 2 full baths, kitchen.
RESTRICTIONS: No smoking, pets by previous arrangement and pet fee.
EXTRAS: Washer, dryer, cable TV/VCR, CD, barbeque, deck, sauna, hot tub, firepit. Walk to Eastsound Village.
SUMMER RATES: $2900 per week, nightly rates available off-season with 2-night minimum.
🚗 From the ferry landing, follow Orcas Road toward Eastsound. Heartwood House is ¼ mile before you reach Eastsound, facing the water.

Wow! Up to ten people can enjoy a fabulous stay at Heartwood House. Local cedar, alder, and madrona woods were used to craft this modern, unique, post-and-beam home. High, arched windows frame the view of East Sound. A sunny sitting area has skylights and windows that wrap from floor to ceiling. The multi-level deck is edged by landscaping and a lawn where kids can work off steam. Eastsound and the waterfront are only a five-minute walk away.

The Homestead 🏠 ♀♂

2195 Deer Harbor Road; Eastsound, WA 98245. Phone: (360) 376-5284; fax (360) 3776-5767; email: *info@homesteadorcas.com*; web site: *homsteadorcas.com*

ACCOMMODATIONS: Home with 2 separate rental units.
- *Seaside:* Loft with queen-size bed; pullout couch and double futon in living room; bath, barbeque, wood stove, kitchen.
- *Blackberry:* Bedroom with queen-size bed, queen fold-down in living area, bath, wood stove, kitchen, washer, dryer, hot tub.

RESTRICTIONS: Children OK, no pets, no smoking.
EXTRAS: Shared hot tub, CD, continental breakfast, private beach, dock (small boats can tie up), rowboat, double kayak.
SUMMER RATES: $350 per night, 3-night minimum. Visa and MasterCard accepted.
🚗 Guests will be given driving directions.

These lodgings on West Sound capture the essence of the San Juans, with a next-to-nature feeling—but lots of creature comforts. Both are modern, bright, and airy, with varnished wooden floors, plenty of windows, and natural touches such as peeled wood posts and driftwood. Seaside has a tiled bath and a loft with a queen-size bed. Both have cathedral ceilings and French doors that open onto a deck. Your own small boat can be moored at the dock, or use the double kayak or rowboat that are provided. A shared hot tub is near the water's edge. The entrance to Turtleback Mountain Preserve is right across the road, if you would like to explore the trails of this new Orcas Island Park.

The setting is so pretty that is a favorite for weddings. The owners will help you with the arrangements, if you wish, or leave the organization up to you.

Huckleberry House 🏠 ♀♂

Eastsound, WA 98245. Phone: (360)0 383-0559; web site: *huckleberryhouse.orcasweb.com*

ACCOMMODATIONS: Rental home with 1 bedroom with queen size bed and trundle, loft with queen-size bed, full bath, kitchen.
RESTRICTIONS: No smoking.
EXTRAS: Washer, dryer, TV/DVD, deck with views of Eastsound, phone, high-speed DSL.
SUMMER RATES: $160 per night, 3-night minimum, $975 per week. Shorter terms off-season.
🚗 Guests will be given driving directions.

Huckleberry House is a quality Craftsman-style home on the forested hillside overlooking Eastsound. You will appreciate the excellent detailing of the house from the polished wood floors and maple cabinets to the fine leather furniture. It is just a short walk to explore the fun shopping and try the fare of restaurants in Eastsound.

The Inn at Ship Bay 🏠 ⛅ ♿

326 Olga Road; Eastsound, WA 98245. Phone: (877) 276-7296 or (360) 376-5886; email: *shipbay@rockisland.com*; web site: *innatshipbay.com*

ACCOMMODATIONS: Inn with 10 rooms and 1 suite, all with king-size bed, private bath, gas fireplace, mini-refrigerator, coffeemaker. The suite also has a queen-size hide-a-bed sofa in the living room, jetted bathtub, separate shower, and wet bar. One room is disabled accessible.

RESTRICTIONS: 1 child per room OK, no pets, no smoking.

EXTRAS: All rooms have a water view, private deck with chairs and table, cable TV. Continental breakfast for inn guests, restaurant serves dinner Tuesday through Saturday and has a full bar. Private party and wedding facilities are available.

SUMMER RATES: $195 to $295. 2-night minimum in high season. Visa and MasterCard accepted.

🚗 Drive through Eastsound Village and continue east and south toward Moran State Park. The inn is on the right-hand side of the road, ¼ mile past a large propane tank that serves as a community bulletin board.

When the owners of a top-rated restaurant decide to run an inn, you know they are going to do it right. The Ship Bay Oyster House has been a long-time, outstanding restaurant on Orcas Island, at the top of East Sound.

The restaurant is now expanded to include this eleven-room inn, located in three two-story units along the bluff overlooking Ship Bay. The buildings are arranged for maximum privacy. Each comfortably decorated room has a private balcony looking out to the waters of East Sound. Luxury linens, down pillows and comforter, and a cheery gas-log fireplace are just a few of the touches to assure your comfort.

The inn also provides full wedding arrangements, tailored to your wishes, with space for up to 65 guests and catered food. For your wedding and reception you can choose a water-view arbor or a canopy on the orchard side lawn, or you can reserve full use of the dining room and bar.

The Inn on Orcas Island 🛏 🏠

114 Channel Road, P.O. Box 309; WA 98243; 888-886-1661 or (360) 376-5227; fax: (360) 376-5228; email: *jeremy@theinnonorcasisland.com*; web site: *theinnonorcasisland.com*

ACCOMMODATIONS: B&B inn with bedrooms, suites, house, and cottage. All except Carriage House have a jetted tub and shower for two.
- 3 bedrooms with queen-size bed, private balcony.
- 3 suites, 2 with king-size bed, 1 with queen-size bed, all with fireplace, private balcony.
- *Carriage House:* Queen-size bed, foldout sofa bed, fireplace, kitchen, full bath.
- *Waterside Cottage:* King-size bed, fireplace.

RESTRICTIONS: No smoking, no pets, no children.

EXTRAS: Multi-course breakfast, satellite TV, robes, kitchen, refrigerators, bicycles, wireless internet. Near Deer Harbor.

SUMMER RATES: Rooms $185, suites $215 to $225, Carriage House $245, Waterside Cottage $285.

🚗 From the ferry, follow Orcas Road for 2½ miles to the intersection of Deer Harbor Road. Turn left on Deer Harbor Road and stay on it for 5 miles, then turn right on Channel Road. The Inn will be on your right, in a short distance.

ORCAS ISLAND
Lodging

This sumptuous B&B inn is arguably the best on the island, with a quality art collection and luxury touches not found elsewhere. The newly-built lodgings, in the style of a classic, elegant inn, was featured in Sunset magazine as one of the West Coast's best seaside getaways. A bottle of chilled champagne welcomes you in your bedroom. Common rooms include a full dining room, sitting room, and sunny conservatory where afternoon tea is served. You will relax in pampered elegance. (Did we say elegant again?)

The inn overlooks a saltwater pond and marsh at the end of Deer Harbor where flocks of birds pause in their migratory flights, or stay longer to nest in the spring. Use the inn's binoculars to spot loons, herons, Canada geese, grebes, and an array of ducks and other waterfowl, or look overhead for eagles and hawks. Deer are regular visitors.

Kangaroo House Bed & Breakfast ⊨ ⅌

P.O. Box 334; Eastsound, WA 98245. Phone: (360) 376-2175; fax: (360) 376-3604; email: *innkeeper@kangaroohouse.com*; web site: *kangaroohouse.com*

ACCOMMODATIONS: B&B inn with suites and rooms. All have private baths.
- 2 suites, one with a king-size bed and double Murphy bed, one with a queen-size bed and twin bed.
- 3 rooms with 2 queen-size beds, 1 double bed, and 1 twin bed.

RESTRICTIONS: Children OK, no pets, no smoking in the inn or on the grounds.

EXTRAS: Full breakfast, hot tub, game room, deck, guest refrigerator, guest microwave, robes, TV/DVD in 2 suites. Wi-fi, bike racks. Near Eastsound.

SUMMER RATES: Rooms $125 to $150, suites $170 to $180, entire inn $770. No minimum stay. Major credit cards deposits accepted at reservation.

🚗 ⛺ From Eastsound, drive north on North Beach Road. The inn, 1459, is on the left, in a little less than a mile.

The kangaroo pet of the historic owner hasn't lived here for quite some time, but the memory of the little 'roo remains in some quaint kangaroo details and photos hanging in the common areas. The kangaroo's owner, Cap'n Ferris, is nearly as interesting—he was a colorful steamship captain. But, even without a live kangaroo and a nautical host, your stay here will be memorable.

The inn is a turn-of-the-century Craftsman-style home with a lovely, old, fieldstone fireplace and beamed ceilings, delightfully furnished in a mix of Craftsman-style antiques and reproductions. The five bedrooms are furnished with antiques, lace curtains, and flowered coverlets. Spend evenings around the fireplace, in the adjacent sitting area of the spacious living room, or in the game room. A hot tub in the garden is for the exclusive use of guests; robes and towels are provided, and you can sign up for a private time.

The inn's property is within walking distance of the marina at Brandt's Landing, Eastsound, and the airport. Usually, one of the inn's hosts, Jill or Charles, will pick you up at the airport or marina, by prior arrangement.

Kingfish Inn Bed & Breakfast ⊨ 👫

4362 Crow Valley Road; Eastsound, WA 98245. Phone: (360) 376-4440; email: *info@kingfishinn.com*; web site: *kingfishinn.com*

ACCOMMODATIONS: B&B inn with 4 rooms, 2 with queen-size bed, 2 with king-size bed, all with private bath, 2 with fireplace. One room has daybed, one has trundle bed.
RESTRICTIONS: Children OK, no pets, no smoking.
EXTRAS: Complimentary breakfast, TV/VCR, video library, 2 with private deck,
SUMMER RATES: $150 to $160. Major credit cards accepted.
🚗 From the ferry, follow Orcas Road for 2½ miles to the intersection of Deer Harbor Road. Turn left on Deer Harbor Road and follow it to Crow Valley Road. The inn shares space with the West Sound Café, at the intersection of Crow Valley Road and Deer Harbor Road.

Any of these very nice, modern rooms, one on the main level and three on the second floor of the West Sound Store, would make an ideal base of operation for all those great Orcas Island activities. Kayaks can be put in at the public dock right across the road. All rooms have windows with views of West Sound. Beds have comfy feather tops that invite you to end your busy day by settling in, sharing a bottle of wine, and watching a vintage video on your VCR while salt-scented breezes drift in the window. Two have little private balconies. Rooms on the upper level have adjoining doors that can be unlocked if you want a suite for several people.

Laughing Moon Farm 🏠 👫

Island View Road; Eastsound, WA 98245. Phone: (360) 376-7879; email: *laughingmoonfarm@yahoo.com*; web site: *laughingmoonfarm.com*

ACCOMMODATIONS: 3 cabins, all with kitchens.
• *Gate House*: 2 bedrooms and a sleeping loft, 2 baths, covered porch. Sleeps 8.
• *Zen House:* 1 bedroom, sleeping loft, full bath, balcony. Sleeps 5.
• *Trout House:* 1 bedroom, bath, covered porch. Sleeps 4.
RESTRICTIONS: No pets, children OK, no smoking.
EXTRAS: Patio or deck, barbeque, TV/DVD, Zen and Trout have fireplaces.
SUMMER RATES: Gate House $1400 per week, Zen and Trout Houses $195 per night, $1200 per week. Visa and MasterCard accepted.
🚗 From the ferry landing follow Orcas Highway for 6 miles to Sunderland Road, which goes through the golf course. Turn right onto Sunderland Road, go ¼ mile, and then turn left onto Island View Road, which becomes gravel. Follow this road up and down a hill for about ½ mile. You will see the gatehouse (a cabin with a green metal roof) and the sign for Laughing Moon Farm. Locate your cabin and call (360) 376-7879 to check in.

These three cabins sit in small clearings on a 22-acre farm, but are well spaced for individual privacy. With the range of accommodations you are sure to find one to meet your needs. All are modern, and nicely furnished, with lots of warm natural wood. Water views, though the trees, are of Eastsound.

ORCAS ISLAND
Lodging

Lieber Haven Marina Resort 🏠 🏘 👪

1945 Obstruction Pass Road, P.O. Box 127; Olga, WA 98279. Phone: (360) 376-2472; web site: *lieberhavenresort.com*

ACCOMMODATIONS: Resort with 12 units (studios, rooms, and 1- and 2-bedroom cottages), all with private bath and patio or deck with picnic table and barbecue. Kitchen in cottages, kitchenette in studios, microwave in rooms. Rooms share a sitting room and deck. Non-cooking rooms are for 2 persons only.

RESTRICTIONS: Children OK, no pets, no smoking.

EXTRAS: Convenience store, boat rental, marina, beach, fishing, scuba diving, no TV. Kayak tours, sailing, fishing, and whale watching charters available. Boat launch nearby.

SUMMER RATES: $125 to $165 for up to 4 persons. $15 for each additional person over 2 years old. Major credit cards accepted.

🚗 ⛰ From Eastsound, drive east, following Crescent Beach Drive and then Olga Road and Point Lawrence Road for 8 miles to the intersection with Obstruction Pass Road. Turn south (right) and follow this road to its end at the Obstruction Pass public dock and launch ramp in 2 miles. The resort is west of the launch ramp. By boat, the resort is on Obstruction Pass, west of the county dock.

Intimate is the word for this corner of Orcas Island. Obstruction Pass is a ¼-mile-wide dog-leg channel that sees less boat traffic than Thatcher Pass, to the south. Lieber Haven, the small resort facing on the pass, offers a casual, nautical setting ideal for a family holiday or a couple's retreat. The accommodations are spacious and comfortably furnished, but not fancy. Most units are strung along the waterfront; others are just a step away. The owners also run the small marina and convenience store.

The natural setting offers a wealth of kid adventures—search the beach for wave-tossed treasures, build fantasylands from driftwood, lure fish to baited hooks dropped from the dock, or check out pilings for bizarre marine life. Moran State Park, with its lakes and hiking trails, is nearby. And for grownups, benches on the dock and shore invite relaxation.

Madrona Hill Bed & Breakfast 🛏 🏠 👪

1285 Victorian Valley Drive, P.O. Box 358; Orcas, WA 98280. Phone: (360) 376-8009; email: *madronahill@rockisland.com*; web site: *madronahillorcas.com*

ACCOMMODATIONS: B&B inn with suite, rooms, and separate guesthouse.
- *Evergreen Suite:* Queen-size bed, 2 window seats fold out to twin beds, bath with jetted tub. $150 per night weekdays, $165 weekends. Additional person 14 and over $15 per night.
- *Orcas Room:* Queen-size bed, private bath. $125 per night.
- *Madrona and Cedar Rooms:* Queen-size beds, 2 rooms share the bath across hall. $99 per night.
- *Guesthouse:* 1 bedroom, queen-size bed, bath, kitchen. $250 per night. Additional person 14 and over $15 per night,

RESTRICTIONS: Child 14 or over OK, no pets, no smoking.

EXTRAS: Full breakfast, wireless internet access, deck.

SUMMER RATES: See above. All rates are double occupancy.

🚐 From the ferry landing turn right on Killebrew Road. In 1 mile turn left on LaPorte Road, and in ¼ mile, at the intersection of Victorian Valley, LaPorte, and John Jones Roads, turn left on Victorian Valley Road and take the first driveway on the right.

A unique geodesic dome and an adjacent guesthouse offer quiet, quality lodgings for escapees from workaday tensions, couples who want a romantic retreat, or those who wish to sample the beauty of Orcas Island life. The lodgings sit on a knoll surrounded by 12 acres of native madrona and evergreen forest. The opportunity to enjoy the unusual space of the modern geodesic dome is worth the stay in itself. The guesthouse deck and a very large cedar deck that wraps around the dome at treetop level have views that include the Olympic Mountains and the Strait of Juan de Fuca.

If you are not familiar with native madrona, your hosts will point it out to you.

Madrona House 🏠 👫

57 Harrison Point Lane; Eastsound, WA 98245; (800) 852-5770 or (360) 376-2108; email: *miamk@centurytel.net*; web site: *orcasmadronahouse.com*

ACCOMMODATIONS: Rental home and separate cottage.
  • House with 3 bedrooms with queen-size beds, queen-size hide-a-bed, 1½ baths, kitchen
  • 1-bedroom cottage with queen-size bed and bath. (Cottage not available until 2008.)
RESTRICTIONS: No smoking.

You Say Arbutus, We Say Madrona

The remarkable evergreen tree known as madrona in Washington State is *Arbutus menziesii*. In British Columbia it is called arbutus, and in California it is madrone or madroño. No matter what its name, there is no mistaking the tree's lovely form and colorful limbs. The distinctive, dark red outer bark peels in large strips to reveal the smooth, yellowish inner bark of its graceful trunks and branches. The deep-green leathery leaves, clusters of small white blossoms, and small, bright-red berries the tree produces provide a beautiful counterpoint to its bark. The trees prefer open banks and often overhang saltwater. There they are battered by storms and twisted into picturesque shapes, to the delight of photographers.

EXTRAS: Fireplace, hot tub, porches, gazebo, private cove. Walking distance to Eastsound.
SUMMER RATES: $486 per night, $2700 per week, 3-night minimum.
🚗 Guests will be given driving directions.

This spot is so pretty it is used for weddings. The waterfront estate facing on Ship Bay dates from the early 1900s. Fruit trees edge the wide lawn that sweeps down to a private cove. The old-fashioned covered veranda has been extended to create a large open deck. Either are just the spot for a cool drink in the afternoon.

The main house sleeps eight people in three bedrooms and a living room foldout couch. Plate rails and beamed ceilings are reminders of the now-modern home's historic past.

Maggie's Manor 🏠 👫 🐴 ♿

P.O. Box 148; Deer Harbor, WA 98243. Phone: (360) 376-4223 or (360) 376-2480; email: *connor@centurytel.net*; web site: *orcasrec.com/maggie*

ACCOMMODATIONS: Rental home that sleeps up to 10 in 4 bedrooms; 3 bedrooms with queen-size beds, 1 with twin beds, and a fifth room on the lower level floor that has 2 roll-aways; 2 baths; large (400-square-foot) kitchen. Ground floor is disabled accessible (not ADA).
RESTRICTIONS: Children welcome, pets by arrangement, no smoking.
EXTRAS: Hot tub, deck, washer, dryer, grand piano, TV, phone, private beach, 180-degree view.
SUMMER RATES: $375 per night, $2250 per week. Major credit cards accepted.
🚗 From the ferry landing follow Orcas Road for about 2½ miles to Deer Harbor Road and turn left. Follow this road through West Sound toward Deer Harbor. Pass Deer Harbor B&B inn (on your left), and at the bottom of the hill turn right onto Channel Road and drive over a small wooden bridge. The Maggie's Manor drive is in 0.5 mile at 508 Channel Road.

A family reunion or wedding in this inspired setting is sure to be a resounding success. Lace curtains, flowered wallpaper, and antiques make this beautiful home a romantic, relaxing getaway. The spacious lawn is ideal for family games of croquet, picnics, or sunbathing on a blanket. The home's 180-degree view of Deer Harbor, the Wasp Island, and the Olympic Mountains is breathtaking. Evenings bring sing-alongs around the grand piano, or a soak in the hot tub while watching the stars. The kitchen is well equipped for preparing meals and snacks for the whole gang.

Have a wedding here, then send the happy couple off to honeymoon at the romantic Gnome House. The same folks who offer that fanciful lodging own Maggie's Manor. They know how to provide truly memorable accommodations.

The home adjoins a 110-acre nature preserve, so don't forget binoculars. You can spot some of the hundreds of species of birds that visit Orcas Island, including spectacular bald eagles, hawks, and osprey. Deer are sure to be seen, and possibly

Massacre Bay Bed & Breakfast & Cottage 🛏 🏠 👫

2098 Deer Harbor Road; Eastsound, WA 98245. Phone: (877) 248-7833 or (360) 376-2766; email: *massacrebay@interisland.net*; web site: *interisland.net/massacrebayb&b*

ACCOMMODATIONS: B&B inn with 3 rooms and separate studio cottage.
  • *Bay View, Island View, and Rose Rooms:* Queen-size beds, baths with showers, Rose Room has queen-size sleeper sofa.

- *Studio cottage:* Queen-size bed, queen-size sleeper sofa, bath with shower, kitchen.
RESTRICTIONS: No pets, children OK, no smoking.
EXTRAS: Full breakfast, each room has small refrigerator, coffeemaker, two have view balcony. House library has TV/VCR, videos, tapes, books, magazines, games. Cottage has barbeque, fireplace, satellite TV/VCR, patio, deck.
SUMMER RATES: Rooms $105 to $135 per night; cottage with breakfast $145 per night, no breakfast $129, $695 per week. Extra person $20 per day, child under 5 $10 per day. Extra person in cottage $10 per day.
🚗⛵ From the ferry landing follow Orcas Road 2½ miles, turn west on Deer Harbor Road. In 2 miles the B&B is on your right.

Your hosts ask that you kick off your shoes when you enter their B&B. You'll want to, anyway—it's that kind of a relaxing spot. The beautiful, spacious rooms are contemporary with lots of comfortable touches. The studio cottage, a short distance away, is ideal for week-long rentals. A hearty breakfast is served to enjoy in your room, on your balcony, or on the main deck. The private bath for Rose Room, on the lower level, is up one flight; robes are provided.

Saunter across the road to the inn's private beach on the north end of West Sound. The small cove, named Massacre Bay, was long ago the site of an Indian battle. Today it is well-known for the flocks of migratory waterfowl that stop by. Stretch out on the driftwood and watch the birds. Kayaks can be put in here to explore West Sound and visit a pair of undeveloped island state parks offshore. The buoy offshore, placed by the inn, is available for mooring your boat.

Meadowlark Guesthouse 🏠 🚶🐄

444 Point Lawrence Road; Olga, WA 98279. Phone: (360) 376-3224; web site: *sanjuanweb. com/meadowlark*

ACCOMMODATIONS: Rental home with 1 bedroom with queen-size bed, queen-size hide-a-bed in living room, private bath, wood stove and electric heat.
RESTRICTIONS: Children OK, pets only by prior arrangement, no smoking.
EXTRAS: Washer, dryer, cable TV/VCR, deck, barbecue, basketball hoop, books, games, video library. Olga Store, community dock, artworks and café all within walking distance.
SUMMER RATES: $135 per night, 2-night minimum.
🚗 Located ½ mile past Orcas Artworks on Point Lawrence Road.

Everything you need for your San Juan Island stay is right here. Owner Barbara Wheeler clearly knows what visitors like to do, and provides storage space for your bicycles, backpacks for your use when hiking in Moran State Park, and a basketball hoop for kids to work off excess energy while parents enjoy a cool drink on the deck. There are laundry facilities to suds out grubby clothes. Although the guesthouse is set up beautifully for a family of four, two couples would find it equally convenient.

The guesthouse sits in 40 acres of open meadow at the end of Buck Bay, on the east side of East Sound, south of Moran State Park. The spectacular view from the deck is out to open meadows, East Sound, Lopez Island, and ferries passing in the distance. The village of Olga is within walking distance, and Moran State Park is less than two miles away.

North Beach Inn 🏠 ⛄ 🐎 ♿

P.O. Box 80; Eastsound, WA 98245. Phone: (360) 376-2660; web site: *northbeachinn.com*

ACCOMMODATIONS: 13 cottages with a mixture of double, twin, and an occasional queen-size bed; all have private baths.
- 4 studio-style cottages, fireplace, kitchenettes, bathroom with shower. Sleep 2 to 3.
- 1 1-bedroom cottage, kitchenette, bathroom with shower. Sleeps 2 to 5.
- 5 2-bedroom cottages, kitchenettes or full kitchens, fireplaces, bathtubs or showers. Sleep 4 or up to 6.
- 3 cottages with 2 bedrooms and a sleeping loft, full kitchens, fireplaces or Franklin stoves, bathtubs. Sleep 4 or up to 7.

RESTRICTIONS: Children OK, pets OK.

EXTRAS: 1800 feet of no-bank shore, seclusion, no TV. Some disabled access.

Rates $135 to $240 per night for basic occupancy level. $820 to $1525 per week. Extra charges for additional persons, additional cars, and dogs. 2-day minimum, weekly rates available. Open year-round. No credit cards.

🚗 Guests will be given driving directions.

North Beach Inn is a grand old standby on Orcas Island's north shore. A long private lane leads to rustic cottages strung along the beach. You'll find it just the spot for a complete escape from the world. Stroll the gravel beach in the cool of the evening, or settle down among the driftwood for an afternoon of solitude with a thick novel.

Facilities vary from older, quite rustic cottages to larger, better appointed lodges big enough to accommodate a family of six or seven. All units but one have fireplaces or wood stoves; all have electric heat and come equipped with bedding and cooking utensils. The main lodge, which is the focal point of the resort, once served as a dining hall for a summer camp. Now it is the owners' private home.

North Shore Cottages 🏠 ⛄ 🐎

271 Sunset Avenue; P.O. Box 1273; Eastsound, WA 98245. Phone: (866) 367-5131 or (360) 376-5131; web site: *northshore4kiss.com*

ACCOMMODATIONS: 4 separate cabins with queen-size beds, 3 with queen-size sleeper sofas, all have full private baths, full kitchens.

RESTRICTIONS: Children OK, pets OK, no smoking.

EXTRAS: Fireplace, deck, private hot tubs, big-screen TV/VCR/DVD in each unit, outdoor grills. Private beach, shared sauna, gardens, walk to Eastsound.

SUMMER RATES: $255 to $355, 2-night minimum; weekly rates available. No credit cards.

🚗 Drive north from Eastsound on North Beach Road. Just opposite the sign to Smuggler's Villa, turn right onto Sunset Avenue. The cabins are on the left in about ¼ mile.

Four gorgeous cottages above the water offer private lodgings for couples or small families. Each unit has its own deck and hot tub. Throughout all the units are unique touches such as leaded-glass windows, mosaics, original art, and antiques. Heron Cove is more sculpture than architecture, with swooping roof, curving walls, and two private decks, one with a hot tub large enough for eight; the other with a gas grill, rotisserie, and bar storage. The upstairs bedroom has a queen-size bed and full bath. Seal Point is a two-level cottage with a door at the head of the stairs to separate the levels into private areas. An additional cottage—actually a treehouse—is planned for 2008. Check to see if it is available when you plan your trip.

A stone arch marks the entrance to Oyster Garth, with its extensive gardens, stone walkways, and path to the beach. We didn't know what a garth is, but we learned it is a small garden or enclosure. This one is so beautiful that it would be ideal for an intimate wedding. The lodging's web site is *northshore4kiss*. Enough said.

The Old Trout Inn ⊨ ⌂

5272 Orcas Road; Eastsound, WA 98245. Phone: (360) 376-7474; email: *nicoles@orcasline.com*; web site: *oldtroutinn.com*.

ACCOMMODATIONS: B&B inn with suites and separate guesthouse.
- 2 suites and 1 room with queen-size bed and private bath with Jacuzzi, private hot tub, private sitting area.
- Guesthouse with queen-size bed, kitchen, private bath, hot tub, gas fireplace, deck.

RESTRICTIONS: No children, no pets, no smoking.

EXTRAS: Full breakfast, satellite TV and VCR, CD, refrigerators, microwaves, coffeemakers, some suites with fireplace, sauna in Pond Suite, all with views of a 3-acre pond, birdwatching. Exercise room available.

SUMMER RATES: Suites: $160 to $205 per night, $860 to $1200 per week. Rooms: $110 per night. Cottage: $195 per night $1200 per week. Optional 3-course á la carte dinner: $45 per person, beverages not included. Massage $75 per hour.

🚗 From Orcas ferry landing, follow Orcas Road north for 3¼ miles. The inn is on the left, ¼ mile past the Deer Harbor Road.

Exquisite settings in the San Juans aren't required to have a beachfront location, as is proved by the Old Trout Inn. With room names such as Water's Edge Cottage, Pond Suite, Greenhouse Suite, and Cattail Room you know the pond is the focal point for this fine lodge. The main house edges right on the beautiful three-acre pond, complete with paddling ducks and a small waterfall.

All rooms are handsomely decorated with a few period pieces and lots of comfortable, country touches. Greenhouse Suite opens onto a sunny garden room. Pond Suite has its own sitting area with a fireplace, wet bar, and TV, and can accommodate four. Breakfast is served in the dining room, with the pond in full view. On request, the innkeepers will prepare an optional three-course dinner for you.

In Water's Edge, a separate (and romantic) cottage a short distance from the main house, guests can retreat to their own world, with their own sitting area overlooking the pond. Guests in the cottage can have their breakfast in the main house, or can opt to have it in the intimacy of their accommodations.

Once in a Blue Moon Farm ⌂ ⋔

412 Eastman Road; Eastsound, WA 98245. Phone: (360) 376-7035; fax: (360) 376-6500; email: *farmgirl@onceinabluemoonfarm.com*; web site: *onceinabluemoonfarm.com*

ACCOMMODATIONS: Suites in several buildings on farm. All units have a microwave and refrigerator.

- *Home (view deck):* 3 bedrooms with queen-size beds, 1½ baths.
- *Home (patio level):* 2 bedrooms with queen-size beds, 1 bath, den, family room (these two can be combined).
- *Main Lodge:* Private suites, community kitchen.
- *Carriage House (loft):* Queen-size bed, 2 singles, sofa, bath; community kitchen.
- *Carriage House (lower):* Double bed plus loft with a queen-size bed, bath, community kitchen.
- *Sunshine Suite:* 1 queen-size bed, 1 double. Pet friendly.

RESTRICTIONS: No smoking, pets and kids OK, pet waiver required.

EXTRAS: Patio with barbeque, satellite TV. Farm animals, gardens, fruit trees, horseback rides.

SUMMER RATES: $150 per couple per night. Small family begins at $185 per night, larger groups $300 to $800 per night. Call for an exact quote.

🚗 From the ferry landing drive 2 miles to Eastman Road, then turn east on it. In ½ mile look for the blue gates on the right.

This tranquil, 35-acre estate offers a very special farm experience with just the lodging to meet your needs. The antique-furnished home has sleeping facilities that can be split between two groups of guests. The same is true of the nearby carriage house. A lodge offers smaller private suites.

The working farm has an arena for horseback riding, alpacas and llamas to pet, chickens to provide fresh eggs, and sheep and goats to enthrall the kids. Walk in the fields and the alpacas will eat right from your hand. Guests can gather organic produce and eggs for their meals and flowers to brighten their lodging. Tours of the sustainable farm can be scheduled—you'll learn about the essential role each organism has in a sustainable environment.

Lodgings on farms give guest an opportunity to enjoy farm animals.

Orcas Cottages 🏠 🍴

Olga, WA 98279; Phone: (360) 779-1296; fax: (360) 779-6293; email: *megb@johnlscott.com*: web site: *orcascottages.com*

ACCOMMODATIONS: 2 cottages.
- *Island Cottage:* 3 bedrooms, 1 queen-size bed, twin beds, 1 double bed and double sofa bed, 2 full baths, kitchen, wood stove.
- *Hidden View Cottage:* Loft with king-size bed and a window seat that can be made into a twin bed, queen-size sofa bed downstairs, bath, kitchen, wood stove.

RESTRICTIONS: No smoking, no pets.
EXTRAS: Cable TV/VCR, telephone, washer and dryer available, views. Moorage on the Olga dock.
SUMMER RATES: $150 and $200 per night, 2-night minimum; $800 and $1400 per week.
🚗 ⛴ Drive past Olga Artworks and turn left at the post office. The cottages are the first property on the left. By boat, the Olga dock is on the east side of East Sound, near its entrance.

Olga Bay and ferry traffic in Harney Channel provide the views for these charming lodgings. Either would be ideal for a family or couples. Island Cottage is a modernized Victorian house, dating from 1884, with three bedrooms. A charming rock stairway leads to Hidden View Cottage, which looks out to Rosario Strait and Lopez Island. You can moor at the Olga dock if you arrive by boat. The innkeeper's buoy was damaged as of 2007; if you might like to use it, check to see if it has been repaired. The cottages are just a short distance uphill from the water.

Orcas Hotel 🏨 🍴

Orcas Landing, P.O. Box 155; Orcas, WA 98280. Phone: (888) 672-2792 or (360) 376-4300; email: *orcas@orcashotel.com*; web site: *orcashotel.com*

ACCOMMODATIONS: Hotel with 12 rooms and suites, queen-size beds, private and shared baths.
RESTRICTIONS: Children by arrangement, no pets, no smoking.
EXTRAS: 2 rooms have Jacuzzis, no TV. Bakery and espresso café (breakfast, lunch), (rooms have complimentary breakfast and espresso), seasonal restaurant (breakfast, lunch, dinner). Walk to ferry and Orcas Landing shopping.
SUMMER RATES: $89 to $208 per night. Reserve entire hotel for $2100 per night. Major credit cards accepted.
🚗 The hotel sits immediately above the Orcas Island ferry landing. Parking is on the north side of the hotel. Open year-round, except for Christmas Eve and Christmas Day.

This quintessential historic inn perched on a hillside above the ferry landing is the grande damé of Orcas Island lodgings. The hotel, built between 1900 and 1904, is on the National Register of Historic Places. It was most recently refurbished in 1985, but it still boasts period furnishings throughout. A veranda wraps around three sides of the inn, and white picket fences complete the turn-of-the-century ambiance.

All rooms have antiques and queen-size or extra-long twin beds with comfy quilts. Two spacious, romantic rooms have view balconies and private baths with Jacuzzis for two. The remaining rooms are cozier, although not cramped; three come with half baths (shower down the hall); others share baths.

Orcas Island Vacation Home 🏠 👪

Phone: (650) 856-2525; email: *melinda_mcgee@hotmail.com*; web site: *orcasislandvacation.com*

ACCOMMODATIONS: Rental home with 2 bedrooms: one with queen-size bed and twin bed, 1 with double bed and twin bed, 1¾ baths, kitchen.
RESTRICTIONS: Children OK, no pets, no smoking.
EXTRAS: Washer, dryer, fireplace, private beach, yard, view.
SUMMER RATES: $985 per week for up to 4 persons, each added person $10 per day. Weekly only.
🚗 Guests will be given driving directions.

Views are always a premium in the San Juans, and this waterfront house on the east side of Orcas Island, midway between Doe Bay and Point Lawrence has some of the best. Sweeping views include Rosario Strait and Cypress, Sinclair, and Blakely Islands. The view is as good from inside the house as it is from the yard or shore. Stairs lead down the high bank to the beach.

Your family will feel at home immediately with the comfortable furnishings, and the yard is a great place for kids to play. Firewood is provided so you can relax in front of the fireplace with a bottle of wine after a day of exploring the island.

The Orcas Tree House 🏠 👪

P.O. Box 168; Olga, WA 98279. Phone: (360) 317-6360; email: *info-no_spam@orcastreehouse.com*; web site: *orcastreehouse.com*

ACCOMMODATIONS: Rental home with 2 bedrooms, king-size and twin bed in one room, double bed in the other, 2 baths, kitchen. 2 resident cats.
RESTRICTIONS: No pets, no shoes in house, no smoking.
SUMMER RATES: $210 per night, 2-night minimum $1260 for 6 nights, 7th night free.
🚗 Between Olga and Doe Bay.

Who wouldn't want to drift off to dreamland in this hillside retreat filled with the scent of the surrounding forest? This lovely, new, two-story cedar home sits on a slope on the south side of Orcas Island. French doors on the decks open out to high views of distant ferries and the snowy peaks of the Olympic Mountains. Everything two couples or a group of four would need for a getaway is here.

The master bedroom occupies the entire top floor, and boasts its own deck. The master bath has a large tub with a skylight and double showerhead ideal for romantic baths with a very close friend. Two residents cats can remain outside for most of your stay, if you wish, or else they will be happy to be your on-site pets.

Otter's Pond Bed & Breakfast 🛏 👪

100 Tomihi Drive, P.O. Box 1540; Eastsound, WA 98245. Phone: (888) 893-9680 or (360) 376-8844; email: *host@otterspond.com*; web site: *otterspond.com*

ACCOMMODATIONS: B&B inn with 5 rooms (king- or queen-size bed), private bath, 2 with fireplace.
RESTRICTIONS: Children over 10 by special arrangement, no pets, no smoking.
EXTRAS: Sumptuous 5-course gourmet breakfast, hot tub, robes, shared sitting room with fireplace and library, TV in Goldfinch Room, Wi-fi in all rooms. Decks, pond, birds, wildlife.

SUMMER RATES: $150 to $225, prefer 2-night minimum stay in summer. Visa, MasterCard and Discovery accepted.

🚗 Take Orcas Road from the ferry terminal to Eastsound Village. From Eastsound, drive east, following Crescent Beach Drive to a T-intersection, and then turn right onto Olga Road. 3 miles from the intersection, turn right on Tomihi Drive, a small, gravel road with a row of mailboxes. Otters Pond is the second property on the right. If you reach Moran State Park, you have missed Tomihi Drive.

You'll fall in love with this French Country-style home. Your attention is first captured by the forest-edged pond, seen through glass doors opening onto the deck. The more you see of the home, the more you marvel at how beautifully it is integrated with its setting, with the natural wood of the home echoed by the cedar and fir forest. Waterfowl often stop at the pond, and feeders on the back deck attract a wide variety of little birds.

The rooms are named after a few of the many birds that come calling: Chickadee, Swan, Bluebird, Hummingbird, and Goldfinch. You will always find fresh flowers in your room, as well as original artwork by local artists. Little niches here and there, both inside and outside, offer privacy to read, sit and chat with a friend, or cuddle with your companion. The second floor has a small library with comfortable chairs, the back deck has a swing, and a small gazebo holds a hot tub enclosed by shoji screens that can be slid to the side for views of stars and moonlight.

Outlook Inn on Orcas Island 🏠 👫🏃♿

171 Main Street, P.O. Box 210; Eastsound, WA 98245. Phone: (888) 688-5665 or (360) 376-2200; email: *info@outlookinn.com*; web site: *outlook-inn.com*

ACCOMMODATIONS: Inn with 40 rooms and suites.
- *Original Inn Rooms:* B&B style with double beds, shared baths.
- *East Wing Rooms:* Either 1 or 2 queen-size beds or 2 double beds, private bath.
- *Bay View Suites:* Luxury rooms with king-size beds, private Jacuzzi baths, private balconies, gas fireplaces; disabled accessible (ADA).

RESTRICTIONS: Children OK, no pets, no smoking.

EXTRAS: TV in Bay View Suites and East Wing; no TV in Original B&B inn. Restaurant (breakfast, dinner), conference/banquet room, chapel on the grounds.

SUMMER RATES: Original B&B inn $84 to $89; East Wing Rooms $165 to $175; Bay View Suites $225 to $289. Major credit cards accepted.

🚗✈ From the Orcas ferry landing, follow Orcas Road north for 8½ miles to Eastsound. The inn is on the left as you enter the business district. For guests arriving by air, the airport is ½ mile to the north.

If your grandparents or great-grandparents ever visited Orcas Island, they might well have stayed at the Outlook Inn. It has a long tradition of providing lodging for island visitors. You may choose to stay in one of the rooms in the historic inn, where the decor has been updated just enough to provide complete modern comfort with 1890s aura. Antiques and framed needlework fill the rooms and halls. All bedrooms have shared baths, B&B-style.

Two adjacent, newer units hold additional rooms that have private baths and

TV, but still with gracious antiques and flower-bedecked Victorian setting. Bayview Suites have deluxe accommodations with sunken living rooms and radiant heated floors. Each of these suites have whirlpool tubs, warmed towels, plush robes, wet bar, TV/VCR, and private balconies opening out to expansive views of the water and surrounding mountains.

The beach lies immediately across the street, and stores and restaurants of Eastsound are just steps away. The inn itself holds New Leaf Cafe, a restaurant that serves breakfast and dinner. See Restaurants & Cafes, page 166.

Palmer's Chart House ⊨ 🏃

102 Upper Deer Harbor Road, P.O. Box 51; Deer Harbor, WA 98243. Phone: (360) 376-4231

ACCOMMODATIONS: B&B inn with 2 rooms with private baths.
RESTRICTIONS: No smoking, no pets, inquire about children.
EXTRAS: Continental breakfast, cable TV, deck, daysails available. Walk to Deer Harbor facilities.
SUMMER RATES: $80 per night. No credit cards.

🚗 From the Orcas ferry landing, drive north on Orcas Road, and in 2½ miles turn west onto Deer Harbor Road and go west for 5 miles. At the entrance to Deer Harbor Village go left on Upper Deer Harbor Road for a few hundred yards. Palmer's is on the right at 102 Upper Deer Harbor Road.

This modern, flower-edged home, overlooking Deer Harbor offers two guest rooms, each with a private bath. Eat breakfast on the sunny deck, or in the evening relax with a good book in the library. You'll enjoy chatting with your well-traveled hosts—they will take you for a daysail on their 33-foot yacht at minimal extra cost. They know these waters well, and possibly you'll see whales or other marine life. Spanish is spoken as well as English.

Pebble Cove Farm 🏡🏃

3341 Deer Harbor Road; Deer Harbor, WA 98243. Phone: (360) 376-6161; email: info@pebblecovefarm.com; web site: pebblecovefarm.com.

ACCOMMODATIONS: B&B inn with 2 suites, both with kitchenettes, hardwood floors.
   • Master suite has separate bedroom with queen-size bed, sofa bed in living room. Dining area, wood-burning fireplace. Sleeps 4.
   • Studio suite has queen-size bed. Sleeps 2.
RESTRICTIONS: Children welcome, no smoking, no pets.
EXTRAS: Organic continental breakfast, VCR, CD, video and CD collection, private decks, walk out to beach, children's play area, garden and farm animals, complimentary bicycles, kayak put-in. Walk to Deer Harbor.
SUMMER RATES: $150 to $225 per night.

🚗 From the Orcas ferry landing, drive north on Orcas Road, and in 2½ miles turn west onto Deer Harbor Road. Continue for another 2¼ miles to the sign for Pebble Cove Farm on the left.

Daisy-fresh might be an overused phrase, but even so, it applies to these bright waterfront lodgings. The outdoors is brought inside with a fanciful twig frame around one window, and a peeled-log bed. Sunlight (and moonlight) streams in through French doors.

The setting is as delightful as the lodgings, with an expansive lawn rolling down to the beachfront and a farm and garden to provide fresh eggs, berries, and a pony who likes to have his ears scratched. If you bring kayaks, you can launch them from shore. Or, you can grab a bicycle and explore country roads.

The Place at Cayou Cove 🏠 👬🐴

P.O. Box 310; Deer Harbor, WA 98243. Phone: (888) 596-7222 or (360) 376-3199; fax: (360) 376-3852; email: *stay@cayoucove.com*; web site: *cayoucove.com*

ACCOMMODATIONS: 4 separate cottages.
- *Carriage House:* King-size bed, 2-person shower and soaking tub, kitchen.
- *Cove Cottage:* Queen-size bed, twin trundle beds, tub and shower, kitchen.
- *Gardeners Cottage:* King-size bed, 2-person shower, kitchen.
- *Allen Cottage:* Queen-size bed, queen-size hide-a-bed, full bath, kitchen; no maid service

RESTRICTIONS: Children and pets OK, no smoking.

EXTRAS: All cottages have satellite TV/DVD, CD, private hot tub, fireplace, barbeque, porch or deck, firepit, private beach. Complimentary ferry or airport pickup. Restaurants and marina nearby.

SUMMER RATES: Rooms $295 to $425 per night, double occupancy, $35 per additional person, per night. 2-night minimum. Rates for Allen Cottage are for the entire unit. Pets $25 per night, 2 pets for $40. Visa and MasterCard accepted.

🚗 ⚓ From the Orcas ferry landing, head north on Orcas Road, and in 2½ miles turn west on Deer Harbor Road. Follow this road as it curves around West Sound. Just before reaching Deer Harbor Marina, turn right on Olympic Lodge Lane. The inn is at the end of the lane. Boats can be moored at the nearby BellPort Deer Harbor Marina, for a fee, or tied to the inn's mooring buoy, by arrangement.

You'll be transported back to bygone times as you enjoy the sun setting over the Olympic Mountains from your deck, porch, or patio of any of these four cottages. The historic Craftsman-style main house on the Deer Harbor waterfront was completed in 1913 by Henry Cayou, whose father homesteaded the property in 1857. The Cove Cottage was built prior to 1910. Families will appreciate the spacious Allan Cottage, on the adjoining property.

The accommodations are warm and elegant—among the best to be found in the San Juans. There's attention to the details that make guests feel pampered, such as thick bath sheets, special soaps, and candles. A full breakfast is served to you right in your cottage, and summer evenings bring wine and hors d'oeuvres. If you are staying offseason, a bottle of champagne welcomes you to your lodging. Dinner can be served in your cottage, with advanced notice.

Rosario Resort and Spa 🏨 👬🐴

1400 Rosario Road; Eastsound, WA 98245. Phone: (800) 562-8820 or (360) 376-2222; fax: (360) 376-2289; email: *info@rosarioresort.com*; web site: *rosario.rockresorts.com*

ACCOMMODATIONS: Resort with 108 rooms and 8 suites with 1 king-size bed or 2 queen-size beds and private bath. Most have fireplaces. Some have separate bedrooms, some have wet bar, some suites with kitchen.

ORCAS SLAND
Lodging

RESTRICTIONS: Children OK, pets OK with permission, no smoking.

EXTRAS: Cable TV in all rooms, most rooms have private balconies with water view, robes, coffeemakers. Exercise rooms, sauna, whirlpool, massage available, 1 indoor pool, 2 outdoor pools (open seasonally), tennis courts, restaurant (breakfast, lunch, and dinner), grocery (open seasonally), lounge, poolside bar and grill (open seasonally), gift shop, boutique, beauty shop, rental cars, meeting facilities, marina, moorage, marine fuel, convenience store, deli.

SUMMER RATES: $219 to $750 per night; special packages available. Major credit cards accepted.

🚗⛴➕ From Eastsound, drive east, following Crescent Beach Drive and then Olga Road. In 4 miles, just before entering Moran State Park, turn south (right) on Rosario Road and follow it downhill for 1¾ miles to the resort. By boat, the resort's marina is on Cascade Bay, on the west side of East Sound. A seaplane float is at the marina for air access.

For many, Rosario is an instant love affair. This elaborate facility, which graces a spectacular setting on Cascade Bay, is billed as "the premier island destination resort in the Pacific Northwest." The sumptuous Moran Mansion was built in 1904, and is on the National Register of Historic Places. It centerpieces the fascinating resort, and holds a restaurant, lounge, gift shop, and spa. The mansion's enormous plate-glass windows that frame the marine view, elegant stained-glass accents, wood parquet flooring, and evening concerts on the historic Steinway and pipe organ, are unparalleled anywhere in the Northwest. On the second floor, several rooms showcase the original furnishings and display photographs from the mansion's heyday.

Some well-appointed rooms and suites are above the waterfront, next to the mansion. Units a short distance away, on the hillside, hold the majority of the rooms and suites; most have balconies opening out to the view. Well-thought out touches such as terry robes, down comforters, coffeemakers, and bottled water add to the luxury. Restaurant cuisine tends to Northwest seafood, but also includes a nice range of other dishes. Marina guests and boaters tied to buoys can take advantage of a landing package that permits use of the pools and spa facilities.

The outside swimming pool is surrounded by glass that shields sunbathers from brisk sea breezes, yet allows views of all the harbor comings and goings. The friendly, helpful staff, the extensive lodging and meeting facilities, and the scenic site make the resort a favorite for weddings, business seminars, and retreats. See also Restaurants & Cafes, page 161 and 165, and Marinas, Launch Ramps & Put-Ins, page 193.

Rose Arbor Cottage 🏠 ♦♦

Eastsound, WA 98245. Phone: (503) 675-7673; web site: *roseair.com*

ACCOMMODATIONS: Rental home with 2 bedrooms (queen-size bed and double bed), 1½ baths, kitchen, sleeps 5.

RESTRICTIONS: No smoking, no pets, no smoking.

EXTRAS: Gas fireplace, entertainment center, private patio, barbeque, washer, dryer, phone and fax. Steps from the waterfront, walk to Eastsound.

SUMMER RATES: $165 per night, 3-night minimum; $960 per week. Package deals available with Rose Air out of Portland.

🚗 Guests will be given driving directions.

Sunsets are usually beautiful, but those in the San Juans are especially spectacular. You will be able to marvel at them right from your living room in this cottage on Orcas Island. The modern, recently remodeled home on the island's north shore has everything a family or small group will need for a fabulous vacation. Kayaks can be put in at the public beach that is just steps away. And, there's a pretty rose arbor, of course.

Sandcastle Guesthouse 🏠 🎏

991 Bartel Road; Eastsound, WA 98245. Phone: (360) 376-6307; email: *pdgrisdale@msn.com*; web site: *aerieonorcas.com*

ACCOMMODATIONS: Rental home with 1 bedroom (queen-size bed), double hide-a-bed, kitchen, fireplace.
RESTRICTIONS: Children OK, no pets, no smoking.
EXTRAS: TV/VCR, CD player, deck, private beach, fresh muffins for breakfast.
SUMMER RATES: $140 per night, 2-night minimum stay.
🚗 From Eastsound head north on North Beach Road to Mount Baker Road. Turn left on Mount Baker Road and drive east about 1½ miles to Terrill Beach Road. Turn left and go ¾ mile and turn left on Bartel Road. The Sandcastle Guesthouse is the first on the right.

If you could find the perfect spot and build your dream vacation getaway, it probably would be just like this tidy guesthouse on Orcas Island's North Shore. The home's spacious deck overlooks a wildlife wetland where ducks and herons gather. Views are north, across the water to Sucia Island and the distant Gulf Islands. Bring a kayak and launch it from the beach for exploring around Orcas Island and nearby state park islands. Orca whales cruise offshore, at times.

The home itself accommodates one or two couples, or a family of four. Furnishings are modern Pacific Northwest, with lots of wood and soothing earth tones.

Sand Dollar Inn Bed & Breakfast 🛏

P.O. Box 152; Olga, WA 98279. Phone: (360) 376-5696; email: *sanddollar@rockisland.com*; web site: *sdollar.com*

ACCOMMODATIONS: B&B inn with 3 rooms (queen-size beds) and private baths; 2 rooms with private baths, 1 with adjacent bath.
RESTRICTIONS: No children, no pets, no smoking.
EXTRAS: Full breakfast, guest refrigerator, phone, water views from sunroom and three bedrooms, no TV. Short distance to Olga.
SUMMER RATES: $135. Visa and MasterCard accepted.
🚗 From Eastsound, drive east, following Crescent Beach Drive and then Olga Road. The inn is on Point Lawrence Road, ¼ mile beyond the Olga intersection, on the north side of the road, 6½ miles from Eastsound.

You can well imagine this gracious home being owned by an old sea captain, with the many antiques being those he had collected on his journeys to the far corners of the world. Although the home once did belong to a ferryboat captain, the present owners are Ric and Ann Sanchez. The lovely Oriental furnishings were collected by Ann, who taught in Japan.

The Sand Dollar Inn sits on a slight hillside overlooking Buck Bay. The shallow bay is a gathering spot for all sorts of waterfowl. Wander down to the county road to birdwatch with binoculars, or you might be able to spot some birds from the inn.

All bedrooms but one have adjoining baths. Robes are provided for occupants of the Library Room, who must take a quick trek across the hall to reach their bath. Hearty breakfasts befitting a sea captain are served in the inn's sunroom.

Seacliff Cottage 🏠 👫

326 Seacliff Trail; Olga, WA 98279. Phone: (360) 317-6810; email: *dcw@rockisland.com*; web site: *seacliffcottage.com*

ACCOMMODATIONS: Rental home with 2 bedrooms (double beds), window seat can be used as a twin bed.
RESTRICTIONS: No smoking, no pets. Not available November through April.
EXTRAS: TV/VCR/DVD, radio, CD player, washer, dryer, outdoor spa, decks.
SUMMER RATES: $310 per night, 4-night minimum, or $270 per night for 7 or more nights.
🚗 Drive to Olga, and then turn left onto Point Lawrence Road. Continue 6 miles, past Doe Bay Resort, to Sea Acres Road. Follow it to Seacliff Trail and turn left on it. At the end, you're there.

This stunning, modern, Arts and Crafts–style home is perched on a high bank on the southeast side of Orcas Island. It overlooks Rosario Strait and islands to the south, and offers bird's eye views of ferries, boat traffic, and (possibly) passing dolphins and whales. Eagles, herons, and seabirds are your companions.

A glass-surrounded window seat is large enough for you to have an afternoon nap, or fall asleep watching the stars.

Smuggler's Villa Resort 🏠 👫

P.O. Box 79; Eastsound, WA 98245. Phone: (800) 488-2097 or (360) 376-2297; fax: (360) 376-5597; email: *smuggler@rockisland.com*; web site: *smuggler.com*

ACCOMMODATIONS: Resort with 20 2-bedroom villas, all with private baths, kitchens, fireplaces.
- *Rambler:* Queen-size bed and two other beds. Sleeps 2 to 4.
- *Honeymoon Rambler:* King-size bed and daybed. Sleeps 2.
- *Townhouse:* 2 queen-size beds and 2 additional beds. Sleeps up to 6.
- *Deluxe Townhouse:* Queen-size bed and 3 other beds. Sleeps up to 6.
RESTRICTIONS: Children OK, no pets, no smoking.
EXTRAS: Washer and dryer, TV/VCR in all units, tennis/basketball court, pickle ball court, hot tub, sauna, heated swimming pool, playground, dock, moorage, beach. Scenic airplane flights nearby, close to Eastsound Village.
SUMMER RATES: $259 to $325 per night, per unit, 4-night minimum. $1599 to $2099 per week. Moorage and ramp fees are extra. Major credit cards accepted.
🚗⛴ From Eastsound, drive north on North Beach Road. Just north of the airport, a road to the left is signed as the entrance to Smuggler's Villa. By boat, the entrance to Smuggler's Villa is due south of Sucia Island. The villa is within walking distance of the Orcas Island airport.

Couples, families, or small groups love these fully appointed, modern, home-style units on Orcas Island's north shore. The spacious accommodations, along with a lot of things to keep kids occupied, make these lodgings a real find. The resort has courts for tennis, basketball, and other sports; the larger courts at Buck Park are just ½ mile down the road. The airport, just a clam toss away, is a transportation advantage for some; others might want to join the gulls with a scenic biplane flight.

All units look out to Brandt's Landing, a private marina that opens to the north shore of Orcas Island. Moorage is available for guests, for a fee. Only a few miles north lie the marine state park islands of Sucia, Matia, and Patos, which can be reached by boat or kayak. En route is Parker Reef, where seals, sea lions, and a host of seabirds hang out.

Spring Bay Inn ▭ ♯♯

464 Spring Bay Trail, P.O. Box 97; Olga, WA 98279. Phone: (360) 376-5531; fax: (360) 376-2193; email: *info@springbayinn.com*; web site: *springbayinn.com*

ACCOMMODATIONS: B&B inn with 5 rooms (queen- or king-size beds), private bath, 1 suite with private outdoor soaking tub.
RESTRICTIONS: Children OK, no pets, no smoking. Maximum of 2 persons per room.
EXTRAS: Full breakfast, hot tub, waterfront, guided kayak tours, forest trails, no TV.
SUMMER RATES: $220 to $260 per night. Entire inn $1189 per night. 2-hour morning, brunch, evening, and group kayak tours $25 per person. Major credit cards accepted.
🚗 From Eastsound, drive east, following Crescent Beach Drive and then Olga Road. At the Olga intersection, turn left on Point Lawrence Road, and in ½ mile turn right onto Obstruction Pass Road. In about a mile, take another right onto Trailhead Road. The road immediately changes from blacktop to dirt, and in ¾ mile a road on the left (Spring Bay Trail) is signed to the inn. It's another ½ mile down this driveway before the inn is reached. You can arrive at the inn by boat, too. There is good anchorage in the protected cove; Spring Bay lies immediately east of Obstruction Pass Campground, on Obstruction Pass.

Spring Bay Inn is a bit off the beaten path, even for Orcas Island, but once you've arrived you will feel as if you have discovered Oz. The magnificent inn is situated on 60 acres of pristine woodland and its own tiny bay. The sumptuous inn holds forth in this rustic setting. In the living room, fourteen-foot-high ceilings and an expanse of windows frame the water view. Huge stone fireplaces anchor either end of this room. There are eight fireplaces throughout the inn! Four bedrooms are on the upper level; Ranger Suite is on the main floor. Each boasts a fireplace. Three units have private decks, and there's a hot tub at water's edge for twilight soaking.

The owners, Carl Burger and Sandy Playa, are former park rangers with great knowledge of nature. Your stay includes a guided kayak tour and basic paddling instruction. Kayaks and all necessary gear are provided. For early risers going kayaking, a continental breakfast is laid out. Upon your return, a full breakfast is ready.

Swannies Inn ⌂♯♯♿

24 Shady Lane; Eastsound, WA 98245. Phone: (360) 376-5686; email: *swannies@webtev.net*; web site: *sanjuanweb.com/orcasisland//swannies*

ACCOMMODATIONS: Inn with 1-bedroom guest quarters with queen-size bed, kitchenette, private entrance. Disabled accessible (1-step only, not ADA).
RESTRICTIONS: Children OK, no pets, no smoking.

EXTRAS: TV/VCR, video library, walk to Eastsound, parking space for boats and RVs.
SUMMER RATES: $90 per night, 2-night minimum.
🚗 In Eastsound, turn north on Prune Alley, and stay on it for about 1 mile. You will see the sign for Swannies on the right.

This charming, 100-year-old home's nearness to Eastsound, and its nice setting, make it a fine spot to stay on Orcas Island. Spend your days exploring the shops and byways of the island, then visit one of Eastsound's excellent restaurants, or bring something home from the Farmer's Market to prepare in your kitchen. Evenings, you'll enjoy relaxing in the pretty, antique-decorated suite, and curling up to watch a movie while warmed by the cozy glow of the wood-burning stove.

Turtleback Farm Inn 🛏 👯

1981 Crow Valley Road; Eastsound, WA 98245. Phone: (800) 376-4914 or (360) 376-4914; fax: (360) 376-5329; email: *info@turtlebackinn.com*; web site: *turtlebackinn.com*

ACCOMMODATIONS: B&B inn with 2 buildings
* *Main Farmhouse:* 7 rooms with queen-size beds; 1 room has double bed, some with additional hide-a-bed, all with private baths, one with private deck.
* *Orchard House:* 4 rooms with king-size bed, fireplace, private bath, private deck.

RESTRICTIONS: Children OK, no pets, no smoking indoors.
EXTRAS: Full breakfast, ponds, evening sherry, sitting room with fireplace, no TV, guest refrigerators, decks.
SUMMER RATES: $100 to $245, 2-night minimum during summer and holidays. Visa, MasterCard, and Discover cards, and personal checks accepted.
🚗 From the Orcas ferry landing, drive north on Orcas Road, and in 2½ miles turn west onto Deer Harbor Road. At the intersection with Crow Valley Road, head north. The inn is on the east side of the road, 2½ miles from the last intersection.

Turtleback Farm Inn is a meticulously restored farmhouse sitting on 80 acres of pastoral land in the shadow of Turtleback Mountain. The property is actually an operating farm, growing apples and raising poultry and sheep. You can spend your day wandering the farm or sunning on the deck.

Antique-filled bedrooms of the old home range from a cozy room with a double bed, to a spacious light-filled room with a queen-size bed and French doors opening onto a private deck. Guests share a sitting room; evening tea or a sherry by the fireplace will send you off to dreamland. The Orchard House, nearby, was built to resemble an old barn, although it is a recent addition. The four spacious, beautifully decorated rooms inside have French doors opening onto private decks that overlook Crow Valley.

Breakfasts are so scrumptious that the inn's recipes, including the one for their acclaimed granola, have been published in a cookbook. In the Orchard House, the full breakfast is served in your room, so you can eat leisurely in your 'jammies, if you wish.

Walking Horse Country Farm (Little House on the Farm) 🏠 🏇

180 West Beach Road; Eastsound, WA 98245. Phone: (360) 376-5306, email: *stay@ walkinghorsefarm.com*, web site: *walkinghorsefarm.com*

ACCOMMODATIONS: Rental home with 2-bedrooms (queen-size beds), kitchen, fireplace, bath.
RESTRICTIONS: Children welcome, no pets, no smoking.
EXTRAS: Washer, dryer, Jacuzzi, VCR, nature trails, ponds, picnic area, farm animals, birdwatching. Carriage rides and trail rides available.
SUMMER RATES: $150 per night, 4-guest occupancy, 2-day minimum.
🚗 From the ferry landing, drive north on Orcas Road for 2½ miles and turn left (west) onto Deer Harbor Road. In 1 mile, at a T-intersection, head north on Crow Valley Road. In 3½ miles, turn left (west) onto West Beach Road. The farm is on the right, just after the intersection.

This beautiful little country home furnished with antiques and collectibles provides truly one-of-a-kind accommodations. The home overlooks the 25-acre horse farm, with its barn-red outbuildings and tidy white fences. You can just enjoy the rural ambiance of the farm, or you can join in on some of the horse-related activities. Farm owners Jeri and Doug Smart offer trail and carriage rides. Also, the farm does weddings with either a Western or English riding theme, complete with a carriage.

Trails on the property are open for walking as well as riding. Picnic tables by the ponds are a nice stop on your tour of the farm. The farm animals include a Belgian draft horse and pony, as well as the elegant Tennessee Walkers. Because of the number of animals on the farm, children must be adult-supervised.

West Beach Resort 🏠 🏇🐴♿

190 Waterfront Way; Eastsound, WA 98245. Phone: (877) 937-8224 or (360) 376-2240; email: *vacation@westbeachresort.com*; web site: *westbeachresort.com*

ACCOMMODATIONS: Resort with 19 cottages (1- and 2-bedrooms with queen-size beds); some have additional hide-a-beds or daybeds. All have private bath, kitchen, electric heat, additional wood stove. Tent and RV campsites (seasonal). Some units disabled accessible.
RESTRICTIONS: Children OK, pets OK (for an additional charge), no smoking.
EXTRAS: Cribs, TV in lobby, DSL internet in lobby and selected cabins. Dock, marine gas, groceries, coin-operated laundry, moorage, beach, hot tub, espresso bar, kayak tours, canoe and rowboat rentals, motorboat rentals, mountain bike rentals. Organized kid and adult activities.
SUMMER RATES: $149 to $239 per night, $975 to $1595 for full week. Maximum of 6 to 8 persons per unit (one unit is 2 persons only). $18 per night for additional persons over age 3. Major credit cards accepted.
🚗 From the Orcas ferry landing, drive north on Orcas Road for 2½ miles to the intersection with Deer Harbor Road. Turn left onto Deer Harbor Road, drive 1 mile, and at a T-intersection, go north on Crow Valley Road. In 3½ miles, turn on West Beach Road, which heads west, and then north. As the road makes another right turn at Enchanted Forest Road, the signed side road to West Beach goes left.

This waterfront resort is ideal for families with restless children. While parents kick back and gull-gaze on their cottage deck or on the beach, kids keep busy exploring the beach, checking out activity at the dock and store, and striking up friendships with kids in the other cottages or campground. In the evening, all can gather around a beach fire to watch the sunset or take a quiet evening mini-cruise. Or, adults and little ones can take part in organized activities. There's never an end to the fun.

Some cabins line the beach, just a step away from the water; others are in the woods above the beach. Furnishings are cozy-comfortable; all have electric heat, but wood stoves add a cheery note on cool evenings. Scuba divers favor West Beach because several of the best dive sites in the San Juans lie north at Point Doughty and south at Lover's Cove. The resort's spacious campground is nearby. See Parks & Campgrounds, page 197

VACATION HOME RENTAL FIRMS
◆

Private homes on Orcas Island provide a nice alternative to commercial lodgings. Brochures picturing and describing homes for short-term rental are available from several real estate firms. Call, email, or fax the company to have theirs sent to you, or check their web site. By the time summer rolls around, accommodations are heavily booked, so try to reserve a home early. Summer rentals are by the week only; during the quiet season there is a two-night minimum. The following firm lists rentals on Orcas Island:

Cherie Lindholm Real Estate
P.O. Box 66; Eastsound, WA 98245. Phone: (360) 376-2204; fax: (360) 376-5699; email: *rentals@lindholm-realestate.com*; web site: *orcashomes.com*

RESTAURANTS, CAFÉS & TAKE-OUT
◆

$	Inexpensive	Most dinner entrées under $12
$$	Moderate	Most dinner entrées $12 to $25
$$$	Expensive	Most dinner entrées $25 and up

▲ = Beer and wine ￥ = Full bar

Bilbo's Festivo $ to $$ ￥
310 A Street; Eastsound, WA 98245. Phone: (360) 376-4728; fax: (360) 376-1112

HOURS: Dinner daily year-round, lunch daily at La Taqueria in the summer. Reservations recommended. Major credit cards accepted.

A hot breath of Mexico in the San Juans! Tables in an outside courtyard surround a firepit; grapevines trail over an arched entryway; adobe walls, cactuses, and handmade tiles accompany the wonderful aroma from the kitchen. Start with a fresh-squeezed lime margarita, then check out the menu for traditional dishes, all done with a light, New Mexican touch. Try offerings from their mesquite grill accompanied by a good Mexican beer. Even local favorites such as oysters and shrimp are given a piquant Southwest treatment. There are soups, salads, and a tempting dessert menu, too.

Boardwalk on the Water $ to $$ 🍷

8292 Orcas Road, P.O. Box 73; Orcas, WA 98280. Phone: (360) 376-2971; email: *mamie@orcasislandboardwalk.com*; web site: *orcasislandboardwalk.com*

HOURS: Breakfast, lunch, and dinner. Major credit cards accepted.

Many of the little side-by-side cottages clinging to the hillside above the Orcas ferry landing are all part of The Boardwalk. As a group, they are a "strolling eatery." The restaurant named Boardwalk on the Water serves up hearty breakfasts, charcoal-grilled hamburgers, and some of the best fish and chips on the island. Beer and wine as well as espresso, coffee, and soft drinks are available. Another cottage offers hot pizza, and the space shared by The Boardwalk gift shop tops it all off with ice cream and frozen yogurt.

The restaurant has inside seating, and for a sunny day, there are also tables outside, scattered between the cottages.

Cabo San Juan and Taqueria $$

134 North Beach Road; Eastsound, WA 98245. Phone: (360) 376-3485

HOURS: Breakfast, lunch, and dinner 6:30 A.M. to 9 P.M., closed Tuesdays. Catering and take-out.

This family began their business by selling tacos at the local Farmer's Market. Their flavorful food was such a hit that they decided to expand their restaurant. They serve classic American breakfasts as well as authentic Mexican lunches and dinners.

Café Olga $ 🍷

Orcas Island Artworks Building; 11 Point Lawrence Road; Olga, WA 98279. Phone: (360) 376-5098

HOURS: Brunch, lunch, and early dinner daily 10 A.M. to 6 P.M. Major credit cards accepted.

Tucked into one corner of the large building that houses the Orcas Island Artworks, Café Olga is a "must" stop for many visitors. The fare includes inexpensive salads, sandwiches, quiche, baked eggs, and pasta, and includes such inviting dishes as lemon pesto pasta, Thai seafood curry, and Mexican chili pie, all made with the freshest of ingredients. Top off your meal with espresso and homemade berry pie or the most incredible cinnamon rolls you'll ever sink a tooth into.

Cascade Bay Grill $ 🍷 on weekends

Rosario Resort; Eastsound, WA 98245. Phone: (360) 376-2222; web site: *rosario.rockresorts.com*

HOURS: Open seasonally 11:30 A.M. to 6 P.M.

Here's the place to stop for chow before you head out on your boat from the Rosario docks, or after your tour of the Rosario Mansion. The café, located next to the dockside grocery store, offers grilled and deli sandwiches, pizzas, and snacks. You can pick up Rosario and San Juan souvenirs here, too.

Chimayo $

Our House Mall; 123 North Beach Road; Eastsound, WA 98245. Phone: (360) 376-6394 (376-MEXI)

HOURS: Lunch and dinner Tuesday through Friday 11 A.M. to 3 P.M., Monday through Saturday 5 P.M. to 9 P.M.

Mexican food is recognized as the new healthy fare. Chimayo does it fast and fresh, with offerings such as black beans and cheese tossed in spicy vinaigrette on a warm tortilla and Redemption Salad (a version of a taco salad with fresh greens). There are the usual tacos and burritos, and you will also find such gourmet specials as roasted eggplant and feta cheese quesadillas topped with roasted tomato salsa. The décor is bright with Mexico-inspired art. Desserts are homemade—'nuf said.

Christina's $$ to $$$ ⦆

Porter Station; 310 Main Street; Eastsound, WA 98245. Phone: (360) 376-4904; web site: *christinas.net*

HOURS: Dinner daily. Reservations recommended. Major credit cards accepted.

Christina's, one of the most widely acclaimed restaurants in the Northwest, occupies the upper floor of a two-story building, a former service station, on Eastsound's waterfront. From such modest surroundings comes sumptuous fare such as six-lilies soup, grilled ahi, truffled lamb ragout with garlic potatoes, and smoked salmon with wild rice cakes. A dish you loved last time might not be on the menu at your next visit, because chef/owner Christina Orchid regularly experiments with new creations. The seafood is the freshest the San Juans produce. The extensive wine list includes fine domestic and imported wines.

Deer Harbor Inn $$ to $$$ 🍾

P.O. Box 142; Deer Harbor, WA 98243. Phone: (360) 376-1040

HOURS: Dinner daily. Reservations recommended. Major credit cards accepted.

This large dining room in the inn on the hillside above Deer Harbor offers gourmet fare in a farmhouse atmosphere. A wood-burning stove sits in one corner, genteel lace tablecloths and small vases of garden flowers decorate well-used wooden tables. An outside deck has seating with a view of the harbor.

Some offerings might remind you of the wonderful meals Grandma made, while others are far better than even she could have conjured up! The homemade soup is accompanied by fresh-baked bread. Entrées include selections of chicken, beef, and local seafood, fettuccines, as well as at least one vegetarian dish. The wine list includes domestic selections as well as some fine French offerings. During summer, you can take an afternoon break for tea and tasty finger sandwiches.

Dockside Galley $

BellPort Deer Harbor Marina, 5164 Deer Harbor Road; Deer Harbor, WA 98243. Phone: (360) 376-3037

HOURS: Breakfast and lunch daily.

This small galley on the marina pier at Deer Harbor has a range of dishes that they'll pop into the microwave for you: frittatas, breakfast burritos, chicken and garden burgers, and Polish dogs. Seating is on the deck or a couple of inside tables. You can also find ice cream, some groceries, beer, and wine as well as ice and bait.

Doe Bay Café $ to $$

107 Doe Bay Road, P.O. Box 437; Olga, WA 98279. Phone: (360) 376-8059; email: *info@ doebay.com*; web site: *doebay.com*

HOURS: Breakfast and lunch daily, dinner Wednesday through Sunday in summer. Weekends only in winter. Major credit cards accepted.

For really healthy food, head to Doe Bay. The natural foods café that is part of the resort serves simple, tasty, inexpensive meals that are good for the body, too. The café is at the back of the lounge, in the historic building. The marine view from inside the rustic little restaurant, overlooking one of the coves of Doe Bay, is as inspiring as the food.

Enzo's Gallery Caffé $

Village Plaza; 365 North Beach Road; Eastsound, WA 98245. Phone: (360) 376-3732

HOURS: 1 P.M. to 9 P.M. Monday through Saturday.

The promise of homemade clam chowder should be enough to assure your pleasure, but you can also try other tasty soups, as well as salads, espresso, specialty teas, gelato, and Italian sodas. The work of local artists is exhibited in the café, and some summer evenings bring performances of singers and local musicians. You'll really get into the Orcas Island scene.

Enzo's Italian Caffé $

Orcas Landing; Orcas, WA 98280. Phone: (360) 376-8057

HOURS: Breakfast and lunch daily.

Located next to the ferry landing, Enzo's is the spot for quick, tasty chow whether waiting for the ferry or just passing through. The small café serves soup, panini, muffins, freshly squeezed juices, gourmet coffees and teas, and a wide selection of gelatos. Seating is inside and on the deck.

The Inn at Ship Bay ᕦ $$–$$$ ⟰

Orcas Road; Eastsound, WA 98245. Phone: (877) 276-7296 or (360) 376-5886; web site: *innatshipbay.com*

HOURS: Dinner daily. Closed in winter. Major credit cards accepted.

The tidy farmhouse edged by an old orchard could well be the home of a retired sea captain. The restaurant's decor befits a sea captain's home too, with nautical prints on the walls. It offers inspired dishes featuring Northwest salmon, Dungeness crab, scallops, and mussels, and fresh local garden produce. You'll find oysters fixed nearly a dozen different ways as appetizers and entrées. If there's someone in your party who doesn't feel like eating seafood at the moment (hard to imagine!), the menu includes Black Angus beef, game hen, or other offerings. The pear tart features fruit picked from their own orchard.

The list of excellent wines includes fine local and California vintages, as well as some imported ones. Try an espresso or one of several apéritifs to go with your dessert. The inn also has excellent wedding facilities, and will cater your festivities.

Kiki's Kafe $

432 North Beach Road; Eastsound, WA 98245. Phone:

HOURS: Daily 7 A.M. to 5 P.M.

If you haven't satisfied your espresso craving by the time you've reached the north end of North Beach Road, Kiki's offers a spot for morning or afternoon refreshment. It serves cookies, espresso, iced drinks, and blended iced drinks.

The Kitchen $ 🍶

249 Prune Alley; Eastsound, WA 98245. Phone: (360) 376-6958

HOURS: Lunch and early dinner. Food is for take-out.

Asian dishes, made from scratch with fresh ingredients, are the mainstay of this shop in the back of the bungalow occupied by clothier Trés Fabu!. Sample a flavorful curry with vegetables and rice, or a soup and traditional rice balls coated with sesame seeds. New, tasty ethnic dishes are added regularly, and there's always a daily special. In nice weather you can eat on their roofed patio.

The Lower Tavern $ 🍶

Langell Street and Orcas Road; Eastsound, WA 98245. Phone: (360) 376-4848

HOURS: Lunch and dinner daily; bar open until 2 P.M.

Local people know this homey tavern in Eastsound is the place to get a really good hamburger. The custom is to slather on horseradish from the big jar on your table—sinuses beware! Other hot and cold sandwiches, chili, and homemade soup round out the menu.

The bar has pool, darts and cards. Grab a seat at the bar or at one of the tables and join in the casual fun, Orcas style. Try out the open mike on Thursday night. The conversation will probably be local politics; you'll gain a lot of insight into what makes this community work.

Lu Lu's Pasta Rustica $ to $$

Prune Alley at A Street; Eastsound, WA 98245. Phone: (360) 376-2335

HOURS: Wednesday through Monday 3 P.M. to 9 P.M. Closed Tuesday.

For flavor and satisfaction it's hard to beat Italian fare. Lu Lu's does it up right, with antipasti, appetizers, soups, and pasta plates piled high with meats or seafood in flavorful sauces. Soups include minestrone made from their own recipe, as well as a daily soup creation. House specials of beef short ribs, chicken, and pork loin are also offered. Pizzas and pasta plates, also available for take-out, offer a great range of toppings.

Main Street Bakery $

29 North Beach Road; Eastsound, WA 98245. Phone: (360) 376-5435

HOURS: Wednesday through Saturday 7:30 A.M. to 6 P.M., Sunday and Monday 7:30 A.M. to 5 P.M. Closed Tuesday.

You can't miss finding this eatery at the corner of Main Street and North Beach Road. Once you've tried their fare, you'll be glad you stopped. All their breads and pastries are homemade, and couldn't be fresher. Breakfasts are assuredly gourmet. There's also espresso, soups, sandwiches (homemade bread, of course), and ice cream. A few tables are inside, and several picnic tables are on the lawn outside.

Mansion Dining Room ৬ $$$ ᵧ

Rosario Resort and Spa; Eastsound, WA 98245. Phone: (800) 562-8820, ext. 400 or (360) 376-2222; web site: *rosario.rockislandresorts.com/info.din.asp*

HOURS: Breakfast 7:30 A.M. to 11 A.M., dinner 5:30 P.M. to 9 P.M. Major credit cards accepted.

If there is a reason that fine San Juan restaurants focus on Northwest fare, it's because it is unbeatable. The Mansion Dining Room at Rosario Resort takes Northwest food to an elegant level. Dishes include seafood done to perfection, as well as steak, pork tenderloin, and even duckling. The view is sublime, and the décor is grand, so if you want to dress for a splendid evening and celebrate a special occasion, this is the place to go. However, your boat shoes and jeans will be just fine, too.

Mom's TLC Café $

18 Umer Street; Eastsound, WA 98245. Phone: (360) 376-7011

HOURS: Tuesday through Saturday 7 A.M. to 3 P.M., Sunday 10 A.M. to 3 P.M.

Sandwiches served with Tender, Loving, Care, just like your Mom did. This café offers old-fashioned comfort food such as ½-pound burgers with a generous range of fixings, grilled sandwiches, barbeque, and classic salads. A prime rib special is offered at times.

Moran Lounge ৬ $$ to $$$ ᵧ

Rosario Resort and Spa; 1400 Rosario Road; Eastsound, WA 98254. Phone: (800) 562-8820, ext. 400 or (360) 376-2222; web site: *rosario.rockislandresorts.com/info.din.asp*

HOURS: Lunch daily from 11:30 A.M. to 5:30 P.M., dinner Sunday through Thursday 5:30 P.M. to 11 P.M. Friday and Saturday dinner until midnight; bar open to 2 P.M.

A relaxed ambiance is the hallmark of the Moran Lounge. Light meals are served, or stop for an early evening cocktail and light appetizer before going on to Rosario's more formal Mansion Dining Room. After a fine meal in the dining room, an after-dinner drink and live music might top off the evening. Entertainment begins at 8 P.M., Wednesday through Sunday in summer, and Saturday year-round.

ORCAS SLAND
Restaurants, Cafés & Take-Out

New Leaf Café $$ 🍷

Outlook Inn; 171 Main Street; Eastsound, WA 98245. Phone: (360) 376-2200; web site: *outlookinn.com*

HOURS: Breakfast Friday through Monday 8 A.M.; dinner Friday through Tuesday 5 P.M.

Its name, New Leaf, hints at the philosophy of its food: fresh, organic, and natural ingredients. The dishes are prepared with a light, often ethnic, touch. The café, in the Outlook Inn, is handy for folks staying there, but even if you are not a guest, you might want to check it out. The glassed-in porch that fronts the dining room is one of the nicest spots in town to enjoy your meal, watch the local activity, and enjoy the view of East Sound and surrounding forested mountains.

Octavia's Bistro $$ 🍸

Orcas Landing; Orcas, WA 98280. Phone: (888) 672-2792 or (360) 376-4300; email: *orcas@ orcashotel.com*; web site: *orcashotel.com*

HOURS: Daily 4 P.M. to 8 P.M.; breakfast Sunday 7 A.M. to noon.

Located in the Orcas Hotel, the setting couldn't be more San Juan: quaint historic inn, bountiful flower garden, and ferries whisking passengers and cars to and fro. The food is typical San Juan, also, but with gusto. Offerings include seafood served with light, flavorful sauces, and beef tenderloin, lamb chops, chicken breasts, and pork medallions with savory accompaniments such as nasturtium peppercorn butter or fresh berry beurre blanc sauce. Sunday breakfasts go beyond the basics, and include tasty omelets, as well as their own fresh-baked breads and pastries.

Octavia's will cater your wedding or other event, too.

Olga's $$ 🍷

Eastsound Square; Eastsound, WA 98245. Phone: (360) 376-5862; web site: *olgasoncorcas.com*

HOURS: Daily 8 A.M. to 3 P.M.

There's no question that San Juan people know good food. If your lunchtime palate is craving more than just another burger, this is the place to go. The offerings are creative and incredibly tasty: caramelized clay pot catfish seasoned with coconut, soy, and ginger; seared, pumpkin-seed breaded ahi tuna; and salad with grilled goat cheese and organic greens. The desert and breakfast menu is equally mouth watering. Seating is both inside and on the deck when the weather's good.

Orcas Hotel Café $$

Orcas Landing; Orcas, WA 98280. Phone: (360) 376-4300; email: *orcas@orcashotel.com*; web site: *orcashotel.com*

HOURS: Breakfast and light lunch.

Stop in for a quick latté, and let yourself be tempted by this cafe's fresh-baked pastries. Or, a slice of quiche or an egg and sausage croissant might be what hits the spot. This small café in one corner of the Orcas Hotel offers light (but really good) breakfasts and lunches.

Our Daily Veg Eatery $

188 A Street; Eastsound, WA 98245. Phone: (360) 376-7834 (376-7VEG)

HOURS: Daily; breakfast 7 A.M. to 10 A.M., lunch 11 A.M. to 3 P.M., dinner 5 P.M. to 8 P.M.

With all the healthy, natural things that are around you in the San Juans, you'll probably be inspired to eat healthy, too. Our Daily Veg Eatery offers vegetarian breakfast sandwiches, burritos, veggie juice tonics, soups, and salads, all prepared fresh daily. Cyclists with hearty appetites will want to check out their all-you-can-eat soup and salad lunch buffet.

Portofino Pizzeria $ to $$ 🍷

274 A Street; Eastsound, WA 98245. Phone: (360) 376-2085; email: *portofino@orcasonline.com*; web site: *portofinopizzeria.com*

HOURS: Lunch and dinner Monday through Saturday 11:30 A.M. to 3:30 P.M., 4:30 P.M. to 9 P.M.; dinner Sunday 4 P.M. to 8:30 P.M. Take-out available.

Pizza by the slice, or by the pie, thin crust, deep dish, country covered, to eat in, or take-out—however you want your pizza, Portofino's has it. They are upstairs, above the Village Stop on A Street. Dine inside or on a large outside deck with a view of Eastsound Village and the water. Hand-tossed pizza crusts give perfect flavor and texture. There are sandwiches, subs, and fresh salads, too.

Rosario Resort and Spa

See Cascade Bay Grill, page 161, Mansion Dining Room, page 165, and Moran Lounge, page 165.

Rose's Bakery Café $$

382 Prune Alley; Eastsound, WA 98245. Phone: (360) 376-5805 (store), (360) 376-4292 (café)

HOURS: Monday through Friday 10 A.M. to 6 P.M., Saturday 10 A.M. to 5 P.M.

This lunch spot is so popular you might find there is a short wait during the busy tourist season—what better testimonial? Owners John and Joni Trumbell have turned fresh local food into a high art form. Rose's menu includes gourmet soups, salads, and sandwiches, pizzas, and daily specials that attract local food enthusiasts. Get a seat at the counter and watch their cooking crew in action. Seating is in a spacious inside room or a covered veranda that stretches across the front of the building.

An adjoining room holds a deli with an excellent selection of wines, sliced meats, cheeses, imported oils and vinegars, and a few kitchen items.

Straight Shot Coffee Bar $

296 Main Street; Eastsound, WA 98245. Phone: (360) 376-2135; email: *darvills@rockisland.com*; web site: *darvillsbookstore.com*

HOURS: Daily.

This espresso shop on the water side of Darvill's Bookstore serves organic espresso and drinks from locally roasted beans. Enjoy your java while browsing. Don't miss the outstanding views of East Sound.

Teezer's Cookies, Etc. $
A Street and North Beach Road; Eastsound, WA 98245. Phone: (360) 376-2913

HOURS: Monday through Saturday 6:30 A.M. to 1:30 P.M.

Not just cookies, although they are so great that would probably be enough. Have a homemade muffin and juice with your morning Starbucks espresso. For an afternoon snack, dig into some scrumptious Håaagen Dazs ice cream.

Thai Sisters Café $
Odd Fellows Hall; 112 Haven Road; Eastsound, WA 98245. Phone: (360) 376-6337; web site: oddshall.org/kitchenstuff

HOURS: Thursday 11:30 A.M. to 6 P.M., Friday 11:30 A.M. to 9 P.M. Take-out available.

You'll find this café on the bottom level of the Odd Fellows Hall. It's a bit out of the way, but the fare is delicious and affordable. The Thai cuisine includes dishes such as Pad Thai, Tom Yumm soup, curries, and sweet and sour beef, chicken, pork or prawns.

Vern's Bayside Restaurant & Lounge $ to $$ ⅄
Main Street; Eastsound, WA 98245. Phone: (360) 376-2231

HOURS: Breakfast, lunch, and dinner daily, 7 A.M. to 3 A.M., Sunday 8 A.M. to 3 A.M. Lounge open to 2 A.M. Pizza to go. Major credit cards accepted.

The setting is right on the water, with huge windows offering a sweeping view the length of East Sound and surrounding hillsides. An outside patio puts you within the sound of lapping waves and mewing gulls.

Breakfasts are good, hearty fare to start the day—steak, eggs, hotcakes, and omelets. For lunch there are hamburgers, fish and chips, sandwiches, salads, and seafood baskets, as well as pizza to eat here or to go. For dinner try New York strip steak, prime rib, barbecued ribs, chicken, or some of their excellent, always fresh, salmon and other seafood choices. Or sample Italian- or Chinese-inspired dishes. There are vegetarian options.

West Sound Café $ 🍴
Crow Valley Road and Deer Harbor Road; Eastsound, WA 98245. Phone: (360) 376-4440

HOURS: Lunch and dinner, breakfast on weekends. Weekdays, 11 A.M. to 7:30 P.M., Saturday 9 A.M. to 7:30 P.M., Sunday 9 A.M. to 2 P.M. Closed Tuesday.

Whether you're bicycling or boating, or are out for a casual car tour of Orcas, this little spot, on a slight hill overlooking the bay, is the perfect place to stop for lunch. Select your soup, salad, or sandwich from the array in the deli case, then settle down at a table in a sunny corner. If the weather's nice, choose a spot on their outside deck, overlooking the water. You can pick up a "loaf of bread and jug of wine" for a picnic to enjoy at Deer Harbor or down on the public boat dock just below.

On weekend mornings there's a full breakfast or fresh pastry and steaming espresso. Lunch specials might be steamed clams (local, of course), fish and chips, grilled sandwiches, or several kinds of burgers. Don't miss their excellent selection of wines and beer. You're sure to find a special one for a friend back home or to open in your B&B in the evening.

GROCERIES, BAKERIES, DELIS & LIQUOR

Country Corner

Corner of Crescent Beach Drive and Terrill Beach Road; Eastsound, WA 98245. Phone: (360) 376-6900

Country Corner is strategically located just as you drive east from Eastsound. Out front you can purchase gas, diesel, or propane, and inside is a broad selection of fast foods and groceries, beers and fine wines. A deli counter offers ice cream, pizza, soups, salads, subs, and sandwiches, and of course, espresso.

A coin-operated laundry is also in the building, so you can freshen your camping clothes while scarfing down lunch and filling your car tank.

The Dockside

Rosario Resort and Spa, 1400 Rosario Road; Eastsound, WA 98245. Phone: (800) 562-8820, or (360) 376-2222; web site: *rosario.rockresorts.com*

Boaters and other visitors to Rosario Resort needing to grab a few supplies or snacks can find them in the building next to the marina. Souvenir T-shirts, sweatshirts, hats, and coffee mugs tend to outnumber grocery items, however. The grill serves pizza, hot dogs, burgers, and other typical grill fare. There's espresso, too, for those of you needing a java jolt, and a small bar, open on weekends in summer.

Island Market

P.O. Box 186; Eastsound, WA 98245. Phone: (360) 376-6000; fax: (360) 376-6001

Island Market, the largest, best-stocked grocery store on Orcas Island, has everything you'll need to replenish your boat's larder, including fresh meat, fresh bakery goods, beer, and wine. They offer video rentals, too.

Stop by the deli for picnic makings to enjoy at Moran State Park. Their great selection of cheeses, meats, and salads will make a repast to rival the scenery. If you're new to the Northwest, discover the ecstasy of Nanaimo bars, a calorie-loaded dessert delicacy.

Boaters wanting to pick up ship's stores can tie up to the public dock at Madrona Point or drop anchor just off it and take their dinghy to the dock. From there, it's just a four-block walk to the market.

Olga Store

4th Street and Olga Road; Olga, WA 98279. Phone: (360) 376-5862

This small grocery store at Olga is generally open only in the summer. It carries souvenir shirts, local cookbooks, and a limited supply of groceries. A deli counter holds sandwiches and salads that can be consumed at a counter inside or at one of the outside tables on the deck. After the long trip downisland, bicyclists find it a welcome spot to pick up sandwich makings and a cold soda.

Orcas Home Grown Market and Deli

138 B North Beach Road; Eastsound, WA 98245. Phone: (360) 376-2009

This oasis of natural and organic foods in the heart of Eastsound provides friendly, personal service, with an emphasis on environmental consciousness. Fresh local produce and seafood are its forte. Hikers, bikers, and boaters delight in the bulk food section with its variety of trail mixes, nuts, and dried fruits. Homeopathic and herbal medications are also sold. The natural foods deli specializes in alternative baking and vegan cooking.

Orcas Village Store

Orcas Ferry Landing; 10 Killebrew Road; Orcas, WA 98280. Phone: (360) 376-8860; fax: (360) 376-8870

This small store right next to the ferry landing is a standby for supplying fresh coffee, ice cream treats, and snacks to ferry-bound travelers. The store's size belies the range of merchandise you'll find inside. You'll be able to put together everything for an Orcas Island picnic. There are groceries, smoked salmon, fresh meat, fresh produce, beer, wine, fishing tackle, magazines, newspapers, candy, toys, and souvenir items. A small deli dispenses hot dogs, pastries, soup, and soft drinks, and there is an ATM for those running short on cash.

Rose's Bakery Cafe

382 Prune Alley; Eastsound, WA 98245. Phone: (360) 376-5805 (store), (360) 376-4292 (café); email: *trumbull@rockisland.com*

After enjoying an excellent lunch at Rose's café, step next door where a deli sells meats and cheeses, both whole and sliced, and a few other food items to take back to your Orcas lodging or tent site. Browse the excellent selection of wines and find one (or more) that piques your interest. Top your purchases off with a few kitchen items such as fancy imported oils, vinegars, and spices.

The Village Stop

A Street; Eastsound, WA 98245. Phone: (360) 376-2093

HOURS: Daily from 7 A.M. to 10:30 P.M.

This convenience store, carries wine, beer, soft ice cream, videos, coffee, and a moderate supply of grocery items.

Washington State Liquor Store—Eastsound

Village Stop Building; A Street; Eastsound, WA 98245. Phone: (360) 376-2616

HOURS: Monday through Saturday 10 A.M. to 6 P.M.

The Eastsound liquor store is on the south side of A Street, in the same building as the Village Stop, and next to the Sunview Movie Theater.

Washington State Liquor Store—Orcas

Orcas Landing; Orcas, WA 98280. Phone: (360) 376-4389

HOURS: Monday through Saturday 10 A.M. to 6 P.M.

At Orcas Landing, you'll find the liquor store in a small building beside the Orcas Village Store.

SHOPPING, GALLERIES & ARTISTS

Artas Usuwil Gallery

330 North Beach Road, Suite 3; Eastsound, WA 98245. Phone: (360) 376-6427, (360) 376-6424; email: *orcastudio@artasusuwil.com*; web site: *artasusuwil.com*

Art as usual—the name of the store reflects the owners' dedication to their craft. Rolf and Gerd Neuwajaar, create stunning one-of-a-kind rings and other pieces of jewelry from gold and precious stones. Pendants reflect the Northwest scenery with representations of evergreens and twisted bonsai. The gallery also features pottery, glass, woodcarvings, and other work of Northwest artists

The Aurora Company Consignment Shop

Our House Mall; 123 North Beach Road; Eastsound, WA 98245. Phone: (360) 376-2249

This consignment outlet has a little of everything for everyone: clothing in silks, sequins, and velvets, jewelry for women and men, and more. The inventory changes daily, so stop in for that special find.

The Barge Gift Shop

BellPort Deer Harbor Marina; 5164 Deer Harbor Road; Deer Harbor, WA 98243. Phone: (360) 376-3037

Located on a barge moored at the BellPort Deer Harbor Marina dock, this tiny shop sells T-shirts, a few kid's toys, fishing gear, books, maps, and charts. They also collect the moorage fees for the marina.

Bucking Doe Studio and Store

199 Main Street; Eastsound, WA 98245. Phone: (360) 376-6808

This eclectic shop offers a collection of antiques, used clothing, and inexpensive prints, along with a few items of new clothing and shoes. They also have an extensive collection of beads for your craft projects.

ORCAS ISLAND
Shopping, Galleries & Artists

Chez Chloé

Eastsound Square; Eastsound, WA 98245. Phone: (360) 376-8896; fax: (360) 376-3949; email: *info@chezchloe.com*; web site: *chezchloe.com*

Ah, France and great cuisine! If cooking is your passion, here is the place to stop. Chez Chloé, in Eastsound Square, carries high quality cooking tools and classic French housewares. They also offer classes in French cooking, catering services, and discussion groups centered on good food. They will even schedule an individual class for you so you can go back home with the mastery of a new cooking technique.

Cottage Gift Shop

Orcas Ferry Landing; Orcas, WA 98280. Phone: (360) 376-4374

You wouldn't want to leave the island without a pair of slug earrings or a gnome wearing an Orcas Island shirt! Here's the place to hit for that last-minute gift. There are games and toys to keep the kids busy; postcards, books, and posters to remind you of your visit; knickknacks to take back to Aunt Edith; and other stuff you'll want for yourself. Their T-shirts, sweatshirts, and jackets are exceptionally nice. The post office shares the same building, so you can mail your cards and gifts right there.

A smaller second store, which sells packaged snacks as well as souvenir items, sits next to the entrance to the ferry lanes. This upper building is also the rental office for Orcas Mopeds.

Crow Valley Pottery and Gallery

2274 Orcas Road; Eastsound, WA 98245; 296 Main Street,; Eastsound. Phone (877) 512-8184 or (360) 376-4260; fax: (360) 376-6495; email: *pottery@rockisland.com*; web site: *crowvalley.com*

HOURS: Eastsound location: Daily 10 A.M. to 5 P.M. Cabin on Orcas Road: Open only from May through October.

🚗 From the ferry landing follow Orcas Road toward the town of Eastsound. In seven miles Crow Valley Pottery is on the left.

A historic log cabin in a natural setting on Orcas Road houses a nifty little gallery. Its location, on the west side of the road, across from the golf course, makes it a perfect place for a first stop after leaving the ferry. Pottery and tiles made from native clays are the main feature; however, there are other selections from the talented hands of numerous artists, many of them local. You can choose from sterling silver jewelry, hand-woven mats and rugs, metalwork, masks, fine photo prints, notecards, and stunning glass creations mouth-blown or made from fused and slumped glass. The gallery also has an "in town" location on Main Street in Eastsound.

Darvill's Bookstore

296 Main Street, P.O. Box 166; Eastsound, WA 98245. Phone: (360) 376-2135; fax: (360) 376-2391; email: *darvills@rockisland.com*; web site: *darvillsbookstore.com*

Many vacationers who really know the San Juans always make a point of checking to find out what Darvill's has that's new. For the dedicated reader, there's sure to be a great mystery, a boating book, or something of local interest. The knowledgeable clerks can help you find the latest book to slake your literary thirst. You'll also find greeting cards, calendars, and books on tape.

Dream

Eastsound Square, Building C; Eastsound, WA 98245

This small shop in the heart of Eastsound Square carries unique clothing, soft beaded chemises, and sheer tops for layering. That's not all, though. They offer jewelry, polished natural seashells, pottery, and beautiful gifts for the home.

Duke Studio

696 A Eastman Road, P.O. Box 271; Eastsound, WA 98245; email: *info@dukestudio.com*; web site: *dukestudio.com*

HOURS: Open only by appointment.

Artist Dwight Duke specializes in bronze sculptures using lost wax casting coupled with modern technology. His studio/foundry is open by appointment, but you might see his work on display at Crow Valley Pottery, the Westcott Bay Institute Sculpture Reserve on San Juan Island, and other sites in the San Juans and Northwest. Duke's college studies included biology and pre-med, leading him to incorporate natural forms such as whales, fish, and insects into his work.

Eastsound Sporting Goods

Templins Center; Eastsound, WA 98245. Phone: (360) 376-5588

Just about everything you need, whatever your favorite sport is, will be found in this shop in Templins Center. If they don't have an item in stock, they should be able to order it for you. The emphasis is on fishing, with gear for both fresh water and saltwater, and a spool-winding machine where you can custom wind your own reel from bulk stock line. There's a lot of hiking and camping gear, too, as well as a full assortment of basketball, baseball, football and jogging equipment.

Faraways Boutique

Our House Mall, 123 North Beach Road; Eastsound, WA 98245. Phone: (360) 376-4534

The name will give you a hint. This shop features marvelous clothing, much of it from foreign countries. The collections include knits, natural fabrics, soft tops for layering, beautiful women's casual wear, hats, lingerie, jewelry, bags, and accessories. You should be able to put together a look that is uniquely "you."

Howe Art Gallery

236 Double Hill Road; Eastsound, WA 98245. Phone: (360) 376-2945; email: *howeart@ centurytel.net*; web site: *howeart.net*

HOURS: Studio visits by appointment.

174 • O<small>RCAS</small> I<small>SLAND</small>: T<small>OURIST</small> N<small>IRVANA</small>

🚗 From the Orcas ferry landing, follow Orcas Road north toward Eastsound. Just ¼ mile before you arrive at Eastsound, you'll see the sign for the studio on the north side of the road.

Spectacular is the only word to describe the Captain Nemolike creations of artist Tony Howe. You can't avoid being amazed and delighted by his work. His kinetic sculptures hang from tree limbs or rest on frames, twirling in the air like huge, silvery aliens or Brobdingnagian cocoons.

Howe's combined studio and gallery is just up the side road, off the highway. The artist works primarily in various metals; however, some of his works incorporate other materials such as fiberglass or painted Mylar stretched over metal frames. Although large, fanciful, sculptures that twirl in the wind and make interesting sounds are his delight, he also creates chairs, tables, fountains, and even chess sets.

James Hardman Gallery
Loft of Orcas Island Artworks; Olga, WA 98279; web site: *jameshardman.com*

Multi-talented artist James Hardman is known for his unique paintings and prints as well as for his choral and chamber music compositions. His paintings, with multiple semi-transparent layers of color, display a style reminiscent of the pointillists. Also displayed are giclee prints of many of his paintings. Hardman has produced seven albums of original instrumental music, and you can also buy them in this shop in the Orcas island Artworks building.

Kay's
Our House Mall; 123 North Beach Road; Eastsound, WA 98245. Phone: (360) 376-4538; email: *kays@rockisland.com*; web site: *sanjuansites.com/kaysantiques*

Kay's is mostly antiques and collectibles, mixed with some contemporary jewelry and other gift items. You'll find unusual antique jewelry, porcelain, dishes, glassware, linens, and some furniture. Prices range from quite inexpensive upwards; all are reasonably priced for their fine quality. Kay's also offers an extensive collection of Persian rugs for sale.

Kizmet
Our House Mall; 123 North Beach Road; Eastsound, WA 98245

Stepping into Kizmet is like traveling to Thailand, India, and Bali. Here are sculptures, fabrics, candles, therapy balls, wooden massage sticks, and items of home décor, all with an Oriental motif. Handmade jewelry is fashioned from silver, ivory, onyx, agate, and other semiprecious stones. Some Northwest art prints are also carried.

Laura's Clothes Horse
138 North Beach Road; Eastsound, WA 98245. Phone: (360) 376-3287

Northwest style is casual, and this boutique in Doty's Marketplace features women's clothing that is both elegant and casual. The collection includes jeans decorated with studs and glitter, soft tops, chemises, and velvet skirts. You will also find jewelry crafted by local artists.

Leapin' Lizards

Number 2 Eastsound Square; Eastsound, WA 98245. Phone: (360) 376-5790; email: *cparks@ rockisland.com*; web site: *sanjuansites.com/leapinlizards*

In this terrific kids' store you might expect to find Orphan Annie just around the corner, engrossed in a puzzle or glow-in-the-dark star chart. You'll enjoy giving a child one of the excellent selections of educational toys and art supplies as much as they'll enjoy receiving it. There's also a colorful and unusual selection of kids' T-shirts and 100-percent cotton clothing.

376-Wear

Village Plaza; 365 North Beach Road, Suite 104; Eastsound, WA 98245. Phone: (360) 376-9327 (376-WEAR)

As the sign says, this shop carries "ordinary clothing for extraordinary people." That means casual men's and women's wear such as Levi's and Red Wing shoes. Comfy blue cambric shirts are just the thing to wear around an evening campfire.

A number of great shops center around Orcas Island's Eastsound Square.

Magpie

Eastsound Square, Building D; Eastsound, WA 98245. Phone: (360) 376-6743; email: *ianine@ magpieoforcas.com*; web site: *magpieoforcas.com*

This shop in Eastsound Square offers a collection of colorful handmade crafts ranging from candles to vases, notecards, soaps and potpourri. Stop for a pretty gift or item for your home that reflects the islands.

Nature's Art

269 Main Street; Eastsound, WA 98245. Phone: (800) 869-2835 or (360) 376-4343; email: *natureart@pacificrim.net*; web site: *sanjuansites.com/naturesart*

Northwest-inspired designs on caps, shirts, bags, and other items are created in this shop. Clothing can be custom embroidered with Orcas Island or Northwest Indian designs, and they will personalize your gifts for friends back home. You'll also find some casual apparel, as well as nature-oriented notecards, CDs, and cassettes. A few select, mouth-watering gourmet food items such as jams and herb vinegars are tucked around the store.

The Nest

238 C North Beach Road; Eastsound, WA 98245. Phone: (360) 376-4580; fax: (360) 376-3727

This greenhouse-style addition to Trés Fabu! on North Beach Road houses a flower shop with a few home décor items. Pick up a bouquet of fresh posies to brighten your vacation home.

Olga Pottery

Corner of 3rd Street and Olga Road; Olga, WA 98279. Phone: (360) 376-4648; web site: *olgapottery.com*

🚗 From Eastsound, drive east, following Crescent Beach Drive and then Olga Road. At the intersection with Point Lawrence Road, continue straight ahead toward Olga. The shop is on the outskirts of the community, on the west side of the road.

This studio is away from the usual shopping lanes of Orcas Island, but it is well worth making the trip to find it. The gate, framed by a Japanese-style fence, opens on a winding pottery-lined path leading to a small studio and sales office. Jerry Waterman produces elegant vases, weed pots, teapots, and other pottery with unique low-luster glazes in lovely earth tones, blues and grays.

Orcas Arts and Gifts

245 Main Street; Eastsound, WA 98245. Phone: (360) 376-5915; email: *suzanneoforcas@ interisland.net*; web site: *sanjuansites.com/orcasartsandgifts*

The focus here is on jewelry and hand-blown glass, much of it created locally. In fact, at times you can watch a resident glassblower at work in an outside gazebo.

The items range from the expected vases, dishes, and knickknacks to unexpected glass seashells, flowers, bugs, and other fanciful items. There are also shirts, hats, and some casual clothing, as well as some prints. You'll be delighted at the useful and decorative items.

Orcas Center Gallery

Orcas Theatre and Community Center; 917 Mount Baker Road, P.O. Box 567; Eastsound, WA 98245. Phone: (360) 376-2281; email: *info@orcascenter.org*; web site: *orcascenter.org*

HOURS: Tuesday through Friday 10 A.M. to 4 P.M., Saturday noon to 4 P.M.

🚗 From Eastsound, drive north on North Beach Road to its intersection with Mount Baker Road. The community center is on the right, in a short distance. Spot the huge metal orca whale on the lawn in front of the center and you will know you are there.

The lobby and Madrona Room of the Orcas Community Center serve as a gallery for local visual artists. Shows are both juried and unjuried, and include a range of art including sculpture, pottery, fanciful beaded objects, photography, and paintings in a range of media. The building has a theater for plays and concerts. Check their schedule and you'll probably find something you would enjoy attending during your stay. See also Events & Attractions, page 185.

The Orcas Island Artworks

Orcas Island Artworks Building, Olga Road at Point Lawrence Road; P.O. Box 125; Olga, WA 98279. Phone: (360) 376-4408 (gallery), (360) 376-5098 (café); web site: *orcasisland. com/artworks*

HOURS: Open daily mid-February through December.

🚗 From Eastsound, drive east, following Crescent Beach Drive and then Olga Road. The building is at the intersection of Olga Road and Point Lawrence Road.

Back in the 1930s, the huge old building at the Olga Road intersection was a strawberry processing plant. Today it holds The Orcas Island Artworks, which belongs to a non-profit artists' cooperative set up to preserve it. The cooperative presents the work of more than 70 artists and craftspeople who work in a wide range of materials and mediums. Everything on display is crafted by local artists, exclusively.

It's a treasure trove! There's no end to the beautiful fine art and functional things. You'll find handmade quilts, quilted wall hangings, tapestries, soft sculptures, wearable art such as fanciful wool hats, ceramics, pottery, porcelain, handmade tiles, sculpture, notecards, jewelry, chess sets, handcrafted wooden toys, paintings...the list goes on. You'll have difficulty prying yourself away.

Orcas Island Board Shop

Village Plaza, 365 North Beach Road; Eastsound, WA 98245. Phone: (360) 376-7233; fax: (360) 376-2151, web site: *orcasislandboardshop.com*

For a skate boarder or snowboarder, this is Nirvana. Boards, clothes, sunglasses, boots, sandals, and every other item a boarder might need (or not need) are available.

Orcas Island Photo and Graphics

Templins Center; Eastsound, WA 98245. Phone: (360) 376-3646; fax: (360) 376-3603

The shop offers both traditional and digital photo finishing. It has film, camera disk storage modules, camera accessories, frames, albums, and more.

Orcas Island Pottery

338 Old Pottery Road; Eastsound, WA 98245. Phone: (360) 376-2813; email: *orcaspots@ rockisland.com*; web site: *orcasislandpottery.com*

HOURS: 10 A.M. to 5 P.M. daily.

🚗 Drive north from West Sound or south from Eastsound on Crow Valley Road, and turn west onto West Beach Road. About 1 mile later, a road to the left is signed to the studio.

One of the greatest spots on Orcas Island! It's not just a place to shop—it's an experience in itself. The studio holds forth in several little log cabins scattered in the woods, with views out to President Channel. After leaving your car in the small parking area, stroll down a woodland path past a trickling, pottery-crafted fountain. Ferns trail over garden sculptures, platters and pottery sculptures decorate outside walls, and wind chimes hang from cabin eaves.

Browse through the cabins, discovering a new pottery or porcelain treasure for your home or garden in every corner. There are unique mugs, pots, platters, soup tureens, and casseroles. Whimsical animals might include turtles with an endearing expression and slugs looking far more appealing than any in your backyard. The works of several potters are represented here, and at times potters can be watched at work, through windows.

A family of turtles waits for a buyer to take them home from Orcas Island Pottery.

Orcas Landing Fine Antiques & Extraordinary Collectibles

Orcas Landing; Orcas, WA 98290. Phone: (360) 376-7368

In the lower level of the old Russell's Landing building, this antique shop buys and sells quality consignments and estate liquidations. Any antique-oholic will want to browse here.

Pawki's Pet Boutique

109 Main Street; Eastsound, WA 98245. Phone: (360) 376-3648; fax: (360) 376-3337; web site: *pawkis.com*

You wouldn't want to take an "All I got was a lousy T-shirt" back to your pet that had to stay at home or in a kennel, but a nice toy might make up for it. Pawki's has a wide assortment of pet toys, baskets, beds, and healthy foods for dogs, cats, gerbils, or whatever other furry friend you might have.

Plan B Gallery

347 North Beach Road; Eastsound, WA 98245. Phone: (360) 376-2667; email: *orcas.girl@yahoo. com*; web site: *planbgallery.org*

Here you can purchase handmade functional, decorative, and wearable art pieces. Vintage cowboy boots become purses, and vinyl LP's are warped into attractive bowls. You will marvel at the creativity. Guest artists display works on a rotating basis.

Poppies

294 A Street; Eastsound, WA 98245. Phone: (360) 376-2686. Phone: (877) 309-8841 or (360) 376-2686; email: *cheryl@poppiesfabric.com*; web site: *poppiesfabric.com*

Many knitters relax best with a pretty project underway. This store has just about everything you'll need to keep your fingers busy while your mind lazes away. Yarns are the major focus, but a few finished items such as felted slippers and hats are also available.

Pyramidion Out of Print

Our House Mall; 123 North Beach Road; Eastsound, WA 98245. Phone: (360) 376-5552

Usually open Thursday through Saturday 11:30 A.M. to 5 P.M.

This treasure house offers used books and CD's. They will buy your used books and CD's by appointment.

Radio Shack

188 A Street; Eastsound, WA 98245. Phone: (360) 376-6939

Every place of any significance must have a Radio Shack, with its collection of electronic gadgets that no one can live without. Or the game to keep the kids happy if the weather turns cruddy. Eastsound's is in the Orcas Athletics Building at the end of A Street.

ORCAS SLAND
Shopping, Galleries & Artists

Ray's Pharmacy

Templins Center; Eastsound, WA 98245. Phone: (360) 376-2230

Ray's is a full-service pharmacy, well stocked with drugs and sundries. It carries a nice selection of souvenirs and gifts with a San Juan flair. You'll find inexpensive toys and games to keep the kids happy in the evening, or while waiting in the ferry line. Drop your film off for quick processing, and pick up several more rolls to take those priceless island photos.

Rhapsody of Orcas Island

1 Templins Center; Eastsound, WA 98245. Phone: (866) 205-5163 or (360) 376-4223; web site: *orcasrec.com/rhapsody*

Truly something out of a fairytale, Rhapsody of Orcas Island is stuffed with enchanting gift items and home furnishings. Enjoy waterfalls, flowers, paintings, antique jewelry, potpourri, decorative accessories for home and self, greeting cards, fleece wear, collectible blankets, silver, glass, lingerie, and locally made gift items.

The Right Place Pottery

2915 Enchanted Forest Road; Eastsound, WA 98245. Phone: (360) 376-4023 ; email: *rightpot@ interisland.net*; web site: *rightplacepottery.com*

🚗 From Eastsound, drive out Enchanted Forest Road and go to the end of the road. Turn left just before you reach the water.

The Right Place Pottery sits on the west side of Orcas Island. Wonderful pots, platters, garden sculptures, and plates are displayed both outside and in the shop. All pottery and glass is made here in this tiny studio; you might be able to watch the owner, Trudy Erwin, at work. She will make personalized pieces for new babies, newlyweds, or other favorite people.

In the summer, no matter what your age, you can try working on a potter's wheel in a "Wheel Experience," or you can paint pre-made pieces.

Rozwear

Village Plaza; 365 North Beach Road; Eastsound WA 98245. Phone: (360) 376-3788; web site: *rozwear.com*

At Rozwear you'll find hand-knit sweaters and caps, hand-woven stoles, and snuggly, stylish fleece jackets that will make you the envy of the cold-weather crowd. Yarn and knitting projects round out the store's offerings.

Rutabaga

P.O. Box 71; Deer Harbor, WA 98243. Phone: (360) 376-5737; email: *info@rutabaga.biz*; web site: *rutabaga.biz*

As most gardeners know, a rutabaga is a rather obscure, usually unloved version of a turnip. However, you'll love this Rutabaga, located in Deer Harbor just a short

SHOPPING, GALLERIES & ARTISTS • 181

walk from the marina. The everchanging, charming collection features gifts, gear, and garb for home and garden; birdhouses, planters, and specialty garden tools, handmade dishware and baskets for your home, and a few great basic clothing items. Many items were crafted on the island; all are of the highest quality.

Sea Shanty Gifts
Orcas Landing; Orcas, WA 98280. Phone: (360) 376-2355

On the lower level of the Orcas Landing building, the Sea Shanty, associated with Orcas Island Eclipse Charters, features original sea-inspired art by local artists. You can also buy gift certificates for a whale watch tour on Eclipse Charters.

Shearwater's Adventure Store
Doty's Marketplace; 138 North Beach Road; Eastsound, WA 98245. Phone: (360) 376-4699; fax: (360) 376-2005; email: *info@shearwateradventures.com*: web site: *shearwateradventures.com*

It's not just kayaking stuff, although you will find plenty of that here. The shop stocks outdoor gear for all sorts of adventurers, including clothing, nautical charts, travel accessories, wildlife identification charts, and gifts. The shop sells new and used kayaks and every kind of kayaking gear from paddles to clothing. Tours, both scheduled and custom can be arranged.

Shinola Jewelry
172 North Beach Road; Eastsound, WA 98245. Phone: (360) 376-4508; email: *vance@ shinolajewelry.com*; web site: *shinolajewelry.com*

The exterior design of this shop, with its fanciful mosaic of cedar shakes, is enough to make you want to stop in. Goldsmith and jeweler Vance Stephens, the shop's owner, specializes in custom-designed fine jewelry with precious and unusual semiprecious stones. Select a stunning pendant for the love of your life, or a one-of-a-kind wedding set.

Slapin Design Studio
P.O. Box 1608; Eastsound, WA 98245. Phone: (360) 376-8855; email: *orcasa12@rockisland.com*; web site: *orcasonline.com/~slapinarts/*

HOURS: Open by appointment.

You might see some of the work of artist Susan Slapin in banks or offices around Eastsound. She doesn't have a gallery, but you can view her work by appointment. The multi-talented artist is a printmaker and painter with a unique eye for naturescapes. Her work includes monotypes and paintings on paper, giclees, prints, photography, and a book of prose poems. Check out her web site—you'll want to watch for her work.

ORCAS ISLAND
Shopping, Galleries & Artists

Smith and Speed Mercantile

284 A Street, P.O. Box 502; Eastsound, WA 98245. Phone: (360) 376-1006; email: *info@ smithandspeed.com*: web site: *smithandspeed.com*

A wonderful alternative general store carries a multitude of hard-to-find hand tools for gardening, and working wood, logs, and timber. They focus on organic products such as non-toxic paints and wood finishes, clay- and casein-base paints, and wool and cotton insulation. Work shirts, pants, socks, towels, blankets, and hats are all of organic cotton or hemp. Organic personal care items, soaps, lotions, and powders are available, as are Amish wagons and products.

Spirit of the Northwest

Templins Center; Eastsound, WA 98245. Phone: (866) 205-5163 or (360) 376-5163; web site: *orcasonline.com/spiritnw*

In the corner of Templins Center, Spirit of the Northwest carries home décor, clothing, food, lamps, and housewares, all with a lodge theme. It has jackets, shirts, and clothing for men and women. There are lots of stuffed bears and moose, a moose footstool, and a multitude of other moose- and bear-inspired items, including clocks, pillows and throws. You'll want to buy a cabin just to use this nifty stuff.

Stark Images Digital Photography

294 A Street; Eastsound, WA 98245. Phone: (360) 376-3306; email: *northwestdarrien@ rockisland.com*

A small gallery at the corner of A Street and North Beach Road displays a half-dozen ceramic pots and some of the photographer's work.

Trés Fabu!

238 North Beach Road; Eastsound, WA 98245. Phone: (360) 376-7673; email: *style@tresfabu.com*

Trés fabu: quite fabulous! You'll agree that this shop is aptly named when you view their collection of casual but very pretty women's clothing. It offers effortless style with separates to dress up or dress down.

The back of the building houses The Kitchen, an Oriental fast food outlet, and on one side is The Nest, a glass-covered flower shop. Where else can you get style, flowers, and a good lunch?

The Waterfront Gallery

Sears Building; Prune Alley; Eastsound, WA 98245. Phone: (360) 376-5949

This prestigious gallery displays the work of a number of Orcas Island's best artists, as well as other well-known wildlife artists such as Robert Bateman. On view are paintings, signed limited-edition wildlife prints, hand-colored etchings and engravings, limited-edition graphics, and fine photography.

Wood's Cove

#1 Eastsound Square; 109 North Beach Road; Eastsound, WA 98245. Phone: (360) 376-2900; email: *customerservice@woodscove.com*; web site: *woodscove.com*

Boots, clogs, slides, sandals, flip-flops, moccasins, slippers—you get the picture. If you are looking for comfortable footwear, this is the spot. The store even has adorable deerskin moccasins for tiny babies. There also are nice selections of jewelry, pottery, soaps, candles, hats, wreaths made from driftwood, and works of local artists in glassware and porcelain.

EVENTS & ATTRACTIONS
◆

Crow Valley School House Museum

Crow Valley Road, Route 1, P.O. Box 83B; Eastsound, WA 98245. Phone: (360) 376-4260

HOURS: Thursday through Saturday 1 to 4 P.M. from Memorial Day to September 15. Tours by appointment.

🚗 On the west side of Crow Valley Road, about 5 miles north of the intersection with Deer Harbor Road. Stop by Crow Valley Pottery at 2274 Orcas Road for information about the school.

Your kids will find it hard to picture themselves in this setting. The Crow Valley School, built in 1888, was for 20 years the place where Orcas youngsters learned their three R's. On display are photographs and other memorabilia from school days on Orcas Island.

Fourth of July Parade

Orcas Island people really know how to have fun. Join them in their community Fourth of July Parade at Eastsound to see them really kick up their heels with good old-fashioned festivities. It's a family event with zany costumes, bands, and that Fourth of July standby—piles of food. Concerts, boat races, and other fun events, underway all day long, are capped off by an evening fireworks display.

The Funhouse Discovery Center

30 Pea Patch Lane; Eastsound, WA 98245. Phone: (360) 376-7177; email: *info@thefunhouse.org*; web site: *thefunhouse.org*

HOURS: Weekdays 3 P.M. to 6 P.M., Saturday 10 A.M. to 3 P.M.

ENTRANCE FEES: 1-day: $5 for individual $20 for family; 3-day: $10 for individual $40 family; annual membership $35 for individual $100 for family.

You'll find a wealth of cool stuff housed in the large, two-story building north of Eastsound at the intersection of North Beach Road and Enchanted Forest Road. There are things here to give both the mind and body a workout. Your family will want to return again and again.

Although The Funhouse is largely geared to kids, grownups will delight in many of the exhibits, too. Brain-teasers and optical illusions baffle and fascinate. There is a climbing wall (children only), softball-pitching cage with an electronic umpire, and an arts and crafts center. A planetarium and other science-oriented exhibits introduce the wonders of the universe. There is internet access, gaming computers,

ORCAS ISLAND
Events & Attractions

and a sound studio. An outside play area with swings, merry-go-round, and tepee offers safe fun for the younger set.

The Lambiel Museum

668 Olga Road; Eastsound, WA 98245. Phone: (360) 3767-4544; web site: *lambielmuseum.com*

HOURS: Tours by appointment only. $10 fee.

🚗 From Eastsound drive east on Crescent Beach Drive to a T-intersection. Turn right (south) onto Olga Road, and the sign for the museum is on the right in about ¼ mile.

Begun more than 20 years ago as a small private collection, this eclectic museum is a work forever in progress. It holds a treasury of Persian rugs, replicas of Egyptian and Greek temples, a grotto containing a labyrinth of surprises, and an array of art created in the San Juan Islands. Multi-colored concrete in the museum's driveway depicts marine life of the area. Two-hour guided tours are led by the owner, Leo Lambiel.

Opening Day of Boating Season

The first Saturday in May the Orcas Island Yacht Club sponsors festivities kicking off the beginning of yachting season. Boats are decorated for display and competition in the yacht parade held on West Sound. Sailboat races and all-around parties complete the gala event.

Orcas Farmers Market

Eastsound Village Square

HOURS: 10 A.M. to 3 P.M.

Every Saturday from May through September, stands are set up in Village Square offering fresh locally grown produce and plants, handmade soaps, textiles, baskets, jewelry, candles, pottery, and much more.

Orcas Island Historical Museum

161 North Beach Road, P.O. Box 134; Eastsound, WA 98245. Phone: (360) 376-4849; email: *orcasmuseum@rockisland.com*; web site: *orcasisland.org/~history*

HOURS: Tuesday through Sunday 1 P.M. to 3 P.M.; from Memorial Day weekend through Labor Day Friday 10 A.M. to 3 P.M. Other times and quiet season by appointment.

🚗 On North Beach Road between Main and A Streets.

Here's a real time-travel adventure. These six linked log cabins were moved to their centrally located site in Eastsound from their original locations on the island. Inside you'll discover what it was like to live on the island in the "good old days." There are household goods, tools, weapons, arrowheads, and all manner of other pioneer memorabilia, as well as photographs of early times on the island.

The collection of Native American artifacts is exceptionally fine. One wall is covered with Chinese coolie hats collected during the time when Asians were illegally smuggled through San Juan waters. An outside shed houses machinery that was used to farm the island long ago.

In November 2006 the museum broke ground for a new building to house offices, archives, storage, and exhibit preparation. The new building will permit archives to be better preserved, and more rotating exhibits to be staged.

Orcas Island Skatepark

Buck Park, Mount Baker Road

The skatepark on Orcas Island would do any city proud. The 20,000-square-foot facilitiy is one of the best in the Northwest, and by any kid's judgement, is awesome, with bowls to match nearly every skater's skill.

Helmets are required. Helmets and boards can be rented from the Orcas Island Board Shop in nearby Eastsound. The park is on Mount Baker Road, north of Eastsound, next to the tennis courts.

Orcas Theater and Community Center

917 Mount Baker Road, P.O. Box 567; Eastsound, WA 98245. Phone: (360) 376-2281; fax: (360) 376-6822; email: *info@orcascenter.org*; web site: *orcascenter.org*

🚗 From Eastsound, drive north on North Beach Road to its intersection with Mount Baker Road. The community center is on the right, in a short distance. Spot the huge metal orca whale on the lawn in front of the center and you will know you are there.

Whether it's a solo recital by a renowned flutist, a presentation of one-act plays by the local theater group, a barbershop quartet concert, or a children's marionette show, you will be amazed at what might be going on at the Orcas Center. The theater presentations are always first rate, whether the artists are local folks or people who come from off-island. The Orcas Island theatrical and choral groups are loaded with talent, and work hard at their craft.

Check the local newspaper to find out what's currently going on, or you might find it posted on the bulletin board at Templins Center. See also Shopping, page 177.

ON-ISLAND TRANSPORTATION

Dolphin Bay Bicycles

Orcas Landing, P.O. Box 1346; Orcas Island, WA 98245. Phone: (360) 376-4157 or (360) 376-6734; email: *dolphin@rockisland.com*; web site: *rockisland.com/~dolphin*

SUMMER RATES: Full day $30, 3-days $70, full week $100.

Avoid the cost and frustrating waits of auto travel to Orcas Island—just leave your car in Anacortes and pick up a bicycle two blocks from the Orcas ferry landing. It's a pedal of 8 miles to Deer Harbor or Eastsound, 16 miles to the entrance of Moran State Park, and 18 miles to Olga. Rates vary by duration of rental; helmets are provided free, and racks and touring packs can be rented. Phone reservations are accepted 48 hours in advance.

ORCAS SLAND
On-Island Transportation

Magic Air Tours

P.O. Box 223; Eastsound, WA 98245. Phone: (800) 376-1929 or (360) 376-2733; email: *rod@ magicair.com*; web site: *magicair.com*

SUMMER RATES: Two persons share the front cockpit for $295.

Shades of the Red Baron! An open cockpit TravelAir biplane makes scenic tours out of Eastsound Airport on Orcas Island, providing travelers with a unique way of becoming acquainted with the many islands and channels of the San Juans. Hand me my goggles and scarf!

Marina Bicycle Rentals

BellPort Deer Harbor Marina; 5164 Deer Harbor Road, P.O. Box 344; Deer Harbor, WA 98243. Phone: (360) 376-3037; fax: (360) 376-6091; email: *deerharbor@rockisland.com*; web site: *deerharbormarina.com*

The BellPort Deer Harbor Marina offers bicycle rentals. It's especially handy if you come in by boat and want to tour the islands.

Orcas Island Shuttle

P.O. Box 208; Orcas, WA 98280. Phone: (360) 376-7433; email: *email@orcasislandshuttle.com*; web site: *orcasislandshuttle.com*

Orcas Island Shuttle offers a combination of public bus, taxi, charter, and rental car services. The bus runs from mid-May to mid-September from the ferry landing to numerous Orcas Island point. They make four trips daily from 8 A.M. to 3:50 P.M., plus a noon run from Eastsound to Rosario Resort.

They also operate a taxi service 24 hours a day, and chartered vehicle service at hourly rates. Mid-size, full-size, mini-van, and SUV rental cars are available.

Orcas Island Taxi

P.O. Box 1251; Eastsound, WA 98245. Phone: (800) 942-1926, or (360) 376-8294; cell: (360) 472-0364; email: *dan@orcastasi.com*; web site: *worcastaxi.com*

Taxi service is on call 24 hours a day to pick you up from any location on Orcas Island and take you where you want to go.

Orcas Mopeds

65 Orcas Hill Road, P.O. Box 265; Orcas, WA 98280. Phone: (360) 376-5266; email: *orcasmopeds@hotmail.com*; web site: *orcasmopeds.com*

SUMMER RATES: Mopeds $20 per hour, $50 per day plus fuel; scootcars $40 per hour, $100 per day plus fuel; bicycles $7 per hour, $35 per day $80 for 3 days.
HOURS: Daily 9 A.M. to 7 P.M.

Orcas Moped, which is located in the building at the head of the ferry lanes, offers a range of rentals. Available are bikes, scootcars, and mopeds. They are also a rental car agent for M & W Autos of Friday Harbor. Bicycles may be taken to other islands.

Orcas Rental Cars

Orcas Landing; Orcas, WA 98280. Phone: (360) 376-7368

Just uphill from the ferry landing, within easy walking distance, Orcas Rental Cars has ten vehicles for rent. Advanced reservations are recommended.

Wildlife Cycles

350 North Beach Road, P.O. Box 1048; Eastsound, WA 98245. Phone: (360) 376-4708; email: *wildlifecycles@rockisland.com*; web site: *wildlifecycles.com*

SUMMER RATES: $7.50 to $10 per hour, $30 to $40 full day, $70 to $90 for 3 days, $105 to 160 for a week.

Begin your bicycle tour of Orcas Island from Eastsound, the hub of the island. This bicycle rental shop is on North Beach Road, north of A Street in Eastsound. It's open daily during summer months. Hours are reduced during the quiet season.

BOAT & KAYAK TOURS, CRUISES & CHARTERS

Amante Sail Tours

P.O. Box 51; Deer Harbor, WA 98243. Phone: (360) 376-4231.

SUMMER RATES: Day sails $35 per person, overnight sails $125 per person, 4-person minimum.

You can either assist as crew, or just relax and enjoy a sail aboard the 33-foot racing sloop *Amante*. Skippered half-day, day, or overnight trips leave from Deer Harbor on Orcas Island. Overnight sails for four to six guests include dinner and a continental breakfast.

Body Boat Blade International

310 Prune Alley, P.O. Box 1487; Eastsound, WA 98245. Phone: (360) 376-5388; fax: (360) 376-5388; cell: (360) 472-0252 or (360) 472-0261; email: *info@bodyboatblade.com*; web site: *bodyboatblade.com*

SUMMER RATES: Single kayak $50 for the first day, $25 for each additional day; wetsuits $15 per day. Major credit cards accepted.

Classes from three hours long to a five-day camp are provided by British Canoe Union (BCU) certified instructors. Also offered are instruction-oriented tours and trips, guide services, expeditions, equipment rental, books, and sales of used boats and equipment. Go back home with a new skill added to your repertoire.

Crescent Beach Kayaks

239 Crescent Beach Drive; Eastsound, WA 98245. Phone: (360) 376-2464; email: *info@crescentbeachkayaks.com*; web site: *crescentbeachkayaks.com*

Both double and single kayaks are available for rent from this business at the head of East Sound, immediately across the road from Crescent Beach. If you don't have kayaking experience they will provide basic instructions before you set out. Paddle along the protected shoreline of East Sound to view a startling variety of underwater life, marine mammals, and birds.

Deer Harbor Charters

5164 Deer Harbor Road, P.O. Box 303; Deer Harbor, WA 98243. Phone: (800) 544-5758 or (360) 376-5989; email: *charter@rockisland.com*; web site: *deerharborcharters.com*

SUMMER RATES: Adults $59, children under 14 $35; quiet season $49 and $32. Discounts for weddings, school groups, 10 or more, and seniors.

Operating out of BellPort Deer Harbor Marina, this company takes you into channels between the San Juan Islands to spot eagles perched in shoreline snags, seals and sea lions hauled out on rocky beaches, or, with luck, orca whales, porpoises, or minke whales. One of their two boats, the 36-foot *Pelagic*, or the larger *Squito* make two excursions daily, at 9:30 A.M. and 2:00 P.M. from both Deer Harbor and Rosario Resort.

Emerald Isle Sailing Charters

5164 Deer Harbor Road, P.O. Box 586; Deer Harbor, WA 98243. Phone: (800) 714-6611 or (360) 376-3472; cell: (360) 317-5332; email: *charters@emeraldislesailing.com*; web site: *emeraldislesailing.com*

SUMMER RATES: San Juans: 3 days $895 per person. San Juans and Gulf Islands: 6 days $1395.

Emerald Isle provides skippered charters with a crew of three on the 54-foot sailing yacht *Na'walak*. Accommodations include space for six passengers in four private staterooms, and use of two single kayaks and a dinghy for exploring. Gourmet meals are prepared for you. Other tours the company offers range as far north as Alaska.

Island Hoppers, Inc., Custom Charters

5164 Deer Harbor Road, P.O. Box 206; Deer Harbor, WA 98243. Phone: (360) 376-7278, (360) 376-5188, (360) 376-5335; web site: *islandhoppersinc.com*

Custom charters are the mainstay of Island Hoppers. They have a 27-foot Sea Sport that can take six persons, rain or shine to any of the San Juan Islands, and weather permitting, a 20-foot, six-passenger jet boat. They also have access to other vessels up to 50 feet for more passengers, or for longer trips. They will do island pick-ups and drop-offs, or charter a boat for a party. Major credit cards accepted.

The Morning Star

149 Orcas Road; Eastsound, WA 98245. Phone: (360) 376-2099; email: *Morningstar@ orcascharters.com*; web site: *orcascharters.com*

SUMMER RATES: 2 hours $350 per group, 3 hours $450, 4 hours $550, all day $1200.

The *Morning Star* is a Chesapeake "Bugeye" 56-foot ketch that offers skippered charters out of Rosario Resort. Built entirely of yellow cedar, and carrying 1064 square feet of sail when under full sail, the boat is a thrill to experience. She is a boat whose beauty more than matches her island surroundings. The captain, an ordained minister, has performed many weddings aboard, and will for you, if you wish.

North Shore Charters

P.O. Box 316; Eastsound, WA 98245. Phone: (360) 375-4855; email: *marty@sanjuancruises.net*; web site: *sanjuancruises.net*

With either of two boats, the *Rock Hopper* a 27-foot custom-built landing craft, or the *Sally J*, a 30-foot Northstar pilothouse cruiser, you can charter trips from the north shore of Orcas to marine state parks on Sucia, Matia, and Patos Islands, or take sightseeing tours on Presidents Channel. Camping and kayaking drop offs and pick ups are available, as are fishing charters. Both vessels accommodate six passengers.

Northwest Classic Daysailing

Deer Harbor, WA 98243. Phone: (360) 376-5581; email: *wardfay@rockisland.com*; web site: *classicdaysails.com*

SUMMER RATES: Adult $60, child $45, $50 per hour after 4 hours.

Take an afternoon, three-hour skippered cruise on the classic Blanchard 33 sloop *Aura*. Trips are between 1 P.M. and 4 P.M. If you'd like, you probably can take the helm for awhile. Blanchards are frequently raced, so if you get the wind for it, and if you want, she'll go at a nice clip. For something really special, arrange for a sunset sail. You can charter for a group as small as two or as large as six.

Orcas Boat Rentals

5164 Deer Harbor Road, P.O. Box 272; Deer Harbor, WA 92843. Phone: (360) 376-7616; email: *moose@interisland.net*; web site: *orcasboats.com*

GROUP SUMMER RATES: $125 to $200 for 4 hours, $175 to $275 for 8 hours, depending on boat. Tax and fuel are additional. Paddleboats $25 for 1 hour, $15 per additional hour.

This firm rents both power boats and sailboats out of the BellPort Deer Harbor Marina—just the thing for a day or afternoon of exploring the harbor, Wasp Channel, and nearby marine state park islands. Boats available include a J/24 sailboat (24 feet, carries 7 persons), 16-foot runabout powered by 50-hp outboard engines that carries up to six persons, and 14-foot, four-person aluminum Duroboat with 15-hp outboard. They also offer skippered charters.

For an unusual bit of fun, rent a paddleboat for duck-level exploring of the protected waters of Deer Harbor.

Orcas Island Eclipse Charters

P.O. Box 353; Orcas, WA 98290. Phone: (800) 376-6566 or (360) 376-6566; fax: (360) 376-4780; web site: *orcasislandwhales.com*

SUMMER RATES: Adult $59, child $35.

Come aboard the 56-foot *Orcas Express* for four-hour cruises among the San Juan Islands. Depart From the ferry landing, stop at marine state parks for a picnic lunch, spot marine mammals and birds, drop a line for bottomfish, or just sightsee. The boat carries up to 64 passengers; four persons are the minimum. All gear and bait are provided, the vessel is equipped with a hydrophone for listening to whales, and a professional naturalist guides trips.

Orcas Island Kayaks

Lieber Haven Resort and Marina, 1945 Obstruction Pass Road; Olga, WA 98279. Phone: (360) 376-2472; web site: *orcasislandkayaks.com*

SUMMER RATES: $10 to $35 per hour.

Obstruction Pass is a great place to begin your kayak adventure. This business, operating out of Lieber Haven Resort, rents single, double, and triple kayaks by the hour, half-day, or full day (8 A.M. to 8 P.M.). Rowboats are also available.

Orcas Island Sailing

P.O. Box 1626; Eastsound, WA 98245. Phone: (360) 376-2113; cell: (360) 310-0100; fax: (360) 376-7543; email: *info@orcassailing.com*; web site: *orcassailing.com*

SUMMER RATES: Skippered day-cruises: $260 for 3 to 4 hours, $410 for all day. Bareboat charters: Half-day $120 to $160, full-day $220 to $260, 3-days or more $200 per day.

Skippered excursions, learn-to-sail cruises, or bareboat charters can be had on any of the boats this firm offers. Their fleet includes an 18-foot, outboard-powered Cape Dory Typhoon, a 21-foot Luders with no engine, and a 26-foot, outboard-powered Pearson Commander.

Orcas Outdoors

Orcas Landing; The Boardwalk, P.O. Box 284; Orcas, WA 98280. Phone: (360) 376-4611, (360) 379-2971; email: *info@orcasoutdoors.com*; web site: *orcasoutdoors.com*

SUMMER RATES: 1- to 3-hour trips $35 to $55 per person; 6 hours $90 per person; overnight, including camping on islands and hiking $299 per person; multi-day $499.

Both guided tours and kayak rentals are available at this convenient location a few hundred feet from the Orcas ferry landing. Tours depart from a private dock west of the ferry slip. Short tours are offered seven days a week. Overnight tours include all kayaking and camping gear, food, and camping fees.

Osprey Tours

P.O. Box 580; Eastsound, WA 98245. Phone: (360) 376-3677; email: *info@ospreytours.com*; web site: *ospreytours.com*

SUMMER RATES: 1 hour $45, half day $75, full day $120, overnight $200, umiak $20 per hour. Kayak launch $10.

Here's a tour where you'll enjoy Native traditions along with the fun of kayaking. Excursions out of Bartwood Lodge, on the north side of Orcas Island, and the beach at The Right Place Pottery, on the west side of the island, use traditionally built, Aleutian-style kayaks for half-day and full-day trips. Osprey's custom-designed, handmade kayaks have wooden frames covered with a tough nylon and hypolon skin, and are extremely light, comfortable, and stable—ideal for beginners.

Osprey also has umiaks, a bathtub-shaped Native canoe that holds six paddlers. These are often at the dock just west of the ferry terminal. Four to six people can rent one and paddle around Harney Channel for an hour—something to do during a long ferry wait. Kayakers walking off the ferry can also launch from this dock, for a fee, and there is some storage space available for their unneeded gear.

The company also sells custom-made kayaks and umiaks.

Sharon L. Charters

P.O. Box 10; Orcas, WA 98280. Phone: (360) 376-4305; email: *sharonl@rockisland.com*

Sail on the classic gaff-rigged schooner *Sharon L*—she's a beauty. A three-hour or longer cruise can be scheduled to meet your individual needs. Skipper Miles McCoy has been sailing local waters for more than 40 years. Who better to show you all the sights?

Shearwater Adventures, Inc.

Doty's Marketplace; 138 North Beach Road, P.O. Box 787; Eastsound, WA 98245. Phone: (360) 376-4699; fax: (360) 376-2005; email: *info@shearwaterkayaks.com*; web site: *shearwaterkayaks.com*

RATES: 3-hour tour $55 per person, full day $85, call for multi-day price quotes.

Shearwater Adventures has offered kayak trips in the San Juan Islands for more than 15 years. Operating out of Rosario Resort, BellPort Deer Harbor Marina, and Doe Bay Resort, they have half-day, full-day, or multiday tours in the islands. Overnight trips include camping on remote islands. Some trips and classes are for women, and are led and taught by women. No experience is necessary; all kayaks are safe, stable, two-person models. You'll be trained in basic paddling techniques and safety before the trip begins.

If you want to sharpen your skills, classes in basic and intermediate-level kayaking are offered. Their three-day advanced first-aid class is geared specifically to people who spend a lot of time outdoors and around the water. Natural history kayak seminars, some of which are offered through the North Cascades Institute, are focused on the unique environment.

Whale Spirit Adventures

P.O. Box 282; Orcas, WA 98280. Phone: (800) 376-8018 or (360) 376-5052; email: *orcashaman@webtv.com*; web site: *nwwhalewatchers.org/whalespirit*

Hearts Desire, a 42-foot wooden trawler, can take up to six guests for a 5½- to 6½-hour nature tour. The boat has a 16-foot heated salon with galley. Tours sail from the West Sound county dock between 10 A.M. and noon. Captain Azuriel Mayo has 21 years of sailing experience and nine years of whalewatching experience. He also plays the flute for the whales' (and your) enjoyment.

ORCAS ISLAND
Boat & Kayak Tours & Charters

MARINAS, LAUNCH RAMPS & PUT-INS

BellPort Deer Harbor Marina &

5164 Deer Harbor Road, P.O. Box 344; Deer Harbor, WA 98243. Phone: (360) 376-3037; fax: (360) 376-6091; VHF channel 78A; email: *deerharbor@rockisland.com*; web site: *deerharbormarina.com*

FACILITIES: 75 guest slips with power and water, restroom with showers, coin-operated laundry, fuel (gas, diesel, kerosene, butane, propane, premix, alcohol), pumpout station, kayak put-in.

BellPort Deer Harbor Marina, located near the head of Deer Harbor offers guest moorage in a spanking new, modern facility. You'll find restrooms and coin-op showers, coin-operated laundry, bicycle rentals, and a grocery/deli (which carries bait) on the dock. All facilities are disabled accessible. A small lawn area behind the post office with picnic tables is available for groups up to thirty. Contact the dock staff for arrangements. Kayaks can be launched from the beach at the marina for a $5 parking fee.

Several boat charter and rental outfits and wildlife tours operate out of here, as well as businesses that offer kayak rentals. The Barge Gift Shop, appropriately on a barge at the head of the docks, has sportswear, fishing gear, books, crafts, toys, and other items.

Deer Harbor Boatworks

155 Channel Road; Deer Harbor, WA 98243. Phone: (360) 376-4056

Located at the far north end of Deer Harbor, the Boatworks offers haul-out, boat repairs, parts, and a small single-lane ramp, usable only at high tides. Parking in the vicinity is very limited.

Obstruction Pass Boat Launch

The Obstruction Pass launch ramp provides quick access to kayakers' and anglers' favorite waters around the south and east side of Orcas Island. To reach the ramp from Eastsound, drive east, following Crescent Beach Drive and then Olga Road through Moran State Park. Turn north on Point Lawrence Road, and in ½ mile turn south on Obstruction Pass Road. Follow this road for 2 miles to a parking lot sitting above a county dock and single-lane launch ramp.

Olga Community Dock

4th Street and Olga Road; Olga, WA 98279.

FACILITIES: Dock with float (removed in winter), guest moorage, toilet, drinking water

Kayaks and other hand-carried boats can be carried down the ramp and put in at the Olga dock. The dock provides quick access to East Sound and Obstruction Pass.

Osprey Tours

P.O. Box 580; Eastsound, WA 98245. Phone: (360) 376-3677; email: *info@ospreytours.com*; web site: *ospreytours.com*

At Orcas Landing, next to the ferry landing, kayakers can launch their paddlecraft from the dock used by Osprey Tours, for a fee. There is a little storage space available for their gear.

Rosario Resort and Spa

1400 Rosario Road; Eastsound, WA 98245-2222. Phone: (800) 562-8820 or (360) 376-2222; VHF channel 78A; email: *info@rosarioresort.com*; web site: *rosario.rockresorts.com*

FACILITIES: Guest slips with power and water, restrooms, showers, coin-operated laundry, mooring buoys, seaplane float, fuel (gas, diesel).

Rosario Resort, on East Sound's Cascade Bay, has a small marina with 15 guest slips with power and water, and numerous mooring buoys offshore. There is a charge for use of mooring buoys for more than six hours. Ashore, you'll find groceries, restaurants, and the full amenities of the historic resort. Boaters are offered a landing package that permits use of the pools and spa. See also Lodging: page 153–154.

West Beach Resort

190 Waterfront Way; Eastsound, WA 98245. Phone: (360) 376-2240; email: *vacation@ westbeachresort.com*; web site: *westbeachresort.com*

FACILITIES: Moorage on floating dock or buoys, restrooms, showers, gas, boat launch ramp.

The only marina on the northwest side of Orcas has floating docks, buoys, and dry storage, as well as a boat launch ramp. Gas, fresh water (not for filling holding tanks), and a fish cleaning station are located on the pier, as well as a dinghy landing area for buoy-moored or anchored boats. No electric service is available on the floats. Groceries are available on shore. Also see Lodging, page 159–160, and Parks & Campgrounds, page 197.

West Sound Marina

P.O. Box 119; Orcas WA 98280. Phone: (360) 376-2314; fax: (360) 376-4634; VHF channel 16; web site: *nwboat.com/westsound*

HOURS: Monday to Friday 8 A.M. to 4: 45 P.M.; Saturday 10 A.M. to 3 P.M.; summers, Sunday 10 A.M. to 3 P.M.

FACILITIES: Some limited moorage with power and water, restrooms, showers, fuel (gas, diesel, kerosene, alcohol), pumpout station.

This full-service marina, midway up the west shore of West Sound, provides permanent moorage plus a limited amount of guest moorage on a 250-foot float on the south side of the marina. Marine facilities include a chandlery, haulouts to 30 tons, and a complete line of maintenance and repair services. West Sound Café, is within walking distance of the marina. See Restaurants page 168–169.

ORCAS SLAND
Marinas & Launch Ramps

PARKS & CAMPGROUNDS

Doe Bay Resort and Retreat Center ⋔

107 Doe Bay Road; P.O. Box 437; Olga, WA 98279. Phone: (360) 376-2291; fax: (360) 376-5809; email: *info@doebay.com*; web site: *doebay.com*

FACILITIES: 14 tent sites some with fire rings and picnic tables, 5 RV sites, 5 yurts, restrooms, showers, guest kitchen (stove, refrigerator, and cookware), hot tubs and sauna (clothing optional), massage available, children's play equipment, convenience store, Doe Bay Art Café (breakfast, lunch and dinner; vegetarian and seafood specialties), volleyball courts, 2 beaches, picnicking, trails, scuba diving, guided kayak trips. Some campsite reservations available.

SUMMER RATES: Campsites $30 per night, $5 surcharge on Friday and Saturday in summer, yurts $70 per night. Major credit cards accepted.

🚍 From Eastsound, drive east, following Crescent Beach Drive and then Olga Road and Point Lawrence Road for 18 miles to Doe Bay.

For those willing to bypass more civilized cabins for a simple campsite, Doe Bay Resort provides tent sites, RV sites, and yurts. Some tent sites are on a large lawn with picnic benches. Numerous smaller campsites are atop the wooded rocky bluff on the east side of the small cove jutting into the main resort area. Campsites are Spartan—most are just a flat spot in the brush, possibly with a fire ring. Views overlook the cove and the main portion of the resort. Yurts are scattered among the campsites, and a few are at other spots on the grounds.

Another camping area uphill from the resort's spa offers a few sites in the woods with an occasional picnic table and another broad, open field for pick-your-spot camping. Restrooms in this area have showers and a bathtub. The campsite fee permits you to use the showers, hot tubs, and sauna. (Clothing is optional in the tubs and sauna.)

The company store carries some basic groceries. See also Lodging, page 132.

Moran State Park ⋔

Star Route 22; Eastsound, WA 98245. Phone: (360) 376-2326, (360) 376-6173 (Camp Moran ELC). Call (888) 226-7688 for reservations; web site: *parks.wa.gov*

FACILITIES: 136 standard campsites, 15 primitive campsites, 2-bedroom vacation house, 54 picnic sites, 5 kitchen shelters, restrooms, vault toilets, trailer dump station, interpretive displays, 2 bathhouses, 2 boat launch ramps (on lakes), 2 docks with boat rentals, swimming areas, children's play equipment, 45 miles of trail (11 miles open to mountain bikes, 6 miles open to horses), 2½ miles of unimproved road, nature trail, Environmental Learning Center. Reservations necessary in summer. Some trails closed or seasonally closed to mountain bikes and horses.

🚍 From the Orcas ferry landing, follow Orcas Road north to Eastsound, and continue east, following Crescent Beach Drive and Olga Road south to the park, a total distance of 13 miles.

Moran, Washington's fourth largest state park, overflows with outdoor recreational activities: camping, picnicking, boating, paddling, sailing, swimming, fishing, bicycling, hiking, horseback riding, and birdwatching. It is one of the most popular

A 50-foot-high tower provides high views of the San Juan Islands from the top of Mount Constitution, in Moran State Park.

destinations in the San Juan Islands, and the park's campsites are nearly always full throughout the summer. Campsite reservations are required between Memorial Day and Labor Day.

The park tops out at 2407-foot-high Mount Constitution, the highest point in the San Juan Islands. You can reach the mountain summit via a steep, winding (but well-paved) road that affords spectacular viewpoints en route. Because of the steep climb and tight curves, RV trailers are not recommended, but other vehicles will have no problems.

At the summit, near the edge of a sheer cliff that breaks from the east face, are incomparable views across Rosario Strait and the Strait of Georgia to the massive ice cone of Mount Baker and the mountains of the Canadian Coast Range. Climb the stairs of the picturesque stone tower atop the mountain, built by the CCC in 1936 to mimic fortifications found in the Russian Caucasus Mountains. The tower offers even broader views of all of the waterways and the many islands of the archipelago. A display identifies surrounding points of interest.

Moran contains five crystal-clear lakes. The second largest is Cascade Lake (with adjoining Rosario Lagoon). The lake, originally much smaller and more shallow, grew to its present size with the damming of its outlet to create a hydroelectric power source for Robert Moran's estate, Rosario, now Rosario Resort. Three of the island's four campgrounds and its primary day-use area are along the shore of the lake. Here also are a swimming beach, paddleboat rentals, and an Environmental Learning Center.

ORCAS SLAND
Parks & Campgrounds

The largest lake in the park, Mountain Lake, lies upstream and up the road in a forested pocket between Mounts Constitution and Picket. It, too, has camping and boat rentals. Cascade Creek, which connects the two lakes, boasts several delightful waterfalls that can be reached via short trails. The largest of these, Cascade Falls, is spectacular in spring and early summer. The park's other three lakes, Summit and the pair of Twin Lakes, are smaller, and require short to moderate hikes to reach.

The heavily wooded park has nearly 50 miles of trails and unimproved roads that offer hikes through beautiful, quiet forests, some of magnificent old cedar, some of tall, stately hemlock, others of densely packed lodgepole pine. Portions of these trails are open to mountain bicycle use and horses, and cyclists and horseback riders may use other sections only during certain periods of the year. Check with the park for current restrictions

Obstruction Pass State Park ⛺

Trailhead Road, Star Route 22; Eastsound, WA 98245. Phone: (360) 376-2326; web site: *parks. wa.gov*

FACILITIES: 9 campsites, Cascadia Marine Trail campsite, 3 mooring buoys, picnic tables, fireplaces, latrines, ½ mile hiking trail. No water.

🚗 From Eastsound, drive east, following Crescent Beach Drive and then Olga Road. At the Olga intersection, turn left on Point Lawrence Road, and in ½ mile turn right onto Obstruction Pass Road. In another mile, take another right onto Trailhead Road (gravel), which is signed to Obstruction Pass State Park. Follow this road to the parking area at its end. Overnight camping is not permitted in the parking lot. By boat, the park is 1 nautical mile south of Olga on East Sound, and ½ nautical mile west of the boat ramp on Obstruction Pass.

Backpack in or boat in to this little state park on the southeast side of Orcas Island. The primitive campground, on a point of land facing on Obstruction Pass, is reached by a nearly level ½-mile trail. The park makes a nice day hike, even if you don't plan to stay overnight.

Turtleback Mountain Preserve

CONTACT: San Juan Preservation Trust; P.O. Box 327; Lopez Island, WA 98261; phone: (360) 468-3202. Or San Juan County Land Bank (360) 378-4402; email: info@sjpt.org, web site: sjpt.org/turtleback.php. For public access map: sjpt.org/pdf/driving_turtleback.pdf

FACILITIES: 1575-acre park. Approximately 6½ miles of trails for pedestrian use only. No fires, no camping, no hunting, dogs must be leashed. No trash containers—please take garbage home with you.

🚗 *North Entrance:* From the ferry, follow Orcas Road north for 3½ miles to the intersection with Nordstrom Lane. Turn left (west) and follow Nordstrom Lane for ½ mile to the intersection with Crow Valley Road and turn right (north) on it. Follow Crow Valley Road for 1¾ miles. The entrance is an unmarked gravel road on the left, opposite a yellow house, just before reaching the Crow Valley Schoolhouse. *South Entrance:* From the ferry drive 2½ miles north on Orcas Road, and then turn left (west) on Deer Harbor Road. Follow Deer Harbor Road through West Sound to the intersection with Wild Rose Lane, in 2½ miles. Turn right (north) onto Wild Rose Lane; parking is on the right, at the top of the field.

Seen from a distance, Turtleback Mountain resembles the head and shell of a turtle. The photo is from the ferry, near Pole Pass. Crane Island is in the center foreground, Orcas Knob is the turtle's "head" on the left.

Turtleback Mountain was acquired for a preserve in what is believed to be the largest fund raising effort in local history. The property, threatened with real estate development, has been saved as a nature preserve and day-use public recreation area.

The mountain, which tops out at 1519 feet, includes wetlands, forests, cliffs, and grassy balds. About 6½ miles of trails and abandoned roads circle the mountain and reach stunning viewpoints. Because of its largely unspoiled nature, it promises to be a recreational, ecological, and geological treasure for generations to come.

And the name? The mountain consists of a long, rounded mass, with a distinct large knob (Ship Peak) on the south. From many vantages on the island and in the water it resembles a turtle, with the mass being the shell, and the knob being the turtle's head. From some views, 1050-foot-high Orcas Knob forms the head.

West Beach Resort ⌂

190 Waterfront Way; Eastsound, WA 98245. Phone: (877) 937-8224 or (360) 376-2240; email: *vacation@westbeachresort.com*; web site: *westbeachresort.com*

FACILITIES: 21 tent sites, 19 RV sites with power, restrooms, showers, coin-operated laundry, boat launch ramp, groceries, children's play equipment. Reservations accepted.

🚗 From the Orcas ferry landing, drive north on Orcas Road for 2½ miles to the intersection with Deer Harbor Road. Turn left onto Deer Harbor Road, drive 1 mile, and at a T-intersection, go north on Crow Valley Road. In 3½ miles, turn on West Beach Road, which heads west, and then north. As the road makes another right turn at Enchanted Forest Road, the signed side road to West Beach goes left.

This popular resort, on a broad bay facing President Channel, offers camping as part of its extensive recreation package. A large, open lawn atop a bluff holds a series of staked-out campsites, each with power, water, and sewer hookups. Nearby are additional sites, but without hookups, for either RV or tent camping.

For kids, there's an assortment of playground equipment and the wonderful sandy beach below. The resort has a small grocery store, cabins, a dock, and a variety of marine rentals and supplies. See also Lodging, pages 159–160.

SAN JUAN ISLAND
WHALES, HISTORY & RACING ZUCCHINIS

SAN JUAN ISLAND IS THE BIG APPLE—Where It's Happening—in the San Juans. OK, so that's a relative thing here in the islands, where the pace rarely quickens beyond a casual mosey. But it's big enough. It boasts a town with diversified stores and gourmet restaurants, it has fascinating historical parks and museums, and it has a golf tournament, boat races, and other events.

Canadians tend to be most familiar with San Juan Island, rather than Orcas or Lopez, because two U.S. Customs check-in sites for boaters are at Friday Harbor and Roche Harbor. During Dominion Day and other Canadian holidays, you'll see an exceptional number of maple leaf ensigns at the docks. Some Canadian and Yankee friends schedule boat rendezvous here.

Friday Harbor, on the east side of San Juan Island, is the major center of commerce. It's the county seat and the only incorporated town in the county. (All of the San Juan Islands constitute San Juan County.) The group of buildings on your right as the ferry enters the harbor are the University of Washington's Friday Harbor labs, a marine research center where faculty and students from the University of Washington and other universities take part in studies of San Juan marine life.

The Friday Harbor business district covers about eight square blocks spreading out from the ferry landing. It's easy to see it all on foot. If you arrive by car, the attendant will direct you to take a right turn off the ferry, and then another quick left turn. You'll be on Spring Street, the main drag.

There's no hokey, planned, "Olde Tyme" ambiance to Friday Harbor; it just grew, and it's terrific! The street layout is haphazard, but that's part of the fun. Little alleys and backstreets lead to great stores tucked in the lower levels or backsides of others. Many businesses are found in remodeled storefronts or old historic homes. Cannery Landing, adjacent to the ferry landing, once housed a fish cannery; in its current reincarnation it holds small shops and offices.

There are celebrations here, too, throughout the summer. Early June brings the Artist's Studio Open House, the Pig War Barbecue is part of Fourth of July festivities. (Where else can you celebrate an historic pig by eating a...uh...pig?) Mid-August heralds the county fair where you can cheer for your favorite zucchini as their owners race their wheeled vegetables down a track. The Shaw Island Classic Sail Race is in August.

Once you leave Friday Harbor, there is rolling farmland and forested hills. In spring, wildflowers paint roadsides with an exuberance of color. Sheep, cattle, horses, llamas, and alpacas graze in velvet pastures, and if you're watchful, you'll spot hawks and eagles soaring overhead or perched in trees. For spectacular beauty, drive or

California poppies brighten a viewpoint on San Juan Island's Westside Road.   199

bicycle along West Side Road, south of Lime Kiln State Park. It's the most scenically splendid road in all the islands, as it winds along the cliffs above Haro Strait.

Other than at Friday Harbor, the only gathering of stores and services on San Juan Island is at Roche Harbor, where there is a small general store, a few shops, and a gas pump—all part of the large resort that is centered on the bay. Numerous resorts and bed and breakfast inns are scattered around the island.

You can't visit the San Juans without realizing orca whales are a very big deal here. Although these whales (also known as killer whales) range throughout the Northern Hemisphere, three pods, or family groups, of orca spend their summers off the islands. Because of this, in 1976 the Orca Survey, sponsored by the Moclips Cetological Society, began a study of their food-gathering habits, communication, and social behavior in the San Juans. By 1980, public interest in whales in general, and orcas in particular, triggered the expansion of the survey beyond its research mission. The organization acquired a building in Friday Harbor, and volunteers converted the top floor into a museum—the only one of its kind in the world.

As a complement to the museum, Lime Kiln State Park, on the west side of San Juan Island, has a whale-watching site with displays describing the various whales. A number of cruise boats will take you out to search for whales or other wildlife. Most of these cruise captains are hooked up to the Whale Hotline, so they receive reports of the latest sightings, increasing your chance of seeing these thrilling mammals.

Much Ado About a Porker

San Juan Island is a cradle of Northwest history, for it was here that the United States and Great Britain very nearly became embroiled in an all-out war. It all began in 1859. The Treaty of 1846 was negotiated to set the boundary between the U.S. and British-ruled Canada. However, the line through the San Juans was not clearly described, and both countries laid claim to them. At this time, a settler, Lyman Cutlar, had scratched out a farm in the middle of a British Hudson's Bay Company sheep pasture on the south end of San Juan Island. One of the Hudson's Bay's pigs persisted in rooting up Cutlar's potatoes, and in desperation he finally settled his problem by shooting the pig. When Cutlar, a U.S. citizen, was threatened with arrest by the British, the question of jurisdiction came to a head.

Troops from both sides were dispatched to the islands, triggering the Pig War. The Americans set up camp on the south end, near the home of the recently deceased pig, while the British chose a site on the west shore, on Garrison Bay. Cooler heads prevailed, and Germany's Kaiser Wilhelm I was asked to arbitrate. Eventually he determined the boundary should be down Haro Strait, making the San Juans property of the U.S. (Little did the pig care, by that point).

A simple enough story—except that it took 13 years to resolve. During this time, the detachments from both sides set up housekeeping at their camps, and life went on. There still remains interesting evidence of their life on the island. Today the two camps make up San Juan Island National Historical Park on Garrison Bay, on the west side of the island, and Griffin Bay, on the southeast.

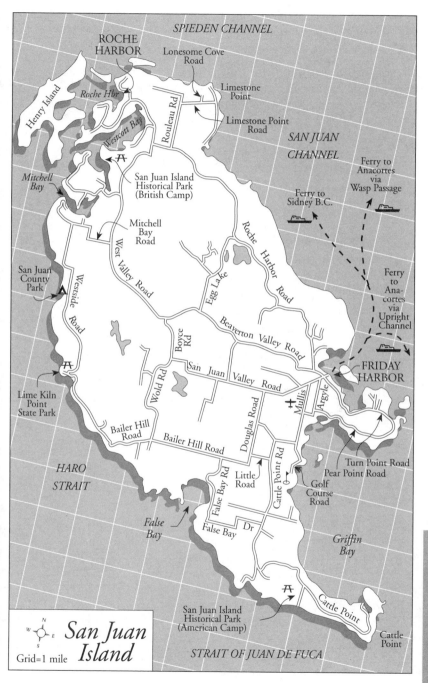

SPIEDEN CHANNEL

ROCHE HARBOR

Lonesome Cove Road

Roche Hbr

Rouleau Rd

Limestone Point

Limestone Point Road

SAN JUAN CHANNEL

Henry Island

Westcott Bay

San Juan Island Historical Park (British Camp)

Mitchell Bay

Mitchell Bay Road

West Valley Road

Ferry to Sidney B.C.

Ferry to Anacortes via Wasp Passage

San Juan County Park

Westside Road

Egg Lake

Roche Harbor Road

Beaverton Valley Road

Ferry to Anacortes via Upright Channel

Lime Kiln Point State Park

Boyce Rd

Wold Rd

San Juan Valley Road

Douglas Road

Beaverton Valley Road

Mullis

Argyle

FRIDAY HARBOR

Bailer Hill Road

Bailer Hill Road

Cattle Point Rd

Turn Point Road

Pear Point Road

HARO STRAIT

False Bay Rd

Little Road

Golf Course Road

Griffin Bay

False Bay

False Bay Dr

San Juan Island Historical Park (American Camp)

Cattle Point

Cattle Point

N
W E
S

San Juan Island

Grid=1 mile

STRAIT OF JUAN DE FUCA

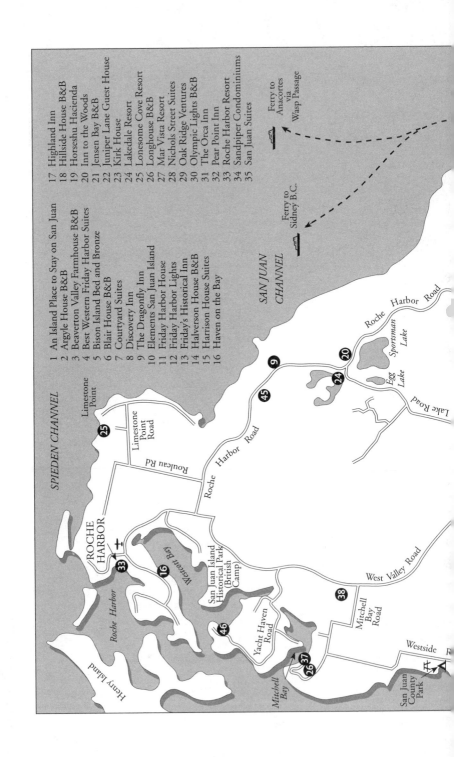

Ferry to Anacortes via Wasp Passage

Ferry to Sidney B.C.

SAN JUAN CHANNEL

SPIEDEN CHANNEL

Limestone Point

ROCHE HARBOR

Henry Island

Roche Island

Roche Harbor

Westcott Bay

San Juan Island Historical Park (British Camp)

Mitchell Bay

San Juan County Park

Limestone Point Road

Rouleau Rd

Roche Harbor Road

Roche Harbor Road

Sportsman Lake

Egg Lake

Lake Road

West Valley Road

Mitchell Bay Road

Yacht Haven Road

Westside R

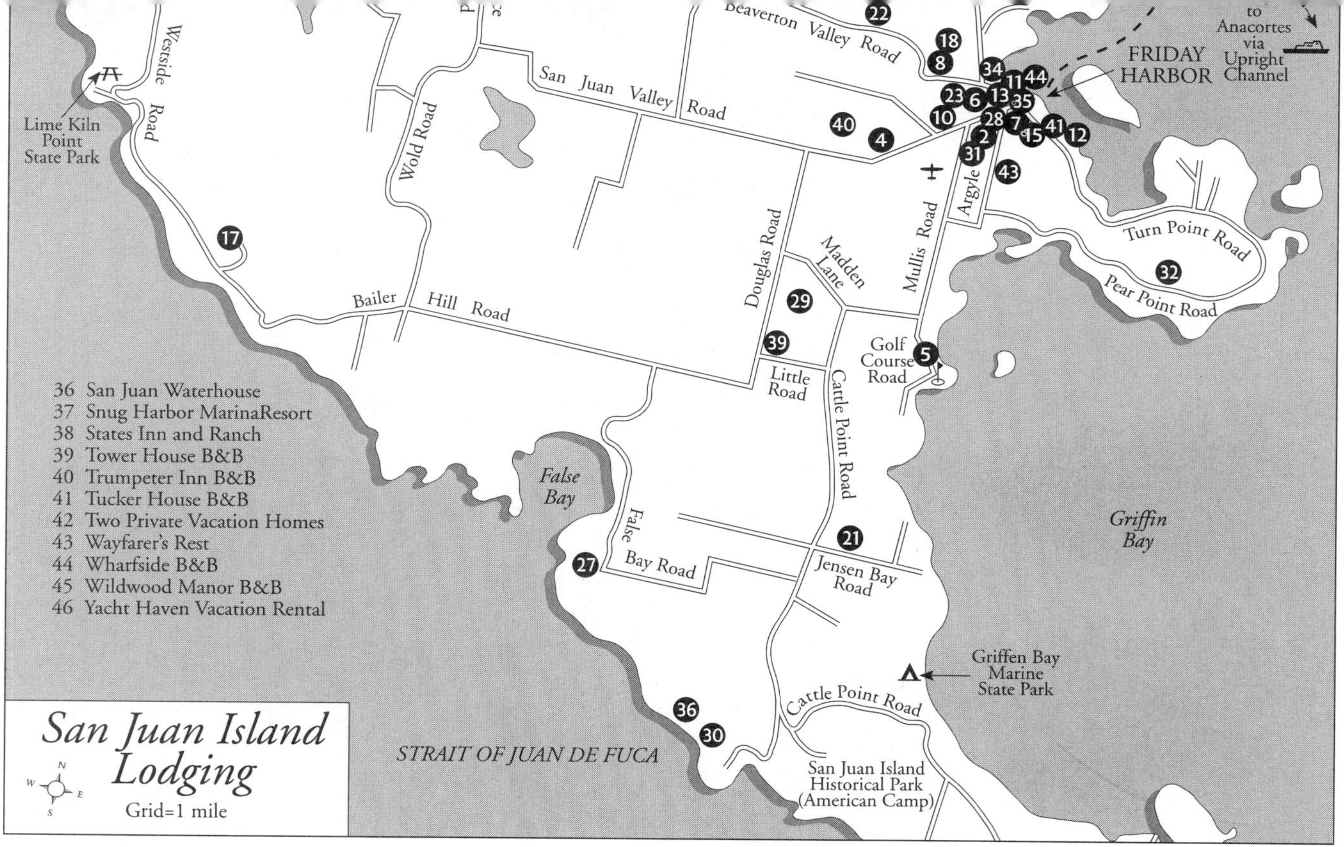

San Juan Island Lodging

Grid=1 mile

36 San Juan Waterhouse
37 Snug Harbor MarinaResort
38 States Inn and Ranch
39 Tower House B&B
40 Trumpeter Inn B&B
41 Tucker House B&B
42 Two Private Vacation Homes
43 Wayfarer's Rest
44 Wharfside B&B
45 Wildwood Manor B&B
46 Yacht Haven Vacation Rental

STRAIT OF JUAN DE FUCA

FRIDAY HARBOR

to Anacortes via Upright Channel

Griffin Bay

Griffen Bay Marine State Park

San Juan Island Historical Park (American Camp)

False Bay

Lime Kiln Point State Park

Westside Road

Turn Point Road

Pear Point Road

Argyle

Mullis Road

Beaverton Valley Road

San Juan Valley Road

Douglas Road

Madden Lane

Cattle Point Road

Little Road

Golf Course Road

Jensen Bay Road

Bay Road

Cattle Point Road

False

Hill Road

Bailer

Wold Road

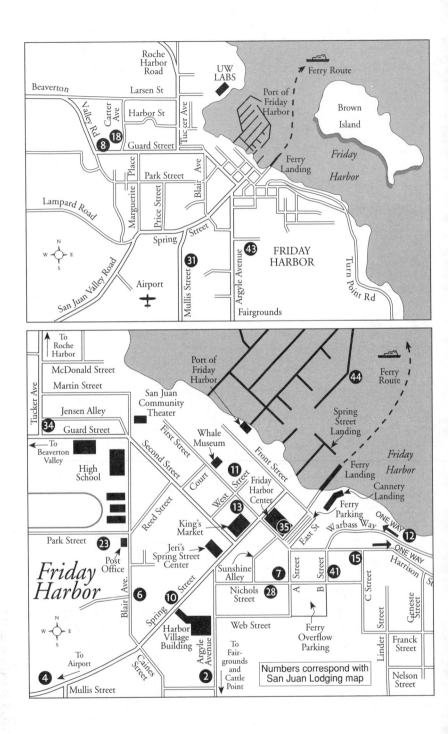

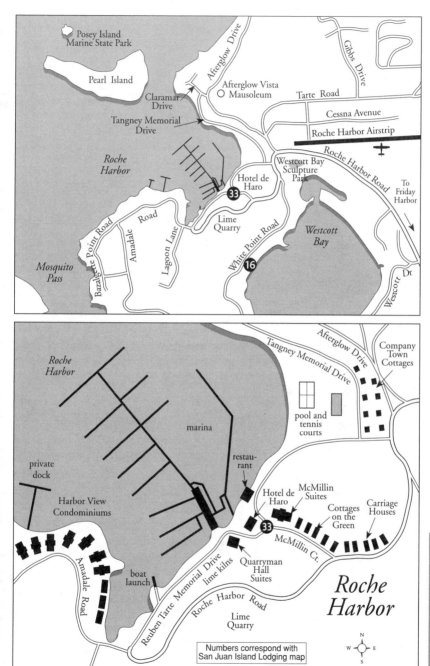

Top map:

Posey Island
Marine State Park

Pearl Island

Claramar
Drive

Tangney Memorial
Drive

Afterglow Drive

Afterglow Vista
Mausoleum

Tarte Road

Gibbs Drive

Cessna Avenue

Roche Harbor Airstrip

Roche Harbor Road

Roche
Harbor

Westcott Bay
Sculpture
Park

Hotel de
Haro

33

Lime
Quarry

White Point Road

Westcott
Bay

To
Friday
Harbor

Bazalgette Point Road

Amadale
Road

Lagoon Lane

16

Mosquito
Pass

Westcott Dr

Bottom map:

Roche
Harbor

Tangney Memorial Drive

Afterglow Drive

Company
Town
Cottages

marina

pool and
tennis
courts

private
dock

restau-
rant

Harbor View
Condominiums

Hotel de
Haro

McMillin
Suites

Cottages
on the
Green

Carriage
Houses

33

McMillin Ct.

Amadale
Road

boat
launch

Reuben Tarte Memorial Drive

lime kilns

Quarryman
Hall
Suites

Roche Harbor Road

Lime
Quarry

*Roche
Harbor*

N
W E
S

Numbers correspond with
San Juan Island Lodging map

LODGINGS

Prices quoted for accommodations are summer rates, per day, double occupancy. However, cottages and vacation homes usually rent for the entire unit. Prices are as of 2007, and are subject to change. Lower rates are usually offered off-season. A tax of 9.7 percent is additional. For a general discussion of lodgings, see Lodging Details, pages 35 to 36.

⊨ = Bed and breakfast inns

⌂ = Cottages, vacation homes, guest suites, condominiums, and hostels

⌂ = Resorts, hotels, motels, and inns

⋔ = Camping (see full descriptions under Parks & Campgrounds)

⋔⋔ = Children OK, however there might be some restrictions

⋔ = Pets OK, however there might be some restrictions

An Island Place to Stay on San Juan ⌂ ⋔⋔ ⋔

P.O. Box 2753; Friday Harbor, WA 98250. Phone: (360) 378-3825; email: *taylors@interisland. net*; web site: *interisland.net/tourist*

ACCOMMODATIONS: 2 homes. Taylor Place can sleep 10, Latta House sleeps 4 to 6, both have kitchens.
RESTRICTIONS: No smoking.
EXTRAS: Barbeque, close to beach, 8¼ miles from Friday Harbor.
SUMMER RATES: Taylor Place $225 to $300 per night, Latta House $155 to $265 per night. Both 2-night minimum.
🚗 Guests will be given driving directions.

Either of these two homes offers a great place for a family or group to stay while recreating on San Juan Island. Taylor Place has room for Grandma and Grandpa and a bunch of cousins, too. The modern home is bright, comfortable, and spacious. The whole mob can gather for a barbeque on the deck, and vie to see who gets the shaded hammock.

Latta House is the place to go if your family is smaller and you want to get *away* from the gang. It, too, is modern and spacious. Touches of driftwood in the décor are very Northwesty.

Argyle House Bed & Breakfast ⊨ ⌂ ⋔⋔ ⋔

685 Argyle Avenue; P.O. Box 823; Friday Harbor, WA 98250. Phone: (800) 624-3459 or (360) 378-4084; email: *info@argylehouse.net*; web site: *argylehouse.net*

ACCOMMODATIONS: B&B inn with guestrooms, suites, and cottages. Some facilities disabled accessible (not ADA).
- 3 guest rooms with queen-size beds, private bath, one room has an additional twin bed. $135 to $139.
- 2-bedroom suite, each room with queen-size beds, one has an additional twin bed, bathroom shared by these two rooms. $245, 4-person occupancy; $25 additional for 5th person.
- *Garden Cottage and Honeymoon Cottage:* 2 studio cottages with queen-size beds, private bath,

satellite TV, mini-fridge, microwave, coffeemaker. Honeymoon cottage has a private deck. $160-165

RESTRICTIONS: No children 8 or under, no pets, smoking outside only.

EXTRAS: Full breakfast, deck, shared hot tub, garden, satellite TV in sitting room of home.

SUMMER RATES: See above. All rates are for 2-person occupancy except for the 2-bedroom suite. Visa and MasterCard accepted.

🚗 From the ferry take Front Street northwest for 1 block then turn left on Spring Street. At a Y intersection in 3 blocks take the left fork, Argyle Avenue, and arrive at the B&B in about 3 blocks.

The gardens surrounding this 1910-vintage Craftsman house provide a lovely accent to the home itself. Even the names of the guest rooms, Robyn's Nest, The Fountain, and Sunflower, reflect the focus on the landscaping. Although the inn is, conveniently, only a half-block from downtown, it sits on a large lot, surrounded by trees and flowers, making it exceptionally quiet and peaceful. Each room is a variation of a fresh color scheme with crisp white walls, charming touches such as lace curtains, and knickknacks tucked into a corner. The two separate cottages, each beautiful enough for a honeymoon getaway, are spacious and airy.

For guests, the innkeepers provide a full, hearty breakfast of fresh fruit, juices, fresh-baked goods, cereal, yogurt, and more.

Beaverton Valley Farmhouse Bed & Breakfast 🛏 🏠 👫🐾

4144 Beaverton Valley Road; Friday Harbor, WA 98250. Phone: (877) 378-3276 or (360) 378-3276; email: *farm@beavertonvalley.com*; web site: *beavertonvalley.com*

ACCOMMODATIONS: B&B inn with 4 rooms and a separate cabin
- *Rose Room:* 2 queen-size beds, private bath.
- *Princess Angeline's Room:* King-size bed, roll-away bed, private bath.
- *Music Room:* Double bed, private bath across the hall (robes provided).
- *Captain's Quarters:* Double bed, private bath.
- *Old Settler's Cabin:* Historic log cabin with queen-size bed, daybed, kitchenette, satellite TV and a VCR/DVD.

RESTRICTIONS: Children OK, pets in the cabin OK by arrangement, no smoking.

EXTRAS: Vegetarian farmhouse breakfast, coffee, tea, guest refrigerator, patio, barbeque.

SUMMER RATES: $100 to $145 for rooms, $170 for cabin. 2-night minimum on weekends. Major credit cards accepted.

🚗 From Friday Harbor, head northwest on Second Street, which becomes Guard Street. It shortly becomes Beaverton Valley Road; follow it for 4 miles. The driveway to the inn, marked by a blue Orca sign, is on the right.

Beaverton Valley Farmhouse is just the ticket for comfortable, beautiful accommodations with a rural ambiance. The two-story farmhouse, built in 1907, was the first licensed bed and breakfast inn on San Juan Island. It has aged gracefully, and been updated over the years in just the right way. It is a grand place to stage a family gathering, with lots of room to kick back and have fun. The living room, with its large stone fireplace, is just the spot for sharing a big bowl of popcorn in the evening and discussing the day's adventures.

SAN JUAN ISLAND
Lodgings

The overall motif is marine life, and very nice artwork carries out the theme. However, the furniture is what is truly marvelous. A number of pieces are hand-carved from teak and are unique. A hearty vegetarian breakfast can be enjoyed in the dining room, or, on sunny days, on the patio.

Best Western Friday Harbor Suites

680 Spring Street; Friday Harbor, WA 98250. Phone: (800) 752-5752 or (360) 378-3031; email: *info@fridayharborsuites.com*; web site: *fridayharborsuites.com*

ACCOMMODATIONS: Inn with 57 suites (63 rooms), king-size or queen-size beds and private baths, kitchenettes. 3 are disabled accessible.

RESTRICTIONS: Children OK, no pets, no smoking.

EXTRAS: Gas fireplaces, cable TV, high-speed internet, private balcony or deck, Jacuzzi, exercise facility, Peppermill Restaurant and Lounge, 3 meeting rooms, continental breakfast, courtesy shuttle service to ferry and San Juan airport. In Friday Harbor.

SUMMER RATES: $148 to $189.

🚐 The suites are on Spring Street, 6 blocks southwest of the ferry landing.

This Best Western franchise offers standard, but quite nice, rooms. Their location is convenient to downtown Friday Harbor. The building was remodeled in 2005, so everything is modern and up-to-date. A conference room and two larger meetings room can be reserved for the use of a group. The Peppermill Restaurant and Lounge are in the building. See Restaurants, page 246

Bison Island Bed and Bronze

87 Bison Place, P.O. Box 1962; Friday Harbor, WA 98250. Phone: (360) 378-4179; fax: (360) 378-4179; email: *bisonisland@centurytel.net*; web site: *bisonisland.com*

ACCOMMODATIONS: Cottage with queen-size bed, full sleeper sofa, bath with shower, kitchenette.

RESTRICTIONS: No young children, no pets, no smoking.

EXTRAS: Living room, 2 decks, cable TV/VCR, barbeque, video library, lakeside firepit, bass fishing gear provided.

SUMMER RATES: $175 per night, other packages to $850 per week (include golf and restaurant credits). 2-night minimum, including Saturday of 3-day holidays. No credit cards.

🚐 From Spring Street, 6 blocks southwest of the ferry, take Mullis Street south alongside the airport. As Mullis turns west it becomes Cattle Point Road. Continue on it for 1½ miles, then look for Bison Place on the left.

This one-bedroom, two-story rental cottage sits on the shore of bass-filled Lake Marion, at the edge of the sixth tee of the San Juan Golf Course. It is modern and nicely appointed, and features a well-equipped kitchenette. Your rental includes fishing gear, and one of the rental packages includes two rounds of golf so you won't miss out on either recreational opportunity.

Bronze artist Doug Bison has his studio on the property, and you are welcome to stop in to see what he is working on. Whether you stay at this cottage or not, you should check out his award-winning art at Bison Studio on First Street in Friday Harbor. See Shopping, page 252–253.

Blair House Bed & Breakfast ⊨ 🕯🐄

345 Blair Avenue; Friday Harbor, WA 98250. Phone: (360) 378-1062, (360) 378-5907; email: *blairhouse@rockisland.com*; web site: *fridayharborlodging.com/blair*

ACCOMMODATIONS: B&B inn with 1 room and 2 2-room suites, queen-size beds, private baths.
RESTRICTIONS: Children and pets by arrangement, no smoking.
EXTRAS: Full breakfast, deck, shared hot tub, TV/DVD/XBox in living room, some rooms have TV. In Friday Harbor.
SUMMER RATES: $115 to $145 weekdays, $165 to $195 weekends. Major credit cards accepted.
🚗 From the ferry terminal, drive north on Spring Street for three blocks and turn right on Blair Avenue. The inn is on the left.

Here's country living within strolling distance of the shops and restaurants of Friday Harbor. Blair House combines the best of both worlds: gracious, relaxed accommodations in a wooded setting, along with a convenient location. Pamper yourself with a soak in the hot tub. Tall Douglas firs and a garden of colorful rhododendrons surround the tidy inn. Sip iced tea on the porch that stretches across the front of the home, or enjoy it on the sun deck.

Furnishings are tastefully charming, with just enough antiques so you don't feel as if you've moved in with your maiden aunt. Bedrooms and suites have private baths. One suite has a private entrance and jetted tub.

Courtyard Suites 🏠 🕯🐄

275 A Street #2 and #4. P.O. Box 2101; Friday Harbor, WA 98250. Phone: (800) 378-1434 or (360) 378-3033; fax: (360) 378-6332; email: *courtyardsuites@rockisland.com*; web site: *courtyardsuites-fridayharbor.com*

ACCOMMODATIONS: Suites in upper level of building.
- 1-bedroom suite sleeps 6 with queen-size bed, sleeper sofa, and futon; kitchen; washer; dryer; water view.
- Studio suite sleeps 5 with queen-size bed and 2 futons; kitchen with courtyard view.

RESTRICTIONS: Children OK, quiet pets OK (cleaning deposit), no smoking.
EXTRAS: Complimentary coffee, tea, and popcorn, cable TV/DVD/VCR, CD, deck, gas grill, parking, wireless internet available nearby. In Friday Harbor.
SUMMER RATES: 1-bedroom suite $225, studio $200; 2-night minimum; rates are double occupancy, $20 per night for each additional person.
🚗 From Front Street turn southwest on Spring Street, and in two blocks turn southeast on Nichols Street. The suites are upstairs above Latitude 48 at the end of the block.

There's no need to bring a car on the ferry if you stay at the Courtyard Suites. Once here, walk the two blocks from the terminal to your reserved suite and settle in. Cars and bicycles are for rent nearby, and taxi service is available. Or, just wander Friday Harbor on foot—there's plenty to see.

The suites, ideal for couples, families, or business travelers, are modern and beautifully appointed, with luxurious linens and down comforters.

Friday Harbor's "main drag," Spring Street, greets you as you leave the ferry.

Discovery Inn

1016 Guard Street; Friday Harbor, WA 98250. Phone: (800) 822-4753 or (360) 378-2000; fax: (360) 378-6232; email: *d-inn@discovery-inn.com*; web site: *discovery-inn.com*

ACCOMMODATIONS: Inn with 20 rooms and 8 suites with 1 or 2 queen-size beds, private bath, some with kitchenette.

RESTRICTIONS: Children OK, no pets, no smoking.

EXTRAS: TV and coffeemaker in rooms, wireless internet, outdoor shared hot tub and sauna (seasonal), barbecue, sun deck, pond, meeting room, bicycle storage. Tennis courts nearby.

SUMMER RATES: Under $119 to $154. Major credit cards accepted.

From Spring Street in Friday Harbor, turn right on Second Street, which becomes Guard Street. The lodge is reached in about ½ mile.

This inn on the outskirts of Friday Harbor, ¾ mile from the ferry terminal, offers standard, nicely furnished rooms in a laid-back setting. The adjoining garden holds natural ponds, sun deck, barbecues, a hot tub, and sauna. Tennis courts are just down the street, at the high school. The innkeepers keep a file of menus from local restaurants that you can check to see where you might want to eat, and the staff will happily perform concierge services.

The Dragonfly Inn ⊨

4770 Roche Harbor Road; Friday Harbor, WA 98250. Phone: 877-378-4280 or (360) 378-4280; email: *host@thedragonflyinn.com*; web site: *thedragonflyinn.com*

ACCOMMODATIONS: B&B inn with 4 rooms, each with a queen-size bed, pulsating two-head shower, 2-person air-massage tub, private patio.
RESTRICTIONS: No children, no pets, no smoking.
EXTRAS: Full breakfast, satellite TV/DVD in common room, afternoon snacks.
SUMMER RATES: $195 to $230 per night. Major credit cards accepted.
🚗 From Spring Street, go right on Second, which bends into Guard. Go right on Tucker, which becomes Roche Harbor Road. Pass Egg Lake Road and Lakedale, then look for the inn on the right at 4770 Roche Harbor Road.

A stunning B&B on the northeast side of San Juan Island is sited in a clearing amid an unspoiled growth of hemlock and madrona. The inn, with a tori-gate at the entrance, is Japanese-inspired throughout. The four rooms, one in each wing of the complex, have Tansu-style vanities, river rock counters, and kimono and obi decorations. Each room's two-person air-massage tub is filled by a flow of water from the ceiling; jetted sides create the sensation of sitting in a bottle of ginger ale. The rooms have private, secluded patios that invite meditation, or just relaxation.

Trails thread through the inn's 15 acres of open timber. Breakfasts are Japanese and Asian fusion cuisine.

Elements San Juan Island Hotel and Spa 🏠 🏡 ⚧ 🐾 ♿

410 Spring Street; Friday Harbor, WA 982504. Phone: (800) 793-4756 or (360) 378-4000: fax: (360) 378-5800; email: *stay@fridayharborinn.com*; web site: *fridayharborinn.com*

ACCOMMODATIONS: Hotel and guesthouse.
• 72 rooms with 1 or 2 queen-size beds, private baths (some jetted tubs). 1 disabled accessible.
• 2-bedroom guesthouse with 2 king-size beds, private bath. Disabled accessible.
RESTRICTIONS: Children OK, pets OK in some rooms, no smoking.
EXTRAS: Full-service onsite spa with massage, facials, manicures, pedicures, body wraps, and more. Inn has indoor heated swimming pool, Jacuzzi, sauna, exercise room, game room, meeting space. Cable TV, phone, coffeemaker, refrigerator, and microwave in all units, some private balconies. Ferry and San Juan airport pickup, conference facilities. In Friday Harbor.
SUMMER RATES: Rooms $189 to $229, guesthouse $369. MasterCard and Visa accepted.
🚗 The hotel is on Spring Street, 4 blocks from the ferry terminal.

On your vacation you like to be pampered, right? Well, here it is. Elements is San Juan Island's inspired hotel and spa, offering a fun, easy-going base for your island adventures. Accommodations range from standard hotel rooms to a spacious, spa-like, two-bedroom guesthouse. Each of the nicely decorated rooms include cable TV. Schedule a conference or business retreat here—the full range of facilities makes it ideal for your function.

You'll enjoy the swimming pool, spa, exercise room, and other amenities such as the colorful beach cruisers available for complimentary guest use. The owners also manage Friday's Historic Inn, where an additional 15 rooms and suites are available.

After settling into your room, visit the spa or stop by the poolside espresso bar. The helpful staff is always full of great suggestions for experiencing the real San Juan Island. A stay here is truly a remarkable and uncommon experience.

Friday Harbor House 🏨 ⅋⅋ ♿

130 West Street, P.O. Box 1385; Friday Harbor, WA 98250. Phone: (866) 722-7356 or (360) 378-8455; fax: (360) 378-8453; email: *fhhouse@rockisland.com*; web site: *fridayharborhouse.com*

ACCOMMODATIONS: Hotel with 23 rooms with queen-size bed, gas fireplace, private bath, oversize jetted tubs. Disabled accessible.

RESTRICTIONS: Children OK, no pets, no smoking.

EXTRAS: Continental breakfast, robes, TV, refrigerator, coffeemaker, telephone with dataport. Friday Harbor House Restaurant (dinner). Meeting rooms and event facilities. In Friday Harbor.

SUMMER RATES: $215 to $360. 2-night minimum summer weekends. Major credit cards accepted.

🚗 From the ferry landing, turn northwest off Spring Street onto First Street. Go 1 block to West Street and turn right. The hotel is at the end of the street.

Friday Harbor House, on the bluff overlooking the harbor, offers the finest modern hotel accommodations in the San Juans. You can luxuriate in your beautifully appointed room. Bedrooms have one or two queen-size beds. Rooms facing on the water enjoy what is probably the best view of Friday Harbor from their balconies, with ferries and boats of the marina just below. The room decor brings the tones and textures of the outside in, with slate floors, wood, and soft earth colors.

The scenic setting makes Friday Harbor House perfect for weddings and other celebrations. Either the dining room or larger San Juan Room can be reserved for your catered event.

Guests receive a complimentary continental breakfast, served in the restaurant or patio. Hotel guests have preferred seating for dinner in the restaurant; however, reservations are recommended. See also Restaurants & Cafés, page 241.

Friday Harbor Lights 🏠 ⅋⅋

250 Warbass Way, P.O. Box 2341; Friday Harbor, WA 98250. Phone: (360) 378-4317; fax: (360) 378-4317; email: *info@fridayharborlights.com*; web site: *fridayharborlights.com*

ACCOMMODATIONS: Condo-style units.
- 1 unit with 3-bedrooms (2 queen-size and a double bed), 3 baths, kitchen. Sleeps 6 to 8.
- 2 studio units, each with queen-size bed, bath with Jacuzzi, kitchen. Sleep 2 to 3.

RESTRICTIONS: Children OK, no pets, no smoking.

EXTRAS: Wood-burning stove, TV/VCR, washer and dryer on property, 40-foot-long deep-water dock free to guests, with power and water available at extra charge. No sleeping on boats, only 1 boat, no rafting.

SUMMER RATES: 3 bedroom $425 for 6-person occupancy, 3-night minimum; suites $185 for 2-person occupancy, 2-night minimum. $20 for each additional person. Visa and MasterCard accepted.

🚗 Take First Street southeast of Harrison (one-way eastbound) to the T-junction with Warbass (one-way westbound). Head back on Warbass to 250. Limited street parking available.

Indeed, you will be able to enjoy the lights of Friday Harbor, along with the comings and goings of the ferry, from these beautiful units. The ferry terminal is just seven blocks away. The units are spacious, sunny, and modern, with big windows opening onto the harbor scene.

Adjacent dock space for a boat comes with the rental. This is one of the few lodgings where you can tie up a good-sized boat, making it an ideal base of operations for your cruises around the islands.

Friday's Historic Inn

35 First Street; P.O. Box 2023; Friday Harbor, WA 98250. Phone: (800) 352-2632 or (360) 378-5848; fax: (360) 378-2881; email: *stay@friday-harbor.com*; web site: *friday-harbor.com*

ACCOMMODATIONS: Inn with 17 units, and guesthouse private baths except for economy rooms.
- 8 deluxe suites with king- or queen-size beds and sleeper sofas, 1 with 2 bedrooms, some with jetted tubs, some with wet bar or kitchenette. $199 to $269.
- 3 standard rooms with queen-size beds, one with sleeper sofa. $149 to $169.
- 4 economy rooms with queen-size and double beds (additional single bed in 1), shared baths. $99 to $129.
- Guesthouse with 2 bedrooms, with king-size bed and king that can be spit into twin beds, 1½ baths, kitchen. Full use of inn facilities. $345.
- Studio apartment with queen bed and hide-a-bed, wet bar. $169.

RESTRICTIONS: Children OK, no pets, no smoking.

EXTRAS: Continental breakfast, some rooms with Jacuzzi, TV/VCR, fireplace, private patio or balcony, private entry, view. In Friday Harbor.

SUMMER RATES: See above. All rates double occupancy. $99 to $269. Cash, checks, or traveler's checks preferred; major credit cards accepted. Honeymoon package available.

🚗 Friday's is on First Street, 2 blocks from the ferry landing.

Whether you're here for whale watching or kayaking, or to tour the island, Friday's will put you right in the heart of Friday Harbor doings. The inn has seen several lives since it originally opened in 1891 to serve San Juan visitors. The building has been handsomely renovated and expanded several times. It now offers upscale lodgings in a range of prices, with the gracious atmosphere of yesteryear.

Many of the accommodations have an island theme, and bear names such as Sucia, Patos, and Matia. Each room is furnished with a tasteful blend of modern and period pieces. Four of the rooms share two nearby baths, although most have private baths. Several boast Jacuzzis. The Orcas Suite, with a king-size bed and Jacuzzi, is a luxurious honeymoon retreat.

A generous continental breakfast includes gourmet coffee, juice, fresh fruit, hot and cold cereal, and fresh-baked scones—just the thing to fuel you for a day's exploring, or to satisfy you while you dive back into bed for 40 more winks in the height of comfort.

SAN JUAN ISLAND
Lodgings

Halvorsen House Bed & Breakfast ⌐ ♦♦

216 Halvorsen Road; Friday Harbor, WA 98250. Phone: (888) 238-4187 or (360) 378-2707; fax: (360) 370-5997; email: *innkeeper@halvorsenhousebb.com*; web site: *halvorsenhouse.com*

ACCOMMODATIONS:
- 2 rooms with queen-size beds, private bath.
- Suite with queen-size bed, private bath Jacuzzi, kitchenette, TV/VCR, and private entrance.
- 1-bedroom apartment with king-size bed, queen-size hide-a-bed in living room, kitchen, dining area, private bath, TV/VCR, private entrance.

RESTRICTIONS: No pets, children 4 years and older OK in apartment, no smoking.

EXTRAS: Gourmet breakfast, shared sitting room with fireplace, TV/VCR, videos, books, games, game table.

SUMMER RATES: $145 to $205 double occupancy, $25 per day each additional person. Major credit cards accepted.

🚗 Take Roche Harbor Road west from Friday Harbor for about 2 miles, then turn south on Halvorsen Road. The house is the first one on the right.

If a gracious setting in a beautifully landscaped, modern home is what you want for your San Juan stay, Halvorsen House should be perfect for you. This beautifully furnished country home, with pastoral views of the nearby valley, is just 2 miles from Friday Harbor. The apartment and suite, on the lower level, each have private entrances and a small patio. The suite, with its privacy and Jacuzzi for two, would be ideal for a honeymoon or other romantic getaway.

A full breakfast is served in the dining room on the main floor. Or, if you are anxious to be out and doing things early in the day, you can have a quick continental breakfast and be on your way.

Harrison House Suites ⌐ 🏠 ♦♦ 🐾

235 C Street; Friday Harbor, WA 98250. Phone: (800) 407-7933 or (360) 378-3587; fax: (360) 378-2270; email: *innkeeper@harrisonhousesuites.com*; web site: *harrisonhousesuites.com*

ACCOMMODATIONS: B&B inn with 4 suites and 5th suite in cottage (studios, 2-bedroom, and 3-bedroom), sleep from 4 to 10 persons; queen-size beds, private baths, kitchens or kitchenette, fireplaces. Three suites have water views.

RESTRICTIONS: Children OK, pets by arrangement, no smoking.

EXTRAS: Complimentary 4-course breakfast delivered to your suite, or in our Garden Café, two suites have private hot tubs, three share a hot tub, decks, guest laundry facilities, TV/VCR. Complimentary bicycles and kayaks. Catered dinners available. In Friday Harbor.

SUMMER RATES: $175 to $375 a night, double occupancy; additional persons $25 per person, per night. Major credit cards accepted.

🚗 From the ferry terminal, take Spring Street and turn left on First, which becomes Harrison in one block as it goes uphill. Turn right on C Street. The lodgings are on the corner of Harrison and C Street; parking is just before C Street, behind the house or in front of it on C Street.

These spacious suites right in Friday Harbor are ideal for a weekend getaway or for an extended family stay. Four of the suites share a 1905 Craftsman-style home;

one suite is on the ground level, one on the main floor, and two are on the upper level. The fifth suites is across the garden in a separate cottage that can sleep up to 4 guests. Several of the suites, or the entire home, can be rented for a retreat, family reunion, wedding, or other group gathering.

The suites are tastefully decorated with a nice blend of modern furnishings and period pieces. Hardwood floors, a formal dining room, a piano, a private sun deck, and a hot tub make the main floor accommodations (San Juan Suite) a true home away from home. This suite has all the architectural details of the historic home.

The inn is a favorite for weddings—the catered food is fabulous!

Haven on the Bay 🏠 ⛺ 🐾

413 White Point Road; Roche Harbor, WA 98250-8102. Phone: (360) 378-2976; email: *sanjuanislandvacations@centurytel.net*; web site: *sanjuanislandvacations.com*

ACCOMMODATIONS: Rental home that sleeps 7 (upper level sleeps 2, separate apartment on lower level sleeps 5), 2½ baths, queen-size beds in upper and lower bedrooms, queen-size hide-a-bed in lower great room, twin-size hide-a-bed in lower study; full kitchens in both upper and lower levels.
RESTRICTIONS: No smoking, small pets OK.
EXTRAS: Satellite TV/VCR/DVD/CD, wireless internet, Jacuzzi in master bath, washer/dryer on both levels. Fireplace and piano in upper level. Balcony and 2 decks, firepit, barbeque, boats, crab pot, fenced yard. Walk to Roche Harbor.
SUMMER RATES: Entire house $2044 for 1 week. Lower level apartment only: $195 per night, $1295 for week.
🚗 Guests will be given driving directions.

This two-story house overlooks medium-bank waterfront on Westcott Bay. The layout of the house offers some flexibility, depending on the size of your group. Each of the home's two levels has a separate entrance. An inner stairway connects the two levels, but a door between the two can be locked. Either the entire house is rented, or just the lower level. The upper level will not be rented out when only the lower level is occupied. The upper level is a bit fancier, with a fireplace, Jacuzzi, and baby grand piano, but both units are modern and very nicely furnished

There is so much to do right out your front door—beachcomb, dig for clams, gather mussels and oysters, set a crab pot (provided), fish, watch for birds and animal life. A paddleboat, 14-foot boat with outboard electric motor, two kayaks, and a buoy for a private yacht are there for your use.

Highland Inn 🛏

439 Hannah Road, P.O. Box 135; Friday Harbor, WA 98250. Phone: (888) 400-9850 or (360) 378-9450; fax: (360) 378-1693; email: *helen@highlandinn.com*; web site: *highlandinn.com*

ACCOMMODATIONS: B&B inn with 2 suites, each with king-size bed, private bath, jetted tub for 2.
RESTRICTIONS: No children, no pets, no smoking.
EXTRAS: Refrigerator, satellite TV/VCR, CD player, phone, gourmet breakfast, afternoon tea and snacks, shared sitting room with fireplace, view veranda, outdoor hydrotherapy tub, video library, art materials, afternoon tea and cookies.

SAN JUAN ISLAND
Lodgings

SUMMER RATES: $275 per night, 2-night minimum for Saturday reservations. Major credit cards accepted.

🚗 From Friday Harbor, follow Spring Street to a Y-intersection at the outskirts of town. Stay left on San Juan Valley Road. In about 1 mile, head south (left) on Douglas Road, which curves west in about 1¾ miles and becomes Bailer Hill Road. As Bailer Hill Road reaches the water and heads north as West Side Road, Hannah Road is on the right. Follow this to the end of the paved road and take the road to the left, Hannah Road, which is marked "private road." The sign for the inn is in just a short distance.

Highland Inn has perhaps the most spectacular marine view of any lodging on San Juan Island. The bedrooms and the 88-foot-long veranda that stretches across the front of the house, look out to Haro Strait, Victoria, B.C., and memorable sunsets. Orca whales frequent the strait, and visitors have a good chance of seeing them offshore in summer.

But, the views are only the beginning—the inn matches the beauty of the view in every way, with landscaping of stepping stones, evergreens, and rhododendrons, and breathtaking interiors. Travel and Leisure magazine named it "Inn of the Month" in September 2000. Each of the spacious suites has a sitting area where you can curl up to enjoy music and a book, or veg out with TV or a video. The suites have jet tubs for two as well as steam cabinet showers. Breakfast can be eaten in the dining room, or, if you want to enjoy privacy or don't feel like dressing, you can enjoy it in your suite.

Hillside House Bed & Breakfast 🛏 ✸✸

365 Carter Avenue; Friday Harbor, WA 98250. Phone: (800) 232-4730 or (360) 378-4730; fax: (360) 378-4715; email: *info@hillsidehouse.com*; web site: *hillsidehouse.com*

ACCOMMODATIONS: B&B inn with 6 rooms with king- or queen-size beds, some have window seat where an additional person can sleep, private or designated bath.

RESTRICTIONS: No children under 10, no pets, no smoking.

EXTRAS: Full breakfast, guest refrigerator, all the banana-chocolate chip cookies you can eat, easy walk to Friday Harbor.

SUMMER RATES: $125 to $275 per night. Major credit cards accepted.

🚗 From Spring Street in Friday Harbor, turn northwest onto Second Street, which angles left and becomes Guard Street. In two more blocks turn right on Carter Street. The inn is on the left in a half block.

This spacious modern home, embraced by native firs and rhododendrons sits on a hillside perch that affords grand views of Friday Harbor, with the town and bay spread below and the mountains rising above. The large deck on the main floor is the perfect spot to soak up the view with a cool drink in hand. Some bedrooms have harbor vistas. Others that face the hillside have an equally interesting view—a two-story atrium with a pond to lull you to sleep.

One of the inn's beautifully decorated rooms is sure to be exactly to your liking. Grandest of all is the secluded Eagle's Nest Retreat on the top floor. It makes the perfect honeymoon hideaway with its comfy king-size bed, Jacuzzi, wet bar, TV, and aerie-like balcony

Horseshu Hacienda 🏠 ⚒ 🐎 ♿

131 Gilbert Lane, P.O. Box 1861; Friday Harbor, WA 98250. Phone: (360) 378-2298; email: *Roxanne@horseshu.com*; web site: *horseshu.com*

ACCOMMODATIONS: Rental home with 3 bedrooms with queen-size beds, 2 baths, Jacuzzi in master bedroom, 1 full-size bed, 2 single roll-away beds, kitchen.
RESTRICTIONS: No smoking.
EXTRAS: Satellite TV/DVD, stereo, telephone, piano, kitchen, wood stove, washer, dryer, deck, patio, barbeque, fax, wireless internet, disabled accessible (not ADA). Horseback trail rides available.
SUMMER RATES: $275 per day, per 6 persons, 2-night minimum, $1400 per week. Additional persons, by arrangement, $12 per person, per day. Rental includes 30-minute complimentary ranch tours for 2 on horseback, and 10 percent discount on horseback rides.
🚐 From the ferry landing drive west on Spring Street, which becomes San Juan Valley Road. In 1 mile from the ferry turn left onto Gilbert Lane. Take the next left, and you will see the entrance archway to Horseshu Guest Ranch.

This spacious ranch-style home has great views across San Juan Valley; better yet, it's part of a terrific guest ranch, so you can arrange for horseback rides or basic instruction during your stay. A thirty-minute horseback tour of the property, for two people, is complimentary with your rental, if the weather permits.

You will feel at home immediately in this modern home, with its skylights, hardwood floors, and large windows looking out to the forest and white-fenced pasture. The master bedroom with its Jacuzzi and satellite TV is a great place to retreat. Just outside the Hacienda is your own chicken coop where you can gather your own fresh eggs daily—what a treat! Kids could throw sleeping bags out on the deck and fall asleep listening to the sounds of the forest and the farm. See also Events & Attractions, page 267.

Inn To The Woods 🛏 ⚒

46 Elena Drive; Friday Harbor, WA 98250. Phone: (888) 522-9626 or (360) 378-3367; email: *intothewoods@rockisland.com*; web site: *inntothewoods.com*

ACCOMMODATIONS: B&B inn with 4 rooms, king or queen-size beds, private baths, one with jetted tub, 3 with hot tubs, 1 room with private entrance.
RESTRICTIONS: No pets, no smoking.
EXTRAS: Full breakfast, satellite TV/DVD/VCR, telephone, robes, massage can be scheduled.
SUMMER RATES: Weekdays $130 to $200, weekends $160 to $230.
🚐 From Spring Street turn right on Second, which turns into Guard. Turn right on Tucker, which becomes Roche Harbor Road. In 4 miles, just past Misty Isle Drive, turn right onto Elena Drive and go uphill to the first driveway.

There's nothing like the sounds and scents of a forest to lull you off to dreamland. As you would expect, Inn To The Woods is situated on five quiet, wooded acres. But, nearby there's an 87-acre lake, too. Sportsman Lake is a bird heaven, with both open water and some marshy edges to attract a wealth of feathered friends for you to watch.

SAN JUAN ISLAND
Lodgings

All rooms feature fine linens, chocolates, and fresh flowers; three have views through the trees of the lake. A full breakfast is served, and fresh-baked treats are available in the afternoon.

Jensen Bay Bed & Breakfast ⊨ ♯♀

363 Jensen Bay Road; Friday Harbor, WA 98250. Phone: (360) 378-5318; email: *stay@jensenbay. com*; web site: *jensenbay.com*

ACCOMMODATIONS: 2-bedroom home with queen-size beds, double futon couch in the living room, bath, kitchen with basic cooking staples.

RESTRICTIONS: Children welcome, no pets, no smoking, 4 persons maximum.

EXTRAS: Continental breakfast, fireplace, TV (no cable), DVD/VCR, CD player.

SUMMER RATES: $195 double occupancy, $20 for each additional person, 2-night minimum. Visa and MasterCard accepted.

🚗 From the Friday Harbor ferry landing, follow Spring Street to Mullis Road and turn left (south). This becomes Cattle Point Road. Turn left on Jensen Bay Road 4¼ miles from the ferry landing. The bed and breakfast is the first house on the left.

This charming, beautifully decorated home, tucked away on five sunny acres south of Friday Harbor is like having your own summer home in the country. It's a great base of operations for your family's island exploring, or it can be a peaceful retreat for absolute solitude.

A continental breakfast of fruit and baked goods is provided, or you can whip up a meal in the kitchen (staples and main breakfast ingredients such as cereal and eggs are on hand—you bring in the main groceries). Have a picnic in the yard, and then spend the evening in front of the living room fireplace, or on the porch enjoying the sunset and mists settling in the surrounding forest.

Owner Manya Pickard is an artist who creates exquisite handmade jewelry of silver and torch-worked glass. Her studio is nearby on the property. If you ask, she will show you her work.

Juniper Lane Guesthouse 🏠 ♯♀

1312 Beaverton Valley Road; Friday Harbor, WA 98250. Phone: (888) 397-2597 or (360) 378-7761; email: *info@juniperlaneguesthouse.com*; web site: *juniperlaneguesthouse.com*

ACCOMMODATIONS: House and separate cabin.
- 3 rooms with queen-size beds, 2 with private baths, 1 with shared bath, 1 with private entrance and porch.
- Hostel-type room with queen-size bed, 4 twin bunk beds, shared bath; 1 with a queen-size bed, 4 twin bunk beds, shared bath.
- Large bedroom for families or groups with queen-size bed, 5 twin bunk beds, 1 twin bed, private bath outside door.
- Cabin with 2 bedrooms, queen-size and full bed, private bath, kitchen, deck.

RESTRICTIONS: No children under 8 in inn unless entire inn is rented, children of any age OK in cabin, no pets, no smoking.

EXTRAS: Fully equipped kitchen for guest use, common area with satellite TV/VCR/DVD, magazines, music. Cabin has deck, satellite TV. Wireless internet access in both guesthouse and cabin.

SUMMER RATES: Rooms $85 to $125 per night, group rooms $30 to $240 per night; cabin $175 per night, 2-night minimum.

🚗 From the ferry landing take Spring Street, turn right on Blair, then left on either Park or Guard, which become Beaverton Valley Road. The inn is at 1312 Beaverton Valley Road, 1¼ mile from the Friday Harbor ferry.

There's always a need for different-style accommodations, and this one's a real winner. The hip, unique inn is a combination of private rooms, hostel-style beds, and a cabin that can sleep up to six people. Single people can be accommodated in the hostel rooms if the rooms are not being used by a group. The décor and furnishings are really nice, with lots of natural wood, cheery colors, and original artwork. Guests can use the shared kitchen to cook meals.

The cabin is rustic, but a real charmer, with natural wood finished walls and its own sunny deck. Both the cabin and inn overlook pastoral Beaverton Valley. There are views of birds and wildlife, as well as neighboring sheep and a llama.

Kirk House 🛏 👫

595 Park Street; P.O. Box 2983; Friday Harbor, WA 98250. Phone: (800) 639-2762 or (360) 378-3757; email: *info@kirkhouse.net*; web site: *kirkhouse.net*

ACCOMMODATIONS: B&B inn with 4 rooms with queen- or king-size beds, all with private entry, private bath, shared common areas.

RESTRICTIONS: No children under 10, no pets, no smoking.

EXTRAS: Full breakfast, afternoon snack, 1 room with double Jacuzzi, 1 room with fireplace, each room with cable TV/DVD, wireless internet. Running track and tennis courts nearby. In Friday Harbor.

SUMMER RATES: $180 to $205 per night. Visa and MasterCard accepted.

🚗 The Kirk House is in Friday Harbor on Park Street, five blocks from the ferry landing.

At the turn of the century, the small town of Friday Harbor boasted few prosperous residents or fancy homes. One exception was the house of Peter Kirk, the founder of the town of Kirkland, who retired in style in this now-classic 1907 Craftsman home. The granite rock used in the foundation, pillared entry, and fireplaces was barged over from Mount Baker. The spacious parlor has 12-foot ceilings, arched doorways, wainscoting, and leaded-glass accent windows. This elegant home now serves as a bed and breakfast inn.

Each of the four large bedrooms of Kirk House features an entry from the parlor, as well as an outside entry. The home is beautifully decorated in Craftsman style, with some antiques. A generous breakfast is provided, but if you plan to leave early to catch a ferry or investigate the island, the innkeepers will pack you a breakfast of select goodies.

The house is adjoined by a pretty, landscaped garden where you can sip your morning coffee or nibble an afternoon snack. Nearby, at the high school, are a public running track and tennis courts that can be used when school is not in session.

SAN JUAN ISLAND
Lodgings

Lakedale Resort 🏠 🏚 ⛰ 🏃 🫎

4313 Roche Harbor Road; Friday Harbor, WA 98250. Phone: (800) 617-2267 or (360) 378-2350; fax: (360) 378-0944; email: *info@lakedale.com*; web site: *lakedale.com*

ACCOMMODATIONS: Resort with cabins, house, and lodge.
- 6 cabins, each with 2 bedrooms with queen-size beds, 2 baths, hide-a-bed in living room, kitchen, fireplace, deck .
- Lake House with 3 bedrooms and sleeping loft, 3 baths (2 with Jacuzzis), kitchen, fireplace, deck.
- 10-room lodge (includes 2 suites) with queen- and king-size beds.

RESTRICTIONS: Children OK (16 or older in lodge rooms), pets OK in cabins, no smoking.

EXTRAS: Clean towels daily, outdoor grill, picnic table, no TV, shared hot tub, lake access, swimming, canoes, rowboats, paddleboats, trout fishing. Lodge has complimentary continental breakfast, banquet/meeting and large great room. Facilities for small weddings. General store on premises.

SUMMER RATES: Cabins $329; house $489 for 4 persons; lodge $239 for 2 persons, $35 for each additional person. Discounts for multidays, 2-night minimum in summer. Major credit cards accepted.

🚗 Take Roche Harbor Road west from Friday Harbor for 4½ miles. Just beyond Egg Lake Road, turn left into the resort.

More than 80 acres of forested parkland, encompassing three private lakes, creates the setting for this resort's really nice lakefront accommodations of varnished peeled logs, with a wonderful, woodsy atmosphere. The park's campground is some distance away, so the cabins have complete privacy.

Each of the cabins features a sunny living room with a cathedral ceiling. The

Cabins at Lakedale Resort have peeled log walls and a cheery, woodsy ambiance.

Lake House is similar to the cabins, but on a much grander scale, with windows filling one end of the cathedral living room providing tree-top views. The large lodge, which faces on the shore of Neva Lake, has rooms furnished in the same Northwest Rustic style as the cabins. They have fireplaces and French doors that open onto a deck. The lodge includes facilities for banquets and meetings, along with a large open-beam greatroom, making it ideal for large groups or seminars. A large lakefront meadow can be used for weddings or family reunions.

Guests have access to all the park's facilities, including the trails and rental boats. The lakes offer good swimming, although there is no lifeguard. Because these are private lakes, a Washington State fishing license is not needed, but the resort charges $4 per day for a fishing permit. Money from the permits is used to restock the lake annually with trout and bass. See also Parks & Campgrounds, page 280–281.

Lonesome Cove Resort 🏠 ⚥

416 Lonesome Cove Road; Friday Harbor, WA 98250. Phone: (360) 378-4477; email: *cabins@ lonesomecove.com*; web site: *lonesomecove.com*

ACCOMMODATIONS: Resort with 6 cabin-suites with double beds, kitchen, private bath, fireplace.
RESTRICTIONS: Children OK, no pets, no smoking.
EXTRAS: Beach, dock with float, trout pond, library, no TV.
SUMMER RATES: $125 to $180. Daily moorage (under 28 feet) $10 to $16, 5-day minimum in summer, 2-day minimum other times. Major credit cards accepted.
🚗⛟ Drive northwest from Friday Harbor on Roche Harbor Road. In 7½ miles, just before reaching Roche Harbor, turn north on Roluleau Road, and in another mile angle right on Limestone Point Road. Lonesome Cove Road, which leads to the resort, is on the left in another ½ mile.

The cove might be lonesome because of its isolation, but you'll never be lonesome with so much to do in such beautiful surroundings. The resort's six hand-built log cabins face on Spieden Channel. You can bring your boat up to the 100-foot-long dock and use the resort as a base for island exploration. Lonesome Cove is centered smack dab in one of the best scuba diving areas in the San Juans—the steep walls of Limestone Point are within swimming distance of the resort beach. For those souls seeking quieter pastimes, there's the beach to stroll, a small library stocked with books, lush grassy lawns to sunbathe on, and lots of wildlife to watch.

All cabins have kitchens, fireplaces, and electric heat. The largest unit accommodates six. They are well spaced for privacy so you don't feel you're living in your neighbor's hip pocket, and the six acres of deep forest that encloses the resort assures solitude.

Longhouse Bed & Breakfast 🛏 🏠 ⚥

2187 Mitchell Bay Road; Friday Harbor, WA 98250. Phone: (360) 378-2568; email: *longhouse@ rockisland.com*; web site: *rockisland.com/~longhouse*

ACCOMMODATIONS: B&B inn and separate cabin.
- 2 rooms with queen-size beds, each with private bath.
- 3-room cabin with queen-size bed, studio bed in living room, kitchen.

RESTRICTIONS: Children OK in cabin by prior arrangement, no pets, no smoking.

EXTRAS: *Rooms:* Full breakfast for guests in rooms, dinners by arrangement, shared greatroom with fireplace and library, deck, beach-front, artifact collection, no TV. *Cabin:* Deck, barbeque, washer, dryer, beach, no breakfast provided.

SUMMER RATES: Rooms $115 to $125 per night. Cabin $130 per night double occupancy, $15 per night for each additional person, 2-night minimum. No credit cards.

🚐 From Friday Harbor, follow Beaverton Valley Road, which becomes West Valley Road, for 6 miles to Mitchell Bay Road. Turn left and continue on the road for 2¼ miles, passing Snug Harbor Marina Resort, to the inn at the road end in about 1 more mile.

A stay at the Longhouse Bed & Breakfast will allow you to really soak in Northwest atmosphere and native culture while enjoying a superb stay. The cedar-sided inn, surrounded by huge cedar and fir trees, faces on Mitchell Bay on the west side of San Juan Island. Innkeepers Jerry and Patty Rasmussen have done a magnificent job of updating the home, yet maintaining its roots as a unique, long-time Mitchell Bay residence. The location is the former site of a Northwest Indian longhouse.

The home has heavy, exposed timbers and a fieldstone fireplace. The greatroom has a cathedral ceiling and an array of windows that look out to the water; the door opening onto the deck is carved with designs similar to the entrance to a longhouse. An extensive collection of artifacts from Northwest Indians, as well as other cultures, is displayed, and a Makah dugout canoe is fastened to a balcony facing on the greatroom.

Patty is a former chef, so you know your breakfast is going to be memorable. Dinners can be prepared for you, on request.

The adjacent rustic cabin, with its own deck and barbecue, offers cozy accommodations for a couple or family of three. The small kitchen is fully equipped with pans and dishes for whipping up snacks or meals. Snug Harbor Marina Resort, a stone's throw away, offers whalewatching and kayak tours.

Mar Vista Resort 🏠 ⚥

1601A False Bay Drive; Friday Harbor, WA 98250. Phone: (360) 378-4448; email: *marvista@rockisland.com*; web site: *marvistaresort.com*

ACCOMMODATIONS: 8 cabins with 1 to 3 bedrooms, mostly queen-size beds, private bath, kitchenette; 1 cabin with fireplace.

RESTRICTIONS: Children OK, no pets, no smoking.

EXTRAS: Children's play equipment, picnic tables, pond, beach, trails, whale watching, no TV.

SUMMER RATES: $120 to $195, 3-night minimum in summer, 2 night minimum the rest of the year. Major credit cards accepted.

🚐 Drive south from Friday Harbor on Argyle, which joins Cattle Point Road. Follow Cattle Point Road to False Bay Drive and turn west. In 1¾ miles False Bay Drive turns north. The signed driveway to Mar Vista Resort is at this road bend. The resort is down the road in 2 miles.

Pack up the kids and head for Mar Vista! This resort has "family fun" written all over it. The cottages are simply furnished, but comfortable—just the thing for carefree relaxation. Mom can settle down with a book and let Dad and the kids take over the cooking and dishwashing; who cares if you have hot dogs for a week? A spacious lawn holds children's play equipment. Trails lead down to the beach where kids can build driftwood castles, collect rocks, or play in the water. As evening settles in, Mom and Dad can sneak in some romantic stargazing as the kids play games with new-found buddies from neighboring cabins.

Spectacular scenery is part of the resort's package; views from the high bluff are out to Haro Strait and the Strait of Juan de Fuca. Bring binoculars and watch for whales that pass by offshore. The cabins are nicely separated so you're not forced to enjoy someone else's kids. One-bedroom cottages have kitchenettes, two-bedroom cottages offer living rooms and kitchens. The three-bedroom cabin has a fireplace.

Nichols Street Suites 🏠 🕴

85 Nichols Street; Friday Harbor, WA 98250. Phone: (866) 374-4272; email: *funkon@rockisland. com*; web site: *lodging-fridayharbor.com*

ACCOMMODATIONS: Building with 2 suites on upper floor.
- 2-bedroom suite with queen-size and double bed, double futon (sleeps 6), bath, kitchen.
- 1-bedroom suite with queen-size, double, and queen-size sleeper beds (sleeps 4), full bath, courtesy kitchen with mini-refrigerator, coffeemaker, microwave, toaster.

RESTRICTIONS: Children OK, no smoking.

EXTRAS: Deck, barbeque, private entrance shared between units. In downtown Friday Harbor.

SUMMER RATES: $165 to $185, double occupancy, $20 for each additional person, 2-night minimum, weekly rates available. Visa and MasterCard accepted.

🚐 On the south side of Nichols Street above Funk & Junk.

Two nicely furnished second-floor suites in the heart of Friday Harbor. Original artwork on the walls add a polished touch. The bedrooms do not have doors; heavy curtains pull across the doorways for privacy, but that adds to the open, airy feel of the lodgings. The suites' location permits easy exploration of Friday Harbor's shops and restaurants. If you enjoy antiquing, you need only wander downstairs to Funk & Junk, the nifty store on the main floor of the building. See also Shopping, page 256.

Oak Ridge Ventures 🏠 🕴

141 Glen Oak Lane, P.O. Box 2083; Friday Harbor, WA 98250. Phone: (800) 687-3558 or (360) 378-6184; email: *oakridge@rockisland.com*; web site: *oak-ridge.net*

ACCOMMODATIONS: Rental home with 4 bedrooms, 3 with queen-size bed, 1 with twin beds and double futon, 2 full baths, 2 half baths.

RESTRICTIONS: Children over 12 OK, no pets, no smoking.

EXTRAS: Kitchen, TV/VCR/DVD and stereo, wi-fi DSL internet.

SUMMER RATES: $1975 per week for 8 persons, 7-day minimum, $100 cleaning fee. No credit cards.

🚐 In Friday Harbor, drive southwest out of town on Spring Street. At a Y intersection turn south on Mullis Road. Follow the main road as it turns west, then south, and becomes Cattle Point Road. About 2½ miles from the ferry terminal, look for the Oak Ridge Lane signpost. Turn right, and go to the top of the paved drive to the home.

Perched on a ridge, surrounded by oaks (thus its name), this pretty yellow Craftsman-style home, with a wide porch looking out to Griffin Bay, provides quiet, gracious lodgings. The house's four spacious bedrooms are tucked under the gables on the second floor. Polished wood floors sport soft rugs, and beds have cushy comforters. Large, lace-curtained windows offer pastoral views of the gardens, San Juan Valley, and Griffin Bay.

To relax, wander through the flower, herb, and vegetable garden, or settle down on comfortable front porch chairs to read and watch boats in Griffin Bay, below, and eagles, above.

Olympic Lights Bed & Breakfast ⊨⋑

146 Starlight Way; Friday Harbor, WA 98250. Phone: (888) 211-6195 or (360) 378-3186; fax: (360) 378-2097; email: *olympiclights@rockisland.com*; web site: *olympiclights.com*

ACCOMMODATIONS: B&B inn with 4 rooms, 2 with queen-size bed, 2 with king-size bed; 2 with private connecting bath, 2 with designated bath a few steps away, robes provided.
RESTRICTIONS: No children, no pets, no smoking.
EXTRAS: Full breakfast, no TV, farm setting.
SUMMER RATES: $140 to $150 per night. No credit cards.

🚗 From Spring Street in Friday Harbor, angle left on Argyle Avenue. Follow the road as it heads south and becomes Cattle Point Road. The lane leading to the inn is on the right in 5½ miles, just before reaching American Camp.

Leave your stress at the gate! This sunny 1895 Victorian farmhouse is sure to lift your spirits. The inn sits in grandeur on a bluff at the south end of San Juan Island, seeming to rise as high as the Olympic Mountains it looks out to. The bright yellow clapboard exterior with white trim hints at the white wicker furnishings and soft pastels of the cheerful country interior. The second floor is carpeted completely in ivory. Guests are asked to remove their shoes before going upstairs—who cannot be relaxed while padding across a cushy carpet in stockinged feet? Fluffy feather comforters that warm the beds hold the sweet scent of salt air and fresh grass. In the morning, innkeepers Christian and Lea Andrade serve a hearty farm breakfast on elegant china in the parlor or in the spacious kitchen.

The setting is as open and airy as the house itself. Rolling grassland spreads south to the tip of the island, with few trees to obstruct the panoramic view. The wide lawn is a perfect spot for a genteel round of croquet in the afternoon or a more energetic game of horseshoes. Evenings bring salty breezes rising off the straits and a sky with more stars than you ever knew existed.

The Orca Inn 🏠 ♦♦ ♿

770 Mullis Street; Friday Harbor, WA 98250. Phone: (877) 541-6722 or (360) 378-2724; fax: (360) 378-1322; email: *theorcainn@adelphia.net;* web site: *orcainnwa.com*

ACCOMMODATIONS: Motel-style accommodations in 75 rooms, 4 with king-size beds, the remainder queen-size or double beds, all with private baths; roll-aways available for rooms with king-size beds. Some disabled accessible.
RESTRICTIONS: Children OK, no pets, smoking permitted in some rooms.

SUMMER RATES: $59 to $104 per night. Credit cards accepted.

🚗 In Friday Harbor, drive southwest out of town on Spring Street. At a Y intersection continue straight on Spring Street and, after a 4-way stop, take the first left onto Mullis Street. The parking lot is on the left side of the road in the second block.

For people coming to the San Juans who want reasonably priced, basic accommodations where they can toss their bags and get on with all that great San Juan recreation, the Orca Inn is probably just what they are looking for. The attractive, nicely landscaped lodgings offer small, motel-type units. The wood-paneled rooms are clean, attractive, and efficient, with comfortable beds and small bathrooms with showers.

Pear Point Inn 🛏 ⁇

2858 Pear Point Road; Friday Harbor, WA 98250. Phone: (360) 378-6655; fax: (360) 378-6659; email: *pearpointinn@interisland.net*; web site: *pearpointinn.com*

ACCOMMODATIONS: B&B inn with 2 units, both with private baths.
- Suite on upper floor with a queen-size bed in separate bedroom, twin beds, kitchenette, private deck.
- Bedroom on main floor with king-size bed.

RESTRICTIONS: Children OK in suite, no pets, no smoking.

EXTRAS: Continental breakfast, satellite TV/VCR, wireless internet, garden hot tub. Transportation to and from the ferry or airport, by arrangement.

SUMMER RATES: $150 to $195 per night, double occupancy. $15 for each additional person in suite. Discount offered if you do not want breakfast.

🚗 From the ferry, follow Spring Street and turn left on First Street. Continue as the road becomes Turn Point Road and then Pear Point Road. It is about 2½ miles to the inn, on the right.

The inn is on the uphill side of the road, with a clearing and broad lawn in front to give terrific views of Griffin Bay. It is located near Turn Point and Jackson Beach, both great recreation areas, so you'll have easy access to kayaking, scuba diving, beach walking, picnicking, kite flying and lots of other San Juan fun.

The spacious rooms are airy and beautifully decorated, with just enough pretty, homey touches to make you comfortable, but not smothered by ruffles and chintz. To give your day a kick-start, a generous continental breakfast can be served in your room or on the deck.

Roche Harbor Resort 🏠 🏠 ⁇

248 Rueben Tarte Memorial Drive, P.O. Box 4001; Roche Harbor, WA 98250. Phone: *resort:* (800) 451-8910 or (360) 378-2155; *marina:* (800) 586-3590; *restaurant:* (360) 378-5757; email: *roche@rocheharbor.com*; web site: *rocheharbor.com*

Accommodations and **SUMMER RATES:** Resort with a range of lodgings.
- 16 Hotel de Haro rooms with king, queen, double, or twin beds, all with shared baths, some with views. $99 to $109.
- 3 Hotel de Haro suites with queen-size beds, sitting areas, private baths, harbor views, one suite with fireplace. $179 to $189.

- 9 Company Town cottages, with queen-size bed, 2 double beds, bath, and kitchen, barbeque, picnic area; larger cottages have propane fireplace; 3-night minimum in July and August. $279 to $299.
- 4 McMillin Suites with king-size beds, private baths, heated floors, 2 TVs, fireplaces, harbor views. $335.
- 8 Quarryman Hall Suites with private veranda, 8 double guestrooms; all have king-size beds, fireplace, plasma TV, marble spa-style bath. $325 to $345.
- Harbor View condominiums, 1, 2, and 3 bedrooms, some with lofts, private baths, kitchens, fireplaces, TV, view decks. $205 to $372.
- Carriage Houses with 2 bedrooms, king and queen-size beds, bath. $425.
- Cottages on the Green with 2 or 3 bedrooms, sleep 4 to 6, king-size and 2 queen-size beds, bath, kitchen. $539.

RESTRICTIONS: Children OK, no pets, no smoking.

EXTRAS: Historic Hotel de Haro, 377-slip marina, mooring buoys, convenience store, gift shop, retail shops, spa, hydro tub, steam rooms, coin-operated laundry, café, restaurant, lounge, outdoor swimming pool, tennis courts, formal gardens, chapel, kiosks featuring work of local artists, outdoor theater, small boat rentals. Airstrip nearby, historic Afterglow Mausoleum nearby.

SUMMER RATES: See above. Some lodgings have 3-night minimum in summer. Major credit cards accepted.

From Friday Harbor, follow Roche Harbor Road northwest to the resort. An adjacent

Roche Harbor is a major vacation destination, with guests from Canada as well as the U.S. and other world points.

airstrip is for guests who fly in. The resort lies on Roche Harbor, at the extreme northwest end of San Juan Island. The large marina has moorage and buoys (for a fee) for guests who arrive by boat.

You won't want to miss scenic Roche Harbor Resort when you visit San Juan Island—it's the premier destination. Boaters flock here to rendezvous with their friends, or just to revel in the marine atmosphere. Even if you're not a boater, it's a fascinating spot. The resort's centerpiece is the historic Hotel de Haro, fronted by a beautiful formal garden. If you want to be right in the heart of harbor activity, you can choose one of the 16 rooms or four suites in the hotel—perhaps it will be the very one where Teddy Roosevelt slept, or you can soak in an oversized bathtub that John Wayne used. The rooms have been updated, of course, but you can't help but feel the history. Three suites have been remodeled to luxury standards.

Still in the historic vein, Cottages on the Green are a number of cabins formerly used by lime kiln workers, which have been renovated and are now resort lodgings. All have kitchens and full baths, and sleep up to six people. They are near the swimming pool and tennis courts—ideal for a family.

However, you might opt for one of the McMillin Suites in the home on the hillside overlooking the harbor, or the condominium-style lodgings around the bay. The condominiums come as one-, two-, or three-bedroom units, and all have kitchens and TVs. Adjacent to the Hotel de Haro, a new building has retail shops and a spa with treatment rooms, a hydro tub, and steam rooms. The upper floors have elegant suites and double guest rooms; French doors in each suite open onto private verandas. No matter which lodging you choose, guests can enjoy full use of the resort's facilities, including the swimming pool and tennis courts.

Roche Harbor is a premium site for weddings and other celebrations. A small chapel can be used for services, and the staff and catering service can meet all your needs for your event.

In summer, several colorful kiosks that line the walkway to the marina sell locally created wares and artworks. See also Restaurants & Cafés, pages 244 and 245, and Marinas, Launch Ramps & Put-Ins pages 279–280.

From Company Town to World-Class Destination

Roche Harbor is the legacy of John S. McMillin, who built a lime quarry empire here more than 100 years ago. The Hotel de Haro was built to house McMillin's business customers and friends. Its proudest moment was in 1906, when President Theodore Roosevelt stayed here.

The limestone eventually played out, and in the 1950s the business closed. Since that time, the once-deteriorating buildings have been restored and the property has been developed as a first-class destination resort. Although the hotel has been renovated, it still maintains much of its historic character. Decks that stretch the width of the two upper stories afford superb views of the harbor.

Sandpiper Condominiums 🏠 🏃🐄

250 Tucker, P.O. Box 383; Friday Harbor, WA 98250. Phone: (360) 378-5610 or (360) 378-8155; fax: (360) 378-2322; email: *bob@sandpiper-condos.com*; web site: *sandpiper-condos.com*

ACCOMMODATIONS: Condominium with 6 studio and 1-bedroom apartments with twin or queen-size beds, kitchenette, and private bath.

RESTRICTIONS: Children OK, well-behaved pets OK, no smoking.

EXTRAS: Cable TV, heated pool, exercise room, wireless internet. Walk to Friday Harbor, tennis courts nearby.

SUMMER RATES: $85 to $115 per day, $450 to $625 per week. Open year-round; rentals daily or weekly. No credit cards.

🚗 From Spring Street in Friday Harbor, head northwest on Second Street, which becomes Guard. Follow Guard and turn right on Tucker; Sandpiper Condominiums are immediately on the right.

If what you're looking for is a moderately priced base of operations, Sandpiper exactly fills the bill, offering daily and weekly studio rentals within walking distance of downtown Friday Harbor. All units are fully furnished and equipped with kitchenettes and cooking equipment. Airbeds are available for added sleeping space.

San Juan Suites 🏠 🏃

150A Spring Street; Friday Harbor, WA 98250. Phone: (800) 722-2939 or (360) 378-8773; email: *reservations@rockisland.com*; web site: *sanjuanislandsuites.com*

ACCOMMODATIONS: Inn with 5 suites, each with king-size bed and full bath, 2 with kitchens.

RESTRICTIONS: No smoking, no pets, children OK.

EXTRAS: Cable TV/DVD, CD, 4 with gas stove and private deck, barbeque, 2 with Jacuzzi's, 2 with washer, dryer. In the heart of Friday Harbor.

SUMMER RATES: $139 to 299 per night, 4-night minimum. Discounted rates are available for various room combinations and extended stays.

🚗 Located on the upper floor of Friday Harbor Center, First and Spring Streets.

In 2002 a disastrous fire wiped out a half block of buildings in the heart of Friday Harbor. The block was rebuilt in a style that reflects the town's historic origins, but the building now houses up-scale businesses and lodgings. Retail spaces fill the lower level, while on the second floor San Juan Suites offers five modern bedrooms that sleep from two and five people. Most have decks overlooking the town and harbor. The beautifully furnished suites have elegant touches such as glass-block tub enclosures and Jacuzzis in some, and private decks in all but one.

San Juan Waterhouse 🏠 🏃

1102 Old Johnson Road, Friday Harbor, WA 98250. Phone: (360) 378-7259; fax: (360) 378-7085 email: *falcon@sanjuanwaterhouse.com*; web site: *sanjuanwaterhouse.com*

ACCOMMODATIONS: House with 3-bedrooms, queen- and king-size beds and 2 twin beds, 2 baths, kitchen.

RESTRICTIONS: Children OK, no pets, no smoking.

EXTRAS: Washer and dryer, living room with fireplace, decks, waterfront.

SUMMER RATES: $2750 per week, 1-week minimum in season.

🚗 In Friday Harbor, head southwest on Spring Street and turn south on Mullis. At the Argyle Avenue intersection Mullis becomes Cattle Point Road. Follow Cattle Point Road south for 4 miles to Old Johnson Road, then turn west on it and follow it west and south to the house at 1102 Old Johnson Road.

Many people consider the west side of San Juan island its best. It is here that orca whales are most often seen (sometimes quite near shore), snowy peaks of the Olympic Mountains add their accent to the blue water, and sunsets build to a stunning display.

This secluded, three-bedroom bungalow sits just above the water. Below are rocky coves that hold tide pools, driftwood, and all sorts of nature's treasures. The home offers everything a group of up to six people would want for a getaway. The kitchen sports a professional Viking stove, where the chefs in the crowd can show off their talents. Two bedrooms are on the main floor. Kids will delight in the loft, which holds twin beds. A small sandy spot nestled between the lawn and rocky shoreline is an ideal sport for sitting in an Adirondack chair to enjoy a book or whale watch. In fall and winter, the home is a great spot for storm watching.

Snug Harbor Marina Resort 🏠 👯 🦌

1997 Mitchell Bay Road; Friday Harbor, WA 98250. Phone: (360) 378-4762; fax: (360) 378-8859; email: *sneakaway@snugresort.com*; web site: *snugresort.com*

ACCOMMODATIONS: Resort with 10 units, studios, 1-bedroom and 2-bedroom waterfront cottages, all with queen-size beds, private bath, and kitchenette. Some have additional queen hide-a-bed and children's loft.

RESTRICTIONS: Children OK, pets OK, no smoking.

EXTRAS: TV. Marina, boat launch, kayak tours, whale watch boat, fuel (gas), propane, convenience store.

Kayak tours leaving from Snug Harbor can explore the west side of San Juan Island.

SUMMER RATES: $169 to $229 per night, pets $10, 2-night minimum, 3-night minimum for Garrison Bay cabin. Major credit cards accepted.

🚐🔺 From Friday Harbor, follow Beaverton Valley Road, which becomes West Valley Road, for 6 miles to Mitchell Bay Road, and turn left. The signed road to Snug Harbor Marina Resort is on the right in ¾ mile.

This friendly little resort on San Juan Island's west side has everything you need for a great island vacation. It is the closest resort to prime kayaking, scuba diving, salmon fishing, and whale watching. The resort's bungalows line the waterfront, with the docks just a few steps away. The nicely furnished accommodations have all the essentials needed for a comfortable stay. All couches are hide-a-beds, so there is space to add an extra person or two (for an added charge).

As of 2007, the resort is in the process of remodeling for the 2008 season, and might have future expansion. Check their web site for their lodging status. See also Marinas, page 280.

States Inn and Ranch 🛏 ♿⚐

2687 West Valley Road; Friday Harbor, WA 98250. Phone: (866) 602-2737, (360) 378-6240; fax: (360) 378-6241; email: *info@statesinn.com*; web site: *statesinn.com*

ACCOMMODATIONS: B&B inn with rooms, suite, and cottage.
- 8 rooms with king- (or 2 twins), queen-size, or double beds, private baths.
- Suite with 2 bedrooms, king-size (or 2 twins), queen-size, and futon beds, full bath, refrigerator
- Cottage with 2 bedrooms, full bath, kitchen, washer, dryer, breakfast basket delivered to your door. TV/DVD.

RESTRICTIONS: Children by arrangement, no pets, no smoking.

EXTRAS: Full breakfast, wi-fi internet access. Working ranch, Ranch Store, pastoral setting. Disabled access for some units. Hiking nearby. Will pick up at ferry or San Juan airport.

SUMMER RATES: Rooms $99 to $169 double occupancy; suite $229 for 4 persons; cottage $249 for 4 persons. Slight charge for additional people. Major credit cards accepted.

🚐 From Friday Harbor, drive northwest on Second Street and follow it as it becomes Guard Street, and then Beaverton Valley Road, which merges into West Valley Road. Approximately 7 miles from Friday Harbor, the sign for the inn is ½ mile north of the Mitchell Bay Road intersection.

Did you ever imagine you could enjoy the splendor of a Louisiana plantation or the laid-back comfort of a Montana ranch right here in the San Juans? At States Inn, you can. Each of the inn's nine bedrooms are decorated with authentic touches from different U.S. states. The Louisiana bedroom has cool, white wicker furniture and soft eyelet curtains; the Southwestern Suite boasts warm southwest tones and Mexican blankets. All bedrooms have adjoining baths except for the Rhode Island room—its bath is just a step down the hall. The Southwestern Suite, with its two separate bedrooms and shared bath and sitting room, is perfect for a family or two couples. The cottage offers a nice lodging for families, along with the opportunity to prepare their own meals.

Getting acquainted with the horses, chickens, and sheep that live on the farm will be a thrill for city kids. Also, the English Camp section of the San Juan Island

Historical Park is just a mile down the road. Guests wanting to stretch their legs can hike down to the park's buildings, or climb to the top of Mount Young for grand views out to Haro Strait.

Tower House Bed & Breakfast 🛏

392 Little Road; Friday Harbor, WA 98250. Phone: (800) 858-4276 or (360) 378-5464; cell: (360) 298-1633 or 1634; email: *chris@san-juan-island.com*; web site: *san-juan-island.com*

ACCOMMODATIONS: B&B inn with 2 large suites, each with king-size bed, private bath, private sitting room, TV/DVD/VCR in each room.
RESTRICTIONS: No children, no pets, no smoking.
EXTRAS: Full breakfast, guest use of refrigerator, TV in living room, hot tub, pond, country setting.
SUMMER RATES: $160 to $175 per night. Major credit cards accepted.

🚗 From Spring Street in Friday Harbor, turn south on Argyle and follow it as it becomes Cattle Point Road. When Cattle Point Road turns south, Little Road is on the right in about ½ mile. The Tower House is on the right in a short ½ mile, just before the intersection with Douglas Road.

When we first saw this fabulous country inn overlooking San Juan Valley, we knew it was a place we wanted to stay. We returned several weeks later, and it fulfilled our dreams. The unique Queen Anne–style home has a round, two-story tower with leaded-glass windows and decorative shingling on the exterior. A romantic sitting room inside the tower adjoins a bedroom. The sitting room for the second bedroom is a cozy library with windows opening out to the garden behind the inn.

Antique furniture blends beautifully with fascinating pieces such as a lacquered Oriental screen and carved animals from Africa, collected by Chris and Joe Luma, the inn's owners. They will tell you how the house itself traveled from afar! It originally sat on Vancouver Island, and was barged to the San Juans.

Feast on the sumptuous vegetarian breakfast, elegantly presented on fine china with crystal and silver, in the dining room.

Trumpeter Inn Bed & Breakfast 🛏 👬 ♿

318 Trumpeter Way; Friday Harbor, WA 98250. Phone: (800) 826-7926 or (360) 378-3884; fax: (360) 378-8253; email: *swan@rockisland.com*; web site: *trumpeterinn.com*

ACCOMMODATIONS: B&B inn with 6 rooms (queen- or king-size bed or twin beds), private bath, some with fireplace and private deck. 1 room has a king-size bed that can be split into 2 twin beds. 1 room disabled accessible.
RESTRICTIONS: Children over 12 by arrangement, no pets, no smoking.
EXTRAS: Full breakfast, TV in sitting room, hot tub, massage service available, country atmosphere.
SUMMER RATES: $155 to $195 per night. Visa, MasterCard, Discover accepted.

🚗 Follow Spring Street out of Friday Harbor, and at a Y-intersection stay left on San Juan Valley Road. The signed lane leading to the inn is on the north in about 2 miles.

With guest rooms named for rosemary, yarrow, and other sweet-scented herbs, you know this is an inn designed to appeal to your senses. Trumpeter Inn proves that a house doesn't have to be old to be charming and comfortable; it's a modern country home with spacious, sunny bedrooms and lovely accents of flowers throughout. All bedrooms are beautifully decorated, and have either king- or queen-size beds and full baths. A disabled-accessible room has a king-size bed that can be split into two twin beds. An upstairs room, Bay Laurel, has sweeping views of San Juan Valley, the Straits of Juan de Fuca, and the Olympic Mountains.

The inn sits on a hillside overlooking rolling, bucolic pastures, with the distant peaks of the Olympic Mountains rising above. Gardens surrounding the inn brim with roses, dahlias, and gladiolus. Spend a quiet evening on the deck listening to the gentle sounds of the country. You might see graceful trumpeter swans (the namesake of the inn) on neighboring ponds and pastures. Bring your cameras and art materials—you will want to capture the beauty of the spot.

Tucker House Bed & Breakfast 🛏️ 🏠 🚻 🐾

260 B Street; Friday Harbor, WA 98250. Phone: (800) 965-0123 or (360) 378-2783; fax: (360) 378-8775; email: *reservations@tuckerhouse.com*; web site: *tuckerhouse.com*

ACCOMMODATIONS: Historic inn with guest rooms, suites, and cottages
- 6 guest rooms with queen-size beds, private baths with 2-person Jacuzzi tubs and showers. Some with fireplaces.
- 2 suites that sleep 4 or 6 guests, private baths, fireplaces. The King Suite has a king-size bed and Jacuzzi tub.
- 2 cottages with queen-size beds, private baths, wood stoves, kitchenettes, private entrances. One has a futon couch and sleeps 4.

RESTRICTIONS: Children welcome, pets OK in cottages, no smoking.

EXTRAS: Full gourmet breakfast, shared hot tub, TV/VCR in all rooms, gardens; private balconies, decks, and patios. Afternoon cookies from the "cookie fairy." 2-block walk from ferry and Friday Harbor.

SUMMER RATES: Rooms $200 to $225, suites $300 to $325, cottages $170 to $250. Rates based on 2-person occupancy; additional person 16 or older $25 per night, under 16 $15, children under 7 free. Major credit cards accepted.

🚐 From Spring Street in Friday Harbor, make the first left on First Street, which becomes Harrison Street. Make a left on B Street. Tucker House is on the left at the end of the block.

You can enjoy the quaint setting of a circa-1898 Victorian inn conveniently located in downtown Friday Harbor. The guest rooms feature tiled bathrooms and 2-person jetted tubs that are like having an in-room spa—admittedly not vintage Victorian, but they certainly add to the pleasure of your stay. Or, if you prefer absolute privacy and the convenience of a kitchenette, opt for one of the cottages. The recently renovated accommodations are appointed with fine, comfortable furnishing and modern luxuries, but retain the inn's turn-of-the-century flavor.

A four-course breakfast, served in the Garden Café or delivered to your suite or cottage, includes seasonal fruit, yogurt and homemade granola, and fresh-squeezed juice. The day's hot entrée might be crêpes, twice-baked goat cheese soufflés, or lemon ricotta pancakes. Recipes are from the inn's own cookbook, *La Cucina Anna Maria: Good Life Recipes from San Juan Island.* Save room for . . . desert? Yes, desert for breakfast. It includes such favorites as crème brulée, Italian parfaits, or strudel.

Two Private Vacation Homes 🏠 👬🐕

P.O. Box 1607; Friday Harbor, WA 98250. Phone: (800) 426-2338 or (360) 378-6284; email: *ge@sanjuanvacationhomes.com*; web site: *sanjuanvacationhomes.com*

ACCOMMODATIONS:
- *Beaverton Valley Country Vacation Home:* 4 queen-size bed, 2 full baths, spa, kitchen, washer, dryer, trout pond with rowing dinghy.
- *Griffin Bay View House:* 2 bedrooms, king-size and queen-size beds, 2 baths, Jacuzzi, kitchen.

RESTRICTIONS: No smoking, children OK, pets OK.
EXTRAS: Satellite TV/VCR/DVD, sun deck, barbeque.
SUMMER RATES: $1290 to $1330 for 3-day stay, $1590 to $1660 for a week. Rates are for up to 8 persons in the Beaverton Valley home, up to 4 persons in the Griffin Bay home.
🚗 Guests will be given driving directions.

Two homes are available for weekly summer rentals. The Beaverton Valley location is a pretty country home on 11 acres, with an orchard, pasture, and trout pond. The Griffin Bay site has water views from nearly every room. Its fully equipped, modern kitchen is ideal for whipping up meals to serve on the large deck.

Wayfarer's Rest 🏠 👬🐕

35 Malcom Street; Friday Harbor, WA 98250. Phone: (360) 378-6428; email: *wayfarersrest@ rockisland.com*; web site: *rockisland.com/~wayfarersrest*

ACCOMMODATIONS: Hostel with lodgings for 18 people. 4 double-occupancy rooms, dorm-style beds in a group room, shared bathroom, sitting room, kitchen.
RESTRICTIONS: Children and pets OK in private rooms, no smoking.
EXTRAS: Shared living room with wood stove, dining area, and kitchen; yard, herb garden.
SUMMER RATES: $30 per person for dorm rooms, private rooms with double beds from $80. Credit cards accepted.
🚗 From the ferry landing, head uphill on Spring Street 3 blocks to Argyle Avenue. Follow Argyle to the south for 2 blocks, then turn east on Malcolm. Wayfarers Rest is the third house on the right side of Malcolm Street, in another 2 blocks.

The great thing about a hostel, aside from the reasonable rates, is the camaraderie between guests as they share their tales of adventure. You might meet people from far corners of the world, and possibly strike up long-lasting friendships.

The hostel's bunk beds in the group room have platforms with comfortable mattresses. In a stroke of creativity, long pieces of driftwood are used to support the outer edges of the platforms. Linens and bedding are provided. Very young children or pets are welcome in the private rooms. All rooms are nicely furnished, and very comfortable. The kitchen has utensils as well as the basic staples and fresh eggs needed for meal preparation; you provide the main ingredients and do your own cooking (and cleanup). Fresh herbs come from the garden. The spacious living room has ample sofas for guests to stretch out, schmooze, and maybe start a songfest.

You won't want to miss reading the guest book, which holds the names of guests from places such as Australia, Italy, and Germany—and be sure to sign it yourself.

Wharfside Bed & Breakfast: Aboard the *Slow Season* |━━| 👫 🐾

Port of Friday Harbor, K Dock; 205 Front Street North; Friday Harbor, WA 98250. Phone: (360) 378-5661, (360) 472-1062; email: *wharfside@rockisland.com*; web site: *slowseason@ rockisland.com*

ACCOMMODATIONS: Boat with 2 staterooms on a 60-foot sailboat with double and queen-size bed and 1 bunk, shared and private bath.

RESTRICTIONS: Children OK, pets by arrangement, no smoking.

EXTRAS: Full breakfast, nautical atmosphere, rowing dinghy, TV, DVD, internet. 2-hour cruise on Tuesday, Thursday, Saturday, and Sunday (time depending on weather). Cruise length and time can be customized. Dinner on board by arrangement. 3-block walk to town and ferry.

SUMMER RATES: $179 (no cruise), $289 (with cruise), 2 persons, 2-night minimum in summer. Major credit cards accepted.

🚗🔺 The *Slow Season* is moored in slip K13 of the Port of Friday Harbor docks.

How can you vacation in the San Juans without getting boating fever? A stay on the *Slow Season* might satisfy that itch. However, beware—you might become so enamored that you'll want to rush out to buy your own boat! Your hosts will welcome you aboard their classic, 60-foot motorsailor. The boat has the warmth and elegance of an old-time sailing ship, with teak and tapestry settees, skylights, and a wood burning stove in the main salon.

When the weather's nice, your breakfast is served on the spacious outside deck. It's so pleasant here you'll want to linger for an afternoon of sunbathing. You can stay tied up to the dock and bask in the salty bustle of the docks. There is an optional two-hour breakfast cruise on weekends.

The aft stateroom, which is ideal for an unforgettable honeymoon retreat, has a private entrance, queen-size bed, and private toilet and sink. The forward stateroom has a double bed and two bunks; the bath is shared. Boaters who arrive at Friday Harbor with a full party will find the *Slow Season* ideal for added sleeping space—but make reservations well ahead of time as it's heavily booked in summer

Wildwood Manor Bed & Breakfast |━━| 👫

5335 Roche Harbor Road, P.O. Box 2255; Friday Harbor, WA 98250. Phone: (877) 298-1144 or (360) 378-3447; fax: (360) 378-6095; email: stay@*wildwoodmanor.com*; web site: *wildwoodmanor.com*

ACCOMMODATIONS: B&B inn with 3 rooms (queen-size beds), private baths; 1 suite with a king-size bed and daybed, private bath.

RESTRICTIONS: No children under 12, no pets, no smoking.

EXTRAS: Full breakfast, each bedroom has TV and DVD, wireless internet; shared patio, dining room, greatroom with fireplace. Walking paths.

SUMMER RATES: Rooms $195, suite $250. Visa and MasterCard accepted.

🚗 From Spring Street in Friday Harbor, turn right on Second Street, then in three blocks angle left on Guard Street. In about one more block, turn right on Tucker Avenue. Follow Tucker, which becomes Roche Harbor Road as it leaves town. The sign for the inn is on your left about 5½ miles from Friday Harbor, just beyond Mineral Point Road.

Located on 11 tranquil acres, Wildwood Manor is a graceful, Queen-Anne–style bed and breakfast inn, with breathtaking water and forest views. The grounds feature beautiful gardens, an expansive lawn, untouched forest, and plenty of space to simply unwind. The surrounding "wildwood" from which the inn takes its name holds deer, fox, squirrels, wild turkeys, and a wealth of smaller birds. The professionally designed inn has distinctive touches that make it exceptionally beautiful and inviting. From the greatroom, guests can watch sailboats on San Juan Channel, with snowy Canadian mountains in the distance.

Each of the accommodations have a different décor. The Decatur Room, the only room on the third floor, has water views and complete privacy. The Shaw Room boasts a sleigh bed and antique French armoire. A custom-designed wing-back padded headboard is featured in the Lopez Room. Both Shaw and Lopez Rooms have woodside views. The two-room San Juan Suite offers spectacular water views, plus additional space.

Yacht Haven Vacation Rental 🏠 👫

423 Shorett Drive, P.O. Box 1893; Friday Harbor, WA 98250. Phone: (408) 395-7600; fax: (408-395-8440; email: *tpworld@aol.com*; web site: *yachthavenvacationrental.com*

ACCOMMODATIONS: Rental home with 2-bedrooms (queen-size bed and twin beds that can be made up as a king-size bed), 2 baths, kitchen; each bedroom has private entrance.

RESTRICTIONS: Children OK, no pets, no smoking.

EXTRAS: Fireplace, deck, satellite TV/VHS/DVD, DSL internet, washer, dryer, indoor heated swimming pool, recreation barn with pool table and pinball, outdoor crab-cooking station, beach with shellfish, private dock with water connection and 30-ampere shore power, dinghy with oars, scuba diving lessons available.

SUMMER RATES: $350 per night, minimum of 3 nights, $2100 per week. Rates discounted for longer stays. Major credit cards accepted.

🚗 Located at the entrance to Garrison Bay, diagonally across from British Camp. Guests will be given driving directions.

This comfortable waterfront bungalow on San Juan Island's west side boasts exquisite marine views and glorious sunsets. Only a clam toss from Roche Harbor, it is just the place to set up housekeeping for a week or two. There's plenty to keep the whole gang happy, including an indoor heated swimming pool, pool table, and pinball machine. It's a boater's dream, as it has its own dock where you can tie up your boat. The bedrooms sleep four in great comfort; couples can move the two twin beds together, or families can split them apart for kids.

The prime location, right on Westcott and Garrison Bays, is near all the boating and resort activity of Roche Harbor, and within rowing distance of San Juan Island Historical Park's English Camp. However, you are far enough away to have plenty of quiet and privacy. You can harvest clams, crab, and oysters right in front of your cabin, and then cook them on the propane barbecue. *(Be aware that a state license is required to harvest shellfish.)* If you don't want to bother with gathering them, you can buy all you can eat from a commercial oyster-growing operation that is within rowing distance at the head of Westcott Bay.

VACATION HOME RENTAL FIRMS

For other lodgings, try one of the two realtors in the San Juans listed below. The firms manage year-round vacation rental properties. The majority of these private homes are on San Juan Island, although a few are on Orcas and other nearby islands. Offerings range from cabins to condos to homes.

Most rentals are for one or two weeks, but some properties are available for longer stays; occasionally two- or three-night rentals might be secured. You can call the companies to request their brochure, or check their web sites.

All Islands Reservations

Friday Harbor, WA 98250. Phone: (360) 378-3845; email: *taylors@interisland.net*; web site: *interisland.net/tourist*

San Juan Island Vacation Rentals

P.O. Box 1133; San Juan Island, WA 98250. Phone: (888) 337-5211 or (360) 378-3190; email: *twobears@rockisland.com*; web site: *sanjuanislandvacationrentals.com*

San Juan Property Management

50A Spring Street, P.O. Box 2717; Friday Harbor, WA 98250. Phone: (800) 742-8210 or (360) 378-2070; email: *sybil@sanjuanpm.com*: web site: *sanjuanpm.com*

Windermere Vacation Rentals

100 First Street, P.O. Box 488; Friday Harbor, WA 98250. Phone: (800) 391-8190; email: *propmgmt@windermeresji.com*; web site: *windermerevacationrentals.com*

RESTAURANTS, CAFÉS & TAKE-OUT

$	Inexpensive	Most dinner entrées under $12
$$	Moderate	Most dinner entrées $12 to $25
$$$	Expensive	Most dinner entrées $25 and up

♦ = Beer and wine ♈ = Full bar

Backdoor Kitchen and Catering $$ to $$$ ♈

400 A Street; Friday Harbor, WA 98250. Phone: (360) 378-9540; email: *hildeman@rockisland. com*; web site: *backdoorkitchen.com*

HOURS: Lunch and dinner Monday through Friday 11 A.M. to 3 P.M.; dinner hours vary seasonally.

Although it is somewhat hard to find, in the back side of a warehouse-type building at the end of A street, Backdoor Kitchen and Catering is worth looking for. Multi-ethnic lunches include soups and salads, sandwiches, curries, nori rolls, and chalupa. Dinners feature salads, oysters, feta cheese wrapped in grape leaves, and esoteric dishes of scallops, lamb, spiced Indian prawns or potato gnocchi. Indoor seating is complemented by tables in the outdoor, landscaped setting.

Beechtree Espresso and Ice Cream Emporium $

Roche Harbor Resort; 248 Rueben Tarte Memorial Drive; Roche Harbor, WA 98250; web site: *rocheharbor.com*

HOURS: Summer 7 A.M. to 8 P.M.; closes at 2 P.M. in spring.

Kiosks under the beech trees near Roche Harbor Resort's formal gardens offer lattes, cappuccino, and mochas made from Starbucks coffees, along with a nice selection of ice creams.

Bella Luna $ to $$ ℐ

175 First Street South; Friday Harbor, WA 98250. Phone: to go (360) 378-4118, business office (360) 378-7789; email: *bellacaters@yahoo.com*

HOURS: Breakfast, lunch, and dinner Tuesday through Sunday 11 A.M. to 9 P.M. Friday and Saturday open until midnight. Reservations recommended. Major credit cards accepted.

Bella Luna is casual enough for the family, but nice enough for a special dinner, with its Mediterranean décor of vine-wrapped beams and tables with tablecloths. The extensive menu ranges from pizza to prawns or prime rib, and there's always a nightly seafood special. For lunch there are salads and sandwiches, including some outstanding burgers. Bella Luna is a popular spot with local people and in-the-know tourists, so reservations are recommended in summer. They are open late on summer weekends, so you can have a late-night drink and dinner.

Colorful flowers and convenient benches make Friday Harbor a pleasant spot to shop and enjoy an ice cream cone.

The Blue Dolphin Café $

185 First Street; Friday Harbor, WA 98250. Phone: (360) 378-6116

HOURS: Breakfast and lunch daily 5 A.M. to 2 P.M. Orders to go.

Here's your best chance for grabbing a quick breakfast or lunch while waiting for the ferry. The Blue Dolphin is right next to the end of the ferry lanes on First Street. They open at 5 A.M. for those riders catching the early boat. It's not just hamburgers—they fix great eggs and delicious deli sandwiches, too.

Bistro Garden $ to $$

180 Web Street; Friday Harbor, WA 98250. Phone: (360) 378-1174

HOURS: Lunch and dinner Tuesday through Sunday 11 A.M. to 9 P.M. Closed Mondays. Take-out available.

The fare is heavily Italian, featuring pizzas, calzones, spaghetti, and lasagna, but the Bistro also offers a wider variety of hot special sandwiches for lunch. They are a bit west of the main Friday Harbor thoroughfares, on Web Street, not far from the ferry overflow parking area. They have take-out, so if you are stuck with a long ferry wait, grab a great pizza.

China Pearl $$ ⅄

51 Spring Street; Friday Harbor, WA 98250. Phone: (360) 378-5254 (restaurant), (360) 378-5551 (lounge); email: *chinapearlrest@yahoo.com*; web site: *sanjuansites.com/chinapearl*

HOURS: Lunch and dinner daily, restaurant 11:30 A.M. to 10 P.M., lounge 12 P.M. to 2 A.M. Orders to go. Lounge, card room. Reservations recommended. Take-out available. Major credit cards accepted.

Whether you've mastered the use of chopsticks or not, Chinese food is always a favorite. China Pearl offers Mandarin, Cantonese, and spicy hot Szechwan cuisines, as well as Japanese and Korean. Select from a wide range of dishes and combinations, or if you want a really gala dinner, order Peking duck.

For an evening of fun, there's a card room, billiard room, pinball, video games, internet jukebox, and live music on weekends.

The Coffee Bar $

1331 Spring Street; Friday Harbor, WA 98250

Jammed between two buildings, this narrow coffee outlet claims to be the world's skinniest latte shop. It sells espresso, iced coffees sodas, juices, bottled water, milkshakes, sandwiches, and chocolate chip cookies.

Cousin Vinnie's $

Jeri's Spring Street Center, 260 Spring Street; Friday Harbor, WA 98250. Phone: (360) 378-8308

HOURS: Daily from 7 A.M. to 11 P.M. Take-out available.

This small New York-style café is tucked into a cubby in the mall on Spring Street. Among the offerings are bagels, pizza, burgers, pasta, desserts, espresso, frappuccino, sorbets, smoothies, ice cream and shakes.

The Doctor's Office $

85 Front Street; Friday Harbor, WA 98250. Phone: (360) 378-8865

HOURS: Lunch daily.

Of course, ice cream is just what the doctor ordered, as well as espresso and healthy juice drinks. This shop in a colorfully painted Victorian home at the head of the ferry landing dispenses delectable homemade ice cream, in cones or hand-packed pints and quarts. Seating is inside or outside on the front porch so you can watch ferry activity and catch your boat on time. They also have a few lunch offerings.

Dos Diablos Taqueria, Restaurant, and Cantina $ to $$ ☿

40 Spring Street; Friday Harbor, WA 98250. Phone (360) 378-8226

HOURS: Taqueria 8 A.M. to 2 P.M., restaurant 11 A.M. to 9 P.M., cantina 11 A.M. to 11 P.M. Take-out available. Major credit cards accepted.

Dos Diablos has a split personality—and all of them Mexican. At street level, on Spring Street, the Taqueria serves quick Mexican breakfasts and lunches such as breakfast burritos, tacos, quesadillas, and nachos. Dos Diablos Restaurant, on the second level, caters to the sit-down lunch and dinner crowd with generous carnita platters, prawns, chile rellenos, and much more. The Cantina, also on the second level, sports rough wooden benches and rough-hewn overhead beams reminiscent of a classic movie-set Mexican bar. It offers 18 specialty tequilas and a 27-ounce Margarita that seems big enough to swim in.

Downrigger's $$ to $$$ ☿

10 Front Street; Friday Harbor, WA 98250. Phone: (360) 378-2700; fax (360) 378-3026; email: *downriggers@rockisland.com*; web site: *downriggerssanjuan.com*

HOURS: Lunch and dinner daily 11 A.M. to 9 P.M.; breakfast at 9 A.M. weekends. Reservations recommended. Major credit cards accepted.

The decor is ship-shape nautical, with lots of blue and brass. The view, especially from the outside deck, is smack-dab above the harbor comings and goings. The food is good old seafood standbys—and that's hard to beat in the San Juans. The menu also includes steak, ribs, and chicken dishes and an extensive array of appetizers, beverages, and desserts. A "Daily Fresh Sheet" tells you which seafood is fresh off the boats.

A children's menu features kid-size burgers and that all-American favorite, grilled cheese sandwiches.

SAN JUAN ISLAND
Restaurants, Cafés & Take-Out

Duck Soup Inn $$$ 🍾

50 Duck Soup Lane; Friday Harbor, WA 98250. Phone: (360) 378-4878; web site: *ducksoupinn.com*

HOURS: Dinners daily at 5 P.M.; weekends only in winter. Reservations recommended. Major credit
   cards accepted.

We can't think of a better way to spend a summer evening than to take a short
drive in the country and stop for a gourmet dinner in a natural setting. Duck
Soup Inn is a scenic six-mile drive from Friday Harbor, on Roche Harbor Road.
The restaurant's interior reflects the surrounding forest, with lots of wood and a
fieldstone fireplace.

The wide-ranging menu draws on such varied cuisines as Northwest, French,
Cajun, and Thai; fresh ingredients and inventive seasonings are the common
thread. Entrées include game, as well as a range of seafood, poultry, and beef
selections. Who could resist such offerings as apple-wood smoked Westcott Bay
oysters, or medallions of beef sautéed with shallots, brandy, and cream. The wine
list features fine wines, both domestic and imported.

Ernie's Café $

744 Airport Circle Drive; Friday Harbor, WA 98250. Phone: (360) 378-6605

HOURS: Summer Tuesday through Sunday 7 A.M. to 7 P.M., off-season 7 A.M. to 2 P.M.

Sitting next to the runway at Friday Harbor Airport, Ernie's is named for Ernie Gann, a
well-known writer and aviation pioneer who lived on San Juan Island. The café offers
simple fare of soups, salads and sandwiches, and is decorated with enough aviation
memorabilia to merit being called a museum. It's worth stopping by to see.

San Juan Island's Greatest Adventurer

The San Juan Islands have had several famous residents. One of the most well-
known is the late Ernest K. Gann, who wrote 21 best-selling novels. Two, *The
High and the Mighty* and *Island in the Sky* became classic movies starring John
Wayne. A third film used his title, *Fate is the Hunter,* but bears little resemblance
to his excellent novel.

Gann's life, as one web site states, "makes Indiana Jones look like Mister
Rogers." As just part of his accomplishments, he began flying commercial airlines in 1938, and later traveled worldwide during World War II as a pilot for
the U.S. Army Air Corps. He eventually became a commercial fisherman. His
novels are largely based on his experiences in those two fields.

Gann and his wife purchased an 800-acre ranch on San Juan Island in
1966, where he continued to write. After his death in 1991, the bulk of the
ranch was donated to the San Juan Island Preservation Trust. In 2003, then-
Washington State Governor Gary Locke awarded Gann the Medal of Merit,
the state's highest honor.

The Flying Burrito $

701 Spring Street; Friday Harbor, WA 98250. Phone: (360) 378-1077 (phone orders)

HOURS: Monday through Saturday 11 A.M. to 7 P.M. Food is primarily for take-out.

With limited seating and a few outside picnic tables, the Flying Burrito is designed for drive-up window take-out fare. The menu includes tacos, burritos, salads, burgers, chips, salsa, and shakes.

Friday Harbor House $$ to $$$ 🍸

130 West Street; Friday Harbor, WA 98250. Phone: (866) 722-7356 or (360) 378-8455; fax: (360) 378-8453; email: *fhhouse@rockisland.com*; web site: *fridayharborhouse.com*

HOURS: Dinner daily 5:30 P.M. to 10 P.M. Reservations recommended. Major credit cards accepted.

You are guaranteed superb dining and one of the finest views in the San Juans at the Friday Harbor House. The restaurant was awarded the prestigious AAA Four Diamond Award, has received the highest of ratings from other "Best" publications, and has been acclaimed in food magazines.

The menu features gourmet seafood selections of Westcott Bay oysters, mussels, king salmon, and Dungeness crab, along with unique offerings such as grilled chicken breasts with sun dried tomatoes, fresh basil, and white wine butter sauce. Locally grown vegetables ensure a fresh taste of the Northwest. You won't be able to pass up delectable dessert selections that include handmade ice creams and sorbets, fruit tart, and chocolate desserts.

Friday Harbor Ice Cream To Go $

1 Spring Street; Friday Harbor, WA 98250

Ice cream, snacks, espresso (open summers only).

Hop off the ferry on a warm summer day and step next door to satisfy your cravings for a nice cool ice cream cone. This stand lays claim to one of the world's largest selections of flavors (72), and, seeing their long counter, it's easy to believe. They offer 16 varieties of chocolate, and as many coffee and candy, nut, and fruit flavors, as well as sherbets, sorbets, frozen yogurt, and sugar-free ice cream.

Friday's Crabhouse $ to $$ 🍾

65 Front Street; Friday Harbor, WA 98250. Phone: (360) 378-8801

HOURS: Lunch and dinner daily, open at 11 A.M. Orders to go. Major credit cards accepted.

You shouldn't leave the San Juans without filling up on local seafood, and Friday's Crabhouse is just the place to do it. In summer you'll find this open-air café on the boardwalk plaza above the ferry terminal. Settle down to a brimming plate of prawns, scallops, fish, oysters, clams, mussels, calamari, or fresh-cracked crab. You can also get smoked clam chowder and shrimp and crab cocktails.

Front Street Ale House $ ℸ

1 Front Street; Friday Harbor, WA 98250. Phone: (360) 378-BEER (378-2337); email: *sanjuanbrewing@rockisland.com*; web site: *sanjuanbrewing.com*

HOURS: Lunch and dinner 11 A.M. to 10 P.M. midweek, Friday and Saturday until midnight, Sunday until 10 P.M. Major credit cards accepted.

The multipage menu alone is worth a stop at the Front Street Ale House. Decorated with hilarious cartoon characters, it will keep you chuckling as you try to decide among the many offerings. The ambiance is British pub, and the menu follows suit with British pub fish and chips. Page after page of the menu reveals more eclectic choices and a sense of humor: "oar D'oeuvres" include oyster shooters and a pint 'o prawns. Other offerings are jalapeño fish and chips, blue oyster burger, chili-stuffed baked potato (with ass-kicking chili), Thai chili sauced chicken, ⅓-pound beef burgers, and a variety of hot sandwiches. Seafood? Try fish and chips, salmon and chips, oysters and chips, scampi and chips, or scallops and chips.

Featured beers come from the San Juan Brewing Company, their own micro-brewery right next door. As of last count, 11 different unique ales, lagers, and stouts were home-brewed on the premises. Other domestic and imported beers are available, too.

Upstairs, the Top Side Gastro Pub and Cocktail lounge offers a living room atmosphere with coffee tables surrounded by comfortable chairs.

Front Street Café $ to $$ 🍾

7 Front Street; Friday Harbor, WA 98250. Phone: (360) 378-2245; fax: (360) 378-2944; email: *frontstreet@beerbreadmix.com*; web site: *sanjuansites.com/frontstcafe*

HOURS: Breakfast and lunch daily 6:30 A.M. to 2 P.M.; early dinner Friday and Saturday. Dinner reservations recommended. Major credit cards accepted.

If you saw the movie "Free Willy," you would have seen this little café overlooking the ferry terminal. But you don't need to be a movie star or extra to enjoy this spot for breakfast while waiting for an early boat, or to pick up a sandwich before heading off on a bike tour of the island. Choose from some of their bakery goodies and an espresso. Lunch offerings include homemade soup, sandwiches, and a hot entrée such as pizza or spinach feta pie. Tables inside the café or on the covered deck provide seating with a close-up view of ferry goings-on.

Golden Triangle Restaurant $$

Friday Harbor Center; 140 First Street; Friday Harbor, WA 98250. Phone: (360) 378-1917

HOURS: Lunch and dinner 11 A.M. to 9 P.M., Tuesday through Saturday. All dishes available for take-out.

This small restaurant with an enormous menu is handily located in Friday Harbor Center. The flavors are mostly Thai, with fried rices, coconut sauce dishes, curries, noodle dishes, and a variety of seafood specials.

Haley's Bait Shop and Grill $ to $$ 𝖸

175 Spring Street; Friday Harbor, WA 98250. Phone: (360) 378-4434

HOURS: Lunch, and dinner, Monday through Saturday 11 A.M. to 10:30 P.M. Bar open until 2 P.M. Major credit cards accepted.

No, you won't find coolers of herring here, as its name might imply—there's something much better. This lively eatery on the Friday Harbor main drag offers reasonably priced family fare, and a full bar in the lounge. The grill, which is a small dining area in front, features burgers, wraps, and Italian cuisine such as pizza and pasta.

The décor is fishing gear, mounted fish, and framed fishing articles. TVs in the dining area and lounge let you keep up on the latest in sports. The lounge also features pool tables, a jukebox, and darts. Some evenings there's live entertainment.

Herb's Tavern $ 🍾

80 First Street South; Friday Harbor, WA 98250. Phone: (360) 378-7076

HOURS: Daily 11 A.M. to 9 P.M.; bar open to 2 A.M.

For more than 30 years Herb's Tavern, at the corner of Spring and First Street, has been a local watering hole. The recently remodeled saloon now offers live music and dancing in its spiffy, all-new digs. You'll want to have one of their great burgers to eat with your cold beer. They offer seafood and appetizers, too. Stop in for a lunch of hearty soup and a sandwich topped off with your favorite microbrew.

The Hungry Clam $ 🍾

205 A Street; Friday Harbor, WA 98250. Phone: (360) 378-FISH (378-3474); email: *hungryclam@adelphia.net*

HOURS: Lunch and dinner daily 11 A.M. to 7 P.M. Take-out available.

When their phone number says FISH, it's pretty clear what you'll get here. The decor is fast-food plain. However, the fish, shrimp, clams, and oysters are served in ample portions. Hamburgers, salads, and vegetarian soups round out the menu. There's inside seating, or take your order out to the restaurant's sun-splashed deck or to the ravenous gang waiting in the car at the nearby ferry landing.

Jimmy's Paradise Café $ to $$ 𝖸

Paradise Lane; 365 Spring Street; Friday Harbor, WA 98250. Phone: (360) 378-3131; email: *jcafe@rockisland.com*

HOURS: Breakfast, lunch, and dinner daily. Many items available for take-out. Major credit cards accepted.

Jimmy's dining room and bar are located in the Paradise Lanes bowling alley, so don't anticipate haute cuisine—just substantial family fare at great prices. The selection is huge: 12 kinds of burgers, seven kinds of hot dogs, eight salads, and 14 varieties of pizza for lunch. Dinner offerings include appetizers, steak, chicken, barbecued ribs, and seafood dinners. Eat at the restaurant, the bar, or the bowling lanes.

Latitude 48 $$ 🍾

275 A Street; Friday Harbor, WA 98250. Phone: (360) 370-5238

HOURS: Breakfast, lunch, and dinner Wednesday through Monday 7 A.M. to 10 P.M. Closed Tuesday.

Latitude 48 is the exact meridian running through Friday Harbor, as well as a fine restaurant at the corner of A Street and Nichols. Breakfasts are imaginative omelets, huevos rancheros, or a smoked salmon bagel plate. Lunches start with seafood appetizers and lead to hearty sandwiches, turkey, French dip, and pulled pork. Dinners include salmon, clams and linguini, chicken breasts, Mongolian pork and slow-roasted baby back ribs.

Lime Kiln Café $

Roche Harbor Resort; 248 Reuben Tarte Memorial Drive; Roche Harbor, WA 98250. Phone: (360) 378-5757; email: *roche@rocheharbor.com*; web site: *rocheharbor.com*

HOURS: Breakfast, lunch, and dinner in summer 7 A.M. to 9 P.M.; breakfast and lunch off-season 8 A.M. to 2 P.M. Major credit cards accepted.

The Lime Kiln Café is so close to the action of the Roche Harbor docks that you could find yourself eating all your meals here. Hearty breakfasts include all the classics, as well as steak with vine-ripened tomatoes. Lunches and dinners list soups, salads, popcorn shrimp, burgers, sandwiches, and chips baskets with oysters, cod, or chicken strips.

Madrona Bar and Grill $$ 🍸

Roche Harbor Resort; 248 Reuben Tarte Memorial Drive; Roche Harbor, WA 98250. Phone: (800) 451-5757, ext 400 or (360) 378-5757, ext 400; email: *roche@rocheharbor.com*; web site: *rocheharbor.com*

HOURS: Lunch and dinner 11 A.M. to midnight mid-May through October. Live music weekends. Reservations recommended.

Mid-range in Roche Harbor dining, between the Lime Kiln Café and the elegant cuisine of McMillin's Dining Room, the Madrona Bar and Grill addresses the light side of Roche Harbor dining. Lunches and dinners offer a menu of Northwest seafood and Pan Asia fare. Their ample summer deck seating overlooking the harbor is just the place to dive into a cold beer, gin and tonic, or daiquiri. The bar's signature cocktail is a Fluffy Duck—you must give it a try.

Maloula Restaurant $ to $$ 🍸

1 Front Street; Friday Harbor, WA 98250. Phone: (360) 378-8485; web site: *sanjuansites. com/maloulas*

HOURS: Lunch and dinner Wednesday through Saturday 11 A.M. to 8:30 P.M. Reservations recommended. Major credit cards accepted.

Ethnic food is always a nice change of pace. Maloula features savory Mediterranean, Middle Eastern, and American cuisines. The food is so good you'll probably become a regular. Lunch features gyros with an assortment of meats, hamburgers, and several choices of green salads, rices, lentils, and hummus. Dinners include more elaborate offerings, such as marinated salmon steak, kabob, seafood, or Cornish game hen. In the mood for a whole leg of lamb? Order it a day ahead and the restaurant will prepare it for six persons or more.

The beverage list includes cocktails and interesting imported wines and beers, as well as domestic ones, that go well with the exotic flavorings of the cuisine. Don't neglect dessert! Choose from incredible Greek pastries, including six different kinds of baklava. In summer, dine outside in a roof garden on tall chairs and tables that improve the view of the harbor.

Marilyn's Garden Path Café $

135 Second Street; Friday Harbor, WA 98250. Phone: (360) 378-6255

HOURS: Breakfast and lunch Monday through Friday 7:30 A.M. to 3:30 P.M. Take-out available.

A great breakfast menu features the standard omelets, eggs, sausages or bacon, but enlivens it with potato pancakes and crepes rolled with mixed berries. The lunch menu lists soups, salads, and half-a-dozen burger offerings. Other sandwiches include turkey on panini with provolone, black olive pesto and tomato, and Swiss cheese with onion.

Market Chef $

225 A Street; Friday Harbor, WA 98250. Phone: (360) 378-4546

HOURS: Open Monday through Friday 10 A.M. to 6 P.M. Food is primarily for take-out.

This shop has a deli-case filled with roast beef, turkey, tuna, and smoked ham sandwiches, which are complemented by homemade soups and salads. A few inside tables and more on an outside deck permit you to enjoy your purchases here. Or, you can take them back to the hungry crowd in the nearby ferry line.

McMillin's Dining Room $$ to $$$ ⟼

Roche Harbor Resort; 248 Rueben Tarte Memorial Drive; Roche Harbor, WA 98250. Phone: (800) 451-8910, ext. A or (360) 378-5757, ext A, (360) 378-2155, ext 400A; email: *roche@rocheharbor.com*; web site: *rocheharbor.com*

HOURS: Dinner daily in summer 5 P.M. to 10 P.M. ; winter Thursday through Monday 5 P.M. to 10 P.M.

Roche Harbor Resort's McMillin's Dining Room offers fine meals to match its fine surroundings. The restaurant is in the former home of John S. McMillin, who founded the Roche Harbor Lime and Cement Company. The home has a welcoming elegance, with lots of richly polished wood, fine art, and beautiful carpets. It's a great spot for a romantic dinner, as well as wedding receptions and other events. They cater, of course.

Menu offerings are varied appetizers of mussels, calamari, crab, and artichoke dip, oysters and wild mushrooms, and goat cheeses. Entrées include pork loin with caramelized apple, seared pretale sole, hazelnut crusted halibut stuffed with crab and Gouda, and rack of lamb with balsamic drizzle. Feast on desserts of five-berry cobbler or crème brulee.

Mi Casita $$ 🍾

95 Nichols Street; Friday Harbor, WA 98250. Phone: (360) 378-6103 or (360) 378-6107

HOURS: Lunch and dinner. Take-out is available.

Mi Casita stresses traditional Mexican fare with its shredded beef and seafood dishes. Outdoor seating and take-out is available. The extensive menu includes nachos, quesadillas, margarita prawns, enchiladas, tamales, tacos, tostados, chile rellenos, chimichangas, burritos, and much more.

One Twenty Nichols $$$ 🍾

120 Nichols Street; Friday Harbor, WA 98250. Phone: (360) 378-6330; email: *johnpeak@ rockisland.com*; web site: *120nichols.com*

HOURS: Dinner Wednesday through Monday 5 P.M. to 9:30 P.M.

One Twenty Nichols offers eclectic Northwest cuisine with a French flavor. The fine dining goes far beyond the usual seafood fare. Appetizers of wild mushroom risotto or smoked mussel ravioli precede entrées of potato-crusted halibut, roasted Cornish game hen, pan-seared duck breast, or New Zealand rack of lamb. Individual entrées or a price-fixed multi-course menu are available.

Pelindaba Downtown $

Friday Harbor Center; 150 First Street; Friday Harbor, WA 98250. Phone: (360) 378-6900; email: *admin@pelindaba.com*; web site: *pelindaba.com*

HOURS: Open all day. Take-out available.

Pelindaba, which operates a large lavender farm on San Juan Island, knows how to mix the herb with food in delectable ways. The restaurant at the back of their retail outlet offers an inspired menu of soups, salads, and savory pies. Many have touches of lavender, such as the Monte Cristo sandwich and lavender herbes de Provence, or the lavender salad crumble. Lavender also laces the cakes, tortes, tarts, breads, cookies, and iced tea. Everything invites a return visit. The café also sponsors evening gatherings for book readings and discussion groups while enjoying the fare.

Peppermill Seafood and Steakhouse $$$ 🍸

Best Western Friday Harbor Suites; 680 Spring Street; Friday Harbor, WA 98250. Phone: (360) 378-7060 (restaurant), (360) 378-6966 (lounge); email: *peppermill@rockisland.com*; web site: *peppermillsanjuan.com*

HOURS: Daily 4 P.M. to midnight, martini happy hour 4 P.M. to 7 P.M. and 10 P.M. to midnight. Major credit cards accepted.

Under the same roof as the Best Western Friday Harbor Suites, the Peppermill Seafood and Steakhouse presents an impressive menu of seafood, prawns, scallops, lobster, and jambalaya, along with beef prime rib, pork tenderloin, and baby back ribs. Pasta and poultry round out the menu.

The full service bar features a widescreen TV for watching sports. The martini happy hours feature large stainless goblets of gin that might humble James Bond.

The Place Bar & Grill $$ to $$$ Y

1 Spring Street; Friday Harbor, WA 98250. Phone: (360) 378-8707; email: *theplace@rockisland.
com*; web site: *theplacesanjuan.com*

HOURS: Dinner 5 P.M. to 9 P.M. daily; Sunday brunch. Reservations. Major credit cards accepted.

This gourmet restaurant started off named The Place Next to the San Juan Ferry Café. However, and as the restaurant's fame grew, it just became The Place Bar & Grill. Once you've sampled their fabulous meals it will become one of your favorite places, and you'll make it a regular stop on your itinerary.

The restaurant offers casual fine dining and a great view of the harbor with its boating and ferry activity. Its menu includes a nice range of fresh seafood, such as halibut, bouillabaisse, linguini with clams, and Northwest staples of salmon and Westcott Bay oysters. Pasta, beef, and chicken, as well as a vegetarian dish, all prepared imaginatively, round out the entrées. You can begin your meal with tempting soups such as wild mushroom bisque, and then end the repast with a flourish by indulging in an inspired dessert such as pudding cake or hazelnut milk chocolate cheesecake. Calories be damned!

Rich's Cannery House Restaurant $ to $$

174 North First; Friday Harbor, WA 98250. Phone: (360) 378-6505

HOURS: Breakfast and lunch Monday through Saturday 7 A.M. to 4 P.M., dinner 5 P.M. to 8 P.M. in
summer. Take-out is available.

Friday Harbor's venerable Cannery House Restaurant changed ownership in 2006, and has been remodeled and updated. It offers continental-style breakfasts with espressos to start the day. Lunches feature sandwiches, chowder, soup de jour, and salads, all with generous servings. Dinners, served in the summer, feature a variety of pastas, daily specials, and mouth-watering pie to top it off. Wireless internet access is available to check your email or surf the internet while munching a burger.

It is on North First, just up the hill from the Whale Museum; its deck has one of the greatest harbor views in the town.

Roche Harbor Resort

See Lime Kiln Café, page 244, Madrona Bar & Grill, page 244, and McMillin's Dining Room, page 245.

Rocky Bay Café $ 🍴

225 Spring Street; Friday Harbor, WA 98250. Phone: (360) 378-5051

HOURS: Breakfast and lunch daily 6:30 A.M. to 3 P.M.

The café is unpretentious, but it offers good hearty food with excellent service. It's where the locals head for breakfast. Basic egg, pancake, and waffle dishes, eggs benedict, and omelets are supplemented with breakfast burritos, huevos rancheros, pork chop breakfast, and chicken-fried steak. Lunches are sandwiches, salads, burgers, fish and chips, and chicken strip platters. Espresso—naturally!

Steps Wine Bar and Café $$ to $$$ 🍷

Friday Harbor Center; 140A First Street; Friday Harbor, WA 98250; (360) 370-5959; email: *dine@stepswinebarandcafe.com*; web site: *stepswinebarandcafé.com*

HOURS: Open for dinner at 4 P.M. Closed Monday and Tuesday.

Located on the Friday Harbor Center walkway across from Pelindaba, Steps Wine Bar offers an extensive wine list and more than 50 wines available by the half glass so you can sample several. Their imaginative meals include dishes such as goat cheese turnover, blackened scallops, sweet potato gnocchi, butter clam croquettes, and mushroom stuffed halibut. You'll have difficulty choosing. Meals, listed on an Early Menu or a full Dinner Menu, can be ordered by either small or large plates. Desserts include Mexican chocolate flan, butternut squash cheesecake, and carrot cake.

The Sweet Retreat & Espresso $

264 Spring Street; Friday Harbor, WA 98250. Phone: (360) 378-1957; email: *dmmorton@ rockisland.com*; web site: *sanjuansites.com/sweet retreat*

HOURS: Monday through Friday 7:30 A.M. to 5 P.M., Saturday 8 A.M. to 2 P.M. Food is for take-out.

This tiny stand, sandwiched between two buildings right on Spring Street, has no sit-down service, but at its counter you can purchase coffee, rolls, muffins, hand-dipped ice cream, and granitas to sample as you stroll. They also offer hot dogs, krautdogs, breakfast sandwiches, soups, and salads for take-out.

The Sweet Spot $

Friday Harbor Center; 180 First Street, Suite 8; Friday Harbor, WA 98250. Phone: (360) 378-5274; fax: (360) 378-1600; email: *pcornlady@sjsweetspot.com*; web site: *thepopcornlady.com*

HOURS: Daily.

Don't sit in the ferry line without crossing First Street to the lower level of Friday Harbor Center to meet The Popcorn Lady. She prepares gourmet flavored popcorn, kettle-popped on the site. Other treats include saltwater taffy, gummy bears, gummy sharks, all sorts of other gummy creatures, licorice, dozens of flavors of jelly beans, and a host of other candies. This is where you'll find justly famous Lopez Island Creamery ice creams.

Top Side Gastro Pub & Cocktail Lounge $ 🍸

1 Front Street; Friday Harbor, WA 98250. Phone: (360) 378-BEER (378-2337); email: *sanjuanbrewing@rockisland.com*; web site: *sanjuanbrewing.com*

HOURS: Lunch and dinner daily 11 A.M. to 10 P.M. midweek, Friday and Saturday until midnight, Sunday until 10 P.M. Major credit cards accepted.

Upstairs from the Front Street Ale House, the Top Side Gastro Pub & Cocktail Lounge has a front room atmosphere, with coffee tables surrounded by lounge chairs. It features a variety of small "share plates" that permit you and your friends to sample from a dozen offerings. Larger meals are available, too. Featured beers come from the San Juan Brewing Company, a microbrewery right next door. Other domestic and imported beers are available, too, as well as mixed drinks.

Vic's Drive Inn $

25 Second Street; Friday Harbor, WA 98250. Phone: (360) 378-8427

HOURS: Breakfast, lunch, and dinner Monday through Friday 7 A.M. to 7 P.M., Saturday 7 A.M. to 2 P.M. Orders to go.

When the gang is clamoring for good old burgers and fries, pizza, or chicken, Vic's will deliciously fill the bill. It's just a block east of the high school. Sit inside, or take your cheeseburger the traditional way—to go.

Vinnie's Ristorante $$ to $$$ 🍸

165 West Street; Friday Harbor, WA 98250. Phone: (360) 378-1934

HOURS: Lunch and dinner daily 5 P.M. to 10 P.M. Major credit cards accepted.

The décor is classy Italian, and so is the menu. Lunches are simple appetizers, salads, lasagna, spaghetti, and hamburgers, but they are far from McDonald's fare. Dinner appetizers include calamari, garlic prawns, oysters, roasted portobello mushrooms, and Mediterranean mussels. Steaks and pastas are joined by scampi, veal or chicken piccata, duck breast, veal or chicken marsala, and cioppino.

GROCERIES, BAKERIES, DELIS & LIQUOR

Big Barn Bakes

895 Spring Street; Friday Harbor, WA 98250. Phone: (360) 378-7089; fax: (360) 378-6567; email: *piet@thevissers.com*

HOURS: Wednesday through Sunday 10 A.M. to 6 P.M.

An artisan bakery, yes, but more. This is also a wine shop and home of the Muffin Man, producing fresh baked goodies.

The Big Store

420 Argyle Avenue; Friday Harbor, WA 98250; (360) 378-2424, (360) 378-3700 (pizza and deli)

HOURS: Daily 7 A.M. to 9:30 P.M.

The Big Store is one of the few gas stations on San Juan Island. In addition to the pumps the associated store carries beer, wine, some limited groceries, deli selections, and video rentals.

Friday Harbor Seafoods

Port Dock Main Pier; P.O. Box 1656; Friday Harbor, WA 98250. Phone: (360) 378-5779; email: *fishcreek@interisland.net*

HOURS: Daily 10 A.M. to 6 P.M.

For the freshest seafood, go right to the source. You can buy cooked Dungeness crab, clams, and shrimp right out of steaming pots at this houseboat on the Friday Harbor docks. Spirit your purchases back to your boat, break out the tartar sauce, and be prepared for paradise! Live tanks hold scallops, Maine lobsters, and crabs. Pick out fresh oysters, salmon, halibut, cod, octopus, mahi-mahi, or other seafood to grill on your hibachi or to have packed in ice to take home.

King's Market Thriftway and Marine Center

160 Spring Street West; Friday Harbor, WA 98250. Market phone: (360) 378-4505 (360); marine center phone: 378-4593; email: *kingsmarket@rockisland.com*; web site: *kings-market.com*

A grocery store as a tourist attraction? It's certainly true of King's. We never go to the San Juans without taking a whirl down its aisles. Besides the usual Cheerios and Pampers, you'll find selections of locally made foods—jams, jellies, sauces, wine—that provide a sampling of the San Juans' bounty. Stop by the deli and pick up everything you need for a picnic lunch or an evening barbecue on the boat. King's will deliver your bags of grub to the dock for you, too. There are also clothing, marine, and variety departments. In an inspired bit of punning, the aisles are named after various San Juan isles.

Fresh seafood, some of it in live tanks, is sold by Friday Harbor Seafood from a houseboat on the main pier in Friday Harbor.

The Little Store

285 Spring Street; Friday Harbor, WA 98250. Phone: (360) 378-4422

HOURS: Deli open 7 A.M. to 5 P.M. daily. The gas pumps are open at the same times.

If you want to fête a bunch of your friends down on your boat, give these folks a call and they'll whip up an extravagant party tray in their deli. For cyclists wanting to get an early start in the cool of the morning, The Little Store is open at 6:30 A.M., ready with all the carbohydrates you'll need for a long day.

Roche Harbor Grocery Store

P.O. Box 948; Friday Harbor, WA 98250. Phone: (360) 378-5562

Boaters needing to replenish their larders can buy what they need at this store on the dock at Roche Harbor. You'll find fresh produce and meat, and other things to spice up tiresome galley meals. Also for sale are fishing gear, bait, some kitchenware, books, magazines, and all sorts of odds and ends.

San Juan Coffee Roasting Co.

18 Cannery Landing; Friday Harbor, WA 98250. Phone: (800) 624-4119 or (360) 378-4443; email: *sjcoffee@rockisland.com*; web site: *rockisland.com/~sjcoffee*

This shop next to the ferry landing has become a San Juan tradition in our family. We always make a point to park in the ferry line in time to saunter down to Cannery Landing and get one of their luscious Håaagen Dazs ice cream cones. It's also a wonderful place to pick up a last minute gift. Who wouldn't love to receive a package of specially roasted Caffé San Juan, select teas, or some gourmet chocolates? If you're not in the mood for ice cream, try a fresh pastry and an espresso.

States Inn Ranch Store

2687 West Valley Road; Friday Harbor, WA 98250. Phone: (866) 602-2737, (360) 378-6240; fax: (360) 378-6241; email: *info@statesinn.com*; web site: *statesinn.com*

🚐 From Friday Harbor, drive northwest on Second Street and follow it as it becomes Guard Street, then Beaverton Valley Road, and merges into West Valley Road. About 7 miles from Friday Harbor, the sign for the inn and ranch is ½ mile north of the Mitchell Bay Road intersection.

That terrific ranch at States Inn now has a store that offers fresh produce from their garden, fresh-baked lunch items, beverages, and some hand-crafted items. Buy eggs that were laid just that morning by the very chickens you see. The store makes a nice stop during your mid-island wanderings.

Washington State Liquor Store

365 Spring Street; Friday Harbor, WA 98250. Phone: (360) 378-2956

HOURS: Monday through Saturday 10 A.M. to 6 P.M.

You'll locate the liquor store in Friday Harbor in the group of shops known as Harbor Village at the Y-intersection of Spring Street and Argyle Avenue.

Westcott Bay Sea Farms

904 Westcott Drive; Friday Harbor, WA 98250. Phone: (360) 378-2489; fax: (360) 378-6388; email: *sandy@westcottbay.com*; web site: *westcottbay.com*

🚗🔺 The Sea Farms are at the end of Westcott Drive, off Roche Harbor Road, 1 mile east of Roche Harbor Resort. Paddlecraft can approach the sea farms from Roche Harbor or nearby homes, but there is no tie-up space for larger boats.

If you feast on oysters at one of the fine restaurants in the San Juans, chances are good that your appetizer or main course came from Westcott Bay Sea Farms. Because of their rich flavor, Westcott Bay oysters are prized by gourmands, and are shipped to markets as far away as Europe. You might dine on them at nearly any place in the world.

This company, one of the San Juan Island's major aquaculture enterprises, runs their large oyster-growing operation off the east shore of the bay, a saltwater inlet east of Roche Harbor. The water temperature in the bay is ideal for raising the two varieties of oysters, one variety of Manila clams, and mussels that the venture specializes in.

Although the company harvests oysters primarily for commercial sales, visitors can stop and choose their fresh gourmet shellfish themselves. Gift packs will be shipped anywhere in the U.S. Visa and MasterCard are accepted. You can view their offerings at their web site, as well, and then phone or fax them with your order.

SHOPPING, GALLERIES & ARTISTS

Alpaca Shop

2nd Floor, Cannery Landing; Friday Harbor, WA 98250. Phone: (360) 378-8445

Very little beats the softness and warmth of alpaca wool, and this shop can introduce you to it in the form of men's and women's sweaters, caps, scarves and other clothing items.

Arctic Raven Gallery

Friday Harbor Center; 130 South First Street, P.O. Box 792; Friday Harbor, WA 98250. Phone: (360) 378-3433; email: *arcticraven@rockisland.com*; web site: *arcticravengallery.com*

This premier gallery in the Friday Harbor Center features "Native art from the source." It specializes in fine art from Inuit, Northwest Coast, and Alaskan Natives. Sculptures, masks, woodcarvings, and a broad range of other media are featured, as well as works of featured Northwest artists.

Bison Gallery

65 Nichols Street, P.O. Box 2837; Friday Harbor, WA 98250. Phone: gallery: (360) 378-5899; studio: (360) 378-4179; cell: (360) 317-8972; email: *gallery@bisonbronze.com*; web site: *bisonbronze.com*

This gallery features art in all mediums by Northwest artists, as well as bronze sculptures by Doug Bison. It also has work by well-known Alaskan artist Rie Muñoz and a collection of Native American pieces, including some antique artifacts. Some of the pieces display unique techniques, such as "Hot Ice" crystal porcelain.

Boardwalk Bookstore

9 Spring Street West; P.O. Box 283; Friday Harbor, WA 98250. Phone: (360) 378-2787; fax: (360) 38.2786; email: *books@boardwalkbookstore.com*; web site: *boardwalkbookstore.com*

A wonderland of books lies in the rear of the little courtyard on Spring Street. There's all the latest fiction, along with a wide selection of guidebooks (such as this one), books of regional interest, beautiful coffee-table volumes, children's books, and something covering your special interest. You're sure to find the ideal book to curl up with on the beach, at your resort, or on the deck of your boat. Store owner Bettye Hendrickson will special order books for you, or will mail them to wherever you wish.

The store also carries maps and nautical charts, as well as postcards and nice greeting cards to go along with that book selection.

Brazenly Lucid Wines

80 Nichols Street; Friday Harbor, WA 98250. Phone: (360) 6300, fax: (360) ; email: stan@ blucid.com; web site: blucid.com

HOURS: Daily, except Tuesday.

This shop is as upbeat as its name, with enthusiastic, knowledgeable owners, and a schedule of fun events. It offers an exceptionally wide range of wines, champagnes, and specialty beers, as well as glassware and wine-related kitchenware. Regularly scheduled events include wine tastings, micro beer tasting, and interesting talks by wine and beer representatives.

Crème Brulee

310 Spring Street; Friday Harbor, WA 98250. Phone: (360) 378-7017; fax: (360) 378-7193; email: *info@mycremebrulee.com*; web site: *mycremebrulee.com*

The offerings in this shop are as delectable as a crème brulee. It features all sorts of nice scented products such as soaps, bath oils, sachets, and candles, as well as decorative accessories, women's clothing, bedding, furniture, baby products, and fancy wrapping papers. The range of goodies is amazing.

Daisy Bloom

5 Front Street; Friday Harbor, WA 98245. Phone: (360) 370-5180; email: *daisybloom@rockisland. com*; web site: *daisybloom.com*

If you are a woman heading up from the Port of Friday Harbor docks to shop, this will probably be the first place you stop. It's a great place to find trendy women's clothing, cashmere tops, knitted shells, and decorated jeans. No matter what your age, you are sure to discover accessories to add just the right touch to your outfit. The shop is next to the Front Street Ale House.

Dan Levin Originals

50 First Street; P.O. Box 1309; Friday Harbor, WA 98250. Phone: (800) 234-5078 or (360) 378-2051

Fine jewelry created by goldsmiths Dan and Diane Levin is known throughout the Northwest. Each stunning piece is hand signed and is sure to appreciate in value over time, as well as bring joy to the wearer. At the artists' studio gallery you might select a pendant of a tiny, exquisitely detailed gold crab with ruby eyes and a diamond clutched in one claw, or a ring with pearls wrapped in a froth of free-form gold.

Dockside Treasures

6 Cannery Landing; Friday Harbor, WA 98250. Phone: (360) 378-4013; fax: (360) 378-4396; email: *vboyd@interisland.net*

This shop, next to the ferry landing in the Cannery Landing Building carries tourist oriented products, refrigerator magnets, T-shirts and children's clothes, all souvenir-imprinted. There's everything for your last minute memories before dashing for the ferry.

Dolphin Arts – Cotton, Cotton, Cotton

165 First Street; Friday Harbor, WA 98250. Phone: (360) 378-3531; email: *vivb@rockisland.com*

Clothing was never before so much fun! This shop features the work of artist Vivien Burnett. You'll find her original designs silk-screened on T-shirts, shirts, and jackets. There are clothes for women and men, and irresistible items for kids. Posters, notecards, and wall hangings also feature her art. Jewelry comes from the creative hands of local artist Deborah Johnsen.

Dominique's House

125 Spring Street; Friday Harbor, WA 98250. Phone: (866) 301-5477 or (360) 378-0877; fax: (360) 378-0897; email: *domhouse@centurytel.net*; web site: *dominiqueshouse.com*

A broad selection of fabulous and fanciful furniture, bath accessories, and home décor is featured. Lamps, pillows, dinnerware, glassware accents, candles, and rugs are just a few of the many items offered. Dominque's House also has an on-line catalog, so you can view their new selections when you get back home.

Dominique's

285 Spring Street; Friday Harbor, WA 98250. Phone: (360) 378-6454; fax: (360) 378-4859; email: *dominiques@rockisland.com*; web site: *dominiquesclothing.com*

This women's clothing shop near the end of Spring Street will help you dress in style. You'll be able to put together a really great outfit from their selection of dresses, separates, accessories, and shoes. The store mixes cutting edge fashion with classic clothing. It has some items, such as picture frames, mirrors, and candles, to decorate your home.

Fire Arts

2217A Wold Road; Friday Harbor, WA 98250; (360) 378-5929; email: *bruceclark@firearts.com*; web site: *firearts.com*

Working out of this home studio, Bruce Clark and Nancy Best produce architectural glass such as tiles, tabletops, clocks, and light sconces. Ceramics include dinnerware, teapots, and tea services as well as sculptural glass and enamel. Commissions and special orders can be accommodated.

Friday Harbor Art Studio and Framing

30 Web Street; Friday Harbor, WA 98250. Phone: (360) 378-5788; email: *howie@ howardrosenfeld.com*; web site: *howardrosenfeld.com*

This back street gallery will professionally frame art you purchase in the San Juans, but that's just the beginning. It is also a studio for Howard Rosenfeld, an artist producing scrimshaw on ivory, pen and ink drawings, and prints from drypoint engraving on copper plates. His work is remarkable for its detailed beauty and accuracy in depicting sailing ships and marine life.

Friday Harbor Drug

210 Spring Street; Friday Harbor, WA 98250. Phone: (360) 378-4421 or (360) 378-4475

In the San Juans, even an ordinary drug store has a different twist. Friday Harbor Drug tucks nautical paraphernalia in with the lipstick and toothpaste. You'll find nautical instruments, log books, charts, maps, tide tables, and boating publications. The store also carries a nice line of gift items, many of which are nautically oriented (of course).

Friday Harbor Souvenir Company

135 Spring Street #F; Friday Harbor, WA 98250. Phone: (360) 378-5711; email: *fridayharborsouvenirco@gmail.com*

The name certainly says it all. From T-shirts, sweatshirts, cups, and caps to tea towels, this store is sure to have something for everyone on your gift list. Shelves are stacked with great merchandise ranging from functional items such as high-quality jackets and sweatshirts to toys and outrageously funny gag gifts. A pair of laptops in one corner offer internet access for a nominal fee.

Friday Harbor Trading Company

180 First Street; Friday Harbor, WA 98250. Phone: (800) 455-0650 or (360) 378-6660; fax: (360) 378-6660; email: *fhtrading@rockisland.com*; web site: *fridayharbortrading.com*

If you've come to the San Juans, you undoubtedly love the sea? This fine shop has a definite nautical bent, with authentically detailed model ships, both historic and contemporary, and marine-inspired home décor. Many handmade items are true works of art, such as fish carved from beautiful wood and stunningly glazed seashell-inspired dishes. Any item would look wonderful in your home, office, or on your boat. Even Christmas ornaments are marine inspired with images of lighthouses, orca whales, and other marine scenes.

Funk & Junk

85 Nichols Street; Friday Harbor, WA 98250. Phone: (360) 378-2638; email: *funkon@rockisland. com*; web site: *lodging-fridayharbor.com/funkandjunkantiques*

Gizmos, gimcracks, and whatcha-ma-callits! Stroll through the aisles of this store crammed with everything from treasures to the kitchen sink. You'll delight in old postcards, books, musical instruments, shoes, quilts, costume jewelry, cookware, used furniture, and on and on. If it's old, it's probably here. There are some true antiques, some wonderful collectibles, and some things that will make you puzzle what they are supposed to be.

Gallery San Juan and Framing Services

210 Nichols Street; Friday Harbor, WA 98250. Phone: (360) 378-1376; fax: (360) 370-5569; email: *mid1@interisland.net*; web site: *gallerysanjuan.com*

The gallery portion of the name indicates that Matt and Barbara Dollahite represent a half-dozen well known San Juan artists and display and sell their works. However, once you acquire a treasured piece of art, you need to have it properly framed, and the shop also provides this service for you.

The Garuda and I

60 First Street; Friday Harbor, WA 98250. Phone: (888) 675-7039 or (360) 378-3733; email: *garuda@interisland.net*

This shop is many things rolled into one: There are imports from Africa, India, Thailand, the Philippines, and other mid- and far-eastern places; there are bins full of gorgeous beads, findings, tools, books, and other crafts supplies to create your own jewelry; and, finally, it's a gallery selling the work of local artists. The fine imports include pillows, baskets, and pottery; you're sure to find the perfect accents or conversation pieces for your home.

The Gourmet's Galley

21 Spring Street West; Friday Harbor, WA 98250. Phone: (360) 378-2251

Who doesn't love to cook—or at least to eat? The Gourmet's Galley is overflowing with good stuff for both cooks and gastronomes, such as fresh-ground coffees, fine wine, beer, teas, spices, cookware, cookbooks, unique teapots, kitchen gadgets, and candy. Many are local brands. For the health-conscious part of you, there are hypoallergenic cosmetics and nutritional foods.

Griffin Bay Bookstore

40 First Street; Friday Harbor, WA 98250. Phone: (360) 378-5511

This nook isn't much wider than a good-size book itself, but it's packed with great literary finds. The store claims more than ten-thousand volumes, and it's easy to believe. There's a good selection of regional books, as well as all the latest fiction and best sellers. And, if they don't have the book you're looking for, they'll order it for you. The store also carries music cassettes and CDs, books on tape, notecards, and maps.

Harbor Bookstore

22 Cannery Landing, P.O. Box 1543; Friday Harbor, WA 98250. Phone: (360) 378-7222; email: *harbor@rockisland.com*; web site: *harborbookstore.com*

Wander up to the second level of Cannery Landing and you'll discover this bookstore. It stocks plenty of good fiction, mysteries, and regional paperbacks. Their excellent selection of children's books also have a regional flair, with tales of ferryboats, whales, seals, and other wildlife. There are cassettes for your tape deck and a nice line of cards, too.

Honey Lane Farms

289 Honey Lane; Friday Harbor, WA 98250. Phone: (360) 378-1895; fax: (360) 378-1895; email: *mpuckett@rockisland.com*; web site: *honeylanefarms.com*

Marjorie Puckett operates an alpaca yarn studio out of her farm, but she spends most summers showing her yarns and alpaca products at one of the art kiosks at Roche Harbor. If she's not at Roche Harbor, you can make an appointment to see her at her at Honey Lane Farm, and she'll tell you how to get there. Her yarns and patterns are also sold online. See also Transportation, page 272.

Island Museum of Art

314 Spring Street, P.O. Box 339; Friday Harbor, WA 98250. Phone: (360) 370-5050; email: *kay@wbay.org*; web site: *wbay.org*

This gallery is managed by the Westcott Bay Institute, which also manages the wonderful sculpture park at Roche Harbor. Their Spring Street gallery mounts exhibits in a range of mediums by well-known local artists. Exhibits change periodically.

Island Studios

270 Spring Street, P.O. Box 3326; Friday Harbor, WA 98250. Phone: (360) 378-6550; email: *info@islandstudios.com*; web site: *islandstudios.com*

This gallery is a cooperative representing more than 100 local artists. You'll enjoy browsing the large store and seeing all the quality, reasonably priced art and crafts created in the San Juan Islands. There are paintings, serigraphs, pottery, leather goods, wreaths, unique Christmas ornaments, jewelry, and quilts. Also included are items such as notecards, vinegars, pepper seasonings, and some handmade clothing. You are sure to find something to fit your budget.

Island Wine Company

2 Cannery Landing Building; P.O. Box 1895; Friday Harbor, WA 98250. Phone: (800) 248-9463 or (360) 378-3229; fax: (360) 378-6299; email: *info@sanjuancellars.com*; web site: *sanjuancellars.com*

The Island Wine Company is just a few steps from the end of the ferry ramp, making it a convenient place to begin, or complete, your visit to Friday Harbor. Several select French, Italian, and Australian wines are available, and some of the lesser known, but highly rated California wines also show up in the racks.

However, the store concentrates on the quality Washington and Oregon wines that make up the bulk of their stock. The company bottles a limited supply of seven different wines, made from Yakima grapes, under its own label, San Juan Cellars. You can sample them in the store's tasting room. This is the only place the label is sold retail. Purchase a bottle or case of fine wine and the store will ship it for you to anywhere in the U.S.

Island Wools

135B Spring Street, P.O. Box 2443; Friday Harbor, WA 98250. Phone: (360) 370-5648; fax: (360) 378-5648; email: *islandwools@rockisland.com*

With all the beautiful yarns available in the San Juans any knitter will want to add some to their collection. This corner of a small mall on Spring Street is filled with an array of yarns and knitting supplies. Even if you don't knit, stop in to choose one of their finished items, such as a hat or scarf.

Joe Friday's Shirt Company

110 Spring Street West; Friday Harbor, WA 98250. Phone: (360) 378-3406

As part of King's Market, Joe Friday's, at the corner of First and Spring, carries a collection of shirts, T-shirts, sweatshirts, and coffee mugs, all carrying San Juan images. It's handy location, right on the corner of First and Spring, makes it an obvious place to stop for your San Juan souvenirs.

King's Video Rental and More

First and West Street; Friday Harbor, WA 98250

Need a movie to pass a few hours on your boat? King's, open seven days a week, offers video and CD rentals, as well as a few soda and candy machines to meet your late-hour jolt requirements.

King's Clothing and Marine Center

110 Spring Street; Friday Harbor, WA 98250. Phone: (360) 378-4593 (marine center), (360) 378-4591 (variety)

The Marine Center of King's Market occupies the floor above the grocery. It has a generous supply of fishing gear, crab traps, marine electronics, charts, and guides. Fishing and crabbing licenses are also sold here. (Better have one!) The clothing portion of the store offers a full line of sportswear, swimsuits, outerwear, windbreakers, pants, sweaters, and jackets to keep you well dressed for San Juan weather.

Krystal Acres Alpaca Farm

152 Blazing Tree Road; Friday Harbor, WA 98250. Phone: (360) 378-6125; fax: (360) 370-5334; email: *info@krystalacres.com*; web site: *krystalacres.com*

HOURS: Daily 10 A.M. to 5 P.M. April through December; Friday through Monday 11 A.M. to 5 P.M. January through March.

🚗 In Friday Harbor, head southwest on Spring Street, and turn right onto 2nd Street, which bends into Guard Street and eventually becomes Beaverton Valley Road. In 5 miles, at an intersection, the road angles north as West Valley Road. In 2 miles from the intersection, Blazing Tree Road and the alpaca farm are on the left.

Drive down West Valley Road south of Roche Harbor Road and you are bound to see a field with strange, long-necked, furry animals looking like a cross between a camel and a teddy bear. They are alpacas. This farm, where they are raised, operates a store that sells warm and wonderful gifts made from their wool: sweaters, scarves, hats, gloves, sofa throws, pillows, and cuddly toys, as well as yarn and knitting patterns if you want to make your own wonderful gifts.

Lavendera Day Spa

Elements San Juan Island Hotel and Spa; 440 Spring Street, P.O. Box 2389; Friday Harbor, WA 98250. Phone: (800) 349-0337 or (360) 378-3637; email: *info@lavenderadayspa.com*; web site: *lavenderadayspa.com*

The spa, associated with Elements San Juan Island Hotel and Spa, provides a full range of massage treatments including La Stone hot rock and Reiki, therapeutic massages, reflexology, and spa treatments including body exfoliation, face glow, and Ayurvedic steamy wonder. Make your vacation *really* relaxing.

Michael Bertrand Photo Gallery

85 Front Street; Friday Harbor, WA 98250. Phone: (360) 317-6622; email: *mbphotos@rockisland.com*; web site: *michaelbertrandphotography.com*

Photographer Michael Bertrand creates dramatic images in color and black and white that reflect the islands, as well as other natural subjects. He has a small, appointment-only studio in the Doctors Office above the ferry landing. Much of the summer he displays his work at an artist's kiosk at Roche Harbor. His works can also be purchased online through his web site.

Moon and Jules Banana Belt Boutique

1 Spring Street, Friday Harbor, WA 98250. Phone: (360) 378-2722; web site: *sanjuansite. com/bananabelt*

You'll find the perfect outfit for lounging around your resort or dining out at one of Friday Harbor's fine restaurants at this shop. The racks are loaded with great women's clothing, including all kinds of casual wear and colorful separates for really chic combinations. Accessorize with some of their interesting jewelry.

Mystical Mermaid

65 Spring Street West; Friday Harbor, WA 98250. Phone: (360) 378-2617; web site: *mysticalmermaid.com*

The shop with this fascinating name occupies a corner of the Friday Harbor Center. Once inside you'll be glad you stopped. The Mystical Mermaid has lots of fun, inexpensive items, as well as some lovely collectibles. It's the perfect place for kids to select something to keep themselves occupied in the camper or boat, or for you to choose gifts for friends back home. Shelves and racks offer books, games, knickknacks, and no end of unusual souvenir items. If you delight in the animal-covered boxes from Harmony Kingdom, as we do, stop in to see the latest irresistible creation.

Nancy's Frame Shop

774 Mullis Street, Suite B; Friday Harbor, WA 98250. Phone: (360) 378-3508

This shop just south of the Orcas Inn offers prints and framing for the art you purchase here or in downtown galleries, as well as beautiful, unique wind chimes.

Nash Brothers Sports

280 Spring Street; Friday Harbor, WA 98250. Phone: (360) 378-4612

Every town needs an outlet selling sporting goods, and Nash Brothers answers that need. Regardless of your sport—golf, darts, tennis, soccer, fishing, archery, baseball, or basketball—they can fill your equipment and apparel needs.

Needlework Boutique

265 Spring Street; Friday Harbor, WA 98250. Phone: (360) 378-2800

To a needleworker there's nothing as enticing as piles of rainbow-hued yarn just waiting for the touch of magic fingers. Island Needlepoint sells canvases, yarns, embroidery floss, novelty threads, and everything else you'll need to create a treasured work of art.

Osito's

120 First Street; Friday Harbor, WA 98250. Phone: (360) 378-4320

From Brio trains to Breyer horses, Osito's will delight the child in your life. This shop in Friday Harbor Center is filled with fantastic toys for the young and young at heart. It also carries a nice selection of children's clothes and sleepwear, a few books, puzzles, and cards. We were intrigued by the tiny "paper dolls" made out of wood, with clothes that attach by Velcro.

Pelindaba Downtown

Friday Harbor Center, 150 Spring Street; Friday Harbor, WA 98250. Phone: (360) 378-6900; email: *admin@pelindaba.com*; web site: *pelindaba.com*

This is the downtown retail outlet for the Pelindaba Lavender Farm. The shop sells almost anything combined with lavender: biscotti, shortbread, gourmet syrup, vinegars, honeys, several types of teas, candles, potpourri, dried wreaths, lotions, and more. The back of the store contains an excellent café featuring lavender-flavored items. See Restaurants, Cafés & Take-Out, page 246.

Pelindaba Lavender Farm

33 Hawthorne Lane, P.O, Box 2389; Friday Harbor, WA 98250. Phone: (360) 378-4248 (farm), (360) 378-3637 (spa); email: *admin@pelindaba,com*; web site: *pelindaba.com*

🚐 In Friday Harbor, head southwest on Spring Street, and angle left onto Argyle Avenue. In 1¾ miles turn right (west) onto Little Road, and in another ½ mile, at a T-intersection go left (south) on Douglas Road, which shortly turns west and becomes Bailer Hill Road. Continue for 2½ miles to Wold Road; turn right and follow it for ½ mile to Hawthorne Lane, on the right. Follow Hawthorne Lane to its end, at the farm.

As much a philosophical statement as a business operation, Pelindaba (Zulu for a place of great gatherings) set out to find a business that would raise a crop that didn't compete with local farming, required little rainfall and artificial fertilizer, and was a stable and economically viable crop. Lavender seemed the answer, and thus the farm on the south end of San Juan Island began.

The Gate House at the entrance to the farm sells much the same array of lavender goods found in their downtown store. The lavender fields, stunning when in bloom, display large, impressive metal sculptures by Micajah Bienvenu. Bring your camera.

Pemberton Sculpture Studio

4965 Pear Point Road, P.O. Box 916; Friday Harbor, WA 98250. Phone: (360) 378-3568; email: *oatmeal@rockisland.com*; web site: *pembertonstudios.com*

HOURS: Thursday though Saturday noon to 5 P.M., or by appointment.

🚐 The studio is about a mile from Friday Harbor. To get there, follow Spring Street and then Argyle Avenue out of town and turn left on Pear Point Road. It is the fourth driveway on the right.

Working in the lost wax casting technique, Tom Pemberton creates exquisite bronze sculptures. Pemberton's art can be whimsical as well as serious. His series of Frog on a Hog bronze sculptures feature croakers-with-an-attitude astride Harleys.

If you stop by, Tom will take you for a tour of his studio.

Robin's Nest

270 Spring Street; Friday Harbor, WA 98250. Phone: (360) 378-6562; web site: *sanjuansites. com/robinsnest*

Whether you are looking for an interesting plant or an urn or container to decorate your garden, you'll undoubtedly discover something to please at Robin's Nest. You'll even find a comfy garden chair to relax in after your gardening's all done. The narrow shop is squeezed between two buildings on Spring Street. However, the greenhouse plastic roof makes it as light-filled as a sunroom. Fresh cut flowers will brighten dinner on your boat, and pre-planted baskets will look great on your patio back home.

Sandpebble

245 Spring Street; Friday Harbor, WA 98250. Phone: (360) 378-2788

If you love Victoriana, you won't be able to drag yourself away from this shop. It's a diverse mix embellished by lace, lace, and more lace. You'll "ooh" and "ahh" over whimsical teapots, gracious china and crystal, beautiful lamps, decorative pillows, brass candlesticks (and candles to go with them), and potpourri by the scoop. There's women's clothing, too: dresses, peignoirs, and lingerie. Their line of high-quality home furnishings includes duvet covers, sheets, shower curtains, rugs, and baskets.

San Juan Florist

Friday Harbor Center, 180 First Street; Friday Harbor, WA 98250. Phone: (800) 582-9978 or (360) 378-2477; email: *sanjuanflorist@rockisland.com*; web site: *sanjuanflorist.com*

A pretty bouquet of flowers might be just what you need to brighten up your boat, or to take as a thank you gift to your San Juan Island host. In addition to a busy florist business, the shop offers extensive gift selections of vases, candles, pottery, cards, and figurines.

San Juan Glassworks

1296 Wold Road, P.O. Box 3003; Friday Harbor, WA 98250. Phone: (360) 378-6725; email: *woodenglass@hotmail.com*; web site: *sanjuanartistcommunity.com/buijs-mancuso*

Artist Yvonne Buijs-Mancuso creates evocative hand blown sun-catchers, glass sculptures, leaded glass lamps, and windows from fused and leaded glass. She does commissions to form exactly the artwork you want.

San Juan Hot Shop

Jeri's Spring Street Center; 260 Spring Street #1; Friday Harbor, WA 98250. Phone: (360) 378-5978; email: *hotshop@rockisland.com*; web site: *sanjuanhotshop.com*

Do you want some spice in your life? Visit the Hot Shop for an almost infinite array of throat-toasting hot sauces and barbecue sauces. Ass-kicking coffees will wake you up with new vigor. Throw in some dishes, T-shirts, cups, and caps, all in the hot spice theme, and you have an unbeatable shop. It's a great place to stop for a laugh, and to buy a unique gift for people back home.

San Juan Jewels, Ltd.

Jeri's Spring Street Center; 260 Spring Street; Friday Harbor, WA 98250. Phone: (360) 378-5877; web site: *sanjuansites.com/sanjuanjewelry*

San Juan Jewels, located in a small indoor mall on Spring Street, stocks fine crystal, dishes, and silver, in addition to timepieces and fine jewelry. They also carry collectible Melody in Motion hand-painted porcelain figurines, Portmeirion china, and figurines. Original works by local artists are displayed in the store and on walls in the mall.

San Juan Vineyards

3136 Roche Harbor Road; Friday Harbor, WA 98250. Phone: (888) 993-9463 or (360) 378-9463; fax: (360) 378-2668; email: *manager@sanjuanvineyards.com*: web site: *sanjuanvineyards.com*

HOURS: Tasting room open daily in summer 11 A.M. to 5 P.M.; Wednesday through Sunday 11 A.M. to 5 P.M. in the fall; Sunday 11 A.M. to 5 P.M. in the spring; January and February by appointment.

🚗 Follow 2nd Street west, then Guard and Tucker to Roche Harbor Road. The winery is on Roche Harbor Road in 3 miles.

Although it's only been open since 1996, this pretty 33-acre vineyard boasts the character and quaintness you'd expect of a long-established facility. Part of its charm comes from the little schoolhouse dating from 1896 that was remodeled to become the winery's tasting room and gift shop. Stop by to sample their offerings and enjoy their outside garden. A few bottles or one of their wine-related gift items will make a nice remembrance of sunny San Juan days. Wines carried are produced in the winery from grapes grown in the Columbia River Valley, as well as from some grown right here. They also carry varietals produced and bottled in Eastern Washington.

The vineyard's small chapel and pretty grounds can be scheduled for a wedding, recommitment ceremony, or other joyous event.

The Second Act

15 North Second; Friday Harbor, WA 98250. Phone: (360) 378-3828

Often the best part of shopping is finding a really terrific buy. This exclusive resale shop is the place to find new and used clothing for men, women, and children at the very best prices.

Serendipity
223 A Street; Friday Harbor, WA 98250. Phone: (360) 378-2665

Books are packed to the rafters in this home-turned-shop. Owners Carol Jackson and Dilys Goodman are former librarians who have a great sense for the kinds of books that will please their customers. Bring in your used paperbacks and swap them two-for-one. There are nautical books for the boat cap'n and fiction for the crew.

Softwear
135 Spring Street; Friday Harbor, WA 98250. Phone: (360) 378-3077

The kids in your crowd are sure to find a place in their wardrobes for some of the terrific, trend-setting clothes in this shop. It's all casual, all comfortable. There are many kinds of separates—sweaters, shirts, T's, pants, and skirts as well as jackets, and a nice line of accessories to top it all off. The eclectic shop also offers lamps, scented candles, candle holders, hair dye, beaded curtains, birdcages, strobe lights, clocks, carved Buddhas, and temporary tattoos. You get the picture.

The Toggery
155 Spring Street West; Friday Harbor, WA 98250. Phone: (360) 378-2299

Friday Harbor doesn't lack for excellent clothing shops, and The Toggery is a dandy one, with a wide selection of apparel. It stocks a full line of clothes for both men and women, with racks full of separates, heavy on comfortable casual clothes, perfect for boat or resort. Jackets, underwear, jewelry, leather goods—you should be able to find whatever you need right here.

The Toy Box
20 First Street; Friday Harbor, WA 98250. Phone: (360) 378-8889; fax: (360) 378-8885; email: *danah@rockisland.com*; web site: *toyboxsanjuan.com*

Toys and games for your kids, or the kid in you. There are lots of inexpensive, educational toys to keep kids happy for long hours. A plastic folding binocular/compass/magnifying glass would be fun for a young camper.

The Toy Box also features fine wooden wind chimes, puzzles, and games. We marveled at some pick-up-sticks crafted of various hardwoods with an elegant leather pouch. Are you old enough to remember that fun game?

West Marine Express
Harbor Village, 313 Spring Street; Friday Harbor, WA 98250. Phone: (360) 378-1086; fax: (360) 378-2469; web site: *westmarine.com*

Most boaters are familiar with West Marine through their stores at other locations, their catalog, and web site. This local outlet has boating supplies, repair items, spare parts, dinghies, life jackets, and crab pots—everything you might have forgotten at home, but absolutely need to enjoy a great San Juans vacation.

Waterworks Gallery

315 Spring Street, P.O. Box 28; Friday Harbor, WA 98250. Phone: (360) 378-3060, (360) 378-5373; fax: (360) 378-3098; email: *info@waterworksgallery.com*; web site: *waterworksgallery.com*

Waterworks Gallery is one of the best places in the islands to find top-drawer original paintings, etchings, lithographs, and sculpture. The artists represented hail from the San Juans and throughout the Northwest. Shows, which are designed to display a group of complementary works, change every five to six weeks, so be sure to stop in regularly. The gallery will also help you chose a perfect frame for your purchase.

Westcott Bay Institute Sculpture Park

P.O. Box 339; Roche Harbor, WA 98250. Phone: (360) 370-5050; email: *kay@wbay.org*; web site: *wbay.org*

🚗 From Friday Harbor, follow Roche Harbor Road northwest toward Roche Harbor Resort. The sculpture park is on the left, just before the entrance to the resort.

More then a hundred pieces of original sculpture are on display in the meadows within walking distance of Roche Harbor Resort. Mowed paths trace the way to the individual pieces of art surrounding a small pond, all of which are for sale. Prices generally begin around $500 and range upward to $40,000. Many of the artists will do commissioned works for you, if you are drawn to their style. Select one for your business' lobby.

A $5 donation is requested of visitors at the park entrance. But, you don't need to purchase a work to appreciate the exhilarating art and the walk in the fine setting.

The Westcott Bay Institute Sculpture Park displays large original artworks in a natural setting. One might just fit your yard or business.

The Whale Museum

62 First Street North. P.O. Box 945; Friday Harbor, WA 98250. Phone: (360) 378-4710, ext 30; fax: (360) 378-5790; email: *store@whalemuseum.org*; web site: *whale-museum.org*

The store at the entrance to the Whale Museum, on the main floor, carries nature-inspired educational toys and games, books, orca identification guides, videos, T-shirts, and other whale-related merchandise. A fine selection of marine photos and paintings are offered for sale.

Wild Things

20 First Street, P.O. Box 391; Friday Harbor, WA 98250. Phone: (360) 378-5000; web site: *wolfhollowwildlife.org*

Wolf Hollow, a wildlife rehabilitation center on San Juan Island, doesn't permit visitors at its recovery site, but it has opened a shop in Friday Harbor to let you know about its activities. To support its work, the shop sells wildlife-oriented gifts such as bird-shaped kites, books, animal puppets, and their own calendar. A display explains the center's work, and a knowledgeable docent is on hand to answer your questions about the center and local wildlife. Adoption packets for birds and animals rehabilitated at the center are available. We adopted a great blue heron, our favorite bird.

EVENTS & ATTRACTIONS

Annual San Juan Island Celebrity Golf Classic

San Juan Golf Club; 2261 Golf Course Road; Friday Harbor, WA 98250. Phone: (360) 378-2254; email: *sjgolf@rockisland.com*; web site: *sanjuangolf.com*

WHEN: Early June.

San Juan Island charities benefit from this popular golf tournament held in early June at the San Juan Golf Club. Pros from clubs around the region are teamed with celebrities from professional sports teams for a day of fun and fundraising.

Aquarium and Marine Interpretive Center

One section of the waiting area at the end of the Spring Street Landing dock contains an interesting 400-gallon saltwater aquarium that holds fish, anemone, and other creatures that live in the saltwater beneath the dock. A 30-foot-long ceramic tile mural on the wall depicts marine life of the islands (with the possible exception of the mermaid).

Fourth of July Parade

We love a parade—we'll bet you do, too! And small-town parades, where everyone joins in, are the best of all. Friday Harbor puts its own special touch on the traditional celebration. There are marching bands, clowns, flags, and fire trucks, of course, but have you ever seen a "pod" of dogs dressed like killer whales, or a solar-powered horse? One year a wheelchair brigade from the Islands' Convalescent Center won the drill team competition. This grand old hometown fun is what America is all about! You can see nighttime fireworks in the harbor from your boat, nearby lodging, or shore.

Horseshu Ranch

131 Gilbert Lane, P.O. Box 1861; Friday Harbor, WA 98250. Phone: (360) 378-2298; email: *Roxanne@horseshu.com*; web site: *horseshu.com*

FACILITIES: Ranch with barn, arena, pasture, trails.

🚗 From the ferry landing drive west on Spring Street, which becomes San Juan Valley Road. In 1 mile from the ferry turn left onto Gilbert Lane. Take the first next left, and you will see the entrance archway to Horseshu Guest Ranch.

SUMMER RATES: Many riding options are offered. Trail ride $89 per person, ranch tour $30, lessons (available for individuals or groups, adult or junior) $28 to $38.

If you have some horseback riding experience, or someone in your family would like to learn riding basics while staying in the San Juans, Horseshu Guest Ranch is the place for you. They start beginners out on a lead line in the arena, so the instructor has control of the horse as the new rider gets accustomed to it. A 4-lesson package will teach the rudiments of horsemanship. People with some riding experience can schedule a 2-hour forest ride on a gentle horse, or can rent a horse to ride in the arena. Guests at the ranch's Horseshu Hacienda qualify for a 10-percent discount.

Isle be Jammin'

335 Argyle Avenue; Friday Harbor, WA 98250. Phone: (360) 378-5151; email: *kirkf@rockisland. com*; web site: *hands-in-harmony.com/*

Musician or not, this is an interesting place to check out. A funky collection of musician-oriented facilities and services includes a musical instrument gallery, music lessons, guitar repair, rehearsal space, jam sessions, and occasional intimate concerts (seating for 20).

Oktoberfest

San Juan County Fairgrounds; Friday Harbor, WA 98250. Phone: (360) 378-4161

WHEN: Mid-October

The San Juan version of the Bavarian celebration takes place in mid-October. Food and drink are provided by local businesses, and a local "oom-pah" band whoops it up. Proceeds benefit the Lions, Kiwanis, and Inter-island Medical Guild. Have fun for good causes.

Opening Day of Boating Season

WHEN: The first Saturday in May.

All of the yacht clubs in the San Juans kick off the boating season with local parades and boats decorated for display and competition. Sailboat races and all-around parties are part of the festivities. The San Juan Island parade is in Friday Harbor.

The Pig War Barbecue Jamboree

Friday Harbor Fairgrounds, 660 Argyle Road, Friday Harbor, WA 98250.

WHEN: Fourth of July.

We doubt the porker that gave up his life, thereby guaranteeing the San Juan Islands a place in history, would appreciate having a barbecue in his honor. Be that as it may, it's a glorious event, and one you won't want to miss if you're on the island when it rolls around.

Teams from all over the region compete for "Best Barbecue in the Northwest," as judged by cooking celebrities. Past entrants have included Lopez Island's Beautiful Butts and Buns, El Porko Loco of Mercer Island, and Pig Al's Chicago Trickynoses.

In addition to some of the best cooking you'll ever taste, this gustatory extravaganza features parades, car exhibits, kids' games, entertainment, music, dancing, and all-round hilarity.

San Juan County Fair

Friday Harbor Fairgrounds, 660 Argyle Road, Friday Harbor, WA 98250. Phone: (360) 378-4310, fax; (360) 378-5433; email: *sjcfair@rockisland.com*; web site: *sanjuancountyfair.com*

WHEN: Mid-August.

Chicken and rabbit races! Oyster barbecues! Largest zucchini awards! A scarecrow contest! Grab the kids and join the fun at an old-fashioned county fair, done up San Juan style. Traditional events such as livestock judging, riding competitions, and displays of homemade goodies are always interesting, but there's a lot more. The island folks really show off their talents in arts, crafts, and performances. You might see a demonstration of basket making, hear a concert on a Native American flute, or listen to a "storytelling" of life in Alaska. The wild Zucchini 500 race features competition between wheel-outfitted zucchinis.

Animal competitions run the gamut of two- and four-legged creatures: chickens, rabbits, sheep, cattle, swine, goats, horses, and camilids (llama/alpaca).

The fairgrounds are on Argyle Avenue, about five blocks from the waterfront, within easy walking distance. Schedules are printed in the local newspaper, and might be posted on bulletin boards in town. Stop by—you'll remember it forever.

San Juan Community Theater

100 Second Street, P.O. Box 1063; Friday Harbor, WA 98250. Phone: (360) 378-3211 (theater), (360) 378-3210 (box office); fax: (360) 378-2398; email: *executivedirector@ sanjuancommunitytheater.org*; web site: *sanjuanarts.org*

World-acclaimed musicians here in the San Juans? Yes, indeed! The very active San Juan Community Theater attracts celebrated musicians, vocalists, and actors. Productions by the local theater group or the local San Juan Singers draw rave reviews. There's also community fun, such as sing-a-longs, school productions, and programs geared for kids. Check the newspaper or community bulletin board to see what's going on. You'll find it a perfect break from an old video in the DVD player.

San Juan Historical Museum

405 Price Street; Friday Harbor, WA 98250. Phone: (360) 378-3949; email: *museum@sjmuseum. org*; web site: *sjmuseum.org*

HOURS: Wednesday through Saturday 1 P.M. to 4:30 P.M. May through September; Thursday and Friday in winter. A nominal admission fee is charged.

🚍 Follow Spring Street southwest from Friday Harbor. Just past the Mullis Road Y, turn right on Price Street. The museum is on the left in a short distance.

In the 1890s, pioneer James King grew grain and apples and raised cattle on the outskirts of the fledging town of Friday Harbor. Today his farmhouse and the property around it are a heritage cherished as the San Juan Island Historical Museum. Most of the rooms in the old King farmhouse retain the homey mood of the original dwelling.

Furnishings, all representative of early days on the island, include an old pump organ dating from the 1900s, a huge St. Clair wood range that dominates the kitchen, a beautiful old wooden hutch that protects antique china and crystal, and the earliest sewing machine used in the San Juans.

A museum room is loaded with relics from the island's past: a switchboard from the old San Juan Hotel that permitted the first telephone communications between Friday Harbor and Roche Harbor, a cannon cover from Pig War days, a family Bible belonging to an American officer on duty during the Pig War. Photos record the history of old-time island residents.

Old buildings are scattered about the grounds; the barn holds antique farm equipment. Other buildings include a cabin, milk barn, root cellar, and jail. Two historic bells decorate the lawn. One once hung in the tower of the Methodist church (now the Grange Hall); the second was the old Friday Harbor fire bell.

In past years the museum has hosted weekly concerts on its lawn during July and August. Check to see if one might be happening while you are there.

San Juan Island Artist's Studio Open House

Phone: (360) 378-5318; email: *artists@sanjuanartists.com*; web site: *sanjuanislandartists.com*

WHEN: First weekend in June.

Yearly, a group of professional San Juan Island artists open their studios and offer their work for sale directly to visitors. This is a terrific opportunity to talk with the artists and learn more about how their works are created. The quality of the work is uniformly outstanding. You'll be able to select from sculpture, handmade furniture, jewelry, weaving, tapestries, stained glass, serigraphs, and paintings in watercolor and oil. It's a fine way to tour the island and discover some out-of-the way spots, too.

The artists are located at nine different spots around the island; by checking the organization's web site or contacting them, you can receive a brochure and map showing the locations of the studios of artists on the current year's tour. Some years a bus is available to take you to the studios.

SAN JUAN ISLAND
Events & Attractions

San Juan Nature Institute

P.O. Box 3110; Friday Harbor, WA 98250. Phone: (360) 378-3646; fax: (360) 378-3646; email: *info@sjnature.org*; web site: *sjnature.org*

This nonprofit organization is dedicated to increasing public understanding and appreciation of the unique natural history of the San Juans. It provides a free lecture series at the UW Friday Harbor Labs and the Camp Orkila Marine Salmon Center. Fee-based classes and field trips are also offered. Past subjects include autumn mushrooms, botanical illustration, ethnobiology, marine life, wildflowers, raptors, and anthropology. Check their web site for a schedule of events.

The Whale Museum

62 First Street North, P.O. Box 945; Friday Harbor, WA 98250. Phone: (360) 378-4710; fax: (360) 378-5790; web site: *whale-museum.org*. Whale Hotline to report sightings: U.W.: (800) 562-8832, B.C.: (800) 665-5939

HOURS: Daily 10 A.M. to 5 P.M.; adult $6, seniors $5, age 5 to 18 and college students with I.D. $3; under 5 free. Group and guided or unguided tour rates available.

Peer eyeball-to-eyeball with a model orca, gaze up to see a humpback whale soaring over your head, duck into a darkened room and listen to strangely musical underwater

The Whale Museum has life-size displays and other fascinating exhibits.

whale conversation, or learn the Native American legend of how the killer whale came to be. It's all here at this outstanding museum in Friday Harbor.

The Whale Museum holds fascinating exhibits of whale skeletons, life-size models of whales, murals, interpretive displays, Native American legends about whales, and an extensive collection of slides and photographs of the orca pod members. In addition, members of the Whale Museum track and maintain a history of the orca whale pods (or families) that spend time in the Washington and British Columbia waters. Whale research is conducted from a lab at Lime Kiln State Park.

The museum also offers in-class and field courses, programs, and workshops on marine mammals, and local ecology and natural history. College credit is offered for some of its field courses in whale biology. As a fund-raising effort, its highly successful Orca Adoption Program issues certificates of adoption for individual members of the San Juan orca pods, and provides you with photos and a biography of your adopted whale. In addition to its displays, there are video programs on the orca pods of the San Juans, and a museum store that carries educational toys and games, books, orca identification guides, videos, T-shirts, artwork, and other whale-oriented merchandise.

Wolf Hollow Wildlife Rehabilitation Center

284 Boyce Road, P.O. Box 391; Friday Harbor, WA 98250. Phone: (360) 378-5000; email: *wolfhollow@wolfhollowwildlife.org*; web site: *wolfhollowwildlife.org*

HOURS: Not open to the public

Thanks to the dedicated staff and volunteers at Wolf Hollow, orphaned or injured wild animals have a better chance at life. Located on Boyce Road, between West Valley Road and San Juan Valley Road, the center is a licensed wildlife rehabilitation center, not a zoo; its goal is to return the orphaned or injured animals to the wild. The more than four hundred animals treated yearly include seal pups, otters, deer, eagles, owls, and other birds. Because Wolf Hollow is a wild animal hospital, random visitors are not permitted, and human contact with the animals is minimal.

Although the center offers educational programs, these folks need your donations (tax deductible) far more than your visit, as the organization receives no government funding. A copy of the organization's newsletter, Wild Times, is available upon request. Wolf Hollow has a retail outlet, Wild Things, at 20 First Street in Friday Harbor. See Shopping, page 266.

DON'T be a Good Samaritan

If you should notice a seal pup on the beach, a fawn without its mother, or any other infant wild animal, and believe it is orphaned or abandoned, do not touch it. Most likely Mom is right nearby and will reclaim her offspring once you are gone. There is a stiff fine for handling marine mammals without a permit. Call Wolf Hollow at (360) 378-4710, and one of the people there will determine if the animal needs help and will take appropriate action.

ON-ISLAND TRANSPORTATION

Bob's Taxi and Limousine Service

2011 Egg Lake Road, P.O. Box 3071; Friday Harbor, WA 98250. Phone: (877) 482-9426 or
(360) 378-6777; fax: (360) 378-6717; email: *bob@egglake.com*

No matter what your transportation needs, this company should be able to help you out. They can provide island tours, transportation from the docks or your lodging to a restaurant, or chauffeuring special occasions such as weddings. If you need transportation to mainland points, they'll take you there, too.

Christina's Carriage Company

221 Heritage Farm Lane; Friday Harbor, WA 98250. Phone: (360) 378-2872; email: *drafthorse@ interisland.net*; web site: *interisland.net/drafthorse*

You'll get right in the mood of the laid-back San Juans with a carriage ride around its quiet roads. In summer, Christina Dahl-Sesby parks her vintage carriage in downtown Friday Harbor. From there she will take up to six people at a time for a fun spin. Her horse accepts tips of a carrot or apple.

You can schedule carriage rides for special occasions, such as birthdays, anniversaries, or weddings—or maybe you can pop The Big Question while taking a romantic tour of the island.

Classic Cab Company

105 Crestview; Friday Harbor, WA 98250; email: *krttrmn@interisland.net*

This full service taxi company offers a range of tour options.

Honey Lane Farms

289 Honey Lane; Friday Harbor, WA 98250; (360) 378-1895; fax: (360) 378-1895; email: *mpuckett@rockisland.com*; web site: *honeylanefarms.com*

Although her major artistic effort is the creation of alpaca yarns, one of Marjorie Puckett's sidelines is offering carriage rides and carriage driving lessons on the south end of the island. Her garage contains a two-person Canadian cart, a two-person Amish cart, and a one-person (plus tailgate) runabout. See also Shopping, page 257

Island Airporter

139 Tarte Road; Friday Harbor, WA 98250. Phone: (360) 378-7438; web site: *islandairporter.com*

RATES: $39.95 to $54.95.

Monday through Saturday the Island Airporter provides non-stop transportation between Roche Harbor and Friday Harbor and SeaTac Airport and return. In typical summers, the coach departs Roche Harbor at 5 A.M., and Friday Harbor at 5: 45 A.M. to arrive at SeaTac at 9:30 A.M. On the return leg the coach departs SeaTac at noon, and arrives at Friday Harbor at 3:15 P.M. and Roche Harbor at 4 P.M. Confirm their schedule before planning a trip.

Island Bicycles

380 Argyle Street, P.O. Box 1609; Friday Harbor, WA 98250. Phone: (360) 378-4941; fax: (360) 378-4706; email: *islbike@islandbicycles.com*; web site: *islandbicycles.com*

HOURS: Daily 10 A.M. to 5:30 P.M.

SUMMER RATES: Hourly $2 to $14, full day $10 to $70, 2-day $15 to $120, 3-day $20 to $160, full week $40 to $300; helmet included with rental. Extra charges for panniers, trailers, car racks and baby strollers.

Leave your car at the Anacortes ferry terminal, enjoy an inexpensive, no-wait passenger ferry trip to Friday Harbor, then tour San Juan Island by bicycle. Island Bicycles is three blocks from the ferry landing; it rents a complete selection of children's one-speed, adult five- and ten-speed, mountain bikes, bike trailers, and baby strollers by the hour, day, or week. Rates vary by type of bicycle and duration of use. Phone reservations are accepted 48 hours in advance. The shop also carries a full line of bicycles for sale, as well as parts, accessories, and repair services.

Island Tours Taxi

Friday Harbor, WA 98250. Phone: (360) 378-4453

Taxi service and island tours.

M & W Auto Sales

725 Spring Street; Friday Harbor; WA 98250. Phone: (800) 323-6037 or (360) 378-2886 (rentals); email: *info@sanjuanauto.com*; web site: *sanjuanauto.com*

RATES: $50 to $100 a day.

If you have walked on the ferry, this company will pick you up at the ferry landing and rent you a car, mini-van, or even a fifteen-passenger van for the duration of your stay on San Juan Island.

Raven Taxi

P.O. Box 848; Friday Harbor, WA 98250. Phone: (360) 378-6868

Full taxi service.

San Juan Concierge

740 Coho Drive; Friday Harbor, WA 98250. Phone: (360) 370-7240; email: *canjuanconcierge@ rockisland.com*

Venita Iverson and James Duke cover all your needs for friendly services such as delivery and drop off of any kind of goods, gift wrapping, party planning and assistance, home care, eldercare and personal shopping.

San Juan Transit, Inc. (San Juan Tours)

Cannery Landing, P.O. Box 2809; Friday Harbor, WA 98250. Phone: (800) 887-8387 or (360) 378-8887; email: *santran@rockisland.com*; web site: *sanjuantransit.com*

RATES: Adults $5 for 1-way trip to $10 for a 1-day pass; senior discount available.

This company runs scheduled bus service to major points of interest on San Juan Island spring through fall. Numerous locations, from Friday Harbor and the San Juan Airport to San Juan National Historical Park (both English and American Camps), are served. Point-to-point fares run $5. Daily commuter passes are available. Call or check their web site for the latest schedules, routes, and rates.

Susie's Mopeds

125 Nichols Street, P.O. Box 1972; Friday Harbor, WA 98250. Phone: (800) 532-0087 or (360) 378-5244; email: *sjmopeds@rockisland.com*; web site: *susiesmopeds.com*

RATES: Mopeds $25 to $50 per hour, $62.50 to $125 a day, no overnights; scootcars $50 per hour, $125 per day; rental cars $32 per hour $96 for 24 hours.

Leave the strenuous pedaling to someone else and enjoy a pleasant two-wheeled tour of San Juan Islands via an easily operated moped, two-passenger scootcar, or rental car. Rent by the hour or by the day from Friday Harbor. A valid driver's license is required. Minimum ages for mopeds 18, scootcars 21, and rental cars 25.

Boat & Kayak Tours, Cruises & Charters

Adventure Charters Northwest

2 Spring Street; Friday Harbor, WA 98250; 2011 Skyline Way; Anacortes, WA 98221. Phone: (800) 258-3119 or (360) 378-7196 (Friday Harbor); (877) 505-2522 or (360) 293-2522 (Anacortes); email: *info@chartersnorthwest.com*; web site: *chartersnorthwest.com*

The Friday Harbor office of Adventure Charters Northwest manages the company's bare boat charter vessels that are located at Friday Harbor. Much of the charter fleet is in Anacortes, the company's main office. Boats available for charter include sailboats from 28 feet to 43 feet ($1080 to $2725 per week), and power boats from 26 feet to 65 feet ($1550 to $11,000 per week). Larger vessels require a USCG licensed master. Skippers can be hired for an extra daily charge.

The office also sells whale watch tickets for San Juan Excursions.

A Trophy Charters

Spring Street Landing, Dock 2, slip 16; P.O. Box 2444; Friday Harbor, WA 98250. Phone: (360) 378-2110; cell: (360) 317-8210; web site: *fishthesanjuans.com*

RATES: Call for prices.

The fully equipped 29-foot Sport Fisher *Halcyon* makes skippered fishing trips in the San Juans, Gulf Islands, and Saanich Inlet. Minimum party size is three; six is the maximum for overnight accommodations.

Bon Accord Kayak Tours

P.O. Box 993; Friday Harbor, WA 98250. Phone: (360) 378-6670; email: *info@bonaccord.com*; web site: *bonaccord.com*

SUMMER RATES:

- *Wildlife boat tours:* 2-hour island loop $29 per person, 3-hour $39 per person, minimum 4 persons.
- *Private 1, 2, or 3 hour tours:* $75 per hour for up to 6 persons.
- *Kayak tours:* ½ day $89 per person, 1-day $119 per person, 2-day $269 per person, 3-day $429 per person, 4-day $529 per person, all kayak tours 2-person minimum.

The 28-foot power boat, *Henrietta*, can be chartered for one- to three-hour cruises for up to six guests. Have a picnic lunch ashore at one of the marine state parks, go scuba diving, search out orca whales, porpoises, seals, and eagles, or just enjoy the beautiful island scenery with no planned whale watching. In addition to a being a USCG-licensed captain, the skipper is a trained naturalist.

The *Henrietta* takes up to three double kayaks and a guide kayak on a rack above the cabin, making it a "mother ship" that can ferry kayaks to any island destination. Guided tours range from a half day to four-days. Kayaks and accessories are provided, or you can bring your own kayak. For multi-day tours, tents, camping gear, food and drink are provided. Normally, three to five hours a day is spent paddling.

Captain Carli's Charters

P.O. Box 2569; Friday Harbor, WA 98250. Phone: (888) 221-1331 or (360) 378-0302; email*: info@carlicharters.com*: web site: *carlicharters.com*

SUMMER RATES: Adults $59 per person, children under 12 $49. Visa and MasterCard accepted.

The 25-foot C-Dory *Soulmate*, cruising at more than 20 knots, is the fastest boat in the whale watch fleet. This increases your chance of seeing orcas on a three- to four-hour wildlife tour. Scheduled tours leave Friday Harbor at 10 A.M. and 2 P.M., and evening trips are available on request. The *Soulmate* carries a maximum of 6 guests.

Crystal Seas Kayaking, Inc.

P.O. Box 3135; Friday Harbor, WA 98250. Phone: (877) 732-7877 or (360) 378-4223; email: *mail@crystalseas.com*; web site: *crystalseas.com*

SUMMER RATES:

- *Kayaking:* 3-hour tour $59 per person, sunset tour $59 per person, west side day tour $79 per person, multi-day (2 to 6 days) camping $299 to $869 per person, inn-to-inn $780 to $2280 per person.
- *Biking and kayaking:* Camping $399 to $1199 per person, inn-to-inn $780 to $2280 per person.

Sea kayaking is one of the most thrilling ways to observe the wildlife of the San Juans—whales, porpoises, seals, and eagles—in their natural habitat. Three-hour tours leaving three times daily, a day-long west side tour, and a sunset tour fill the simple paddle tour sheet. Custom tours can be arranged. To assure a personal touch, groups are limited to six persons. No experience is needed; each tour includes a kayaking and safety lesson, and all kayaks are extremely stable two-person models. The kayaks leave from Snug Harbor, on the west side of San Juan Island, but transportation is furnished from Friday Harbor.

For longer paddles, Crystal Seas offers two- to six-day trips with all kayak camping, kayaking and bike camping, kayak and B&B "camping" or any combination of the above. It all depends on where you want to tuck yourself in for the night.

Discovery Sea Kayaks

1 Spring Street, P.O. Box 2743; Friday Harbor, WA 98250. Phone: (360) 378-2559; email: *info@ discoveryseakayak.com*; web site: *discoveryseakayak.com*

SUMMER RATES: Day tour (6½ hours) $79 per person, sunset tour (4½ hours) $69; 2-day tour $190 per person, 3-, 4-, and 5-day tours $255 to $395 per person. 8 persons maximum for multi-day tour.

This firm offers day and sunset tours on the west side of San Juan Island seven days a week. For multi-day tours, kayaks, paddling, and safety gear are provided, but clients are responsible for their own camping equipment and food, and share camp chores.

The Discovery retail outlet in Friday Harbor sells kayaks, outdoor sports wear, PFDs, paddles and kayaking accessories.

Maya's Whale Watch Charters

210 Madrona Drive; Friday Harbor, WA 98250. Phone: (360) 378-7996; cell: (360) 317-4462; email: *captjim@interisland.net*; web site: *mayaswhalewatch.biz*

SUMMER RATES: $65 per person, children $55.

Depart from Snug Harbor, on the west side of San Juan Island, aboard the 22-foot *Annie Mae*, which carries a maximum of six passengers. Your three-hour tour in Haro Strait covers the main feeding grounds of the San Juan orca pods. Captains Jim Maya and Terry Domico are intimately familiar with the whale's habits, and have one of the faster boats in the whale watch fleet to reach their area quickly.

Outdoor Odysseys

82 Cedar Street, Friday Harbor, WA 98250 or 12003 23rd Avenue NE, Seattle, WA 98125. Phone: (800) 647-4621, or (360) 378-3533 (summer), (206) 361-0717 (winter); email: *ceekayaker@aol.com*; web site: *outdoorodysseys.com/sanjuans*

SUMMER RATES: Day tours $59 to $79 for adults, reduced rates for children 5 to 11; 2-, 3-, 4-, and 5- day tours $229 to $725; Women on Water 3-day B&B and walking tour $749.

Paddling, camping, and wildlife watching in the San Juans are the focus of adventures provided by Outdoor Odysseys. A range of trips is offered out of Friday Harbor, including a Women on Water tour that combines paddling, hiking, and B&B stopovers. Groups are small, equipment is state-of-the-art, and guides are experienced and knowledgeable. (Also, the food is great!) The company, operating out of San Juan County Park, has worked in conjunction with REI and the Seattle Aquarium, so you know how highly they are respected.

Salish Sea Charters

P.O. Box 4446; Roche Harbor, WA 98250. Phone: (877) 560-5711 or (360) 378-8555; email: *info@salishsea.com*; web site: *salishsea.com*

SUMMER RATES: $59, children under 12 $49.

Salish Sea Charters' 40-foot cruiser, *The Stellar Sea*, leaves from Snug Harbor Marina Resort on the west side of San Juan Island, in prime whale-viewing territory, and makes three three-hour tours daily from April 1 through the end of October. A reduced schedule is offered during the quiet season. The vessel holds up to 18 passengers, and has a viewing deck and heated cabin for brisk days. Coffee, tea, cocoa, and snacks are available.

San Juan Excursions

#2 Spring Street Landing, P.O. Box 2508; Friday Harbor, WA 98250. Phone: (800) 809-4253 or (360) 378-6636; fax: (360) 378-6552; email: *sanjuanex@watchwhales.com*; web site: *watchwhales.com*

SUMMER RATES:
- *Whale watch/wildlife cruises:* Adults $65, children 4 to 12 $45.
- *Private charters:* (39 persons or fewer) $450 per hour, first 4 hours; $300 per hour thereafter; (40 to 80 persons) $600 per hour $400 per hour thereafter, plus catering fees and banquet permit, if needed.
- *Kayak tours:* 3 hours $59 per person; 5 hours $75 per person. Visa and MasterCard accepted.

This cruise company offers whale watch tours and private charters aboard the classic 64-foot yacht *Odyssey,* as well as sea kayak tours. The Odyssey has two levels of wrap-around decks, two heated salons, four staterooms, a galley, and two heads with showers. It has a capacity of 97, with room for 60 inside. Daily sailings are for 3½ to 4 hours. Sea kayak tours are three to five hours.

San Juan Safaris

Marine Activity Center at Roche Harbor; P.O. Box 2749; Friday Harbor, WA, 98250. Phone: (800) 450-6858 or (360) 378-1323; email: *fun@sanjuansafaris.com*; web site: *sanjuansafaris.com*

SUMMER RATES: Whale watch tours: 3 to 4 hours, adults $65, children $45. Kayak tours: 3 hours, $59 per person, 5 hours $75 per person.

Operating out of both Friday Harbor and Roche Harbor, San Juan Safaris conducts kayak treks and whale watch cruises that have easy access to the western "wild side" of San Juan Island. Guides take kayak parties of up to ten persons each on daily three-hour nature tours in the morning, afternoon, and evening. No prior kayaking experience is necessary. Shakedown training is conducted in protected Roche Harbor, then the tours paddle past nature preserve islands in San Juan Channel.

For those who prefer to be a little farther out of the water when observing nature, a daily three-hour whale watch cruise from Roche Harbor and Friday Harbor is offered aboard the 30-foot *Kittiwake*, the 42-foot *Sea Hawk*, or the 55-foot *Sea Lion*.

SAN JUAN ISLAND
Boat & Kayak Tours & Charters

Scamper Charters

685 Spring Street, #191; Friday Harbor, WA 98250. Phone: (877) 314-3532 or (360) 472-0212, (360) 471-1323; email: *scamper@rockisland.com*; web site: *scampercharters.com*

SUMMER RATES: Sunset cruises $55 per person, 3 or more; private charters $100 per hour, minimum of 4 hours. Visa and MasterCard accepted.

Launched in 1920, the elegant, 36-foot fantail launch *Scamper* is available for water taxi service and private charters for up to six persons. The fully restored yacht exudes the elegance and history of an earlier era of Prohibition, flappers, and that "scandalous" jazz.

Sea Quest Kayak Expeditions

Zoetic Research, P.O. Box 2424F; Friday Harbor, WA 98250. Phone: (888) 589-4253 or (360) 378-5767; email: *quest@sea-quest-kayak.com*; web site: *sea-quest-kayak.com*

SUMMER RATES: ½ day $55 per person, 1-day $79 per person; 2-, 3-, and 5-day trips $299 to $699 per person. Surcharge on 1-day Saturday trips in July and August. Women-only tours available.

Sea Quest Expeditions, a non-profit organization, is dedicated to environmental education, scientific investigation, and financial support of environmental and conservation causes. Trips are led by experienced sea kayak guides and accompanied by environmental instructors; the trip is a learning experience, not just a "look at the whales and seals" tour. No previous kayaking experience is required; brief safety and paddling instructions are provided.

Between May and October, the group offers one-day tours to seek out orca whales, porpoises, seals, bald eagles, and other marine birds and mammals. Two- and three-day tours are also offered, with overnight stays at marine state parks. Special five-day research expeditions to B.C. islands for observing and photographing minke whales are part of an ongoing ten-year study of these mammals. Kayaks, accessories, camping equipment, breakfast and dinners are provided. Special trips for families, school groups, and women only are available.

Western Prince Cruises

#2 Spring Street, P.O. Box 418; Friday Harbor, WA 98250. Phone: (800) 757-6722 or (360) 378-5315; fax: (360) 378-4240; email: *contact@orcawhalewatch.com*; web site: *westernprince.com*

SUMMER RATES: Adults $65, children 4 to 12 $45. Discount on tickets purchased 14 days ahead of sailing.

Based at the main dock in the Port of Friday Harbor, the 46-foot *Western Prince II*, which holds up to 33 guests, offers daily, four-hour wildlife cruises in the San Juans. Although orca whales are the star attractions, playful Dall's porpoise might escort your boat. Watch for eagles soaring above and harbor seals basking on rocky islets. An on-board naturalist will help make your trip more meaningful. The cruise price includes free admission to the Friday Harbor Whale Museum. Reservations are strongly advised. Children under four years old and pets are not permitted aboard.

Discovery Sea Kayaks offers companion kayak tours with discounts available for booking with them and Western Prince at the same visit.

MARINAS, LAUNCH RAMPS & PUT-INS

Jackson Beach Boat Launch

To find this public launch ramp, operated by the Port of Friday Harbor, take Argyle Avenue south out of Friday Harbor, and in ¾ mile turn east onto Pear Point Road. When the road reaches a sand and gravel operation, turn downhill on Jackson Beach Road. A two-lane concrete ramp with an adjoining boarding float dips into North Bay at the tip of a narrow spit. A pair of vault toilets are located at the head of the ramp. Kayaks and other beachable boats can be put in anywhere along the spit.

Port of Friday Harbor

204 Front Street N, P.O. Box 889; Friday Harbor, WA 98250. Phone: (360) 378-2688 (office), (360) 378-3114 (fuel pier); fax: (360) 378-6114; VHF channel 66A; email: *tarrih@ portfridayharbor.org*; web site: *portfridayharbor.org*

FACILITIES: 130 guest slips (power and water), fuel dock (gas, diesel, propane), pumpout station, restrooms, showers, U.S. Customs.

SUMMER RATES: Under 74 feet varies between 65¢ and 75¢ per foot, depending on month; over 74 feet varies between 90¢ and $1.20 per foot. Power additional 10¢ per foot for 30 amp 20¢ per foot for 50 amp.

This large port facility boasts several hundred permanent moorage slips as well as extensive facilities for guest boaters. A U.S. Customs office is in a building near the port offices. During summer months, a Customs booth is staffed on the breakwater near the seaplane float. Several yacht charter companies and cruise boats operate from Spring Street Landing. During the summer you can purchase fresh fish, crab, and shrimp, either raw or cooked, at a "fish deli" on the main port float. The port dock is just two blocks from downtown Friday Harbor.

The long pier at the foot of Spring Street serves as a pickup point for wildlife cruises and other large boats. The two halves of the building on the pier frame an open, roofed area with benches and phones. Public restrooms are on one side. One half of the building contains an interesting 400-gallon saltwater aquarium.

Roche Harbor Resort

248 Reuben Tarte Memorial Drive, P.O. Box 4001; Roche Harbor, WA 98250. Phone: (360) 378-2155, (360) 378-2080 (Customs), VHF channel 78A; email: *roche@rocheharbor.com*; web site: *rocheharbor.com*

FACILITIES: Guest moorage on floats (power and water) and buoys, fuel dock (gas, diesel, kerosene, butane, propane, outboard mix, alcohol), restrooms, showers, coin-operated laundry, groceries, boat launch ramp, U.S. Customs, lodging.

This first-class resort and marina are on the northwest corner of San Juan Island on Roche Harbor. Large guest floats, with power and water, line the waterfront below the resort, mooring buoys are offshore in the harbor, and a boat launch ramp sits to the south of the large landfill pier. A U.S. Customs office is maintained on the outer end of the main dock during summer months. A general store at the head of the dock carries groceries, hardware, and sundries. The resort hotel, restaurants, lounge, and several shops are among the shore-side amenities. See also Lodging, pages 225–227, Restaurants, Cafés & Take-Out, pages 244 and 245, and Groceries, Bakeries, Delis & Liquor, pages 251.

San Juan County Park Boat Launch

This county park is on West Valley Road on the west shore of San Juan Island. It holds a single-lane public launch ramp that drops into Smallpox Bay, a small cove off Haro Strait. See also Parks & Campgrounds, page 282,

Snug Harbor Marina Resort

1997 Mitchell Bay Road; Friday Harbor, WA 98250. Phone: (360) 378-4762; fax: (360) 378-8859; email: *sneakaway@snugresort.com*; web site: *snugresort.com*

Located on Mitchell Bay on the west side of San Juan Island, the marina has 24 guest slips with power and water, a fuel dock (gas and premix), restrooms, showers, and a coin-operated laundry. Haulouts of boats up to 26 feet and dry storage are available. The marina store stocks some groceries, and bait and tackle. See also Lodging, pages 229–230.

PARKS & CAMPGROUNDS

Fairgrounds Family Park and Skatepark

660 Argyle Road, Friday Harbor, WA.

🚐 The park is in the southwest corner of the fairgrounds on Argyle Avenue, about five blocks from the waterfront, within easy walking distance.

When traveling with a family, a place to let the kids have fun and work off their energy becomes pretty important. Grab some picnic makings at a Friday Harbor deli, and stop here for some quality time. The small park has a children's play area, a picnic shelter with tables, barbecue, and a sanican. The skatepark boasts some interesting concrete bowls where teens will have a blast working out their skateboards, or watching local kids showing off their stuff.

Lakedale Resort ⋒

4313 Roche Harbor Road; Friday Harbor, WA 98250. Phone: (800) 617-2267 or (360) 378-2350; fax: (360) 378-0944; email: *info@lakedale.com*; web site: *lakedale.com*

FACILITIES: 73 standard campsites, 15 waterfront sites, 10 bicycle campsites, 12 RV sites, 6 group campsites, token-operated showers, restrooms, groceries, bait and tackle, ice, wood, camping equipment, boat rentals (paddleboat, rowboat, canoe). Open March 15 to October 15. Reservations accepted.

🚐 Take Roche Harbor Road west from Friday Harbor for 5 miles; just beyond Egg Lake Road, turn into the campground.

Here's a terrific private campground that rivals any state park. In fact, it was voted the number-one campground in the Northwest by The Bicycle Paper. You'll find it along the south side of Roche Harbor Road, just west of Egg Lake Road.

The park's acreage includes three shallow, trout- and bass-stocked lakes. Campsites are scattered about in a grassy area or nestled in the woods between the lakes. A few are right on the lakeshore. Swimming is permitted in two roped-off areas of the lakes, although there are no lifeguards. Because the lakes are on private property, you don't need a fishing license to try for pond fish, but Lakedale does charge a daily fee.

The general store at the entrance to the campground stocks the usual groceries, bait, ice, and wood for sale, and in addition rents fishing tackle, tents, stoves, lanterns, and sleeping bags. See also Lodging, pages 220–221.

Lime Kiln State Park

6158 Lighthouse Road; Friday Harbor, WA 98250. Phone: (360) 378-2044; web site: *parks.wa.gov*

🚗 Take Roche Harbor Road west from Friday Harbor 9 miles to West Valley Road. Turn south on it, and in 3¼ miles, turn west on Mitchell Bay Road. In just under a mile, turn south on West Side Road, and follow it 6½ miles to the park.

What are all those people doing standing on the bluff, staring out to sea with their faces fused to binoculars? They undoubtedly are trying to spot whales offshore at this, the world's only park dedicated to watching for these magnificent creatures. You might spot orca, minke, and pilot whales, or their smaller relatives, harbor and Dall's porpoises. The major salmon runs heading for Fraser River spawning grounds pass through Haro Strait, along the west side of San Juan Island, attracting whales that feed on them.

A trail leads from the parking lot to the rocky shoreline south of Lime Kiln lighthouse. Here, interpretive panels describe the various marine mammals that might be seen. Picnic tables scattered along the beach make comfortable spots to wait for them to appear. Because their appearance is not choreographed, sighting them requires patience, time, and sharp eyes to spot a dorsal fin breaking through waters offshore. We recommend binoculars and cameras with telephoto lenses.

A pair of lime kilns operated here until the 1920s, processing limestone quarried from nearby cliffs. Displays describe the work done here; one of the kilns has been restored and can be reached by trail.

At the north side of the parking lot, a small interpretive center, open in summer. It has further displays on whales, limestone, and lime kilns. T-shirts, books, orca identification charts, and a few stuffed toy seals and whales are for sale.

Mitchell Bay Landing ⋔

2101 Mitchell Bay Road; Friday Harbor WA 98250. Phone: (360) 378-9296; cell: (360) 472-1699; fax: (360) 378-8393; email: *retreat@mitchellbaylanding.com*; web site: *mitchellbaylanding.com*

ACCOMMODATIONS: Campground with sanicans, no showers or potable water.
- 3 tent sites on a waterfront lawn.
- RV sites with electric hookups.
- 10-foot tent trailers with push-out beds, refrigerator, outside cooking.
- 2 family-size trailers with queen-size or double beds, dinette, kitchenette, barbeque.

RESTRICTIONS: Children OK, pets under control and on leash OK, no smoking.

EXTRAS: Rentals of single and double kayaks, rowing scull, 2 skiffs, fishing gear, crab pots.

SUMMER RATES: Tent site $25, RV site $50, tent trailers $75, full trailers $104 to $149. Kayak rentals $55 to $85 per day, boat rentals $25 to $65 per hour, $129 to $329 per day. Kayak tours from $59. Major credit cards accepted.

🚗 From Friday Harbor take Beaverton Valley Road, then West Valley Road for 6 miles to Mitchell Bay Road, and in 2 miles stay right and follow Mitchell Bay Road to Mitchell Bay Landing.

This small campground includes space for tents on a waterfront lawn, RV hookup sites, and several on-site trailers. This is a quiet waterfront retreat, popular with families and low budget campers. Unfortunately, there is no potable water, so bring your own for drinking and cleanup, or purchase bottled water. Sanitary facilities are well-maintained sanicans. Pay showers can be found at Roche Harbor, not far away.

Kayaks can be rented for trips exploring the west side of the island. Two skiffs and a rowing scull are also available for closer-to-home prowling around Mitchell Bay.

San Juan County Park ⛺

380 Westside Road North; Friday Harbor, WA 98250. Phone: (360) 378-1842 (reservations only), (360) 378-8420 (information); email: *parks@co.san-juan.wa.us*; web site: *co.san-juan. wa.us/parks/sanjuan*

FACILITIES: 20 campsites, hiker/biker/kayaker campsites, group camp, picnic tables, picnic shelter, fireplaces, fire rings, restrooms, groceries, boat launch ramp, mooring buoys. Reservations recommended.

RATES: Campsites $25 per night for 4 persons and 1 vehicle (site 18 is $34), extra adult $5 each, extra child $3 each, extra vehicle (maximum 2) $5 each; Hiker/biker/kayaker site, adult $6, child $3, maximum 10 persons, no vehicles.

🚗 Take Roche Harbor Road west from Friday Harbor 9 miles to West Valley Road. Turn south on it, and in 3¼ miles, turn west on Mitchell Bay Road. In just under a mile, turn south on West Side Road, and follow it 3¾ miles to the park.

Grassy slopes dotted with trees reach down to the edge of Haro Strait, with cross-channel views of Victoria, B.C. This is the site of San Juan County Park, on the west side of San Juan Island, the only public camping facility on the island. Natural attractions, plus a boat launch ramp on Smallpox Bay, and outstanding scuba diving along the shoreline and nearby Low Island, make it a popular (and crowded) site during the summer.

The park holds only 20 campsites, plus a small group camp and a camping area for those who arrive via foot, bicycle, or kayak. The campground office and a small store that sells groceries and fishing supplies sits above the launch ramp.

San Juan Island National Historical Park

640 Mullis Street, Suite 100, P.O. Box 429; Friday Harbor, WA 98250. Phone: (360) 378-2240; fax: (360) 378-2615; web site: *nps.gov/sajh*

FACILITIES: *English Camp:* Dinghy dock, picnic tables, toilets, hiking trail. *American Camp:* Picnic tables, restrooms, drinking water, fire pits, hiking trails, historical displays and interpretation.

🚙 *English Camp:* Take Roche Harbor Road west from Friday Harbor, and in 8½ miles, turn south on West Valley Road. Follow it for 1½ miles to the park. *American Camp:* From Friday Harbor, take Argyle Avenue south, then west, to Cattle Point Road. Continue south on Cattle Point Road to the park. The total distance is about 5 miles.

The U.S. and Great Britain at war? Over a *pig*? Yes, it nearly happened here. A visit to this fascinating national park will take you back to the mid-1800s when it all happened. For a full description, see the introduction to San Juan Island, page 200, which describes the war.

Begin your investigation of the park at English Camp, on Garrison Bay, where three of the original buildings have been restored. One has historical displays and a video program describing events that led to the Pig War.

The building with the most colorful history is the blockhouse, built on the beach to protect the marines (from marauding Indians, not Americans). It was later used as a guardhouse for miscreant troopers. The formal flower garden that once graced the grounds has been replanted. Interpretive displays are found above the camp, where the officers' quarters were built on hillside terraces. A trail from the park leads across the road and up a hillside to a small cemetery at the base of Young Hill, in ½ mile. The cemetery holds the graves of British marines who died accidentally during the long occupation; there were no war-related casualties, other than the pig. The trail continues for another mile to the top of Mount Young with magnificent views over Garrison Bay to the Canadian Gulf Islands

American Camp shows historical displays in the park headquarters building; interpretive trails lead past two restored buildings, Pickett's Redoubt, and the Hudson's Bay Company farm site. Other hiking trails lead to great views from the rolling top of 290-foot Mount Finlayson, and along several secluded lagoons on the Griffin Bay shoreline. If you've brought your picnic lunch along, there are tables with views at South Beach, fronting on the Strait of Juan de Fuca, and on the more protected shore of Griffin Bay.

Town and Country Mobile Home Park ⛺

595 Tucker Avenue North; Friday Harbor, WA 98250. Phone: (360) 3789-4717

FACILITIES: 40 tent and RV sites with hookups, restrooms, showers, coin-operated laundry. Reservations accepted.

🚙 From Spring Street in Friday Harbor, turn northwest on Second Street, which becomes Guard Street in about four blocks. Continue on Guard for two blocks to Tucker Avenue. Head north on Tucker, then northwest on Roche Harbor Road for two blocks to the RV park.

Although the majority of the facilities at Town and Country are dedicated to permanent mobile home sites, the park has some transient sites along its perimeter. All have full hookups. Half-a-dozen tent sites are scattered among the trees along one side. Restrooms, showers, and a coin-operated laundry are available in the transient RV area. Because the bulk of the patrons are long-term guests, it is advisable to call ahead to find out if space is available.

THE OTHER ISLANDS

◆

THE FERRY-SERVED ISLANDS are well described in earlier chapters, but what about all those remaining islands? There are more than 170 of them, in total, and they represent a fair amount of real estate. People cruising by admire their beauty and "ooh" and "ahh" at the snug little waterfront cabins and gracious bluff-top homes that dot some of their edges. These other islands fall into one of several categories:

- Some are private residential sites.
- Some are privately held, but are either too small or lacking in potable water to support a home.
- A number are marine state parks.
- A few choice ecological locations (entire islets as well as sections of larger islands) are held by The Nature Conservancy as preserves.
- Finally, the remaining number of little isles and inhospitable rocks and reefs are part of the 84 sites of the San Juan National Wildlife Refuge.

THE RESIDENTIAL ISLANDS

Nearly all the non-ferry islands that have private residences utilize private airstrips to allow residents access; some private homes have docks, and a few of the islands, such as Waldron and Decatur, have private community docks. None of these docks are open for use to the general public.

Two of the larger residential islands, Blakely and Decatur, flank either side of Thatcher Pass, where the ferry usually enters the archipelago. Both are strictly residential islands, although Blakely, which is nearly as large as Shaw Island, is owned by a small corporation that wisely sells only a few lots a year to ensure controlled growth on the fragile site. Obstruction, another island that holds a few homes, lies north of Blakely and south of Orcas Island, in the middle of Peavine Pass and Obstruction Pass.

The ferry passes a number of small islands that lie on Harney Channel and Wasp Passage, in the heart of the islands, giving passengers "Better Homes and Gardens" views of picturesque property. Some islands are dotted with homes, while others host only a summer cottage each. Additional islets passed by the ferry are lacking in water or are too small to support even a cabin. These include Frost, Crane, Cliff, McConnell, Coon, Low, Bell, Reef, and Double.

Waldron, a large, mostly flat island immediately west of Orcas Island, is a study in self-sufficiency. On the island, all power for electricity, radiotelephones, appliances, and furnaces comes from private gasoline generators or propane tanks; water comes from private wells. Neighbors rely on neighbors in the tightly knit community.

The list of privately owned islands lying scattered about the edges of the San

The sun rises on a quiet anchorage at Jones Island Marine State Park.

Juans includes Trump and Center Islands, in Lopez Sound; Canoe, in Upright Channel off the southeast side of Shaw; Pearl and Henry, at the entrance to Roche Harbor; and at the northeast corner, Spieden, Satellite, Johns, and Stuart (with the exception of Stuart Island Marine State Park). Other privately owned islands include Brown (so obvious it's almost overlooked, facing on Friday Harbor) and Barnes, lying on the north side of the San Juans, parallel to Clark Island Marine State Park. Of the multitude of islands at the south end of Lopez Island, Long, Charles, and Iceberg Islands are the only ones that are not designated as wildlife refuges.

A small marina and general store on the north side of Blakely Island is the only commercial development on any of these islands.

Blakely Island General Store and Marina

1 Marine Drive; Blakely Island, WA 98221. Phone: (360) 375-6121; fax (360): 375-6141; email: *nparker@gmail.com*

FACILITIES: Guest moorage (power, water), restrooms, showers, coin-operated laundry, fuel (gas, diesel), groceries

⚓ The marina is on a bay on the north side of Blakely Island, facing on Peavine Pass.

A dredged channel behind a rock breakwater leads to a small marina basin that offers both permanent and guest moorages. The long fuel dock fronting on Peavine Pass leads ashore to a general store that carries groceries, ice, beer, wine, and fishing and marine supplies. Customers and guests may use a picnic shelter and barbecue in the broad lawn adjacent to the store. The marina is a free wi-fi hot spot.

THE NATURE CONSERVANCY HOLDINGS

In an entire set of islands that seem like a nature preserve in themselves, it's to be expected that forces are hard at work keeping it that way. The Nature Conservancy, one of the forerunners in the quest for environmental preservation, is a non-profit, nationwide environmental organization that uses contributed funds to purchase property of unique ecological value. They hold the land under a protected status until appropriate government agencies can muster the public support and financial resources to assure its long-term preservation. Several San Juan Island properties have been saved from private or commercial development by this organization.

YELLOW ISLAND. The most westerly of the Wasp Islands, Yellow Island, was purchased by The Nature Conservancy in 1980 to preserve its fields of exotic and endangered plants and wildflowers. No formal boat access is provided, although visitors may land small boats ashore, providing that they restrict their travel to designated trails and don't endanger the island's plant and animal biosystems. Kayakers are prohibited from landing on the long sandy spits on either end of the island.

WALDRON ISLAND. On the west side of Waldron Island, on Cowlitz Bay, a section of beach, meadow, and marshland property of unique biological value has been purchased by The Nature Conservancy. The property is open to the public, but access is discouraged to preserve the ecosystems for which it was acquired. Additional property in the vicinity of Point Disney was added to their holdings in 2000.

SENTINEL ISLAND. Sentinel Island, in Spieden Channel on the south side of Spieden Island, is a miniature version of its larger nearby companion. The Nature

A view from the ferry: Blakely and Decatur Islands, two of the residential islands, in the foreground and distance, and small Willow Island, part of the San Juan Islands National Wildlife Refuge, in the center right.

Conservancy purchased the island to preserve its nesting areas for bald eagles and other marine birds. Landing on the island is permitted only with prior permission from The Nature Conservancy.

WILDLIFE REFUGE ISLANDS

The San Juan Islands National Wildlife Refuge consists of 84 rocks, reefs, and islets in the San Juan Archipelago, ranging from ¼-acre to 140 acres in size. These are nesting and breeding grounds for sea birds such as glaucous-winged gulls, Brant's and pelagic cormorants, tufted puffins, pigeon guillemots, rhinoceros auklets, and black oystercatchers. An estimated two-hundred other species of birds visit the islands annually. You might sight harbor seals, porpoises, and whales in the surrounding waters, or hauled out on sunny rocks. Bald eagles use larger grassy islands for feeding areas; a few weasels and river otters are also found there.

Although this fascinating collection of marine mammals and birds is wonderful to watch and photograph from a distance, it is unlawful to go ashore on any refuge property, or to disturb the wildlife.

THE MARINE STATE PARKS

For many boaters, the greatest treasures of the San Juans are the numerous islands acquired over the years by the Washington State Parks and Recreation

Commission and designated as marine state parks. Accessible only by boat, canoe, kayak, or float plane, these sites are used for recreational boating, hiking, scuba diving, and camping.

All (with the exception of Posey and Doe Islands) have mooring buoys available for public use in their more protected bays or coves. These buoys, which are on a first-come, first-serve basis, are set in 20 to 50 feet of water at mean low tide. Sucia and Stuart State Parks have lineal moorage systems to provide more tie-ups. Some parks also have docks with floats for overnight moorage and easy access to land; however, many floats are removed in winter to prevent storm damage. Fees are charged for moorage on buoys or floats, and any one boat's stay is limited to 36 consecutive hours.

Campsites at marine state parks are termed "primitive," which means that they consist of only a picnic table and fire ring, and a flat space to pitch a tent. Designated Cascadia Marine Trail sites have been created as part of a water trail system stretching from Olympia to the Canadian border. The campsites are open to all users of paddle-powered craft.

Sanitary facilities are either pit, vault, or self-composting toilets. Only a few of the islands have water, and even on those the source might dry up, especially toward the end of a long, dry summer. Park budgets have been pared to the bone in recent years, and most marine state parks have no garbage pick up or disposal. Please take all garbage away with you—and perhaps pick up any left by other, less-considerate visitors.

Following are brief descriptions of the parks that have developed boating and camping facilities. In addition, there are numerous undeveloped islands and strips of public access shoreland owned by state parks or the Department of Natural Resources. All are more fully described and mapped in our companion volume, *The San Juan Islands: Afoot and Afloat.* The developed park islands are listed on the following pages, along with other campgrounds.

A mooring buoy in Sucia Island's Shallow Bay offers prime sunset views.

What's Dragging?

A lineal mooring system consists of a 200-foot-long cable strung between a pair of pylons anchored to the sea floor. Mooring eyes are provided along the cable, and boats can tie up to the eyes on either side. This system allows more moorage in a small area, and in addition is easier on the environment, as it greatly reduces the damage done to the seabed by dragging buoy anchor blocks and boat anchor chains. For environmental reasons, we urge you to use the lineal mooring system whenever possible.

If anchored or tied to a buoy, please use the minimum amount of anchor scope to allow your boat to be secure. Contrary to some boating "bibles," a scope of seven times the water depth generally is not necessary, and is almost impossible to achieve in many of the small coves found in the San Juans. In all but the most severe weather, a three-to-one scope is adequate with a well-set anchor, and is considerably more environment friendly, as dragging anchor chains damage the seabed. It is also more courteous for others who might wish to share a crowded anchorage. Rafting with a friend is also a good way to preserve the seabed, but be sure to not overload a buoy.

PARKS, CAMPGROUNDS & CAMPS

Blind Island Marine State Park ⋒

CONTACT: Sucia Island State Park; Star Route, Box 177; Olga, WA 98279. Phone: (360) 376-2073

FACILITIES: 4 primitive camping/picnic sites, Cascadia Marine Trail campsites, vault toilet, 4 mooring buoys, no water or garbage collection.

⚠ The island sits in the entrance to Blind Bay, west of the Shaw Island ferry landing.

Blind Island is a tiny island that protects a series of mooring buoys along its south side in Blind Bay. Decorated only with tufts of grass and scruffy brush, the main attraction of this islet is its incomparable view of boat and ferry traffic plying busy Harney Channel.

Canoe Island

See Canoe Island French Camp, pages 47–48.

Clark Island Marine State Park ⋒

CONTACT: Sucia Island State Park; Star Route, Box 177; Olga, WA 98279. Phone: (360) 376-2073

FACILITIES: 2 primitive campsites, 2 picnic sites, 2 fire rings, vault toilets, 9 mooring buoys, no water or garbage collection.

⚠ Clark Island lies in the Strait of Georgia, 2¼ nautical miles north of the northeast tip of Orcas Island.

Erase the visiting boats riding on buoys or at anchor offshore, and you almost expect to see Robinson Crusoe stroll across the broad beach to greet you. Campsites lie hidden in a midisland strip of trees and brush. The north end of this long, narrow island is cliff rimmed at waterline, and covered with a dense, barely penetrable jungle inland. As a result, all recreational use (except scuba diving) is confined to the lobe at the south end of the island. Here the center strip of woods is flanked by wide, open beaches, sandy on the west, and cobble on the east.

The Sisters, a collection of rocks, reefs, and islets, are but a stone's throw away from a series of tiny rock coves on the south end of the island. The cacophony of marine birds on these rocks makes it clear that they are part of the San Juan National Wildlife Refuge.

Doe Island Marine State Park ⋀

CONTACT: Sucia Island State Park; Star Route, Box 177; Olga, WA 98279. Phone: (360) 376-2073

FACILITIES: 5 primitive campsites, vault toilets, dock with float, no water or garbage collection.
⚠ The island lies in Rosario Strait off the southeast side of Orcas Island, ¼ nautical miles south of Doe Bay, or 2¼ nautical miles north of Obstruction Pass.

This tiny, flower garden island enjoys beautiful sunrise views across Rosario Strait to the rugged 800-foot face of Eagle Cliff on Cypress Island. A dock with a float that lies in the small protected bay between Doe Island and Orcas Island offers some limited moorage space; because no mooring buoys are provided, boats planning overnight stays must be able to be beached or ride at anchor. Primitive campsites on headlands

A classic ketch anchors off James Island Marine State Park.

between its small coves are favorite overnight spots for kayakers. A rough trail along the shoreline overlooks nearby rocks crowded with flocks of marine birds.

Griffin Bay Marine State Park ⋀

CONTACT: Spencer Spit State Park; 521A Bakerview Road; Lopez Island, WA 98261. Phone: (360) 468-2251

FACILITIES: 4 primitive campsites, Cascadia Marine Trail campsite, fire circle, toilets, 2 mooring buoys.

⚠ The park is on the east side of Lopez Island on Griffin Bay, due west of Halftide Rock, and south of Low Point. There is no land access.

This tiny marine state park on the east side of Lopez Island is primarily of interest to paddlers. Two mooring buoys lie offshore. Unfortunately, the danger of Half-tide Rock, other submerged rocks, and old rotted-off pilings tend to discourage an approach by boats that have any draft. It's great for kayakers who can easily land on the gentle shore. The offshore reefs are part of the San Juan Island Wilderness Area, and so afford the opportunity to spot seals, gulls, and other seabirds that frequent them.

James Island Marine State Park ⋀

CONTACT: Sucia Island State Park; Star Route, Box 177; Olga, WA 98279. Phone: (360) 376-2073

FACILITIES: 13 primitive campsites, 3 Cascadia Marine Trail campsites, picnic shelter, toilets, dock with float, 5 mooring buoys, 1½ miles of trail, no water or garbage collection.

⚠ The island lies in Rosario Strait off the east side of Decatur Island, south of Thatcher Pass.

This dogbone-shaped island, just off the main ferry route from Anacortes, is the easternmost doorkeeper to the San Juans. It is often used as a first stop by boaters heading into the islands, or for a wistful pause on the way home before acknowledging that an idyllic vacation is over. Steep, cliffy headlands are broken by only three small coves. The cove on the west side of the island holds a dock and float; the side-by-side pair of bays on the east side share five mooring buoys. Shoreside facilities are Spartan.

Johns Island

See Camp 'Norwester, page 47.

Jones Island Marine State Park ⋀

CONTACT: Sucia Island State Park; Star Route, Box 177; Olga, WA 98279. Phone: (360) 376-2073

FACILITIES: 21 primitive camping/picnic sites, 2 Cascadia Marine Trail campsites, water, dock and float, 7 mooring buoys, hiking trails.

⚠ The island lies off the southwest tip of Orcas Island, on the west side of Spring Passage, at the junction of San Juan and President Channels.

Jones Island is the hub of boating activity in the heart of the San Juans. It is only a short cruise away from marinas and shore-side amenities at Friday Harbor and Deer Harbor, and is within an easy paddle of the rock pile cluster of the Wasp Islands.

Deer are often seen in the marine state parks, especially Jones Island. They sometimes swim between the islands.

Three small coves indent the shoreline of the wooded island. The largest, on the north, has a dock, float, and mooring buoys. Two smaller side-by-side coves on the south side of the island on San Juan Channel have only mooring buoys. A short hiking trail across the island links the two camping areas.

Matia Island Marine State Park ⋀

CONTACT: Sucia Island State Park; Star Route, Box 177; Olga, WA 98279. Phone: (360) 376-2073

FACILITIES: 6 primitive campsites, 7 picnic tables, self-composting toilet, dock and float, 2 mooring buoys, 1 mile of hiking trail, no water or garbage collection.

⚓ The island lies in the Strait of Georgia, 2¾ nautical miles north of Orcas Island. The park is on the west end of the island above Rolfe Cove.

Although most of Matia Island is part of the San Juan Island National Wildlife Refuge, 5 acres on its west tip are managed as a marine state park. Snug little Rolfe Cove is surrounded by wave-cut sandstone cliffs, on the island itself, and on a small, steep-walled islet on the north side of the cove. The gravel beach at the head of the cove holds a dock and float that access the park's small camping and picnic area. A crude trail seeks out other coves on the south and west ends of the island, and a long, shallow indentation in its southeast shoreline. The east end of the island is closed to hikers because of its refuge status.

Patos Island Marine State Park ⋀

CONTACT: Sucia Island State Park; Star Route, Box 177; Olga, WA 98279. Phone: (360) 376-2073

FACILITIES: 7 primitive campsites, vault toilets, 2 mooring buoys, 1¼ miles of hiking trail, no water or garbage collection.

⚓ Patos Island lies at the confluence of Boundary Pass and the Strait of Georgia, 4¼ nautical miles north of Orcas Island.

The northernmost outpost of the San Juan Islands is Patos Island, sitting on the U.S.–Canada border at the junction of Boundary Pass and the Strait of Georgia. The one-time lighthouse reserve now holds only the Patos Island light at the tip of Alden Point, which marks the change of boat course required to head north to Vancouver, B.C. The remainder of the island is a state park. A primitive campground at the head of Active Cove is the starting point of a trail around the perimeter of the island that offers access to a mile-long hike of the island's incomparable north shore beaches.

Point Doughty Marine State Park ⛺

CONTACT: Sucia Island State Park; Star Route, Box 177; Olga, WA 98279. Phone: (360) 376-2073

FACILITIES: 2 primitive campsites, Cascadia Marine Trail campsite, picnic sites, vault toilets, no water or garbage collection.

⚓ Point Doughty is on the north side of Orcas Island, 1 mile northeast of YMCA Camp Orkila.

The only access to this small park on a cliffy headland is by boats that can be drawn up on shore. It is primarily used by paddlers because it has no buoys, and anchoring offshore is rather tenuous due to the rocky bottom and strong current. A former land path from Camp Orkila became unsafe due to erosion, and a beach walk access is also prohibited. A rough log staircase climbs steep rocks from the beach, reaching an open grassy bluff. Views are north and east to Sucia and Matia Islands, the Canadian Coast Range, and Mount Baker.

Posey Island Marine State Park ⛺

CONTACT: Sucia Island State Park; Star Route, Box 177; Olga, WA 98279. Phone: (360) 376-2073

FACILITIES: 2 primitive campsites, 1 Cascadia Marine Trail campsite, vault toilet, no water or garbage collection.

⚓ The island lies in Spieden Channel, off the north side of Pearl Island at the entrance to Roche Harbor.

This tiny, low islet barely emerges from the shallow waters over a rocky shelf just east of the entrance to Roche Harbor. The island sees few boaters, because it can be reached only by kayaks or small boats that can be beached, and its amenities are limited to a pair of weathered picnic tables. Because of heavy use by kayakers, the park has a limit of 16 people for overnight camping. In late spring, the profusion of wildflowers that intertwine with the cover of low grass and brush justify a visit for nature photography.

Satellite Island

See YMCA Camp Orkila, page 49.

Stuart Island Marine State Park ⛵

CONTACT: Sucia Island State Park; Star Route, Box 177; Olga, WA 98279. Phone: (360) 376-2073

FACILITIES: 19 primitive campsites, 4 Cascadia Marine Trail campsites, picnic units, vault toilets, 22 mooring buoys, 2 docks with floats, 2 offshore floats, 2 lineal mooring systems, marine pumpout station, water, hiking trails.

⚠️ The park straddles a narrow isthmus between Stuart Island's Prevost and Reid Harbors, and wraps around the head of the latter.

The tip of Stuart Island thrusts northwest toward the U.S.–Canada border that runs down the centers of adjoining Haro Strait and Boundary Pass. The arrowhead-shaped island has a deep, narrow shaft-slot cut into it from the southeast by Reid Harbor, and a chip in its north side formed by companion Prevost Harbor. The state park spans the high, narrow, rocky spine between the two harbors, and laps around the broad, low beach at the head of Reid. Each bay has mooring buoys, a lineal mooring system, and a dock with a float; Reid also has a pair of midharbor floats tethered to pilings.

Campsites are scattered across the top of the narrow strip of land between the two harbors, or are hidden in dense growth at the head of Reid Harbor. Hiking trails beyond the park boundary lead to island roads that can be used to reach Turn Point, on the northwest tip of the island. The Coast Guard lighthouse site here presents dramatic overviews of heavy-vessel traffic in Haro Strait and Boundary Pass, and smaller craft fishing the tide rips around the point. The unmanned light is automated.

Sucia Island Marine State Park ⛵

CONTACT: Sucia Island State Park; Star Route, Box 177; Olga, WA 98279. Phone: (360) 376-2073

FACILITIES: 55 primitive campsites, 2 group camps, picnic shelters, composting toilets, docks with floats, 53 mooring buoys, 2 lineal mooring systems, 6½ miles of hiking trails, artificial underwater reef.

⚠️ The island lies at the confluence of the Strait of Georgia and President Channel, 2½ nautical miles north of Orcas Island.

Among a treasure-chest of jewels, Sucia Island is the prize. Its unique horseshoe shape gives it a half-dozen coves offering the finest anchorages, protected in most weather. In addition, its shape provides nearly 14 miles of shoreline for beachcombing, picnicking, wading, sunbathing, clam digging, or sand-castle building.

Each of the bays holds numerous mooring buoys, as well as space for additional anchorages. Fossil Bay, on the south side of the island, offers docks and floats. Moorages range from elbow-to-elbow mooring buoys in Fossil Bay to four tide-swept buoys in lonesome little Ewing Cove; one buoy lies over the hulls of three sunken vessels that form an artificial reef—a prime scuba diving site.

Most of the coves are framed by fancifully shaped sandstone rocks and cliffs, sculpted and pocked by wave erosion. Trails on the long wooded fingers of the island lead to open bluffs overlooking its many picturesque bays.

Astonishing sandstone formations, carved by water and wind, contribute to Sucia Island's legendary beauty.

Turn Island Marine State Park ⚓

CONTACT: Sucia Island State Park; Star Route, Box 177; Olga, WA 98279. Phone: (360) 376-2073

FACILITIES: 13 primitive campsites, picnic site, vault toilets, 3 mooring buoys, 3 miles of trail, no water or garbage collection.

Turn Island lies in San Juan Channel, off the east tip of San Juan Island, 2 nautical miles east of Friday Harbor.

Although it is part of the San Juan Islands National Wildlife Refuge, tacit recognition of its popularity as a recreation site has led to joint management of Turn Island by the Fish and Wildlife Service and the State Parks and Recreation Commission. Primitive camping and picnicking is limited to the low southwest corner of the island; the remainder retains its wild status and nature, except for a narrow trail around the island perimeter. The narrow channel that separates Turn from San Juan Island can be easily crossed by kayak or hand-carried boat from a public access off Turn Point Road, two miles east of Friday Harbor.

FOR ADDITIONAL INFORMATION

Bed & Breakfast Association of San Juan Island
P.O. Box 3016; Friday Harbor, WA 98250. Phone: (866) 645-3030 or (360) 378-3030; web site: *san-juan-island.net*

Lopez Island Chamber of Commerce
Lopez Village, Old Post Road, P.O. Box 102; Lopez Island, WA 98261. Phone: 877-433-2789 or (360) 468-4664; email: *lopezchamber@lopezisland.com*; web site: lopezisland.com

Orcas Island Chamber of Commerce
P.O. Box 252; Eastsound, WA 98245. Phone: (360) 376-2273; web site: *orcasislandchamber.com*

San Juan Chamber of Commerce
135 Spring Street, P.O. Box 98; Friday Harbor, WA 98250. Phone: (360) 378-5240; email: *chamberinfo@sanjuanisland.org*; web site: sanjuanisland.org

San Juan Island.com
P.O. Box 912; Friday Harbor, WA 98250. Phone: (800) 722-2939 or (360) 378-4244; email: *info@sanjuanisland.com*; web site: sanjuanisland.com
This web site offers a single point of contact for various bookings for San Juan Island lodging, tours, charters, rentals, dining, and activities and special events.

SanJuanSites.com
web site: *sanjuansites.com*
This web site offers some limited links to lodging, restaurants, and activities in the San Juans. Interactive maps show the various bed and breakfast inns.

San Juan Islands Visitors Bureau
P.O. Box 1330; Friday Harbor, WA 98261. Phone: (888) 463-3701 or (360) 378-3277; email: *info@visitsanjuans.com*; web site: guidetosanjuans.com

FOR MORE INFORMATION ON PARKS:

San Juan County Parks and Recreation
Friday Harbor, WA 98250. Phone: (360) 378-8420
For reservations March 1 to August 1, (360) 378-1842; email: *parks@co.san-juan.wa.us*; web site: co.san-juan.wa.us/parks

Washington State Parks and Recreation Commission
7150 Cleanwater Lane, KY-11; Olympia, WA 98504. Phone: (360) 902-8844, (for reservations) 888-226-7688; email: *infocent@parks.wa.gov*;web site: parks.wa.gov

FOR OTHER INFORMATION:

Red Tide Hotline
(800) 562-5632

Whale Hotline
(800) 562-8832 (US), (800) 665-5939 (BC)

Washington State Ferries
2901 Third Avenue, Suite 500; Seattle, WA 98121-3014
Administrative offices: (206) 515-3400
24-hour schedule information: 800-843-3779
Seattle: (206) 464-6400
Reservations to and from Sidney BC: 888-808-7977 or (206) 464-6400
TT/TDD relay services for the hearing impaired: 800-833-6385; Seattle: (206) 515-3460
email: *wsinfo@wsdot.wa.gov*; web site: wsdot.wa.gov/ferries
Web camera view of Anacortes, Orcas, and Friday Harbor terminal lots: *wsdot.wa.gov/ferries/ cameras*

United States Customs
Anacortes: (360) 293-2331
Friday Harbor and Roche Harbor: (360) 378-2080
Participants in I-68 an/or NEXUS/SENTRI programs: (800) 562-5943

INDEX

About the Authors

Marge and Ted Mueller are outdoor enthusiasts and environmentalists who have explored Washington State's waterways, islands, and other natural features for more than forty years. Ted has taught classes on cruising in Northwest waters, and both Marge and Ted have instructed mountain climbing classes through the University of Washington. They are members of The Mountaineers and The Nature Conservancy.

The Muellers are the authors of twelve regional guidebooks, including the *Afoot & Afloat* series, published by The Mountaineers, which covers the waters and shorelines from the Gulf Island to the ends of Puget Sound. Their book, *Afoot & Afloat: The San Juan Islands*, now in its fourth edition, is a companion to this volume.